W9-BAF-800

Parallel Programming
with MPI

Parallel Programming
with MPI

Peter S. Pacheco

University of San Francisco

Morgan Kaufmann Publishers, Inc.
San Francisco, California

Sponsoring Editor   Jennifer Mann
Production Manager   Yonie Overton
Production Editor   Julie Pabst
Editorial Assistant   Jane Elliott
Cover Design   Ross Carron Design
Text Design   Rebecca Evans & Associates
Illustration   ST Associates, Inc.
Composition   Ed Sznyter, Babel Press
Indexer   Ty Koontz
Printer   Courier Corporation

Morgan Kaufmann Publishers, Inc.
Editorial and Sales Office
340 Pine Street, Sixth Floor
San Francisco, CA 94104-3205
USA
Telephone   415/392-2665
Facsimile   415/982-2665
Email   mkp@mkp.com
WWW   http://www.mkp.com
Order toll free   800/745-7323

©1997 by Morgan Kaufmann Publishers, Inc.
All rights reserved
Printed in the United States of America

01   00   5   4

No part of this publication may be reproduced, stored in a retrieval system,
or transmitted in any form or by any means—electronic, mechanical, photo-
copying, recording, or otherwise—without the prior written permission of the
publisher.

Library of Congress Cataloging-in-Publication Data
Pacheco, Peter S.
     Parallel programming with MPI / Peter S. Pacheco.
          p. cm.
     Includes bibliographical references and index.
     ISBN 1-55860-339-5
     1. Parallel programming (Computer science) I. Title.
QA76.642.P3 1997
005.2'752–dc21   96-39324

E Pluribus Unum

Foreword

DEVELOPMENT OF THE MESSAGE-PASSING INTERFACE (MPI) began as a community effort. The MPI Forum wanted to define a standard and portable message-passing system that would support parallel applications and libraries. This MPI standardization effort involved over 80 people from 40 organizations, mainly from the United States and Europe. Most of the major vendors of concurrent computers at the time were represented, along with researchers from universities, government laboratories, and industry.

MPI defines the syntax and semantics of a core of library routines useful to a wide range of users writing portable message-passing programs in Fortran 77 or C. MPI also forms a possible target for compilers of languages such as High Performance Fortran. Both commercial and free public-domain implementations of MPI already exist. These run both on tightly coupled, massively parallel machines (MPPs) and on networks of workstations (NOWs).

Though much of MPI serves to standardize the "common practice" of existing systems, it goes further. MPI defines advanced features such as user-defined datatypes, persistent communication ports, powerful collective communication operations, and communication contexts. No previous system incorporates all these features. MPI is beginning to foster the development of a parallel software industry, and there is excitement among computing researchers and vendors that the development of portable and scalable, large-scale parallel applications is now feasible.

This timely book by Peter Pacheco, who participated in the MPI standardization effort, gives you a quick introduction to the standard and provides examples and insight into the process of constructing and using message-passing programs on a distributed-memory computer. In light of the fact that the MPI effort produced a final statement of the standard and an annotated reference manual, it's important to know that this book is far from a reworking of the standard. It presents introductory concepts of parallel computing, from simple send/receive to debugging (both logical and performance), as well as covering advanced topics and issues relating to the use and building of a numerical library within the MPI framework. Throughout the book, programming assignments help reinforce the concepts that have been presented.

The book is required understanding for anyone working with distributed-memory parallel computers. It explores parallel computing in depth and provides an approach to many problems that may be encountered. It is especially useful to application developers, numerical library writers, and students and teachers of parallel computing.

I have enjoyed and learned from this book, and I feel confident that you will as well.

JACK DONGARRA

Contents

Foreword   **vii**

Preface   **xvii**

Chapter 1   **Introduction**   **1**

    1.1   The Need for More Computational Power   1
    1.2   The Need for Parallel Computing   3
    1.3   The Bad News   5
    1.4   MPI   6
    1.5   The Rest of the Book   7
    1.6   Typographic Conventions   9

Chapter 2   **An Overview of Parallel Computing**   **11**

    2.1   Hardware   11
      2.1.1   Flynn's Taxonomy   12
      2.1.2   The Classical von Neumann Machine   12
      2.1.3   Pipeline and Vector Architectures   13
      2.1.4   SIMD Systems   14
      2.1.5   General MIMD Systems   15
      2.1.6   Shared-Memory MIMD   16
      2.1.7   Distributed-Memory MIMD   19
      2.1.8   Communication and Routing   24

2.2   Software Issues   25
      2.2.1 Shared-Memory Programming   26
      2.2.2 Message Passing   29
      2.2.3 Data-Parallel Languages   32
      2.2.4 RPC and Active Messages   34
      2.2.5 Data Mapping   34
2.3   Summary   36
2.4   References   38
2.5   Exercises   38

Chapter 3   Greetings!   41

3.1   The Program   41
3.2   Execution   42
3.3   MPI   43
      3.3.1 General MPI Programs   44
      3.3.2 Finding Out about the Rest of the World   44
      3.3.3 Message: Data + Envelope   45
      3.3.4 Sending Messages   47
3.4   Summary   50
3.5   References   51
3.6   Exercises   52
3.7   Programming Assignment   52

Chapter 4   An Application: Numerical Integration   53

4.1   The Trapezoidal Rule   53
4.2   Parallelizing the Trapezoidal Rule   56
4.3   I/O on Parallel Systems   60
4.4   Summary   63
4.5   References   63
4.6   Exercises   63
4.7   Programming Assignments   64

Chapter 5   Collective Communication   65

5.1   Tree-Structured Communication   65
5.2   Broadcast   69
5.3   Tags, Safety, Buffering, and Synchronization   71
5.4   Reduce   73
5.5   Dot Product   75
5.6   Allreduce   76

5.7   Gather and Scatter   78
5.8   Allgather   82
5.9   Summary   83
5.10 References   86
5.11 Exercises   86
5.12 Programming Assignments   87

Chapter 6   **Grouping Data for Communication**   **89**

6.1   The count Parameter   89
6.2   Derived Types and MPI_Type_struct   90
6.3   Other Derived Datatype Constructors   96
6.4   Type Matching   98
6.5   Pack/Unpack   100
6.6   Deciding Which Method to Use   103
6.7   Summary   105
6.8   References   107
6.9   Exercises   108
6.10 Programming Assignments   109

Chapter 7   **Communicators and Topologies**   **111**

7.1   Matrix Multiplication   111
7.2   Fox's Algorithm   113
7.3   Communicators   116
7.4   Working with Groups, Contexts, and Communicators   117
7.5   MPI_Comm_split   120
7.6   Topologies   121
7.7   MPI_Cart_sub   124
7.8   Implementation of Fox's Algorithm   125
7.9   Summary   128
7.10 References   132
7.11 Exercises   132
7.12 Programming Assignments   133

Chapter 8   **Dealing with I/O**   **137**

8.1   Dealing with stdin, stdout, and stderr   138
8.1.1   Attribute Caching   139
8.1.2   Callback Functions   141
8.1.3   Identifying the I/O Process Rank   142

8.1.4 Caching an I/O Process Rank   144
8.1.5 Retrieving the I/O Process Rank   148
8.1.6 Reading from `stdin`   149
8.1.7 Writing to `stdout`   150
8.1.8 Writing to `stderr` and Error Checking   152
8.2 Limited Access to `stdin`   154
8.3 File I/O   156
8.4 Array I/O   158
8.4.1 Data Distributions   159
8.4.2 Model Problem   161
8.4.3 Distribution of the Input   162
8.4.4 Derived Datatypes   162
8.4.5 The Extent of a Derived Datatype   164
8.4.6 The Input Code   166
8.4.7 Printing the Array   168
8.4.8 An Example   170
8.5 Summary   171
8.6 References   176
8.7 Exercises   176
8.8 Programming Assignments   177

Chapter 9   Debugging Your Program   179

9.1 Quick Review of Serial Debugging   179
9.1.1 Examine the Source Code   180
9.1.2 Add Debugging Output   182
9.1.3 Use a Debugger   184
9.2 More on Serial Debugging   188
9.3 Parallel Debugging   188
9.4 Nondeterminism   188
9.5 An Example   191
9.5.1 The Program?   192
9.5.2 Debugging The Program   196
9.5.3 A Brief Discussion of Parallel Debuggers   196
9.5.4 The Old Standby: `printf/fflush`   199
9.5.5 The Classical Bugs in Parallel Programs   200
9.5.6 First Fix   202
9.5.7 Many Parallel Programming Bugs Are Really Serial Program-
        ming Bugs   203
9.5.8 Different Systems, Different Errors   205
9.5.9 Moving to Multiple Processes   206
9.5.10 Confusion about I/O   208
9.5.11 Finishing Up   210

9.6   Error Handling in MPI   210

9.7   Summary   212

9.8   References   215

9.9   Exercises   215

9.10   Programming Assignments   215

Chapter 10   Design and Coding of Parallel Programs   217

10.1   Data-Parallel Programs   218

10.2   Jacobi's Method   218

10.3   Parallel Jacobi's Method   220

10.4   Coding Parallel Programs   225

10.5   An Example: Sorting   226

    10.5.1   Main Program   227

    10.5.2   The "Input" Functions   230

    10.5.3   All-to-all Scatter/Gather   232

    10.5.4   Redistributing the Keys   233

    10.5.5   Pause to Clean Up   236

    10.5.6   `Find_alltoall_send_params`   236

    10.5.7   Finishing Up   239

10.6   Summary   240

10.7   References   241

10.8   Exercises   241

10.9   Programming Assignments   242

Chapter 11   Performance   245

11.1   Serial Program Performance   245

11.2   An Example: The Serial Trapezoidal Rule   247

11.3   What about the I/O?   248

11.4   Parallel Program Performance Analysis   249

11.5   The Cost of Communication   250

11.6   An Example: The Parallel Trapezoidal Rule   252

11.7   Taking Timings   254

11.8   Summary   256

11.9   References   257

11.10   Exercises   257

11.11   Programming Assignments   258

Chapter 12	**More on Performance**	**259**

12.1 Amdahl's Law   259
12.2 Work and Overhead   261
12.3 Sources of Overhead   262
12.4 Scalability   263
12.5 Potential Problems in Estimating Performance   265
   12.5.1 Networks of Workstations and Resource Contention   265
   12.5.2 Load Balancing and Idle Time   266
   12.5.3 Overlapping Communication and Computation   267
   12.5.4 Collective Communication   269
12.6 Performance Evaluation Tools   269
   12.6.1 MPI's Profiling Interface   271
   12.6.2 Upshot   272
12.7 Summary   275
12.8 References   277
12.9 Exercises   277
12.10 Programming Assignments   278

Chapter 13	**Advanced Point-to-Point Communication**	**279**

13.1 An Example: Coding Allgather   280
   13.1.1 Function Parameters   280
   13.1.2 Ring Pass Allgather   282
13.2 Hypercubes   284
   13.2.1 Additional Issues in the Hypercube Exchange   286
   13.2.2 Details of the Hypercube Algorithm   288
13.3 Send-receive   293
13.4 Null Processes   295
13.5 Nonblocking Communication   296
   13.5.1 Ring Allgather with Nonblocking Communication   298
   13.5.2 Hypercube Allgather with Nonblocking Communication   299
13.6 Persistent Communication Requests   301
13.7 Communication Modes   304
   13.7.1 Synchronous Mode   305
   13.7.2 Ready Mode   306
   13.7.3 Buffered Mode   307
13.8 The Last Word on Point-to-Point Communication   309
13.9 Summary   309
13.10 References   313
13.11 Exercises   313
13.12 Programming Assignments   314

Chapter 14 **Parallel Algorithms**   **315**

14.1 Designing a Parallel Algorithm   315
14.2 Sorting   316
14.3 Serial Bitonic Sort   316
14.4 Parallel Bitonic Sort   320
14.5 Tree Searches and Combinatorial Optimization   324
14.6 Serial Tree Search   325
14.7 Parallel Tree Search   328
    14.7.1 Par_dfs   330
    14.7.2 Service_requests   332
    14.7.3 Work_remains   332
    14.7.4 Distributed Termination Detection   334
14.8 Summary   335
14.9 References   336
14.10 Exercises   336
14.11 Programming Assignments   337

Chapter 15 **Parallel Libraries**   **339**

15.1 Using Libraries: Pro and Con   339
15.2 Using More than One Language   340
15.3 ScaLAPACK   342
15.4 An Example of a ScaLAPACK Program   345
15.5 PETSc   350
15.6 A PETSc Example   352
15.7 Summary   358
15.8 References   359
15.9 Exercises   359
15.10 Programming Assignments   359

Chapter 16 **Wrapping Up**   **361**

16.1 Where to Go from Here   361
16.2 The Future of MPI   362

Appendix A **Summary of MPI Commands**   **363**

A.1 Point-to-Point Communication Functions   363
    A.1.1 Blocking Sends and Receives   363
    A.1.2 Communication Modes   364
    A.1.3 Buffer Allocation   365

A.1.4 Nonblocking Communication   365
A.1.5 Probe and Cancel   369
A.1.6 Persistent Communication Requests   369
A.1.7 Send-receive   371
A.2 Derived Datatypes and `MPI_Pack/Unpack`   372
A.2.1 Derived Datatypes   372
A.2.2 `MPI_Pack` and `MPI_Unpack`   375
A.3 Collective Communication Functions   376
A.3.1 Barrier and Broadcast   376
A.3.2 Gather and Scatter   376
A.3.3 Reduction Operations   379
A.4 Groups, Contexts, and Communicators   381
A.4.1 Group Management   381
A.4.2 Communicator Management   383
A.4.3 Inter-communicators   385
A.4.4 Attribute Caching   386
A.5 Process Topologies   387
A.5.1 General Topology Functions   387
A.5.2 Cartesian Topology Management   387
A.5.3 Graph Topology Management   389
A.6 Environmental Management   391
A.6.1 Implementation Information   391
A.6.2 Error Handling   391
A.6.3 Timers   392
A.6.4 Startup   392
A.7 Profiling   393
A.8 Constants   393
A.9 Type Definitions   396

Appendix B   MPI on the Internet   399

B.1 Implementations of MPI   399
B.2 The MPI FAQ   400
B.3 MPI Web Pages   400
B.4 MPI Newsgroup   400
B.5 MPI-2 and MPI-IO   401
B.6 Parallel Programming with MPI   401

Bibliography   403

Index   407

Preface

IT IS NOW CLEAR THAT PARALLEL COMPUTING is here to stay: our voracious need for ever greater computing power simply cannot be satisfied by conventional, single-processor architectures. More and more companies are investing in architectures with multiple processors, and more and more colleges and universities are including parallel computing in their curricula.

The increase in the use of parallel computing is being accelerated by the development of standards for programming parallel systems. Developers can now write portable parallel programs and hence expect to obtain a reasonable return on the huge investment required in a large parallel software development project.

About MPI

The *Message-Passing Interface* or *MPI* is the most widely used of the new standards. It is not a new programming language; rather it is a library of subprograms that can be called from C and Fortran 77 programs. It was developed by an open, international forum consisting of representatives from industry, academia, and government laboratories. It has rapidly received widespread acceptance because it has been carefully designed to permit maximum performance on a wide variety of systems, and it is based on message passing, one of the most powerful and widely used paradigms for programming parallel systems. The introduction of MPI makes it possible for developers of parallel software to write libraries of parallel programs that are both portable and efficient. Use of these libraries will hide many of the details of parallel programming and, as a consequence, make parallel computing much more accessible to students and professionals in all branches of science and engineering.

About this Book

As parallel computing has moved more into the mainstream, there has been a clear need for an introductory text on parallel programming—a text that can be used by students and professionals who are not specialists in parallel computing, but who still want to learn enough about parallel programming so that they can exploit the vastly greater computational power provided by parallel systems. *Parallel Programming with MPI* has been written to fill this need. This text aims to provide students, instructors, and professionals with a tool that can ease their transition into this radically different technology.

Parallel Programming with MPI or *PPMPI* is first and foremost a "hands-on" introduction to programming parallel systems. It was written for students and professionals who have no prior experience in programming parallel systems. It was designed for use both as a self-paced tutorial and as a text in a more conventional classroom/computer laboratory setting. The only prerequisite to reading it is a nodding acquaintance with the first-year college math sequence and a knowledge of a high-level, procedural computing language. *PPMPI* provides both a complete introduction to MPI and an elementary introduction to parallel programming. It covers all the features of MPI, it provides a brief overview of parallel computing, and it provides an introduction to such topics as parallel debugging, parallel program design and development, and parallel program performance analysis. It also contains an introduction to the use of MPI libraries. In the belief that "teaching by example" is the most useful approach, *all* of the concepts are introduced through the use of fully developed program examples. The source for all of the programs can be downloaded from `http://www.usfca.edu/mpi`.

Except for the material in Chapters 3–8 the chapters are mostly self-contained and can be read in any order. Chapters 3–7 form a self-contained tutorial introduction to MPI and, as such, should probably be read in order, and before the remaining chapters. There are, however, parts of these chapters that can be omitted with no loss of continuity. The material on gather, scatter, and allgather in Chapter 5 and the material on topologies in Chapter 7 can be safely omitted on a first reading.

Before actually writing a larger parallel program, you will probably want to at least familiarize yourself with some of the problems involved in carrying out I/O on parallel systems. So Chapter 8 should receive at least a cursory initial examination. If you're anxious to make use of non-blocking communications, Chapter 13 can be read at any point after completing Chapter 7. Section 1.5 provides a more detailed overview of the contents of each chapter.

Since space considerations don't permit the presentation of programming examples in both C and Fortran, a choice had to be made between the two. For students, using C is the clear choice, since most learn to program in Pascal or C++, both of which are closer to C than to Fortran 77. However, Fortran would probably be the language of choice for most practicing scientists and engineers. Believing that the greater experience of the professional audience will make it easier for them than for students to follow examples in an unfamiliar language, I decided to use C throughout. However, I have tried to write all of the C source in a style that should be relatively accessible to a Fortran programmer. I have made very limited use of pointers and dynamic memory allocation, and I have tried to avoid the use of C's more obscure constructs. In addition, all of the example programs are available online in Fortran 77, thanks to a former student, Laura Koonce, who has done the translation. They can be downloaded from `http://www.usfca.edu/mpi`.

All of the examples in the text have been written in ANSI C rather than Kernighan and Ritchie C. So if your system uses a K&R C compiler, you will probably want to get a different compiler. The GNU C compiler, `gcc`, uses ANSI C, it is freely available from a number of sites on the internet, and it has been ported to virtually all currently available systems.

All of the programs in the text have been tested on a network of Silicon Graphics workstations running the `mpich` implementation of MPI. They have also been tested on an nCUBE 2 running a slightly optimized version of `mpich`. Please report any errors that do surface, in either the code or the text, to `peter@usfca.edu`. I'll pay the usual bounty of $1 to the first person reporting each error. A list of errata will be available at `http://www.usfca.edu/mpi`.

Classroom Use

Parallel programming will soon be a basic part of every computer scientist's education, and *PPMPI* will be well-suited for use in the second or third semester of the basic computing sequence. At this time, however, most colleges and universities introduce parallel programming in upper-division classes on computer architectures or algorithms. For these classes, I've used *PPMPI* as a supplement to existing, conventional texts. I assign the material in Chapters 3–10 as reading at appropriate places in the course and cover the remaining material as needed in the classroom. For example, in USF's parallel algorithms class, I spend a couple of weeks covering the material in Chapters 1 and 2. Parts of Chapters 3–10 are assigned as reading at various points during the course—usually when a programming assignment makes use of the material. The material on performance is covered in detail in class and applied to some basic parallel algorithms (e.g., dot product and matrix-vector multiplication). Fox's algorithm in Chapter 7 and bitonic sort and parallel tree search in Chapter 14 provide our initial examples of "significant" parallel algorithms. In the remainder of the course we cover more parallel algorithms from texts such as Kumar et al. [26].

We also teach an upper division class in parallel programming at USF. *PPMPI* is followed more or less on a chapter-by-chapter basis. The details of what is covered in the classroom are tailored to the level of the students. For well-motivated students, very little time is spent on syntax, and the course turns out to be very close to the previously described parallel algorithms class. For less motivated students, I run the class in much the same way as an "Introduction to Programming Class." Each week or two I introduce a new problem and then spend a week or two discussing the development of a solution. This typically involves fairly extensive discussions of the syntax and semantics of MPI functions.

I also teach a class for seniors and graduate students in which they spend a year working on a parallel programming project sponsored by a company or government agency. In this class, I usually spend a week or two on an overview of parallel computing. The students learn parallel programming by working through *PPMPI* on their own.

Support Materials

Problems in the text are divided into "Exercises" and "Programming Assignments." Most of the exercises involve some programming, but they focus on the mastery of a single basic concept and the effort involved in writing a solution to an exercise is minimal compared to that needed to complete a programming assignment.

In order to save instructors from the labor-intensive activity of designing major programming assignments, there will be a repository available online at `http://www.usfca.edu/mpi`. In order to make this repository as large as possible, I would like to make this a group effort, and I encourage instructors to send exercises and programming assignments (and, if you have them, solutions) to me at `peter@usfca.edu`. Morgan Kaufmann will make solutions available to faculty. Please contact Morgan Kaufmann at `orders@mkp.com` or 1-800-745-7323 to obtain your copy, or visit their home page `http://www.mkp.com`.

Acknowledgments

With a project that extends over several years, you tend to lose track of all that has happened in its day-by-day evolution. While it seemed at the time that a certain piece of advice, a tidbit of information, or a nudge in the right direction could never be forgotten, now that the time has come to acknowledge all of those who contributed to this book, the task seems impossible. So let me begin by thanking all of you who contributed to the development of this book. Please accept my sincerest apologies if I have overlooked any of you in the following acknowledgments.

The MPI Forum did an excellent job of designing a portable standard for programming parallel systems. My thanks to each and every one of them. I should also thank the developers of the free, portable implementations of MPI: Argonne National Laboratory and Mississippi State University for `mpich`, the Ohio Supercomputer Center for LAM, and the Edinburgh Parallel Computing Centre for CHIMP. A very large part of the development of the text involved writing and testing the code examples. Without these excellent implementations of MPI, I wouldn't have been able to write the book.

Some members of the Forum went above and beyond in helping me with the development of the text. Rusty Lusk of Argonne National Laboratory arranged to provide access to Argonne's SP2. Jack Dongarra of the University of Tennessee and Oak Ridge National Laboratory arranged for funding for the MPI Forum and very generously contributed the Foreword. Gary Howell of FIT, Alan Sussman of the University of Maryland, and Eric Van de Velde of Caltech kindly agreed to review an early proposal for the text. My thanks to all of them.

Support for my participation in the MPI Forum was provided by the University of San Francisco's Faculty Development Fund and the Advanced Research Projects Agency. The work on MPI that was supported by the Advanced Research Projects Agency under contract number NSF-ASC-9310330 was administered by the National Science Foundation's Division of Advanced Scientific Computing. My thanks to all of these institutions.

Access to computing facilities was provided by nCUBE, Argonne National Laboratory, the San Diego Supercomputer Center, and the Concurrent Supercomputing Consortium parallel computer system operated by Caltech. The Argonne National Laboratory High-Performance Computing Research Facility is funded principally by the U.S. Department of Energy Office of Scientific Computing. I'm grateful to all of these organizations for their generosity.

I owe a great debt of gratitude to the individuals who reviewed the manuscript: Jay Jackson of the University of Southwestern Louisiana, Don Breazeal of Intel, Allan Porterfield of Tera, Suresh Damodaran-Kamal of the HP Convex Technology Center, Jeffrey J. Nucciarone of Penn State, and one anonymous reviewer. They all made tremendous contributions—the book was immensely improved by their excellent suggestions. Of course I am to blame for any remaining errors.

My thanks to Gene Golub, who provided me with office space and computing facilities at Stanford during my sabbatical in the fall of 1995. He was also a great source of advice and encouragement throughout the project.

The staff at Morgan Kaufmann have been a great help to me. I'm grateful to Bruce Spatz for convincing me that I didn't have to do *everything*. Jennifer Mann and Jane Elliott did a great job of getting feedback on the manuscript and helping me apply it. Julie Pabst did a very thorough job in making sure that the manuscript was as consistent and error-free as possible and showed great patience in having my illegible scribbles converted into clear figures.

Many of the staff at nCUBE provided valuable assistance and advice. I want particularly to thank Shomit Ghose for his inspiring views of the future of parallel computing and his great sense of humor and Peter Madams for arranging the loan of a 32-processor nCUBE 2 to USF.

Closer to home, I want to thank all of the members of the mathematics department at USF. I'm sure the book would have never been completed without my colleagues' encouragement and advice. I owe special debts of gratitude to

Tristan Needham and Stanley Nel. Tristan acted as a sort of secretary of state, trying to make sure that in my zeal to get the book done I offended as few people as possible. I'm deeply grateful to him (and my correspondents during this period should be grateful to him, as well). The book would have never made it beyond an outline without the support of Stanley Nel, who is also dean of the College of Arts and Sciences. He arranged for financial support during the early stages of research and did everything in his power to help me with the book's completion. I'm deeply grateful to him also.

Of course there wouldn't be a book if it hadn't been for my students. When I first taught parallel computing in the fall of 1990, I discovered the horrors that relatively inexperienced students face when trying to learn parallel computing, and this compelled me to find ways to make learning a little easier. They have been very helpful in more ways than they're probably aware of: they showed me what was easy, what was way too hard, and what kinds of exposition might be expected to work. I am especially grateful to J.M. del Rosario, Noriko Hosoi, Edward Janne, Laura Koonce, Michael Ong, Tariq Rashid, and Thomas J. Willis.

These acknowledgments wouldn't be complete without an expression of gratitude to my parents. They have always been a source of support and encouragement.

My greatest debt is to my wife, Ginny. She put up with the late nights and early mornings for longer than either of us would care to remember. She gave me much needed advice at every stage. I'm delighted that I can finally start to repay her by saying, "It's done."

CHAPTER 1

Introduction

THIS BOOK HAS BEEN WRITTEN for people who want to learn how to program parallel computers. In this introduction, we'll talk about why we continue to need ever greater computing power and why parallel computers can be used to meet this need. We'll also touch on one of the most important forces driving our need for increased computing power: the development of computational science and engineering as a fundamental part of how scientists and engineers carry out research and development.

We'll also briefly discuss some of the difficulties associated with parallel computing, why it is so important that people who program learn to write portable parallel software, and the importance of the Message-Passing Interface (MPI) standard for programming parallel computers.

We'll close the chapter with an overview of the rest of the book and a few suggestions on how best to read it (section 1.5). If you're already an experienced parallel programmer and are reading this book because you want to learn about MPI, you may want to skip ahead to this section.

1.1 The Need for More Computational Power

As in politics, the lust for more power has been one of the main driving forces in the development of computers. Before the dawn of the computer era, scientists and engineers thought that the ability to carry out a few hundred arithmetic computations each second was nearly unimaginable. However, almost as soon as they found themselves with this much computational power, they began to clamor for more. They wanted to be able to carry out thousands of operations each second. The story is an old one. After thousands, it was millions, then billions, and the current goal is trillions (although many are already talking about quadrillions of operations per second).[1]

A not entirely philosophical question in this connection is, Why? What is causing this ever-escalating need for greater computational power? Science, engineering, finance, and even entertainment all provide impetus. Since we're primarily addressing scientists and engineers, let's talk about one of their major motivations.

For centuries, science has followed the basic paradigm of first observe, then theorize, and then test the theory through experimentation. Similarly, engineers have traditionally first designed (typically on paper), then built and tested prototypes, and finally built a finished product. However, it is becoming less expensive to carry out detailed computer simulations than it is to perform numerous experiments or build a series of prototypes. Thus the experiment and observation in the scientific paradigm, and design and prototyping in the engineering paradigm, are being increasingly replaced by computation. Furthermore, in some cases, we can now simulate phenomena that could not be studied using experimentation; e.g., the evolution of the universe. Of course, our reach always exceeds our grasp, and before we have even solved one problem, we can imagine an even more complex variation that will require computing power several orders of magnitude greater than what we require to solve our current problem. The more knowledge we acquire, the more complex our questions become.

But one trillion operations each second? Surely this is excessive? Here's a simple example illustrating that one trillion operations each second is actually somewhat modest. Suppose we wish to predict the weather over the United States and Canada for the next two days.[2] Also suppose that we want to model the atmosphere from sea level to an altitude of 20 kilometers, and we need to make a prediction of the weather at each hour for the next two days.

A standard approach to this type of problem is to cover the region of interest with a grid and then predict the weather at each vertex of the grid. So suppose we use a cubical grid, with each cube measuring 0.1 kilometer on each side. Since the area of the United States and Canada is about 20 million square kilometers, we'll need at least

$$2.0 \times 10^7 \, \text{km}^2 \times 20 \, \text{km} \times 10^3 \, \text{cubes per km}^3 = 4 \times 10^{11} \, \text{grid points.}$$

If it takes 100 calculations to determine the weather at a typical grid point, then in order to predict the weather one hour from now, we'll need to make about 4×10^{13} calculations. Since we want to predict the weather at each hour for 48 hours, we'll need to make a total of about

$$4 \times 10^{13} \, \text{calculations} \times 48 \, \text{hours} \approx 2 \times 10^{15} \, \text{calculations.}$$

---

1   We're using the American system of denominations: one billion $= 10^9$, one trillion $= 10^{12}$, and one quadrillion $= 10^{15}$.

2   This is a slight modification of an example presented in [26].

If our computer can execute one billion (10^9) calculations per second, it will take about

$$2 \times 10^{15} \text{ calculations}/10^9 \text{ calculations per second} = 2 \times 10^6 \text{ seconds}$$
$$\approx 23 \text{ days!}$$

In other words, the calculation is hopeless if we can only carry out one billion operations per second. If, on the other hand, we can carry out one trillion (10^{12}) calculations per second, it will take us about half an hour to carry out the computations. So we'll actually be able to make a complete prediction of the weather over each of the next 48 hours.

It's not difficult to imagine simple modifications to this problem so that one trillion operations per second won't be sufficient. For example, we might replace the United States and Canada with the entire earth. Then the area would go from 2×10^7 to about 5×10^8 square kilometers. So the required computation time would increase from about 30 minutes to about 13 hours, and our first 12 predictions would be useless. Furthermore, it's not difficult to find completely different problems requiring vastly greater computational power than we currently possess. For example, detailed atomic-level simulations of bio molecules and numerous types of simulations that would expedite the design and manufacture of integrated circuits all require vastly greater computational power than we currently possess. Indeed, the U.S. government has spent millions of dollars funding research for the development of algorithms and computing equipment that can be used to solve a collection of so-called grand challenge problems, problems in science and engineering whose solution will make fundamental contributions to both our theoretical and practical knowledge.

Before proceeding to a discussion of how we might be able to obtain the computational power to solve these problems, we should mention that although we have focussed on the problem of computational speed, another fundamental problem in the development of greater computational power is the development of vastly greater storage requirements. Even if we build a computer that is capable of performing trillions of operations each second, if it only has access to a few millions of words of memory, this computer is likely to be of little use. Thus, the development of greater computational power subsumes the development of both greater speed and greater storage.

1.2 The Need for Parallel Computing

Suppose we wanted to build a computer capable of carrying out one trillion operations each second.[3] Perhaps the most obvious approach is to simply extend well-understood technologies. That is, we might try to build a more

---

3   This example is based on an example in [11].

or less conventional von Neumann computer with an extremely fast processor and a very large amount of memory. Now suppose we want a computer that can execute the following code in one second:

```
/* x, y, and z are arrays of floats, each containing */
/* one trillion entries */
for (i = 0; i < ONE_TRILLION; i++)
    z[i] = x[i] + y[i];
```

On a conventional computer, we would successively fetch $x[i]$ and $y[i]$ from memory into registers, add them, and store the result in $z[i]$. Thus, in order to execute this code, we would need to be able to carry out at least 3×10^{12} copies between memory and registers each second. If data travels from memory to the CPU at the speed of light (3×10^8 meters/second), and if r is the average distance of a word of memory from the CPU, then r must satisfy

$$3 \times 10^{12} r \text{ meters} = 3 \times 10^8 \text{ meters/second} \times 1 \text{ second},$$

or $r = 10^{-4}$ meters. Now, our very fast conventional computer must contain at least three trillion words of memory in order to store x, y, and z. Typical memory hardware has the words laid out in a regular rectangular grid. If we use a square grid with side length s and connect the CPU to the center of the square, then the average distance from a memory location to the CPU is about $s/2$. So we want $s/2 = r = 10^{-4}$ meters, or $s = 2 \times 10^{-4}$ meters. If our memory words form a square grid, a typical "row" of memory words will contain

$$\sqrt{3 \times 10^{12}} = \sqrt{3} \times 10^6$$

words. Thus we need to fit a single word of memory into a square with side length measuring

$$\frac{2 \times 10^{-4} \text{ meters}}{\sqrt{3} \times 10^6} \approx 10^{-10} \text{ meters.}$$

This is the size of a relatively small atom! In other words, unless we figure out how to represent a 32-bit (or, more likely, 64-bit) word with a single atom, we'll find it impossible to build our computer.

So how do we build a computer capable of carrying out one trillion operations each second? Consider an analogous problem. Peter is a Roman contractor who specializes in excavation. His single laborer, Paul, can excavate 1000 cubic feet a day. However, there's a huge surge in demand for his services when it's reported that Attila the Hun is going to pay a visit to Rome next week. Peter figures that in order to meet the demand, he needs to excavate about 100,000 cubic feet a day for the next week. He's no fool. He solves his problem by simply hiring 99 more men, increasing his workforce from 1 to 100.[4]

---

4 Incidentally, Attila didn't sack Rome after all. Tradition has it that Pope Leo I met with him and convinced him to leave Italy.

The analogy should be clear: our single laborer is our processor and memory, and our 100,000 cubic feet a day is a grand challenge problem or other computationally demanding problem. Our solution is also clear: we should obtain more laborers or more processors and memory modules to solve the problem. A *parallel computer* is simply a computer (or collection of computers) with multiple processors that can work together on solving a problem.

1.3 The Bad News

OK, we know how to solve grand challenge problems, or more accurately, we know, in theory, how to obtain virtually unlimited computational power. The bad news is that we haven't said *how* our processors will work together. Presumably, Peter just told each of his men where to dig and handed him a shovel. The analogy might be to give each processor a program and let it compute. However, it's not easy to think of a problem that can be solved by humans or processors working completely independently of each other. For example, suppose that, Peter, instead of specializing in excavation, was a general contractor, and Pope Leo asked him to redesign and rebuild Rome after it was sacked by Genseric. Certainly, he wouldn't be able just to hire a bunch of unskilled laborers and hand each one a shovel. Rather, he would have to hire urban planners, architects, carpenters, stone masons, etc. Then he would have to organize them—get the urban planners talking to the architects, the architects talking to the stone masons and carpenters, and on and on.

To make matters worse, the analogous situation for processors is *much* more complicated. Indeed, a better analogy for the processors would be that Peter, instead of hiring urban planners, architects, etc., hired a large number of men, each ignorant of whatever work he has been hired to carry out, and it was up to Peter to instruct each of the men in the appropriate art.

When we set out to predict the weather we won't be able to buy California weather-predicting processors, jet-stream-predicting processors, and Gulf Coast weather-predicting processors. Rather, it will be up to us as programmers to insure that each processor receives the appropriate instruction in how to perform the calculations. Furthermore, implicit in the fact that processor A receives instructions for predicting the weather in San Francisco is the fact that processor A will need to communicate with processors responsible for predicting the weather at nearby locations.

So having obtained our collection of processors and memory, there is still a huge amount of work to be done. We must

1. decide on and implement an interconnection network for the processors and memory modules,
2. design and implement system software for the hardware,
3. devise algorithms and data structures for solving our problem,
4. divide the algorithms and data structures up into subproblems,

5. identify the communications that will be needed among the subproblems, and

6. assign subproblems to processors and memory modules.

As we've hinted in the preceding discussion, these are the critical problems in the development of parallel computing as a truly effective alternative to conventional serial computing.

1.4 MPI

In this book we'll be mainly concerned with items 3–6. We'll assume that someone else has taken on the job of building the physical machine and designing and implementing system software, although we'll discuss a number of aspects of these problems in Chapter 2, and we'll find ourselves frequently pointing out how decisions that were made about these issues will affect the performance of our programs. In other words, we'll be mainly concerned with the development of application programs, although we won't be able to ignore hardware and system software issues. Indeed, until recently, we might have had to learn two entirely new programming languages if we wanted to program two different parallel machines. However, this unfortunate state of affairs has been much improved. Two groups have taken on the formidable job of developing standards for programming parallel systems.

The first group, the High Performance Fortran Forum, has developed a set of extensions to Fortran 90 that allows programmers to easily write **data-parallel** programs. A data-parallel program achieves parallelism by dividing the data (e.g., vectors or matrices) among processors and having each processor apply (more or less) the same operations to its portion of the data. High Performance Fortran (HPF) provides a number of primitives for conveniently distributing arrays and operating on them in parallel. It is an extremely powerful and well-designed programming system. However, there are many parallel algorithms that cannot be efficiently converted into machine language by the current generation of HPF compilers.

The second group, the Message-Passing Interface (MPI) Forum, has taken a different approach to developing a standard for programming parallel systems. Rather than specifying a new language (and hence a new compiler), it has specified a *library* of functions that can be called from a C or Fortran program. The foundation of this library is a small group of functions that can be used to achieve parallelism by **message passing.** A message-passing function is simply a function that explicitly transmits data from one process to another. Message passing is a powerful and very general method of expressing parallelism. Message-passing programs can be used to create extremely efficient parallel programs, and message passing is currently the most widely used method of programming many types of parallel computers. Its principal drawback is that it is very difficult to design and develop programs using message passing. Indeed, it has been called the "assembly language of parallel computing" because it forces the programmer to deal with so much detail. In spite of this, the history of parallel computing suggests that it is possible to develop message-passing programs, and that if the design process is sufficiently deliberate, it doesn't take an undue effort to design extremely sophisticated programs. Furthermore, as more and more software is developed that uses MPI, more and more sophisticated algorithms will be encapsulated in *portable* MPI libraries, and the inclusion of these algorithms into a program will be simply a matter of calling a function. Indeed, within a year of the completion of MPI, virtually every maker of parallel systems supplied a version, there were at least three freely available portable implementations, and a number of excellent libraries had been written using MPI.

In this text we'll focus on the nuts and bolts of how to program parallel machines using MPI. We'll provide a brief overview of the current state of the art in parallel hardware and software, a tutorial introduction to basic message passing with MPI, and a tutorial introduction to the problem of designing, developing, and evaluating parallel programs.

1.5 The Rest of the Book

In Chapter 2 we'll provide a very brief overview of parallel computing. We'll discuss some of the issues we alluded to in the preceding sections: interconnection networks and system software. We'll also discuss some of the main approaches to programming parallel computers. If you're new to parallel computing, you should read this chapter either before or concurrently with Chapters 3–7. If you already have a good deal of experience with parallel computers, you can probably get away with just skimming or even skipping the chapter.

Chapters 3–7 provide a tutorial introduction to basic MPI. Chapter 3 discusses the details of how to write a minimal MPI program that uses only blocking sends and receives. Chapter 4 discusses a simple example: how to parallelize the trapezoidal rule for numerical integration using only blocking sends and receives. Chapter 5 provides an introduction to some of the collective communication operations available in MPI. Collective communications typically involve more processes than the so-called point-to-point communications. For example, one process may wish to "broadcast" a value to all other processes. This chapter also discusses some technical details of MPI terminology. Since communication between processes is usually an expensive operation, Chapter 6 discusses methods for reducing the number of communication operations by combining data that might be split across several messages into a single message. Chapter 7 discusses communicators and topologies. Communicators are one of the fundamental innovations available in MPI. They provide a natural way of partitioning the "communication universe" of a parallel program so that messages are properly received. Topologies provide a simple way of addressing processes that have some logical structure (e.g., a two- or three-dimensional grid). These chapters are fundamental to the remainder of the book. So, if you are new to MPI, regardless of whether you are new to parallel programming, you should read these chapters. If you're new to parallel programming, you should also make sure you do the exercises and write the programs in the programming assignments.

Chapter 8 discusses some approaches to the problem of carrying out I/O on parallel computers. It does not discuss any of the efforts currently underway to standardize I/O on parallel machines, nor does it make any attempt to develop high-performance I/O functions. Rather, it discusses some of the problems associated with I/O and attempts to develop some functions that will be reasonably portable. If you are using a system that provides convenient I/O access to parallel programs (e.g., every process can use `printf` and `scanf`), then you can ignore much of this material. However, if you have never dealt with the mapping problem, the problem of distributing a dataset across a collection of processes, then you should definitely read section 8.4.

Chapter 9 takes up the thorny problem of debugging parallel programs. Although you may consider yourself an expert in debugging, unless you already have a good deal of experience debugging parallel programs, we strongly encourage you to read this chapter. It's very easy to get extremely frustrated if you're debugging a parallel program: indeed, your attempts to simply find bugs may introduce new bugs. So this chapter could save you a lot of grief.

Chapters 10–12 take up the problem of putting what we've learned together: they address the problem of how to design and develop a substantial parallel program that meets the performance requirements of its specification. Chapter 10 addresses the problem of simply designing and coding, while Chapters 11 and 12 are devoted to the analysis and prediction of program performance.

Chapter 13 discusses the advanced point-to-point communications functions available in MPI. In particular, it discusses nonblocking communication. Together with the MPI tutorial in Chapters 3–7 it provides an overview of the functions available in MPI.

Chapter 14 provides a very brief discussion of parallel algorithms. We look at some of the issues involved in the design of parallel algorithms and go through detailed developments of two algorithms.

One of the best features of MPI is its support for the development of portable parallel libraries. Chapter 15 provides a short introduction to the use of two libraries that use MPI: ScaLAPACK and PETSc. Both are libraries for solving problems in scientific computing. ScaLAPACK is a library for solving problems in dense linear algebra. PETSc is a library for use in the design and development of programs to solve linear, nonlinear, and differential equations.

Chapter 16 provides pointers to additional information on MPI and a brief discussion of future directions in the development of MPI.

Except for the material in Chapters 3–8, the chapters are largely independent of each other. Chapters 3–8 should be read in order and before any of the subsequent chapters. The two chapters on performance, Chapters 11–12, should also be read in order. The remaining chapters can be read in any order. In particular, Chapter 13, on advanced point-to-point communications, can be read at any time after Chapter 8.

In summary, if you're new to parallel programming, you should read the book sequentially, and do as many of the exercises and write as many of the programs as possible. If you're already an experienced parallel programmer (or you feel that you can't take the time to read all that other stuff), you should read the tutorial chapters (Chapters 3–7) and Chapter 13. You can then read the remaining chapters as needed, using Appendix A as a guide to the rest of MPI.

1.6 Typographic Conventions

We'll make use of the following typefaces in the text:

- Program text, displayed or within running text, will use the following type:

```
#include <stdio.h>

main() {
    printf("Hello World!\n");
}
```

- When a term is defined, we'll use boldface type: A **blocking** function will not return until the arguments can be reused by the calling program.
- We'll also occasionally need to refer to the environment in which a program is being developed. In these examples, we'll assume that the programmer is working on a UNIX system, and we'll use % to indicate the shell prompt.

CHAPTER 2

An Overview of Parallel Computing

THIS CHAPTER CONTAINS A BRIEF SURVEY of parallel comput-
ing. In it we'll discuss the architecture of current parallel systems and try to
give a short overview of the current state of the art in methods for programming these systems. The chapter is mostly independent of the rest of the book.
It can be used as a reference chapter if some of the hardware/software issues
that arise in later chapters are not completely clear. However, since message
passing may not be the last word in parallel computing, we suggest that you
look it over so that you'll have an idea of some of the major ideas and issues
in parallel computing.

2.1 Hardware

There are as many varieties of parallel computing hardware as there are stars
in the sky ... well, not quite, but there are *many* different architectures, and
trying to impose some logical order on them may strike some as rather akin
to Procrustes' attempts to extend hospitality to his visitors.[1] But we must
persevere.

---

1   "Procrustes or the Stretcher ... had an iron bedstead, on which he used to tie all travellers
who fell into his hands. If they were shorter than the bed, he stretched their limbs to make
them fit it; if they were longer than the bed, he lopped off a portion. Theseus served him as
he had served others" [5].

2.1.1 Flynn's Taxonomy

The original classification of parallel computers is popularly known as **Flynn's taxonomy.** In 1966 Michael Flynn classified systems according to the number of instruction streams and the number of data streams. The classical von Neumann machine has a single instruction stream and a single data stream, and hence is identified as a **single-instruction single-data (SISD)** machine. At the opposite extreme is the **multiple-instruction multiple-data (MIMD)** system, in which a collection of autonomous processors operate on their own data streams. In Flynn's taxonomy, this is the most general architecture. Intermediate between SISD and MIMD systems are SIMD and MISD systems. We'll discuss each of these architectures.

2.1.2 The Classical von Neumann Machine

The classical von Neumann machine is divided into a CPU and main memory. The CPU is further divided into a control unit and an arithmetic-logic unit (ALU). The memory stores both instructions and data. The control unit directs the execution of programs, and the ALU carries out the calculations called for in the program. When they are being used by the program, instructions and data are stored in very fast memory locations, called **registers**. Of course, fast memory is more expensive, so there are relatively few registers.

Both data and program instructions are moved between memory and the registers in the CPU. The route along which they travel is called a **bus.** It's basically a collection of parallel wires together with some hardware that controls access to the bus. Faster busses will have more wires; e.g., a 32-bit bus is faster than a 16-bit bus.

The classical von Neumann machine needs some additional devices before it can be useful: input and output devices, and usually extended storage devices such as a hard disk.

The **von Neumann bottleneck** is the transfer of data and instructions between memory and the CPU: no matter how fast we make our CPUs, the speed of execution of programs is limited by the rate at which we can transfer the (inherently sequential) sequence of instructions and data between memory and the CPU. As a result, few computers today are strictly classical von Neumann machines. For example, most machines now have a hierarchical memory: in addition to the main memory and registers, there is an intermediate memory, faster than main memory but slower than registers, called **cache**. The idea behind cache is the observation that programs tend to access both data and instructions sequentially. Hence, if we store a small block of data and a small block of instructions in fast memory, most of the program's memory accesses will use the fast memory rather than the slower main memory.

2.1.3 Pipeline and Vector Architectures

The first widely used extension to the basic von Neumann model was **pipelining.** If the various circuits in the CPU are split up into functional units, and the functional units are set up in a pipeline, then the pipeline can, in theory, produce a result during each instruction cycle. As an example, suppose we have a program containing the following code:

```
float x[100], y[100], z[100];
for (i = 0; i < 100; i++)
    z[i] = x[i] + y[i];
```

Further suppose that a single addition consists of the following sequence of operations:

1. Fetch the operands from memory.
2. Compare exponents.
3. Shift one operand.
4. Add.
5. Normalize the result.
6. Store result in memory.

Now, suppose we have functional units that perform each of these basic operations, and these functional units are arranged in a pipeline. That is, the output of one functional unit is the input to the next. Then, while, say, x[0] and y[0] are being added, one of x[1] and y[1] can be shifted, the exponents in x[2] and y[2] can be compared, and x[3] and y[3] can be fetched. Thus, once the pipeline is "full," we can produce a result six times faster than we could without the pipelining.

A further improvement can be obtained by adding *vector* instructions to the basic machine instruction set. In our example of adding 100 pairs of floats, if we don't have vector instructions, an instruction corresponding to each of our basic operations will have to be fetched and decoded 100 times. With vector instructions, each of the basic instructions only needs to be issued once. The difference is somewhat analogous to the difference between the Fortran 77 code

```
      do 100 i = 1, 100
          z(i) = x(i) + y(i)
  100 continue
```

and the equivalent Fortran 90 code

```
      z(1:100) = x(1:100) + y(1:100)
```

Another improvement in vector machines is the use of multiple memory banks: operations that access main memory (fetch or store) are several times slower than operations that only involve the CPU (e.g., add). The use of independent memory banks can, to a degree, overcome this problem. For example, suppose that we can execute a CPU operation once every CPU cycle, but we can only execute a memory access every four cycles. Then if we have four memory banks, and our data is properly distributed among the banks, we can access memory once per cycle. In our example, if, say, z[i] is stored in memory bank i mod 4, then we can execute one store operation per cycle.

Some authors regard vector processors as MISD machines; others state that there is no such thing as an MISD machine, and that these machines are a variant of SIMD machines. Still others say that they aren't really parallel machines at all.

Some examples of vector processors are the CRAY C90 and the NEC SX4. See the references at the end of the chapter for information on performance benchmarks.

The great virtue of vector processors is that they are well understood and there are extremely good compilers. So it is relatively easy to write programs that obtain very high performance, and, as a consequence, they continue to be very popular for high-performance scientific computing.

There are, however, several drawbacks. The principles of pipelining and vectorization don't work well for programs that use irregular structures or use many branches—the key to performance is filling the pipeline and keeping it full. If operands aren't laid out properly in memory, this is impossible. Further, if a program has lots of conditional branches, there will be little opportunity for the use of vector instructions. Perhaps the greatest drawback is that they don't seem to *scale* well. That is, it's not clear how to modify them so that they can handle ever larger problems. Even if we add several pipelines and manage to keep them full, the upper limit on their speed will be some small multiple of the speed of the CPU.

2.1.4 SIMD Systems

A pure SIMD system (as opposed to a vector processor) has a single CPU devoted exclusively to control, and a large collection of subordinate ALUs, each with its own (small amount of) memory. During each instruction cycle, the control processor broadcasts an instruction to all of the subordinate processors, and each of the subordinate processors either executes the instruction or is idle. For example, suppose we have three arrays x, y, and z, distributed so that the memory of each processor contains one element of each array. Now suppose that we want to execute the following sequence of (serial) instructions:

```
for (i = 0; i < 1000; i++)
    if (y[i] != 0.0)
        z[i] = x[i]/y[i];
    else
        z[i] = x[i];
```

Then each subordinate processor would execute something like the following sequence of operations:

Time Step 1. Test local_y != 0.0.

Time Step 2.

a. If local_y was nonzero, z[i] = x[i]/y[i].
b. If local_y was zero, do nothing.

Time Step 3.

a. If local_y was nonzero, do nothing.
b. If local_y was zero, z[i] = x[i].

Note that this implies completely synchronous execution of statements. In other words, at any given instant of time, a given subordinate process is either "active" and doing exactly the same thing as all the other active processes, or it is idle.

The example makes the disadvantages of an SIMD system clear: in a program with many conditional branches or long segments of code whose execution depends on conditionals, it's entirely possible that many processes will remain idle for long periods of time.

However, the example doesn't make clear that SIMD machines tend to be relatively easy to program if the underlying problem has a regular structure. Furthermore, although communication is quite expensive in distributed-memory MIMD systems, it is basically no more expensive than computation in SIMD machines. (We'll try to explain why this is so, after we've talked about MIMD systems.) Finally, they do scale well, as the following examples show.

The most famous examples of SIMD machines are the CM-1 and CM-2 Connection Machines that were produced by Thinking Machines. The CM-2 had up to 65,536 1-bit processors and up to 8 billion bytes of memory. Maspar also produced SIMD machines. The MP-2 has up to 16,384 32-bit ALUs and up to 4 billion bytes of memory.

2.1.5 General MIMD Systems

The key difference between MIMD and SIMD systems is that with MIMD systems, the processors are autonomous: each processor is a full-fledged CPU with both a control unit and an ALU. Thus each processor is capable of executing its own program at its own pace. In particular, unlike SIMD machines, MIMD systems are *asynchronous*. There is often no global clock, and, unless, the processors are specifically programmed to synchronize with each other, there may be no correspondence between what is being done on different processors—even if the processors are executing the same program.

The world of MIMD systems is divided into shared-memory and distributed-memory systems. Some authors distinguish between the two architectures by

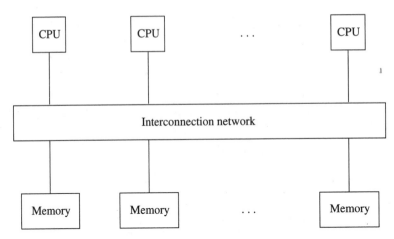

Figure 2.1   Generic shared-memory architecture

calling shared-memory systems **multiprocessors** and distributed-memory systems **multicomputers.** However, this terminology hasn't gained universal acceptance, and it is quite common to hear "multiprocessor" used as a synonym for "parallel processor."

2.1.6 Shared-Memory MIMD

As the name implies, the generic shared-memory machine consists of a collection of processors and memory modules interconnected by a network (see Figure 2.1).

Bus-Based Architectures

The simplest interconnection network is bus based. However, if multiple processors are simultaneously attempting to access memory, the bus will become saturated, and there may be long delays between starting a fetch or store and actually copying the data. Thus each processor usually has access to a fairly large cache (see Figure 2.2). Because of the limited bandwidth of a bus, these architectures do not scale to large numbers of processors. For example, the largest configuration of the currently popular SGI Challenge XL has only 36 processors.

Switch-Based Architectures

Most other shared-memory architectures rely on some type of switch-based interconnection network. As an example, the basic unit of the Convex SPP1200 is a 5×5 **crossbar switch.** A crossbar can be visualized as a rectangular mesh of wires with switches at the points of intersection, and terminals on its left and top edges. Processors or memory modules can be connected to the termi-

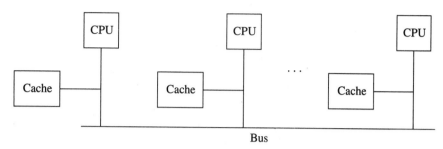

Figure 2.2   Bus-based shared-memory architecture

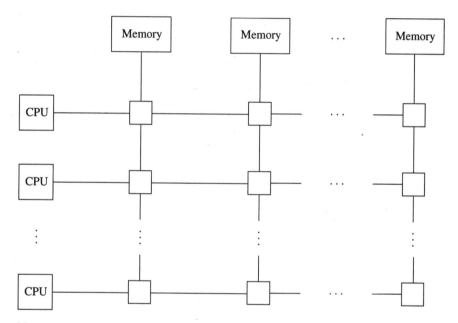

Figure 2.3   Crossbar switch

nals (see Figure 2.3). The switches can either allow a signal to pass through in both the vertical and horizontal directions simultaneously, or they can redirect a signal from vertical to horizontal or vice versa (see Figure 2.4). Thus, for example, if we have processors on the left and memory modules on the top of the crossbar, then any processor can access any memory module. Further, any other processor can simultaneously access any other memory module. That is, communication between two units will not interfere with communication between any other two units. So crossbar switches don't suffer from the problems of saturation that we encountered with busses.

Unfortunately, they tend to be very expensive: an $m \times n$ crossbar will need mn hardware switches. Thus, they tend to be fairly small. For example,

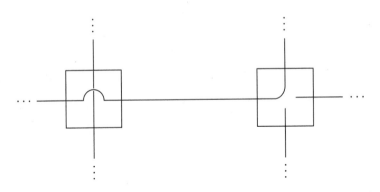

Figure 2.4   Configurations of the internal switches

in the Convex SPP1200, in order to have more than eight processors in a single machine, two or more crossbars are connected in a ring.

Note that this implies that when a processor accesses memory attached to another crossbar, the access times will be greater. This is, of course, undesirable, but it is a compromise that has been reached by virtually all designers of shared-memory machines. That is, nonuniform access times are the rule rather than the exception. Such systems are called **nonuniform memory access** or NUMA systems.

Cache Coherence

A problem that is encountered with any shared-memory architecture that allows the caching of shared variables is *cache consistency* or *cache coherence.* If a processor accesses a shared variable in its cache, how will it know whether the value stored in the variable is current? That is, suppose processor A wants to access a shared variable x in its cache. How does A know that some other process B hasn't modified its copy of x, rendering A's copy out of date? There are a number of cache consistency protocols, and they vary considerably in complexity. The simplest is probably the **snoopy protocol**, and it is suitable for small bus-based machines. The basic idea is that in addition to the usual hardware associated with a CPU, each processor has a cache controller. Among other things, the cache controllers "snoop" on the bus; i.e., they monitor the bus traffic. When a processor updates a shared variable, it also updates the corresponding main memory location. The cache controllers on the other processors detect the write to main memory and mark their copies of the variable as invalid. Notice that the bus makes this possible: any traffic on the bus can be monitored by all the controllers. Thus this approach is unsuitable for other types of shared-memory machines.

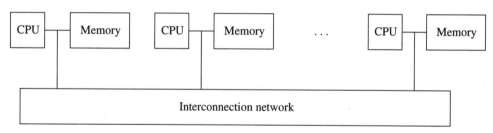

Figure 2.5   Generic distributed-memory system

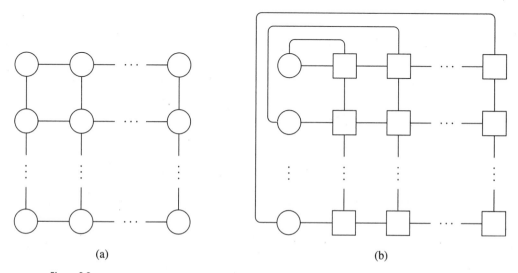

(a)   (b)

Figure 2.6   Different types of distributed-memory systems: (a) a static network (mesh) and (b) a dynamic network (crossbar)

2.1.7   Distributed-Memory MIMD

In distributed-memory systems, each processor has its own private memory. Thus, a generic distributed-memory system can be represented as in Figure 2.5. If we view a distributed-memory system as a graph, where the edges are communication wires, then there are two broad types of graphs: those in which each vertex corresponds to a processor/memory pair, or **node**, and those in which some vertices correspond to nodes and others correspond to switches. Figure 2.6 illustrates the distinction: round vertices are nodes and square vertices are switches. Networks of the first type are called **static networks** and networks of the second are called **dynamic networks**.

From a performance and programming standpoint, the ideal interconnection network is a fully connected network, in which each node is directly connected to every other node (see Figure 2.7). With a fully connected network, each node can communicate directly with every other node. Furthermore, the

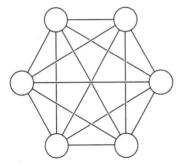

Figure 2.7   A fully connected interconnection network

communication involves no delay, and any node can communicate with any other node at the same time that any other communication is taking place. Unfortunately, the cost of such a network makes it impractical to construct such a machine with more than a few nodes.

Dynamic Interconnection Networks

Perhaps the closest we can come, in practice, to a fully connected network is a crossbar switch in which each process is connected to a terminal on the left edge and a terminal on the right edge (see the illustration on the right in Figure 2.6). Essentially the only delay in communication comes from the setting of a single switch, and if node i is communicating with node j, then any other pair of distinct nodes can communicate simultaneously. However, as we noted in section 2.1.6, these networks are also very expensive, and it is unusual to see crossbars with more than 16 processors. A notable exception is the Fujitsu VPP 500, which uses a 224×224 crossbar with 224 nodes.

A less expensive solution is to use a **multistage** switching network. There are a number of different types of multistage network. An example, an **omega** network, is illustrated in Figure 2.8. If we have p nodes, then an omega network will use $p \log_2 (p)/2$ switches, and, as a consequence, is a good deal less expensive than the crossbar, which uses p^2 switches. With the omega network, any node can communicate with any other node. However, there is a relatively high probability that communication between two nodes will interfere with communication between two other nodes. Further, the delay in transmitting a message is increased, since $\log_2 (p)$ switches must be set. In its SP series of computers, IBM has compromised between the two switching strategies: it uses an omega network, but the individual switches (represented in Figure 2.8 as 2×2 crossbars) are 8×8 crossbars. Currently the largest installed machine has 512 nodes.

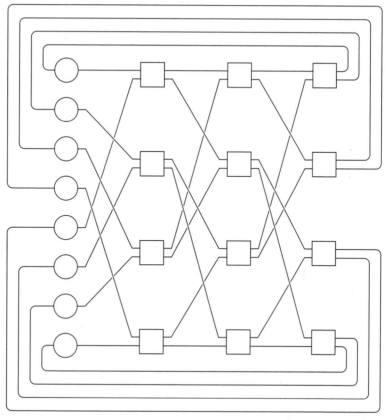

Figure 2.8   An omega network

Static Interconnection Networks

At the opposite extreme from a fully connected network is a **linear array**, a static network in which all but two of the nodes have two immediately adjacent neighboring nodes. A **ring** is a slightly more powerful network. This is just a linear array in which the "terminal" nodes have been joined (see Figure 2.9). The virtue of these networks is that they are relatively inexpensive: beyond the cost of the nodes, there is only an additional cost of $p-1$ or p wires. They also scale well: it's quite easy and inexpensive to increase the size of the network so that it includes arbitrarily many nodes. The principal drawback is that the number of available wires is extremely limited: if two nodes are communicating, it's very likely that other nodes attempting to communicate will be unable to do so. Furthermore, in a linear array, two processes that are attempting to communicate may have to forward the message along as many as $p-1$ wires, and in a ring it may be necessary to forward the message along as many as $p/2$ wires.

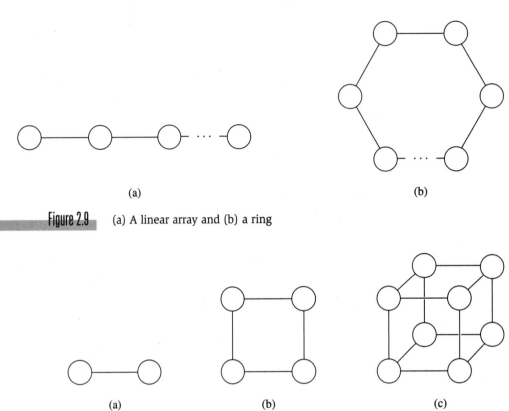

Figure 2.9   (a) A linear array and (b) a ring

Figure 2.10   Hypercubes of (a) dimension 1, (b) dimension 2, and (c) dimension 3

The practical static interconnection network that is closest to the fully connected network is the **hypercube**. Hypercubes are defined inductively. A dimension 0 hypercube consists of a single node. In order to construct a hypercube of dimension $d > 0$, we take two hypercubes of dimension $d - 1$ and join the corresponding nodes with communication wires. Hypercubes of dimensions 1, 2, and 3 are illustrated in Figure 2.10. Since we double the number of nodes with each increase in dimension, a hypercube of dimension d will contain $p = 2^d$ nodes. Since we add a wire to each node when we increase the dimension by one, in a hypercube of dimension d, each node is directly connected to d other nodes. Thus, it is relatively easy (compared to the linear array or the omega network) to arrange that communicating nodes don't interfere with other communications. Furthermore, it's not difficult to show that if we follow a shortest path between any two nodes in a hypercube of dimension d, then we'll traverse at most d wires (use induction on the dimension). Thus, the maximum number of wires a message will need to be forwarded along is $d = \log_2(p)$ wires. This is much better than the linear array or ring. The principal drawback to the hypercube is its relative lack

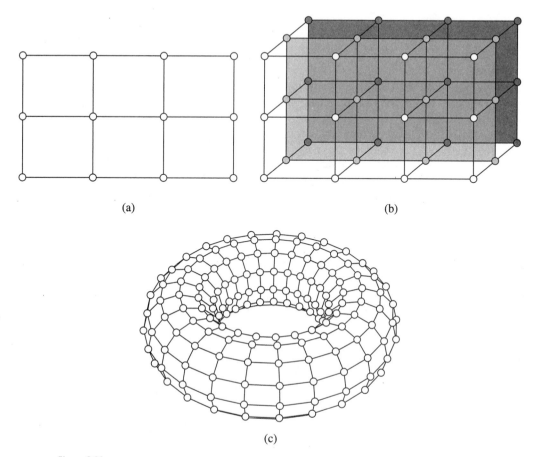

(a)

(b)

(c)

Figure 2.11   (a) Two-dimensional mesh, (b) three-dimensional mesh, and (c) two-dimensional torus

of scalability. In spite of the fact that the first "massively parallel" MIMD system was a hypercube (an nCUBE 10 with 1024 nodes), each time we wish to increase the machine size, we must *double* the number of nodes and add a new wire to each node.

Intermediate between hypercubes and linear arrays are meshes and tori, which are simply higher dimensional analogs of linear arrays and rings, respectively. Figure 2.11 illustrates a two-dimensional mesh, a two-dimensional torus, and a three-dimensional mesh. Observe that an n-dimensional torus can be obtained from an n-dimensional mesh by adding "wrap-around" wires to the nodes on the border. Also observe that, as we increase the dimension, it becomes less and less likely that two pairs of communicating nodes will interfere with each other, and that if a mesh has dimensions $d_1 \times d_2 \times \cdots \times d_n$, then the maximum number of wires a message will have to traverse is

$$\sum_{i=1}^{n}(d_i - 1).$$

So if a mesh is square, i.e., $d_1 = d_2 = \cdots = d_n$, the maximum will be $n(p^{1/n} - 1)$. More or less the same reasoning applies to tori; e.g., in a "square" torus, the maximum will be $\frac{1}{2}np^{1/n}$. Furthermore, meshes and tori scale better than hypercubes (although not as well as linear arrays and rings). For example, if we wish to increase the size of a $q \times q$ mesh, we simply add a $q \times 1$ mesh and q wires. More generally, we need to add $p^{(n-1)/n}$ nodes if we wish to increase the size of a square n-dimensional mesh or torus. Meshes and tori are currently quite popular. The Intel Paragon is a two-dimensional mesh, and the Cray T3E is a three-dimensional torus. Both scale to thousands of nodes.

Bus-Based Networks

The last, and probably the simplest, network is a bus. A cluster of workstations on an ethernet provides a popular example. Of course, busses tend to be fairly slow, and even worse, busses, especially ethernets, soon become saturated if there are more than a few nodes or more than absolutely minimal communication. Thus, although they are very useful for program development, currently available bus-based systems don't show much promise for very large-scale applications.

2.1.8 Communication and Routing

An issue that soon appears when we study communication in distributed-memory MIMD systems and larger shared-memory systems is that of routing. If two nodes are not directly connected or if a processor is not directly connected to a memory module, how is data transmitted between the two? Let's take a look at this problem on distributed-memory systems using a static interconnection network. Before proceeding, however, we should note that this problem is not necessarily completely solved with hardware: many systems implement parts of their routing using software.

The problem of routing subsumes two additional subproblems: If there are multiple routes joining the two nodes or processor and memory, how is a route decided on? Is the route chosen always a "shortest" path? Most systems use a deterministic shortest-path routing algorithm. That is, if node A communicates with node B, then the route that the communication uses will always be the same, and there will be no other route that uses fewer wires. This issue arises whether the intermediaries are other nodes or switches.

Another problem in this connection is the question of how intermediate nodes forward communications. There are two basic approaches. In order to understand them, let's suppose that node A is sending a message to node C, and node B lies between A and C. Node B has essentially two choices: it can

Time	Node A				Data Node B				Node C			
0	z	y	x	w								
1		z	y	x				w				
2			z	y			x	w				
3				z		y	x	w				
4					z	y	x	w				
5						z	y	x				w
6							z	y			x	w
7								z		y	x	w
8									z	y	x	w

Figure 2.12   Store-and-forward routing

Time	Node A				Data Node B	Node C			
0	z	y	x	w					
1		z	y	x	w				
2			z	y	x				w
3				z	y			x	w
4					z		y	x	w
5						z	y	x	w

Figure 2.13   Cut-through routing

read in the entire message, and then send it to node *C*, or it can immediately forward each identifiable piece, or **packet**, of the message. The first approach is called **store-and-forward routing.** The second is called **cut-through routing.** Store-and-forward routing is illustrated in Figure 2.12. Cut-through routing is illustrated in Figure 2.13. In the figures, the message is composed of four packets, w, x, y, and z. As we can see, using store-and-forward routing the message takes twice as long as the time it takes to send a message between adjacent nodes, while the time it takes using cut-through routing only adds the time it takes to send a single packet. Furthermore, store-and-forward routing uses considerably more memory on the intermediate nodes, since the entire message must be buffered. Thus, most systems use some variant of cut-through routing.

2.2 Software Issues

The idea of a **process** is a fundamental building block in most paradigms of parallel computing. Intuitively, a process is an instance of a program or a subprogram that is executing more or less autonomously on a physical processor.

A program is parallel if, at any time during its execution, it can comprise more than one process. In order to create useful parallel programs, there must be ways that processes can be specified, created, and destroyed, and there must be ways to coordinate interprocess interaction. In this section, we'll take a brief look at how these issues are addressed in different programming paradigms.

2.2.1   Shared-Memory Programming

Although we conventionally think of a shared-memory system as one in which the processors have more or less equal access to all the memory locations, it is perfectly reasonable to *emulate* shared memory with physically distributed memory if we have a mechanism for creating a global address space. Thus, it may be possible to program a distributed-memory system using shared-memory programming primitives, and this discussion may be applicable to a variety of underlying hardware configurations.

Shared-memory systems typically provide both **static** and **dynamic** process creation. That is, processes can be created at the beginning of program execution by a directive to the operating system, or they can be created during the execution of the program. The best-known dynamic process creation function is `fork`. A typical implementation will allow a process to start another, or **child**, process by calling `fork`. The starting, or **parent**, process can wait for the termination of the child process by calling `join`.

Coordination among processes in shared-memory programs is typically managed by three primitives. The first specifies variables that can be accessed by all the processes. The second prevents processes from improperly accessing shared resources. The third provides a means for synchronizing the processes. To illustrate these ideas, let's look at a very simple example. Suppose that each process has computed a *private* int `private_x`. By a private variable, we mean a variable whose contents are accessible to only one process. Thus, each process has defined a distinct variable `private_x` that cannot be accessed by any of the other processes. The program should compute the sum of these private ints, and a single process will print the sum.

We can use the first primitive to allocate a shared variable `sum`. One approach might be to simply prefix the definition of the variable with the keyword `shared`. So part of the variable definition component of our program might be

```
int private_x;
shared int sum = 0;
```

Things get a little more complicated when we start trying to compute the sum. We can't simply have each process compute

```
sum = sum + private_x;
```

In order to understand why this is a problem, recall that a typical system will

Time	Process 0		Process 1	
0	Fetch sum	= 0	Finish calculation of private_x	
1	Fetch private_x	= 2	Fetch sum	= 0
2	Add	2 + 0	Fetch private_x	= 3
3	Store sum	= 2	Add	3 + 0
4			Store sum	= 3

Figure 2.14   One scenario for shared-memory addition

execute something like the following sequence of machine instructions when it performs the add:

```
Fetch sum into register A
Fetch private_x into register B
Add contents of register B to register A
Store contents of register A in sum
```

Now suppose we have two processes, 0 and 1, the value of process 0's private_x is 2, and the value of process 1's private_x is 3. Then, depending on when the processes try to execute the addition of private_x to sum, we can compute a value of 2, 3, or 5 for sum. For example, consider the sequences of events depicted in Figure 2.14. Of course, sum should be 5, but since the sequences of machine commands making up sum = sum + private_x overlapped, the value computed by process 0 was overwritten by process 1.

Thus, we must make sure that the command

```
sum = sum + private_x;
```

is executed by only one process at a time. When we wish to ensure that only one process can execute a certain sequence of statements at a time, we are trying to arrange for **mutual exclusion,** and the sequence of statements is called a **critical section.**

One of the simplest approaches to solving the problem of mutual exclusion is called a **binary semaphore.** The basic idea is that there is a shared variable s whose value indicates whether the critical section is free. If s is 1, the section is free. If it's 0, the region cannot be accessed. Thus we would like to do something like this on each process:

```
shared int s = 1;

while (!s);              /* Wait until s = 1   */
s = 0;                   /* Close down access  */
sum = sum + private_x;   /* Critical section   */
s = 1;                   /* Re-open access     */
```

The problem is that the operations involved in manipulating s are not **atomic**. That is, while one process is fetching s = 1 into a register to test whether it's

OK to enter the critical region, another process can be storing $s = 0$. We need to be able to arrange that once a process starts to access s, no other process can access it until the original process is done with the access, including the reset of its value.

Thus, in addition to the shared variable, a binary semaphore consists of two special functions:

```
void P(int*  s  /* in/out */);
void V(int*  s  /* out    */);
```

The first function, P, has an effect similar to

```
while (!s);
s = 0;
```

However, it prevents other processes from accessing s once one process gets out of the loop. Similarly V sets s to 1, but it does this "atomically." The mechanics of achieving atomicity are system dependent. A simple solution is the addition of machine commands that "lock" and "unlock" variables: when a variable is locked, only the process that locked it can write to it.

The final issue we need to address is how to make sure that the correct sum is printed. In other words, if, say, process 0 is printing the sum, how can it know when all the processes have completed adding in their private_xs to sum? In view of the preceding discussion, we could create another shared variable that we could use to maintain a count of the number of processes that have updated sum. However, this is usually carried out with a somewhat higher-level operation called a **barrier.** A barrier is usually implemented as a function (which may or may not take an argument). Once a process has called the function, it will not return until every other process has called it. Thus, if we have a barrier after our sum, process 0 will know that the additions have been completed once it returns from the call to the barrier. In summary, then, our program body should look something like this:

```
int private_x;
shared int sum = 0;
shared int s = 1;

/* Compute private_x */
        ⋮
P(&s);
sum = sum + private_x;
V(&s);

Barrier();

if (I'm process 0)
    printf("sum = %d\n", sum);
```

The concept of shared variables and barriers is quite natural and appealing to programmers that have some experience with conventional systems. The idea of a binary semaphore, however, is not so appealing. It is somewhat error-prone and forces serial execution of the critical region. Thus, a number of alternatives have been devised. Monitors provide a higher-level alternative available on many systems. Basically, they encapsulate shared data structures and the operations that can be performed on them. In other words, the shared data structures are defined in the monitor, and the critical regions are functions of the monitor. When a process calls a monitor function, the other processes are prevented from calling the function.

Unfortunately, monitors do nothing to solve the serialization problem. It's not difficult to imagine alternative approaches to our addition program that don't enforce serial access to the shared variables. However, the obvious solutions tend to be extremely complicated in that they introduce other shared variables and critical regions. There are other solutions, but discussion of them is beyond the scope of this brief overview. See the references at the end of the chapter for information on other solutions.

2.2.2 Message Passing

The most commonly used method of programming distributed-memory MIMD systems is message passing, or some variant of message passing. In basic message passing, the processes coordinate their activities by explicitly sending and receiving messages. For example, at its most basic, the Message-Passing Interface (MPI) provides a function for sending a message:

```
int MPI_Send(void*       buffer       /* in */,
             int         count        /* in */,
             MPI_Datatype datatype    /* in */,
             int         destination  /* in */,
             int         tag          /* in */,
             MPI_Comm    communicator /* in */)
```

and a function for receiving a message:

```
int MPI_Recv(void*       buffer       /* out */,
             int         count        /* in */,
             MPI_Datatype datatype    /* in */,
             int         source       /* in */,
             int         tag          /* in */,
             MPI_Comm    communicator /* in */,
             MPI_Status* status       /* out */)
```

The current version of MPI assumes that processes are statically allocated; i.e., the number of processes is set at the beginning of program execution, and no additional processes are created during execution. Each process is assigned a unique integer rank in the range 0, 1, ... , $p - 1$, where p is the number of processes.

To illustrate the use of the functions, suppose that process 0 wishes to send the float x to process 1. Then it can call MPI_Send as follows:

```
MPI_Send(&x, 1, MPI_FLOAT, 1, 0, MPI_COMM_WORLD);
```

Process 1 needs to call MPI_Recv. In order that the data be received properly, it needs to match the tag and communicator arguments, and the memory available for receiving the message, which is specified by the buffer, count, and datatype parameters, must be at least as large as the message sent. The status parameter returns information on such things as the actual size of the message received. Thus, process 1 can call MPI_Recv as follows:

```
MPI_Recv(&x, 1, MPI_FLOAT, 0, 0, MPI_COMM_WORLD, &status);
```

There are several issues that need to be addressed here. First, note that the commands executed by process 0 (MPI_Send) will be different from those executed by process 1 (MPI_Recv). However, this does not mean that the programs need to be different. We can simply include the following conditional branch in our program:

```
if (my_process_rank == 0)
    MPI_Send(&x, 1, MPI_FLOAT, 1, 0, MPI_COMM_WORLD);
else if (my_process_rank == 1)
    MPI_Recv(&x, 1, MPI_FLOAT, 0, 0, MPI_COMM_WORLD, &status);
```

This approach to programming MIMD systems is called **single-program, multiple-data** (SPMD). In SPMD programs, the effect of running different programs is obtained by the use of conditional branches within the source code. This is the most common approach to programming MIMD systems.

Another issue we need to address is the semantics of the send/receive pairing. Suppose process 0 calls MPI_Send, but process 1 doesn't call MPI_Recv until some time later. Does process 0 simply stop and wait until process 1 calls MPI_Recv? Even worse, suppose process 0 calls MPI_Send, but process 1 fails to call MPI_Recv. Does the program crash or hang? The answers will, in general, depend on the system. The key issue is whether the system software provides for buffering of messages.

Buffering

Let's assume that process 0 and process 1 are running on distinct nodes, say, 0 is running on node *A* and 1 is running on node *B*. In this case there are several ways of dealing with the first situation: 0 can send a "request to send" to 1 and wait until it receives a "ready to receive" from 1, at which point it begins transmission of the actual message. Alternatively, the system software can **buffer** the message. That is, the contents of the message can be copied into a system-controlled block of memory (on *A* or *B*, or both), and 0 can continue executing. When 1 arrives at the point where it is ready to receive the message, the system software simply copies the buffered message into the appropriate memory location controlled by 1. The first approach, i.e., process 0 waits until process 1 is ready, is sometimes called **synchronous** communication. The second approach is called **buffered** communication.

The clear advantage of buffered communication is that the sending process can continue to do useful work if the receiving process isn't ready. Disadvantages are that it uses up system resources that otherwise wouldn't be needed (e.g., the memory for buffering), and, if the receiving process is ready, the communication will actually take longer, since it will involve copying between the buffer and the user program memory locations.

Most systems provide some buffering, but the details vary widely. Some systems attempt to buffer all messages. Others buffer only relatively small messages and use the synchronous protocol for large messages. Others let the user decide whether to buffer messages, and how much space should be set aside for buffering. Some systems buffer messages on the sending node, while others buffer them on the receiving node.

Note that if the system provides buffering of messages, then our second problem—process 0 executes a send, but process 1 doesn't execute a receive—shouldn't cause the program to crash; the contents of the message will simply sit in the system-provided buffer until the program ends. If, on the other hand, the system doesn't provide buffering, process 0 will probably hang; it will wait forever for a "ready to receive" from process 1.

Before proceeding, it should be noted that SIMD systems don't incur the overhead of buffering or waiting since every operation is synchronous across all the processes. Thus, process 0 "knows" process 1 is ready to receive, and the message can be immediately transmitted. It should also be noted that there are other approaches to the problem of how to deal with messages if there is no guarantee of synchronization among the processes. We'll discuss one such approach in section 2.2.4.

Blocking and Nonblocking Communication

We also need to look at what happens if we reverse the arrival at the communication points. That is, suppose process 1 executes the receive, but process 0 doesn't execute the send until some later time. The function we used for the receive, `MPI_Recv`, is **blocking.** This means that when process 1 calls `MPI_Recv`, if the message is not available, process 1 will remain idle until it becomes available. Note that this isn't quite the same thing as synchronous communication. In synchronous communication, the two processes directly communicate: process 0 won't begin sending the message until it has received explicit permission from process 1. In blocking communication, it may not be necessary for 0 to receive permission to go ahead with the send. For example,

0 may have already buffered the message when 1 is ready to receive, but the communication line joining the processes might be busy.

Most systems provide an alternative, **nonblocking** receive operation. In MPI, it's called MPI_Irecv. The *I* stands for *immediate.* That is, the process returns "immediately" from the call. It has one more parameter than MPI_Recv: a **request.** If, instead of calling MPI_Recv, process 1 called MPI_Irecv, the call would notify the system that process 1 intended to receive a message from 0 with the properties indicated by the argument. The system would initialize the request argument, and process 1 would return. Then process 1 could perform some other useful work (that didn't depend on the message from process 0) and check back later to see if the message had arrived. It would inform the system which message it was looking for through the request argument that was initialized by the original call to MPI_Irecv.

The use of nonblocking communication can be used to provide dramatic improvements in the performance of message-passing programs. If a node of a parallel system has the ability to simultaneously compute and communicate, the overhead due to communication can be substantially reduced. For example, if each node of a system has a communication coprocessor, then we can start a nonblocking communication (e.g., MPI_Irecv), perform computations that don't depend on the result of the communication, and when the computations are completed, finish the nonblocking operation. While the computations are being carried out, the communications co-processor can do most of the work required by the nonblocking operation. Since communication is very expensive relative to computation, overlapping communication and computation can result in tremendous performance gains.

2.2.3 Data-Parallel Languages

One of the simplest approaches to programming parallel systems is called **data parallelism.** In it, a data structure is distributed among the processes, and the individual processes execute the same instructions on their parts of the data structure. Clearly this approach is extremely well suited to SIMD machines. However, it is also quite common to use it on MIMD systems. One of its most attractive aspects is that for very regular structures it is possible for the user program to simply indicate that the structure should be distributed across the processes, and the compiler will automatically replace the user directive with code that distributes the data and performs the data-parallel operations. Let's look at a very simple example.

As we noted in Chapter 1, HPF is a set of extensions to Fortran 90 designed to make it relatively easy for a programmer to write highly efficient data-parallel programs. Here's a simple example that performs a distributed array addition:

```
      program add_arrays
!HPF$ PROCESSORS p(10)
```

```
                    real x(1000), y(1000), z(1000)
          !HPF$ ALIGN y(:) WITH x(:)
          !HPF$ ALIGN z(:) WITH x(:)
          !HPF$ DISTRIBUTE x(BLOCK) ONTO p

          C      Initialize x and y
                 ⋮
                 z = x + y
                 end
```

We begin by specifying a collection of 10 abstract processors with the first HPF directive. After defining our arrays, the first ALIGN directive specifies that y should be mapped to the abstract processors in the same way that x is. That is, for each i, y(i) is assigned to abstract processor q if and only if x(i) is. The second ALIGN statement has a similar effect on z. The DISTRIBUTE statement specifies which elements of x will be mapped to which abstract processors, and since y and z have been aligned with x, it will automatically map the corresponding elements of y and z. BLOCK specifies that x will be mapped by *blocks* onto the processors. That is, the first $1000/10 = 100$ elements will be mapped to the first processor, the next 100 to the second, etc. Once the arrays are distributed and initialized, we can simply add corresponding entries on the appropriate abstract processors with the Fortran 90 array addition statement

```
          z = x + y
```

A few observations are in order here. HPF doesn't provide a mechanism for specifying the mapping of abstract processors to physical processors. The actual mapping is usually done at execution time, and most systems provide (nonportable) means for a program to determine what the mapping is.

Explicitly aligning the arrays in the HPF directives will probably result in a more efficient executable program. In our example, the compiler will "know" that there won't be any communication when the addition is carried out. If the arrays weren't explicitly aligned, they might not be mapped in the same way to the processors, and hence communication might be necessary.

Finally, the problem of mapping data structures to processors is, in general, a very difficult one, unless the structure is static and very regular (e.g., a dense matrix). This can be a serious problem in *any* parallel program. However, it is especially problematic in data-parallel programs, where a mapping is specified at compile time. We'll return to the problem of mapping data structures to processes in section 2.2.5 and section 8.4.1.

It should be noted that "data parallel" is used in a somewhat different way in other contexts. It can be used to describe a methodology for designing a parallel program. In this context, it is usually contrasted with control-parallel programming, in which parallelism is obtained by partitioning the control or instructions of the program rather than the data. In general, most parallel programs use both approaches to obtain parallelism.

2.2.4 RPC and Active Messages

Although message-passing and data-parallel languages are the most widely used methods for programming distributed-memory systems, there are a number of other approaches to programming these systems. Two that have been very successful are RPC (Remote Procedure Call) and active messages. They share the assumption that the communication among processes should be more general than the simple transmission of data: they provide constructs for processes to execute subprograms on *remote* processors. The similarities end here however. RPC is essentially synchronous. In order to call a "remote procedure," one process, the client process, calls a *stub* procedure that sends an argument list to another process, the server process. The argument list is used by the server process in a call to the actual procedure. After completing the procedure, the (possibly modified) arguments are returned to the client process. The client is idle while it waits for the results to be returned by the server. This inefficiency reflects the origin of RPC: it was originally developed for use in distributed systems. The model environment is a collection of autonomous multitasking computers, and client and server processes are running on different computers. While the client process is waiting for the return of the arguments, its host system can perform useful work on other jobs. Clearly this will result in inefficiencies if the host systems are dedicated processors.

Active messages remedy this problem by eliminating the synchronous behavior of the process interaction. The message sent by the source process contains, in its header, the address of a handler residing on the receiving process's processor. When the message arrives, the receiving process is notified via an interrupt, and it runs the handler. The arguments of the handler are the contents of the message. Thus, there is no synchronicity: The first process "deposits" its message in the network and proceeds with its computations. Whenever the message ultimately arrives on the receiving process, the receiving process is interrupted, the handler invoked, and the receiving process continues its work. Thus, active messages provide features of both RPC and nonblocking message passing.

2.2.5 Data Mapping

The issue of **data locality** came up several times in our discussion of data-parallel programming. It is also a critical issue in the programming of both distributed-memory systems and nonuniform memory access (NUMA) shared-memory systems. In general, communication is much more expensive than computation. In conventional systems, it is almost a commonplace that instructions that access memory are much slower than operations that only involve the CPU. This difference in cost is even more dramatic if the memory is remote; i.e., if it is the local memory of another node in a distributed-memory system or if it is a "distant" memory module in a NUMA shared-memory system. Thus, considerable effort has been devoted to the problem of optimal data mapping, that is, the problem of how to assign data elements to processors so that communication is minimized. There is an easy (silly) solution: on a distributed-memory system map all the data-elements to the memory of a single node and have that process do *all* the calculations. (A similar mapping applies to NUMA shared-memory systems.) Of course, this would result in a considerable waste of computational resources. So the problem of **load balancing** is counterpoised to our data locality problem. That is, we want to assign the same amount of work to each processor, or else we'll be wasting our computation resources. Any mapping must take into consideration both load balance *and* data locality.

In this section, we'll take a brief look at what is probably the simplest case of the mapping problem: how to map a linear array to a collection of nodes in a distributed-memory system. For the sake of explicitness, suppose that our array is $A = (a_0, a_1, \ldots, a_{n-1})$. Let's also think of our processors as a linear array: $P = (q_0, q_1, \ldots, q_{p-1})$. We'll assume that the amount of computation associated with each array element is about the same. In other words, if we assign the same number of elements to each processor, we'll have achieved the goal of load balancing.

If the number of processors, p, is equal to the number of array elements, n, then there is only one mapping that balances the load equally among the processors:

$$a_i \rightarrow q_i$$

for each i, and our problem seems a trivial one. Indeed, if p evenly divides n, then it might at first seem that there are only two mappings that balance the load. A **block mapping** partitions the array elements into blocks of consecutive entries and assigns the blocks to the processors. Suppose, for example, that $p = 3$ and $n = 12$. Then a block mapping would look like this:

$$a_0, a_1, a_2, a_3 \rightarrow q_0,$$
$$a_4, a_5, a_6, a_7 \rightarrow q_1,$$
$$a_8, a_9, a_{10}, a_{11} \rightarrow q_2.$$

The other "obvious" mapping is a **cyclic mapping**. It assigns the first element to the first processor, the second element to the second, and so on. When each processor has one element of the array, we go back to the first processor, and repeat the assignment process with the next p elements. This process is repeated until all the elements are assigned. If $p = 3$ and $n = 12$, we'll have the following mapping:

$$a_0, a_3, a_6, a_9 \rightarrow q_0,$$
$$a_1, a_4, a_7, a_{10} \rightarrow q_1,$$
$$a_2, a_5, a_8, a_{11} \rightarrow q_2.$$

But we've only scratched the surface! Consider, for example, the following mapping:

$$a_0, a_1, a_6, a_7 \rightarrow q_0,$$
$$a_2, a_3, a_8, a_9 \rightarrow q_1,$$
$$a_4, a_5, a_{10}, a_{11} \rightarrow q_2.$$

This is a **block-cyclic mapping**. It partitions the array into blocks of consecutive elements as in the block mapping. However, the blocks are not necessarily of size n/p. The blocks are then mapped to the processors in the same way that the elements are mapped in the cyclic mapping. In our example, the blocks have size 2. If we start considering the (very real) possibility that the blocksize and/or p don't evenly divide n, we see that there are a huge number of different mappings just for linear arrays, and if we start looking at higher-dimensional arrays or trees or general graphs, the problem becomes astronomically complex.

So, how do we decide on the appropriate mapping? Not surprisingly, it's highly problem dependent. The literature is filled with discussions of mappings. See the references at the end of the chapter for pointers to information on matrix mappings. We'll come back and look at the nuts and bolts of how to actually distribute an array in section 8.4.1.

2.3 Summary

In this chapter we've touched on a large variety of issues in parallel computing. We began with a discussion of parallel architectures and continued with a discussion of some issues that arise in programming parallel systems.

Pipeline/vector processors obtain parallelism by "pipelining" functional units in the CPU and issuing vector instructions. They continue to be very popular, mainly due to the relative ease with which they can be programmed to solve problems with regular structures. However, they are less successful with irregular structures and don't scale to arbitrarily large problems.

SIMD systems have one control unit and many subordinate arithmetic and logic units. They scale well, and they don't suffer from many of the problems inherent in communicating between asynchronous processes. However, their relative difficulty with irregular structures and their difficulties with conditional branches have led many to believe that they cannot be good general-purpose systems. At this time, it appears that they will probably continue to be niche machines.

The concept of *shared-memory MIMD* is appealing and intuitively natural to programmers accustomed to programming conventional systems. Hence, they have achieved a much wider acceptance than distributed-memory systems. The principal difficulty they have encountered is *scalability*: the hardware needed to allow many processors uniform access to memory is very expensive. The compromise that has been reached is to settle for *nonuniform access.* That is, each processor sees a hierarchy of memory speeds, and it is up to the programmer to keep this in mind when she designs her software. At the top of the hierarchy, most shared-memory systems use fairly large local *caches.* Assuring that these caches are consistent adds to the cost of shared-memory designs.

Distributed-memory MIMD systems continue to scale better than shared-memory systems, and meshes and switch-based systems are currently the most popular architectures. *Routing* is of critical importance in the design of distributed-memory systems; we briefly discussed *store-and-forward* and *cut-through routing.* The principal drawback to distributed-memory MIMD systems has been that they are very difficult to program.

While *processor* and *memory* are the fundamental conceptual units of parallel hardware, the *process* is the fundamental conceptual unit of parallel software. Roughly speaking, a process is an instance of a program that is executing on a physical processor.

Most shared-memory systems provide facilities for both static and dynamic creation of processes. A commonly used method for the dynamic creation/destruction of processes is the familiar `fork/join`. In order to program shared-memory systems, we need programming primitives for defining shared variables—variables that each process can access. We saw that the existence of shared resources can lead to errors if we're not careful to limit access to the shared resources. Sections of code that should only be accessed by one process at a time are called *critical sections.* We used *binary semaphores* to limit access. We may also need to synchronize the processes. A common means for doing this is called a *barrier.*

Message passing is the most commonly used method for programming distributed-memory systems. We saw that message passing can be *synchronous* or *asynchronous.* If a system provides *buffering,* then the system can copy the sender's message to a system buffer, and the sender can continue with its work. However, if there is no buffering, the processes must synchronize; i.e., the sender must receive permission from the receiver to transmit the message. Message-passing functions can also be either *blocking* or *nonblocking.* In blocking message passing, a call to a communication function won't return until the operation is complete. For example, a blocking receive function will not return until the message has been copied into the user process's memory. Nonblocking communication consists of two phases. During the first phase, a function is called that starts the communication. During the second phase, another function is called that completes the communication. Thus, if the system has the capability to simultaneously compute and communicate, we can overlap communication and computation by doing some useful computation between the two phases of the operation.

Parallel programs are usually broadly divided into two categories: *data parallel* and *control parallel.* In data-parallel programs, we obtain parallelism by partitioning the data among the processes; in control-parallel programs, we partition the instructions. Typical parallel programs usually use both methods.

Data-parallel languages are explicitly designed to facilitate data-parallel programming. They have convenient language constructs for distributing data structures among processes and having each process carry out more or less the same operations on its part of the data. Data-parallel languages are very efficient and easy to use, provided the structure of the underlying problem is fairly regular.

RPC and *active messages* generalize message passing. Processes can communicate both by exchanging data and by executing instructions on other processes. RPC is synchronous. Active messages are asynchronous.

We closed the chapter with a brief discussion of *data mapping* or *data distribution*. The problem arises from the conflicting goals of *data locality* and *load balancing*. In distibuted-memory and NUMA shared-memory systems, accessing remote data is relatively expensive, so we would like to have as much data as possible stored in local or nearby memory. However, we also want the workload distributed as evenly as possible among the processes, so we would also like to assign each process an equal amount of data. We took a brief look at three data distributions that attempt to resolve these conflicting goals: *block, cyclic,* and *block-cyclic* mappings of linear arrays.

2.4 References

Almasi and Gottlieb [1] is an excellent reference for most of the material in this chapter. They have an especially nice discussion of other approaches to obtaining mutual exclusion. Kumar et al. [26] also discusses a number of the issues we've touched on here.

Michael Flynn's now classic paper [16] was published in *Proceedings of the IEEE*.

The Performance Database Server [31] can be accessed over the World Wide Web. It provides a comprehensive summary of system performance figures.

Active messages were first discussed by von Eicken et al. in [37]. Demmel [11] discusses matrix mappings in the context of Gaussian elimination.

Foster [17] provides a more extensive discussion of HPF.

2.5 Exercises

1. Suppose that node A is sending an n-packet message to node B in a distributed-memory system with a static network. Also suppose that the message must be forwarded through k intermediate nodes.

   a. Estimate the cost of sending the message using store-and-forward routing.

   b. Estimate the cost using cut-through routing.

Write your estimate in terms of the cost of sending a message between directly connected nodes.

2. Write pseudocode for sorting a shared n-element list of ints in an n-process shared-memory program.

3. Consider the following fragment of pseudocode for a shared-memory program:

```
shared int s = 1;
        ⋮
while (1) {
    P(&s);
    /* Critical section */
        ⋮
    V(&s);
}
```

If we run this program with a large number of processes, what problem(s) might occur with access to the critical region?

4. The different mappings we discussed for linear arrays can be generalized to two-dimensional arrays.

   a. A *block-row* mapping corresponds to a block mapping of a linear array, except that the array elements are the rows of the matrix. Illustrate a block-row distribution of a 6 × 6 matrix among three processes.

   b. Similar definitions apply for block-column mappings. Illustrate a block-column distribution of a 6 × 6 matrix among three processes.

   c. A similar definition applies for cyclic-row mappings. Illustrate a cyclic-row distribution of a 6 × 6 matrix among three processes.

   d. In the preceding definitions, we can think of our processes as forming a "virtual" linear array. If we think of our processes as forming a "virtual" grid, a more natural mapping is a *block-checkerboard* mapping, or *block-block* mapping. In a block-block mapping the matrix is partitioned into rectangular block submatrices, and the submatrices are mapped in row-major order to the processes. Illustrate a block-checkerboard distribution of a 6 × 6 matrix among four processes. The block submatrices should have order 3 × 3, and the virtual grid should have order 2 × 2.

   e. How should we define a *cyclic-cyclic* mapping? Illustrate your answer with a 6 × 6 matrix distributed among four processes.

   f. How would we form hybrid mappings in which one dimension used a block distribution, and the other used a cyclic distribution? Illustrate your answer with a 6 × 6 matrix distributed among four processes.

CHAPTER 3

Greetings!

WE'LL BEGIN OUR STUDY of *practical* parallel computing by using `MPI_Send` and `MPI_Recv` to write a simple program. This chapter is shorter than most of the other chapters because we want you to start writing parallel programs as soon as possible.

3.1 The Program

The first C program that most of us saw was the "hello, world" program in Kernighan and Ritchie's classic text, *The C Programming Language* [24]. It simply prints the message "hello, world." A variant that makes some use of multiple processes is to have each process send a greeting to another process.

On most parallel systems, the processes involved in the execution of a parallel program are identified by a sequence of nonnegative integers. If there are p processes executing a program, they will have ranks $0, 1, \ldots, p - 1$. So one possibility here is for each process other than 0 to send a message to process 0. Of course, we want to know that process 0 received the messages. So we'll have it print them out. Here is an MPI program that does this.

```
#include <stdio.h>
#include <string.h>
#include "mpi.h"

main(int argc, char* argv[]) {
    int         my_rank;    /* rank of process      */
    int         p;          /* number of processes  */
    int         source;     /* rank of sender       */
    int         dest;       /* rank of receiver     */
```

```
int          tag = 0;          /* tag for messages      */
char         message[100];     /* storage for message   */
MPI_Status   status;           /* return status for     */
                               /* receive               */

/* Start up MPI */
MPI_Init(&argc, &argv);

/* Find out process rank   */
MPI_Comm_rank(MPI_COMM_WORLD, &my_rank);

/* Find out number of processes */
MPI_Comm_size(MPI_COMM_WORLD, &p);

if (my_rank != 0) {
    /* Create message */
    sprintf(message, "Greetings from process %d!",
        my_rank);
    dest = 0;
    /* Use strlen+1 so that '\0' gets transmitted */
    MPI_Send(message, strlen(message)+1, MPI_CHAR,
        dest, tag, MPI_COMM_WORLD);
} else { /* my_rank == 0 */
    for (source = 1; source < p; source++) {
        MPI_Recv(message, 100, MPI_CHAR, source, tag,
            MPI_COMM_WORLD, &status);
        printf("%s\n", message);
    }
}

/* Shut down MPI */
MPI_Finalize();
} /* main */
```

3.2 Execution

The details of compiling and executing this program depend on the system you're using. Compiling may be as simple as

```
% cc -o greetings greetings.c -lmpi
```

However, there may also be a special script or makefile for compiling. So ask your local expert how to compile and run a parallel program that uses MPI. When the program is compiled and run with two processes, the output should be

```
Greetings from process 1!
```

If it's run with four processes, the output should be

```
Greetings from process 1!
Greetings from process 2!
Greetings from process 3!
```

Although the details of what happens when the program is executed vary from system to system, the essentials are the same on all systems, provided we run one process on each processor.

1. The user issues a directive to the operating system that has the effect of placing a copy of the executable program on each processor.
2. Each processor begins execution of its copy of the executable.
3. *Different processes can execute different statements by branching within the program based on their process ranks.*

This last point is very important. In the most general form of MIMD programming, each process runs a different program. However, in practice, this generality is usually not needed, and the appearance of "each process running a different program" is obtained by putting branching statements within a single program. So in the "Greetings!" program, even though the statements executed by process 0 are essentially different from those executed by the other processes, we avoid writing several distinct programs by including the branching statement

```
if (my_rank != 0)
        ⋮
else
        ⋮
```

This form of MIMD programming is frequently called **single-program multiple-data (SPMD)** programming. Don't confuse it with SIMD programming, since it is a form of MIMD programming. All of the programs in this book will use the SPMD paradigm.

3.3 MPI

Notice that the program consists entirely of conventional C statements and preprocessor directives. MPI is not a new programming language. It's simply a library of definitions and functions that can be used in C (and Fortran) programs. So in order to understand MPI, we just need to learn about a collection of special definitions and functions.

3.3.1 General MPI Programs

Let's begin at the beginning and discuss the MPI statements in the program. Every MPI program must contain the preprocessor directive

```
#include "mpi.h"
```

This file, mpi.h, contains the definitions and declarations necessary for compiling an MPI program.

MPI uses a consistent scheme for MPI-defined identifiers. All MPI identifiers begin with the string "MPI_." The remaining characters of most MPI constants are in capitals (e.g., MPI_CHAR). The first character of the remainder of the name of each MPI function is capitalized and subsequent characters are lowercase (e.g., MPI_Init).

Before any other MPI functions can be called, the function MPI_Init must be called, and it should only be called once. Its parameters are pointers to the main function's parameters—argc and argv. It allows systems to do any special setup so that the MPI library can be used. After a program has finished using the MPI library, it must call MPI_Finalize. This cleans up any "unfinished business" left by MPI—e.g., it frees memory allocated by MPI. So a typical MPI program has the following layout:

```
        ⋮
#include "mpi.h"
        ⋮
main(int argc, char* argv[]) {
        ⋮
    /* No MPI functions called before this */
    MPI_Init(&argc, &argv);
        ⋮
    MPI_Finalize();
    /* No MPI functions called after this */
        ⋮
} /* main */
        ⋮
```

Note that it is not necessary to call MPI_Init as the first executable statement in the program, or even in main: it must be called *before any other MPI function is called.* Similarly, it is not necessary to call MPI_Finalize as the last executable statement or even in main: it must be called *at some point following the last call to any other MPI function.*

3.3.2 Finding Out about the Rest of the World

Since the flow of control in an SPMD program depends on the rank of a process, MPI provides the function MPI_Comm_rank, which returns the rank of a process in its second parameter. The first parameter is a **communicator**. Essentially a communicator is a collection of processes that can send messages to each other. For now, the only communicator we'll need is MPI_COMM_WORLD. It is predefined in MPI and consists of all the processes running when program execution begins.

Many of the constructs in our programs also depend on the number of processes executing the program. So MPI provides the function MPI_Comm_size for determining this. Its first parameter is a communicator. It returns the number of processes in a communicator in its second parameter.

3.3.3 Message: Data + Envelope

The actual message passing in our program is carried out by the MPI functions MPI_Send and MPI_Recv. The first command sends a message to a designated process. The second receives a message from a process. These are the most basic message-passing commands in MPI.

Before we discuss the details of their parameter lists, let's look at some of the problems involved in message passing. Suppose process A wants to send a message to process B, and there is some type of physical connection between A and B—e.g., a wire. Consider an analogous situation: Amy wants to send a message to Bob. In this case the physical connection is the route the postal service uses when it collects and delivers the letter. Amy proceeds by composing the letter, putting it in an envelope, addressing and stamping the envelope, and dropping the letter in a mailbox. The postal service collects the mail in the mailbox and delivers the letter to Bob's house. Bob checks his mail, finds the letter, opens it, and reads Amy's message.

The analogy with Amy's composing the message is clear: A must compose the message; i.e., put it in a buffer. A must "drop the message in a mailbox" by calling MPI_Send. In order for the postal service, or message-passing system, to know where to deliver the message, it must be addressed. This is done by "enclosing the message in an envelope" and adding an address. Physically this corresponds to adding some information to the actual data that A wishes to send. But just the address isn't enough. Since the physical message is just a sequence of electrical signals, the system needs to be able to determine where the message ends. One solution is to also add the size of the message. Another solution is to mark the end of the message with a special symbol. In either case, the number of elements in the message and their type can be used to identify the end of the message. Thus, typical message-passing systems "enclose" messages in **envelopes**. Among other things, the envelope contains the destination of the message and information identifying the size or end of the message. Certainly this information, destination and size of message, should be enough for B to receive the message, and in order to receive the message, it calls MPI_Recv.

However, let's see if we can make some trouble for Bob and our processes. Bob receives three types of correspondence at his office: junk mail, personal mail from acquaintances, and personal mail from strangers, and he wants his secretary to sort his mail into these three categories. Bob is planning to reply to the mail from the acquaintances, read the personal mail from strangers, and toss the junk mail. An analogy for the processes might be that *A* sends messages to *B* that ask for data, while *C* sends messages to *B* that contain information *B* needs in order to do calculations, and *D* sends data that should be printed. Bob's secretary will sort his mail by looking at the return addresses on the envelopes. The obvious analogy for message-passing computing is to add the address of the source process to the envelope so that *B* can take appropriate action.

Now suppose the Presto Computer Corporation is sending some advertising information to Bob, and an employee of Presto, whom Bob doesn't know, is also sending Bob some information that Bob requested on Presto's new superchip. What should Bob's secretary do? He's received junk mail and personal mail from a single source—the Presto Computer Corp. His secretary will probably be able to distinguish between the junk mail and the personal mail by looking at the size of the envelope or the amount of postage. An analogy for processes might be that *B* receives floats from several processes. Some of these floats should be printed, while others should be stored in an array, and a single process can send both floats to be printed and floats to be stored. How is *B* to distinguish between the two different types? Neither the source nor the size of the message is sufficient. Two possible solutions come to mind:

- Each process sends two messages. The first specifies whether the float is to be printed or stored, and the second contains the actual float.
- Each process can send a single message, a string, that contains both the float and whether the float is to be printed or stored.

There are problems with both. The biggest problem with the first is that it is very expensive on current generation systems to send messages—the general rule of thumb is to send as few as possible. Another problem with the first is that if *B* is receiving lots of messages, the first message of a pair may get "separated" from the second by other messages, and it may be difficult, or impossible, to decide which messages should be paired. If we use the second approach, the sending process must "encode" the data into a string before sending, and the receiving process must "decode" the data from the string after receiving it. This is time-consuming. Furthermore, there may be a loss of precision when the float is encoded as a string and then decoded.

The solution to this problem that has become standard on message-passing systems is the use of **tags** or **message types**. A tag or message type is just an int specified by the programmer that the system adds to the message envelope. In our setting, for example, the programmer might decide that floats to be printed should have tag 0, and floats to be stored should have tag 1. When *B* receives the message, it checks the tag on the envelope and acts accordingly. There is nothing special about these numbers. MPI guarantees that the integers

0–32767 can be used as tags. Most implementations allow much larger values. Since message type can be easily confused with datatype, in order to avoid confusion, in the remainder of the book we'll always use tag rather than type.

A final issue for Bob: Bob has two occupations. To his coworkers he's known as a mild-mannered programmer, but he is also a secret agent, and as part of his work as a secret agent, he routinely conducts huge financial transactions with some disreputable characters. Of course he doesn't want his perfectly respectable secretary reading mail from these characters. So he rents a post office box, and all of his secret correspondence is sent to the post office box.

An analogous problem for the processes might occur in this situation: Amy has written a large program that solves a system of differential equations. As part of her solution, she needs to solve systems of linear equations, but she doesn't feel that she has the expertise necessary to write code that will do this efficiently. So she acquires a library of functions that solves systems of linear equations, and her program simply calls functions from this library. If the routines in the library need to do message passing (and they will in this case), how can Amy's program distinguish between messages it sends and messages sent by routines in the library? They might accidentally use the same tags. The solution adopted by MPI is to add a further piece of information to the message envelope: a *communicator*. We mentioned before that a communicator is a collection of processes that can send messages to each other. Further, two processes using distinct communicators cannot receive messages from each other. So Amy can get her program to distinguish between its messages and the library's messages by passing a communicator to the library that is different from any communicator(s) she uses in the parts of the program that she has written. Thus, a final piece of information for the envelope is a communicator.

In summary, then, the message envelope contains at least the following information:

1. The rank of the receiver
2. The rank of the sender
3. A tag
4. A communicator

3.3.4 Sending Messages

OK. Now it should be fairly clear what most of the parameters of MPI_ Send and MPI_Recv are. The exact syntax for the two functions is

```
int MPI_Send(
        void*         message     /* in */,
        int           count       /* in */,
        MPI_Datatype  datatype    /* in */,
        int           dest        /* in */,
```

Table 3.1   Predefined MPI datatypes

MPI datatype	C datatype
MPI_CHAR	signed char
MPI_SHORT	signed short int
MPI_INT	signed int
MPI_LONG	signed long int
MPI_UNSIGNED_CHAR	unsigned char
MPI_UNSIGNED_SHORT	unsigned short int
MPI_UNSIGNED	unsigned int
MPI_UNSIGNED_LONG	unsigned long int
MPI_FLOAT	float
MPI_DOUBLE	double
MPI_LONG_DOUBLE	long double
MPI_BYTE	
MPI_PACKED	

```
            int             tag          /* in */,
            MPI_Comm        comm         /* in */)

    int MPI_Recv(
            void*           message      /* out */,
            int             count        /* in */,
            MPI_Datatype    datatype     /* in */,
            int             source       /* in */,
            int             tag          /* in */,
            MPI_Comm        comm         /* in */,
            MPI_Status*     status       /* out */)
```

The contents of the message are stored in a block of memory referenced by the parameter message. The next two parameters, count and datatype, allow the system to determine how much storage is needed for the message: the message contains a sequence of count values, each having *MPI* type datatype. This type is not a C type, although most of the predefined MPI datatypes correspond to C types. The predefined MPI types and the corresponding C types (if they exist) are listed in Table 3.1. The last two types, MPI_BYTE and MPI_PACKED, don't correspond to standard C types—we'll discuss them later. It should be noted that there may be additional MPI types if the system supports additional C types. For example, if the system has type long long int, then there should be an MPI type MPI_LONG_LONG_INT.

Note that the amount of space allocated for the receiving buffer does not have to match the exact amount of space in the message being received. For example, when our program is run, the size of the message that process 1 sends, strlen(message) + 1, is 26 chars, but process 0 receives the message in a buffer that has storage for 100 characters. This makes sense. In general,

the receiving process may not know the exact size of the message being sent.
So MPI allows a message to be received as long as there is sufficient storage
allocated. If there isn't sufficient storage, an overflow error occurs.

The parameters dest and source are, respectively, the ranks of the receiving and the sending processes. MPI allows source to be a wildcard. There is
a predefined constant MPI_ANY_SOURCE that can be used if a process is ready
to receive a message from any sending process rather than a particular sending
process. There is not a wildcard for dest.

As we noted earlier, MPI has two mechanisms specifically designed for
partitioning the message space: tags and communicators. The parameters tag
and comm are, respectively, the tag and communicator. The tag is an int, and,
for now, our only communicator is MPI_COMM_WORLD, which is predefined on
all MPI systems and consists of all the processes running when execution of
the program begins. There is a wildcard, MPI_ANY_TAG, that MPI_Recv can
use for the tag. There is no wildcard for the communicator. In other words, in
order for process A to send a message to process B, the argument comm that A
uses in its call to MPI_Send must be identical to the argument that B uses in
its call to MPI_Recv, while A must use a tag and B can receive with either an
identical tag or MPI_ANY_TAG.

Note that the possible use of wildcards for the arguments source and
tag by MPI_Recv, but not by MPI_Send "matches a 'push' communication
mechanism, where data transfer is effected by the sender (rather than a 'pull'
mechanism, where data transfer is effected by the receiver)" [28, 29].

The last parameter of MPI_Recv, status, returns information on the data
that was actually received. It references a struct with at least three members—
one for the source, one for the tag, and one for an error code. Their names
are

```
status -> MPI_SOURCE
status -> MPI_TAG
status -> MPI_ERROR
```

So if, for example, the source of the receive was MPI_ANY_SOURCE, then status -> MPI_SOURCE will contain the rank of the process that sent the message. There may be additional, implementation-specific members.

The status parameter also returns information on the size of the message
received. However, this is not directly accessible to the user as a member. In
order to determine the size of the message received, we can call

```
int MPI_Get_count(
        MPI_Status*     status       /* in  */,
        MPI_Datatype    datatype     /* in  */,
        int*            count_ptr    /* out */)
```

The status doesn't contain a member for the count since this may involve
an unnecessary computation. For example, if the system records the number

of bytes received, then every call to MPI_Recv would have to carry out a division to convert bytes to the number of elements received. In most cases, this information probably won't be needed. So in the relatively rare instances when it is needed, the program can call MPI_Get_count.

As with almost all other MPI functions, both MPI_Send and MPI_Recv have integer return values. These return values are error codes: if the function detected an error, it can return an int indicating the nature of the error. However, the default behavior of MPI implementations is to abort execution of the program if an MPI function detects an error. In Chapter 9 we'll discuss how to change this default behavior, but for the time being we'll ignore the return values.

3.4 Summary

MPI is not a new programming language. It is a collection of functions and macros, or a *library* that can be used in C programs.

The programs that we will write in this text use the *single-program multiple-data (SPMD)* model. In this model, each process runs the same executable program. However, the processes execute different statements by taking different branches in the program: the branches are determined by the process rank.

Every MPI program must include the preprocessor directive

```
#include "mpi.h"
```

This includes the declarations and definitions necessary for compiling an MPI program. MPI uses a consistent scheme for MPI-defined identifiers. All MPI identifiers begin with the string "MPI_." The remaining characters of most MPI constants are capital letters. The first character of the remainder of the name of each MPI function is capitalized and subsequent characters are lowercase (e.g., MPI_Init).

Before any other MPI function is called, our program must call

```
int MPI_Init(
        int*    argc      /* in/out */,
        char**  argv[]    /* in/out */)
```

After our program is finished using MPI, it must call

```
int MPI_Finalize(void)
```

In order for a process to find out how many processes are involved in the execution of a program, it can call

```
int MPI_Comm_size(
        MPI_Comm   comm                        /* in  */,
        int*       number_of_processes         /* out */)
```

A *communicator* is a collection of processes that can send messages to each other. `MPI_COMM_WORLD` is a predefined communicator: it consists of all the processes running when program execution begins. In order for a process to find out its rank, it can call

```
int MPI_Comm_rank(
        MPI_Comm   comm       /* in  */,
        int*       my_rank   /* out */)
```

Actual message passing is accomplished using the two functions

```
int MPI_Send(
        void*        message    /* in */,
        int          count      /* in */,
        MPI_Datatype datatype   /* in */,
        int          dest       /* in */,
        int          tag        /* in */,
        MPI_Comm     comm       /* in */)

int MPI_Recv(
        void*        message    /* out */,
        int          count      /* in  */,
        MPI_Datatype datatype   /* in  */,
        int          source     /* in  */,
        int          tag        /* in  */,
        MPI_Comm     comm       /* in  */,
        MPI_Status*  status     /* out */)
```

The parameter `message` refers to the actual data being transmitted. The parameters `count` and `datatype` determine the size of the message. `MPI_Recv` doesn't need to know the exact size of the message being received, but it must have at least as much space as the size of the message it's trying to receive.

The `tag` and `comm` are used to make sure that messages don't get mixed up. Since `MPI_Recv` can use wildcards for `source` and `tag`, the `status` parameter returns the source and tag of the message that was actually received.

Each message consists of two parts: the data being transmitted and the envelope. The envelope of a message contains

1. the rank of the receiver
2. the rank of the sender
3. a tag
4. a communicator

3.5 References

A detailed discussion of the syntax and semantics of the various MPI functions is contained in the MPI Standard [28, 29]. There are also very complete discussions in [34] and [21]. Both [21] and [17] provide introductory discussions of MPI.

3.6 Exercises

1. Create a C source file containing the "Greetings!" program. Find out how to compile it and run it on different numbers of processors. What is the output if the program is run with only one process? How many processors can you use?

2. Modify the "Greetings!" program so that it uses wildcards in the receives for both source and tag. Is there any difference in the output of the program?

3. Try modifying some of the parameters to MPI_Send and MPI_Recv (e.g., count, datatype, source, dest). What happens when you run your program? Does it crash? Does it hang (i.e., stop in the middle of execution without crashing)?

4. Modify the "Greetings!" program so that all the processes send a message to process $p - 1$. On many parallel systems, every process can print to the screen of the terminal from which the program was started. Have process $p - 1$ print the messages it receives. What happens? Can process $p - 1$ print to the screen?

3.7 Programming Assignment

1. Write a program in which process i sends a greeting to process $(i + 1)\%p$. (Be careful of how i calculates from whom it should receive!) Should process i send its message to process $i + 1$ first and then receive the message from process $i - 1$? Should it first receive and then send? Does it matter? What happens when the program is run on one processor?

CHAPTER 4

An Application: Numerical Integration

NOW THAT WE KNOW HOW TO SEND MESSAGES with MPI, let's write a program that uses message passing to solve a problem: calculate a definite integral with the trapezoidal rule. If you remember the trapezoidal rule, you can skip section 4.1.

4.1 The Trapezoidal Rule

Recall that the definite integral from a to b of a nonnegative function $f(x)$ can be thought of as the area bounded by the x-axis, the vertical lines $x = a$ and $x = b$, and the graph of the function $f(x)$. See Figure 4.1.

One approach to estimating this area or integral is to partition the region into regular geometric shapes and then add the areas of the shapes. In the trapezoidal rule, the regular geometric shapes are trapezoids; each trapezoid has its base on the x-axis, vertical sides, and its top edge joining two points on the graph of $f(x)$. See Figure 4.2.

For our purposes, we'll choose all the bases to have the same length. So if there are n trapezoids, the base of each will be $h = (b - a)/n$. The base of the leftmost trapezoid will be the interval $[a, a + h]$; the base of the next trapezoid will be $[a + h, a + 2h]$; the next, $[a + 2h, a + 3h]$; etc. In general, the base of the ith trapezoid will be $[a + (i - 1)h, a + ih]$, $i = 1, \ldots, n$. In order to simplify notation, let x_i denote $a + ih$, $i = 0, \ldots, n$. Then the length of the left side of the ith trapezoid will be $f(x_{i-1})$, and its right side will be $f(x_i)$. See Figure 4.3. Thus, the area of the ith trapezoid will be

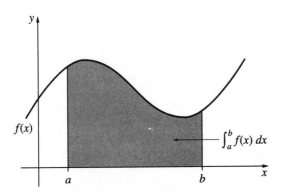

Figure 4.1   Definite integral of a nonnegative function

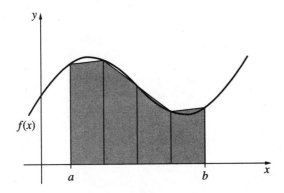

Figure 4.2   Trapezoids approximating definite integral

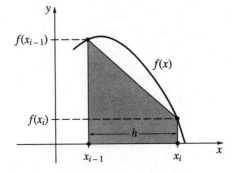

Figure 4.3   The ith trapezoid

$$\frac{1}{2}h[f(x_{i-1}) + f(x_i)],$$

and the area of our entire approximation will be the sum of the areas of the trapezoids:

$$\frac{1}{2}h[f(x_0) + f(x_1)] + \frac{1}{2}h[f(x_1) + f(x_2)] + \cdots + \frac{1}{2}h[f(x_{n-1}) + f(x_n)]$$

$$= \frac{h}{2}[f(x_0) + 2f(x_1) + 2f(x_2) + \cdots + f(x_n)]$$

$$= [f(x_0)/2 + f(x_n)/2 + f(x_1) + f(x_2) + \cdots + f(x_{n-1})]h.$$

So by putting $f(x)$ into a subprogram, we can write a *serial* program for calculating an integral using the trapezoidal rule.

```
/* Calculate definite integral using trapezoidal rule.
 * The function f(x) is hardwired.
 * Input: a, b, n.
 * Output: estimate of integral from a to b of f(x)
 *     using n trapezoids.
 */

#include <stdio.h>

main() {
    float   integral;   /* Store result in integral   */
    float   a, b;       /* Left and right endpoints    */
    int     n;          /* Number of trapezoids        */
    float   h;          /* Trapezoid base width        */
    float   x;
    int     i;

    float f(float x);   /* Function we're integrating */

    printf("Enter a, b, and n\n");
    scanf("%f %f %d", &a, &b, &n);

    h = (b-a)/n;
    integral = (f(a) + f(b))/2.0;
    x = a;
    for (i = 1; i <= n-1; i++) {
        x = x + h;
        integral = integral + f(x);
    }
    integral = integral*h;

    printf("With n = %d trapezoids, our estimate\n", n);
    printf("of the integral from %f to %f = %f\n",
        a, b, integral);
} /* main */
```

Table 4.1 Assignment of subintervals to processes

Process	Interval
0	$[a, a + \frac{n}{p}h]$
1	$[a + \frac{n}{p}h, a + 2\frac{n}{p}h]$
$\vdots$	$\vdots$
i	$[a + i\frac{n}{p}h, a + (i + 1)\frac{n}{p}h]$
$\vdots$	$\vdots$
$p - 1$	$[a + (p - 1)\frac{n}{p}h, b]$

```
float f(float x) {
    float return_val;
    /* Calculate f(x).  Store calculation in return_val. */
         ⋮
    return return_val;
} /* f */
```

4.2 Parallelizing the Trapezoidal Rule

As we saw in Chapter 2, there are several approaches to parallelizing a serial program. Perhaps the simplest approach distributes the data among the
processes, and each process runs essentially the same program on its share of
the data. In our case, the data is just the interval $[a, b]$ and the number of
trapezoids n. So we can parallelize the trapezoidal rule program by assigning
a subinterval of $[a, b]$ to each process, and having that process estimate the
integral of f over the subinterval. In order to calculate the integral over $[a, b]$,
the processes' local calculations are added.

An obvious question here is, How does each process know which subinterval it should integrate over, and how many trapezoids it should use? In
order to answer this, suppose there are p processes and n trapezoids, and,
in order to simplify the discussion, also suppose that n is evenly divisible by
p. Then it is natural for the first process to calculate the area of the first n/p
trapezoids, the second process to calculate the area of the next n/p, etc. Recall
that MPI identifies each process by a nonnegative integer. So if there are p
processes, the first is process 0, the second process 1, ... , and the last process
$p - 1$. Using the notation we developed in our discussion of the serial program,
we have each process calculating integrals over the subintervals indicated in
Table 4.1.

Thus each process needs the following information:

- The number of processes, p
- Its rank
- The entire interval of integration, $[a, b]$
- The number of subintervals, n

Recall from Chapter 3 that the first two items can be found by calling the MPI functions `MPI_Comm_size` and `MPI_Comm_rank`. The last two items should probably be input by the user. But this (perhaps surprisingly) can raise some difficult problems. So for our first attempt at calculating the integral, let's "hardwire" these values by simply setting their values with assignment statements.

A second obvious question is, How are the individual processes' calculations added up? One straightforward approach would be to send each process's result to, say, process 0, and have process 0 do the final addition.

With these assumptions we can write our first "real" MPI program.

```
/* Parallel Trapezoidal Rule
 *
 * Input: None.
 * Output:  Estimate of the integral from a to b of f(x)
 *    using the trapezoidal rule and n trapezoids.
 *
 * Algorithm:
 *    1.  Each process calculates "its" interval of
 *        integration.
 *    2.  Each process estimates the integral of f(x)
 *        over its interval using the trapezoidal rule.
 *    3a. Each process != 0 sends its integral to 0.
 *    3b. Process 0 sums the calculations received from
 *        the individual processes and prints the result.
 *
 * Note:  f(x), a, b, and n are all hardwired.
 */
#include <stdio.h>

/* We'll be using MPI routines, definitions, etc. */
#include "mpi.h"


main(int argc, char** argv) {
    int         my_rank;   /* My process rank           */
    int         p;         /* The number of processes   */
    float       a = 0.0;   /* Left endpoint             */
    float       b = 1.0;   /* Right endpoint            */
    int         n = 1024;  /* Number of trapezoids      */
    float       h;         /* Trapezoid base length     */
    float       local_a;   /* Left endpoint my process  */
```

```
    float       local_b;    /* Right endpoint my process */
    int         local_n;    /* Number of trapezoids for  */
                            /* my calculation            */
    float       integral;   /* Integral over my interval */
    float       total;      /* Total integral            */
    int         source;     /* Process sending integral  */
    int         dest = 0;   /* All messages go to 0      */
    int         tag = 0;
    MPI_Status  status;

    float Trap(float local_a, float local_b, int local_n,
              float h);     /* Calculate local integral  */

    /* Let the system do what it needs to start up MPI */
    MPI_Init(&argc, &argv);

    /* Get my process rank */
    MPI_Comm_rank(MPI_COMM_WORLD, &my_rank);

    /* Find out how many processes are being used */
    MPI_Comm_size(MPI_COMM_WORLD, &p);

    h = (b-a)/n;    /* h is the same for all processes */
    local_n = n/p;  /* So is the number of trapezoids */

    /* Length of each process's interval of
     * integration = local_n*h.  So my interval
     * starts at: */
    local_a = a + my_rank*local_n*h;
    local_b = local_a + local_n*h;
    integral = Trap(local_a, local_b, local_n, h);

    /* Add up the integrals calculated by each process */
    if (my_rank == 0) {
        total = integral;
        for (source = 1; source < p; source++) {
            MPI_Recv(&integral, 1, MPI_FLOAT, source, tag,
                MPI_COMM_WORLD, &status);
            total = total + integral;
        }
    } else {
        MPI_Send(&integral, 1, MPI_FLOAT, dest,
            tag, MPI_COMM_WORLD);
    }

    /* Print the result */
    if (my_rank == 0) {
        printf("With n = %d trapezoids, our estimate\n",
            n);
```

```
            printf("of the integral from %f to %f = %f\n",
                a, b, total);
    }

    /* Shut down MPI */
    MPI_Finalize();
} /*  main  */


float Trap(
            float   local_a    /* in */,
            float   local_b    /* in */,
            int     local_n    /* in */,
            float   h          /* in */) {

    float integral;    /* Store result in integral  */
    float x;
    int i;

    float f(float x); /* function we're integrating */

    integral = (f(local_a) + f(local_b))/2.0;
    x = local_a;
    for (i = 1; i <= local_n-1; i++) {
        x = x + h;
        integral = integral + f(x);
    }
    integral = integral*h;
    return integral;
} /*  Trap  */


float f(float x) {
    float return_val;
    /* Calculate f(x). */
    /* Store calculation in return_val. */
        :
    return return_val;
} /* f */
```

Observe that this program also uses the SPMD paradigm. Even though process 0 executes an essentially different set of commands from the remaining processes, it still runs the same program. The different commands are executed by branching based on the process rank.

Also note that we were careful to distinguish between variables whose contents were significant on all the processes, and variables whose contents were only significant on individual processes. Examples of the former are a, b, and n. Examples of the latter are `local_a`, `local_b`, and `local_n`. Variables whose contents are significant on all the processes are sometimes called **global variables**, and variables whose contents are significant only on individual processes are sometimes called **local variables**. If you learned to program in Pascal, this terminology may at first seem somewhat confusing. However, it's usually very easy to tell from the context which meaning is implied.

It's extremely important that we, as programmers, distinguish between global and local variables: it can be very difficult or impossible to decipher a program that makes no distinction between the two. One of the most insidious things a parallel programmer can do is to use the same variable for both global and local storage with no documentation. In general, separate variables should be allocated for global and local scalar variables. For composite variables it may be necessary to use the same storage for both global and local variables. However, if this is done, it should be clearly documented.

4.3 I/O on Parallel Systems

One obvious problem with our program is its lack of generality. The function, $f(x)$, and the input data, a, b, and n, are hardwired. So if we want to change any of these, we must edit and recompile the program. Different functions can be incorporated by revising the `Trap` function so that it takes an additional parameter—a pointer to a function. Since this has nothing to do with parallel computing, we'll leave it as an exercise to modify the program to use function pointers. However, the issue of changing the input data has everything to do with parallel computing. So we should take a look at it.

In our `greetings` and serial `trapezoidal` programs we assumed that process 0 could both read from standard input (the keyboard) and write to standard output (the terminal screen). Many parallel systems provide this much I/O. In fact, many parallel systems allow all processors to both read from standard input and write to standard output. So what's the problem?

In the first place, we were careful to say "many" (not "all") systems provide this much I/O. But even if we could say "all," there would still be issues that need to be resolved.

Let's look at an example. Suppose we modify the `trapezoidal` program so that each process attempts to read the values a, b, and n by adding the statement

```
scanf("%f %f %d", &a, &b, &n);
```

Suppose also that we run the program with two processes and the user types in

```
0 1 1024
```

What happens? Do both processes get the data? Does only one? Or, even worse, does, say, process 0 get the 0 and 1, while process 1 gets the 1024?

If all the processes get the data, what happens when we write a program in which we want process 0 to read the first input value, process 1 to read the second, etc.? If only one process gets the data, what happens to the others? Is it even reasonable to have multiple processes reading data from a single terminal?

Further, what happens if several processes attempt to simultaneously write data to the terminal screen? Does the data from process 0 get printed first, then the data from process 1, etc.? Or does the data appear in some random order? Or, even worse, does the data from the different processes get all mixed up— say, half a line from 0, two characters from 1, three characters from 0, two lines from 2, etc.?

Regardless of how you feel these questions should be answered, there is not (yet) a consensus in the parallel computing world.

Thus far, we have assumed that process 0 can at least write to standard output. We will also assume that it can read from standard input. In most cases, we will only assume that process 0 can do I/O. It should be noted that this is a fairly weak assumption, since, as we noted, many parallel systems allow multiple processes to carry out I/O.[1] You might want to ask your local expert whether there are any restrictions on which processes can do I/O.

OK. If only process 0 can do I/O, then we need for process 0 to send the user input to the other processes. This is readily accomplished with a short I/O function that uses MPI_Send and MPI_Recv.

```
/* Function Get_data
 * Reads in the user input a, b, and n.
 * Input parameters:
 *      1.  int my_rank:  rank of current process.
 *      2.  int p:  number of processes.
 * Output parameters:
 *      1.  float* a_ptr:  pointer to left endpoint a.
 *      2.  float* b_ptr:  pointer to right endpoint b.
 *      3.  int* n_ptr:  pointer to number of trapezoids.
 * Algorithm:
 *      1.  Process 0 prompts user for input and
 *          reads in the values.
 *      2.  Process 0 sends input values to other
 *          processes.
 */
void Get_data(
          float*  a_ptr       /* out */,
          float*  b_ptr       /* out */,
```

---

1   If your system won't allow you to do this, skip forward to Chapter 8 for a discussion of how to deal with systems with limited I/O capabilities.

```
        int*     n_ptr      /* out */,
        int      my_rank    /* in  */,
        int      p          /* in  */) {

    int source = 0;      /* All local variables used by */
    int dest;            /* MPI_Send and MPI_Recv       */
    int tag;
    MPI_Status status;

    if (my_rank == 0){
        printf("Enter a, b, and n\n");
        scanf("%f %f %d", a_ptr, b_ptr, n_ptr);
        for (dest = 1; dest < p; dest++){
            tag = 0;
            MPI_Send(a_ptr, 1, MPI_FLOAT, dest, tag,
                MPI_COMM_WORLD);
            tag = 1;
            MPI_Send(b_ptr, 1, MPI_FLOAT, dest, tag,
                MPI_COMM_WORLD);
            tag = 2;
            MPI_Send(n_ptr, 1, MPI_INT, dest, tag,
                MPI_COMM_WORLD);
        }
    } else {
        tag = 0;
        MPI_Recv(a_ptr, 1, MPI_FLOAT, source, tag,
            MPI_COMM_WORLD, &status);
        tag = 1;
        MPI_Recv(b_ptr, 1, MPI_FLOAT, source, tag,
            MPI_COMM_WORLD, &status);
        tag = 2;
        MPI_Recv(n_ptr, 1, MPI_INT, source, tag,
                MPI_COMM_WORLD, &status);
    }
} /* Get_data */
```

Note that we used different tags for the messages containing a_ptr, b_ptr, and n_ptr. Although MPI guarantees that a sequence of messages sent from one process to another process will be received in the order they will be sent, this certainly doesn't hurt, and it provides a little extra assurance when we're developing the program that our messages are being received where they should be.

4.4 Summary

We didn't learn any new MPI commands in this chapter, but we did write a program that solved a problem. The process we used is typical when writing a parallel program:

1. First we recalled a serial algorithm for solving our problem: we studied the trapezoidal rule for estimating a definite integral.

2. In order to parallelize the serial algorithm, we simply partitioned the data among the processes, and each process ran essentially the same program on its data: we partitioned the interval of integration, $[a, b]$, among the processes, and each process estimated an integral over its subinterval.

3. The "local" calculations produced by the individual processes were combined to produce the final result: each process sent its integral to process 0, which summed them and printed the result.

We noted the importance of distinguishing between global variables—variables whose contents have significance on all processes—and local variables—variables whose contents only have significance on individual processes.

We briefly discussed I/O on parallel systems. We noted that many parallel systems allow each process to read from standard input and to write to standard output. However we saw that there may be difficulties in arranging that input is read by the correct process and whether output appears in the correct order. We will avoid this problem (for the time being) by only assuming that process 0 can do I/O.

4.5 References

A discussion of the trapezoidal rule and other methods of numerical integration can be found in [19]. A discussion of the issues involved in parallel I/O can be found in [9, 10].

4.6 Exercises

1. Type in the first version of the parallel trapezoidal rule program. Define $f(x)$ to be a function whose integral you can easily calculate by hand (e.g., $f(x) = x^2$). Compile it and run it with different numbers of processes. What happens if you try to run it with just one process?

2. Modify the parallel trapezoidal rule program so that a, b, and n are read in and distributed by process 0—use the Get_data function. Where should the function be called? Do you need to make any modifications other than including the definition of Get_data and a call to Get_data?

4.7 Programming Assignments

1. Modify the parallel trapezoidal rule program so that it has several different functions it can integrate, and the chosen function is passed to the Trap subroutine. Have the user select which function is to be integrated by giving him a menu of possible functions.

2. A more accurate alternative to the trapezoidal rule is Simpson's rule. The basic idea is to approximate the graph of $f(x)$ by arcs of parabolas rather than line segments. Suppose that $p < q$ are real numbers, and let r be the midpoint of the segment $[p, q]$. If we let $h = (q - p)/2$, then an equation for the parabola passing through the points $(p, f(p))$, $(r, f(r))$, and $(q, f(q))$ is

$$y = \frac{f(p)}{2h^2}(x - r)(x - q) - \frac{f(r)}{h^2}(x - p)(x - q) + \frac{f(q)}{2h^2}(x - p)(x - r).$$

If we integrate this from p to q, we get

$$\frac{h}{3}[f(p) + 4f(r) + f(q)].$$

Thus, if we use the same notation that we used in our discussion of the trapezoidal rule and we assume that n, the number of subintervals of $[a, b]$, is even, we can approximate

$$\int_a^b f(x)dx \doteq \frac{h}{3}[f(x_0) + 4f(x_1) + 2f(x_2) + 4f(x_3)$$
$$+ \cdots + 2f(x_{n-2}) + 4f(x_{n-1}) + f(x_n)].$$

Assuming that n/p is even, write

a. a serial program and

b. a parallel program that uses Simpson's rule to estimate $\int_a^b f(x)dx$.

CHAPTER 5

Collective Communication

THERE ARE PROBABLY A FEW THINGS in the trapezoidal rule program that you think we can improve on. For example, there is the I/O issue. There are also a couple of problems we haven't discussed yet. Let's think about what happens when the program is run with eight processes.

All the processes begin executing the program (more or less) simultaneously. However, after carrying out the basic setup tasks (calls to MPI_Init, MPI_Comm_size, and MPI_Comm_rank), processes 1–7 are idle while process 0 collects the input data. We don't want to have idle processes, but in view of our restrictions on which processes can read input, there isn't much we can do about this. However, after process 0 has collected the input data, the higher rank processes must continue to wait while 0 sends the input data to the lower rank processes. This isn't just an I/O issue. Notice that there is a similar inefficiency at the end of the program, when process 0 does all the work of collecting and adding. Of course, this is highly undesirable: the main point of parallel computing is to get multiple processes to collaborate on solving a problem. If one of the processes is doing most of the work, we might as well use a conventional, single-processor machine.

5.1 Tree-Structured Communication

Let's try to improve our code. We'll begin by focussing on the distribution of the input data. How can we divide the work more evenly among the processes? A natural solution is to imagine that we have a tree of processes, with 0 at the root.

During the first stage of the data distribution, 0 sends the data to, say, 1. During the next stage, 0 sends the data to 2, while 1 sends it to 3. During the

65

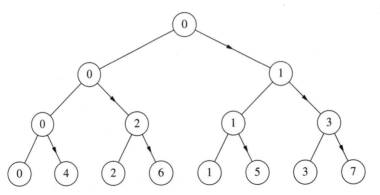

Figure 5.1 Processes configured as a tree

last stage, 0 sends to 4, while 1 sends to 5, 2 sends to 6, and 3 sends to 7. (See Figure 5.1.) So we have reduced our input distribution loop from seven stages to three stages. More generally, if we have p processes, this procedure allows us to distribute the input data in $\lceil \log_2(p) \rceil$ stages,[1] rather than $p - 1$ stages. This can be a huge savings. For example, $\log_2(1024) = 10$. That is, if we use this tree-structured scheme with 1024 processes, the time required for our program to complete the data distribution will be reduced by a factor of 100!

Let's modify our Get_data function to use a tree-structured distribution scheme. Essentially, the distribution is a loop:

```
for (stage = first; stage <= last; stage++)
    if (I_receive(stage, my_rank, &source))
        Receive(data, source);
    else if (I_send(stage, my_rank, p, &dest))
        Send(data, dest);
```

The I_receive function returns 1 if, during the current stage, the calling process receives data. Otherwise it returns 0. If the calling process receives data, the parameter source is used to return the rank of the sender. The I_send function performs a similar function, testing whether a process sends during the current stage.

In order to implement this code, we need to calculate

- whether a process receives and, if so, the source, and
- whether a process sends and, if so, the destination.

As you can probably guess, these calculations can be a bit complicated, es-

---

1   The **ceiling** of a real number x is the smallest whole number greater than or equal to x. It is denoted by $\lceil x \rceil$.

pecially since there is no canonical choice of ordering. In our example, we chose

1. 0 sends to 1.
2. 0 sends to 2; 1 sends to 3.
3. 0 sends to 4; 1 sends to 5; 2 sends to 6; 3 sends to 7.

We might also have chosen (for example)

1. 0 sends to 4.
2. 0 sends to 2; 4 sends to 6.
3. 0 sends to 1; 2 sends to 3; 4 sends to 5; 6 sends to 7.

Indeed, unless we know something about the topology of our system, we can't really decide which scheme is better. However, it's fairly easy to see how to calculate the required information using the first scheme, so let's use it. Let's also use the C convention that counting begins at 0. So the first stage is stage 0, the second, stage 1, etc. If

$$2^{stage} \leq \text{my\_rank} < 2^{stage+1},$$

then I receive from

$$\text{my\_rank} - 2^{stage}.$$

If

$$\text{my\_rank} < 2^{stage},$$

then I send to

$$\text{my\_rank} + 2^{stage}.$$

To summarize, our second version of the Get_data function, together with the functions it calls, should look something like this:

```
/* Ceiling of log_2(x) is just the number of
 * times x-1 can be divided by 2 until the quotient
 * is 0.  Dividing by 2 is the same as right shift.
 */
int Ceiling_log2(int  x  /* in */) {
    /* Use unsigned so that right shift will fill
     * leftmost bit with 0
     */
    unsigned temp = (unsigned) x - 1;
    int result = 0;

    while (temp != 0) {
        temp = temp >> 1;
        result = result + 1 ;
    }
```

```
        return result;
} /* Ceiling_log2 */

int I_receive(
        int    stage       /* in  */,
        int    my_rank     /* in  */,
        int*   source_ptr  /* out */) {

    int    power_2_stage;

    /* 2^stage = 1 << stage */
    power_2_stage = 1 << stage;
    if ((power_2_stage <= my_rank) &&
            (my_rank < 2*power_2_stage)){
        *source_ptr = my_rank - power_2_stage;
        return 1;
    } else return 0;
} /* I_receive */

int I_send(
        int    stage    /* in  */,
        int    my_rank  /* in  */,
        int    p        /* in  */,
        int*   dest_ptr /* out */) {
    int power_2_stage;

    /* 2^stage = 1 << stage */
    power_2_stage = 1 << stage;
    if (my_rank < power_2_stage){
        *dest_ptr = my_rank + power_2_stage;
        if (*dest_ptr >= p) return 0;
        else return 1;
    } else return 0;
} /* I_send */

void Send(
        float  a     /* in */,
        float  b     /* in */,
        int    n     /* in */,
        int    dest  /* in */) {

    MPI_Send(&a, 1, MPI_FLOAT, dest, 0, MPI_COMM_WORLD);
    MPI_Send(&b, 1, MPI_FLOAT, dest, 1, MPI_COMM_WORLD);
    MPI_Send(&n, 1, MPI_INT, dest, 2, MPI_COMM_WORLD);
} /* Send */

void Receive(
        float*  a_ptr  /* out */,
        float*  b_ptr  /* out */,
```

```
                        int*    n_ptr  /* out */,
                        int     source /* in  */) {

                MPI_Status status;

                MPI_Recv(a_ptr, 1, MPI_FLOAT, source, 0,
                    MPI_COMM_WORLD, &status);
                MPI_Recv(b_ptr, 1, MPI_FLOAT, source, 1,
                    MPI_COMM_WORLD, &status);
                MPI_Recv(n_ptr, 1, MPI_INT, source, 2,
                    MPI_COMM_WORLD, &status);
        } /* Receive */

        void Get_data1(
                        float*  a_ptr    /* out */,
                        float*  b_ptr    /* out */,
                        int*    n_ptr    /* out */,
                        int     my_rank  /* in  */,
                        int     p        /* in  */) {

                int source;
                int dest;
                int stage;

                if (my_rank == 0){
                    printf("Enter a, b, and n\n");
                    scanf("%f %f %d", a_ptr, b_ptr, n_ptr);
                }
                for (stage = 0; stage < Ceiling_log2(p); stage++)
                    if (I_receive(stage, my_rank, &source))
                        Receive(a_ptr, b_ptr, n_ptr, source);
                    else if (I_send(stage, my_rank, p, &dest))
                        Send(*a_ptr, *b_ptr, *n_ptr, dest);
        } /* Get_data1*/
```

5.2 Broadcast

A communication pattern that involves all the processes in a communicator is
a **collective communication.** As a consequence, a collective communication
usually involves more than two processes. A **broadcast** is a collective communication in which a single process sends the same data to every process in the
communicator. As we saw in section 5.1, a tree-structured broadcast can be
much more efficient than a broadcast based on a sequence of sends all origi-
nating from the **root** of the broadcast. However, we also saw that the details
involved in writing the code to carry out this tree-structured broadcast were
fairly complicated.

Furthermore, without knowing the details of the topology of the system we're using, we can't be sure that our hand-coded broadcast is the most efficient broadcast possible. So we would like to have someone with detailed knowledge of our system write an optimized broadcast that we can use. Not surprisingly, MPI has allowed for this: each system that runs MPI has a broadcast function, MPI_Bcast. Since MPI only specifies the syntax of the function call and the result of calling it, it's possible for implementors to write a highly optimized function.

The syntax of MPI_Bcast is

```
int MPI_Bcast(
        void*       message    /* in/out */,
        int         count      /* in     */,
        MPI_Datatype datatype  /* in     */,
        int         root       /* in     */,
        MPI_Comm    comm       /* in     */)
```

It simply sends a copy of the data in message on the process with rank root to each process in the communicator comm. It should be called by *all* the processes in the communicator with the same arguments for root and comm. Hence a broadcast message cannot be received with MPI_Recv. The parameters count and datatype have the same function that they have in MPI_Send and MPI_Recv: they specify how much memory is needed for the message. However, unlike the point-to-point functions, in most cases count and datatype should be the same on all the processes in the communicator. The reason for this is that in some collective operations (see below), a single process will receive data from many other processes, and in order for a program to determine how much data has been received, it would need an array of return statuses. Since there is no tag in collective communication functions, making count and datatype the same on all processes removes the need for a status parameter.

Note that in the syntax specification, message is identified as an in/out parameter. In conventional serial programs, in/out parameters have values that are both used and modified by the function. In parallel programs, another interpretation can be attached to in/out parameters of collective communication functions: on some processes the parameter may be in, while on others it may be out. In the case of MPI_Bcast, message is in on the process with rank root, while it is out on the other processes.

Just to make sure that we understand how to use MPI_Bcast, let's rewrite Get_data.

```
void Get_data2(
        float*  a_ptr     /* out */,
        float*  b_ptr     /* out */,
        int*    n_ptr     /* out */,
        int     my_rank   /* in  */) {
```

Table 5.1 Broadcast times (times are in milliseconds; version 1 uses a linear loop of sends from process 0, version 2 uses MPI_Bcast; all systems running mpich)

	nCUBE2		Paragon		SP2	
Processes	Version 1	Version 2	Version 1	Version 2	Version 1	Version 2
2	0.59	0.69	0.21	0.43	0.15	0.16
8	4.7	1.9	0.84	0.93	0.55	0.35
32	19.0	3.0	3.2	1.3	2.0	0.57

Table 5.2 Send/receive sequence of events

Time	Process A	Process B
1	MPI_Send to B, tag = 0	Local work
2	MPI_Send to B, tag = 1	Local work
3	Local work	MPI_Recv from A, tag = 1
4	Local work	MPI_Recv from A, tag = 0

```
if (my_rank == 0) {
    printf("Enter a, b, and n\n");
    scanf("%f %f %d", a_ptr, b_ptr, n_ptr);
}
MPI_Bcast(a_ptr, 1, MPI_FLOAT, 0, MPI_COMM_WORLD);
MPI_Bcast(b_ptr, 1, MPI_FLOAT, 0, MPI_COMM_WORLD);
MPI_Bcast(n_ptr, 1, MPI_INT, 0, MPI_COMM_WORLD);
} /* Get_data2 */
```

Certainly this version of Get_data is much more compact and readily comprehensible than both the original and our hand-coded tree-structured broadcast. Furthermore, it's probably a good deal faster. Table 5.1 shows the runtimes of the data distribution phase of our first and third versions (Get_data and Get_data2).

5.3 Tags, Safety, Buffering, and Synchronization

Note that MPI_Bcast (and all the other collective communication functions in MPI) do not use tags. In order to understand the reasons for this, let's look at a couple of examples.

Recall our example from Chapter 3 in which we discussed the need for tags in MPI_Send and MPI_Recv. In that example, process A sent several messages to process B, and B decided how to handle these messages on the basis of the tag. In particular, consider the sequence of events outlined in Table 5.2. Note that this sequence of events requires that the system **buffer** the messages being sent to process B. That is, memory must be set aside for

Table 5.3   Broadcast sequence of events

Time	Process A	Process B	Process C
1	MPI_Bcast &x	Local work	Local work
2	MPI_Bcast &y	Local work	Local work
3	Local work	MPI_Bcast &y	MPI_Bcast &x
4	Local work	MPI_Bcast &x	MPI_Bcast &y

storing messages before a receive has been executed. Recall that the message envelope contains

1. The rank of the receiver
2. The rank of the sender
3. A tag
4. A communicator

There is no information specifying where the message should be stored by the receiving process. Thus, until *B* calls MPI_Recv, the system doesn't know where the data that *A* is sending should be stored. When *B* calls MPI_Recv, the system software that executes the receive can see which (if any) buffered message has an envelope that matches the parameters specified by the receive. If there isn't a message, it waits until one arrives.

If a system has no buffering, then *A* cannot send its data until it knows that *B* is ready to receive the message, and consequently memory is available for the data. When a send cannot complete until the receiver is ready to receive the message, the send is said to use **synchronous mode.**

Programming under the assumption that a system has buffering is very common (most systems automatically provide some buffering), although in MPI parlance, it is **unsafe**. This means that if the program is run on a system that does not provide buffering, the program will **deadlock**. If the system has no buffering, *A*'s first message cannot be received until *B* has signalled that it is ready to receive the data with tag 0. So *A* will hang while it waits for *B* to receive the first send, and *B* will hang while it waits for *A* to execute the second send.

Now consider a somewhat analogous example that uses broadcasts. Suppose we have three processes, *A*, *B*, and *C*, and *A* is broadcasting two floats, x and y, to *B* and *C*. Also suppose that on process *A*, x = 5 and y = 10. See Table 5.3. When the broadcasts are completed on all three processes, x = 5 and y = 10 on processes *A* and *C*. However, on process *B* the values will be reversed: x = 10 and y = 5. Why? When people first started programming parallel processors, broadcasts (and all other collective communication functions) were points of **synchronization**. On a given process the broadcast would not return until every process had received the broadcast data. On current systems this restriction has been relaxed. If the system has adequate buffering, it's OK for A to complete (from its point of view) two broadcasts before the other processes even begin their calls. However, in terms of the data communicated, the *effect* must be the same as if the processes synchronized. So the first MPI_Bcast on B matches the first MPI_Bcast on A, and B stores the first value it receives, 5, in y.

At first this may seem a little confusing. However, its net effect is that a sequence of collective communications on distinct processes will be matched in the order in which they're executed.

5.4 Reduce

In the trapezoidal rule program after the input phase, every process executes essentially the same commands until the final summation phase. So unless our function $f(x)$ is fairly complicated (i.e., it requires considerably more work to evaluate over certain parts of $[a, b]$), this part of the program distributes the work equally among the processes. As we have already noted, this is not the case with the final summation phase, when, once again, process 0 gets a disproportionate amount of the work. However, you have probably already noticed that by reversing the arrows in Figure 5.1, we can use the same idea we used in section 5.1. That is, we can distribute the work of calculating the sum among the processes as follows:

1. a. 4 sends to 0; 5 sends to 1; 6 sends to 2; 7 sends to 3.
   b. 0 adds its integral to that of 4; 1 adds its integral to that of 5; etc.
2. a. 2 sends to 0; 3 sends to 1.
   b. 0 adds; 1 adds.
3. a. 1 sends to 0.
   b. 0 adds.

Of course, we run into the same question that occurred when we were writing our own broadcast: is this tree structure making optimal use of the topology of our system? Once again, we have to answer that this depends on the system. So, as before, we should let MPI do the work by using an optimized function.

The "global sum" that we wish to calculate is an example of a general class of collective communication operations called **reduction operations**. In a global reduction operation, all the processes in a communicator contribute data that is combined using a binary operation. Typical binary operations are addition, max, min, logical and, etc. The MPI function for performing a reduction operation is

```
int MPI_Reduce(
        void*           operand     /* in  */,
        void*           result      /* out */,
        int             count       /* in  */,
```

Table 5.4   Predefined reduction operators in MPI

Operation Name	Meaning
MPI_MAX	Maximum
MPI_MIN	Minimum
MPI_SUM	Sum
MPI_PROD	Product
MPI_LAND	Logical and
MPI_BAND	Bitwise and
MPI_LOR	Logical or
MPI_BOR	Bitwise or
MPI_LXOR	Logical exclusive or
MPI_BXOR	Bitwise exclusive or
MPI_MAXLOC	Maximum and location of maximum
MPI_MINLOC	Minimum and location of minimum

```
MPI_Datatype  datatype  /* in  */,
MPI_Op        operator  /* in  */,
int           root      /* in  */,
MPI_Comm      comm      /* in  */)
```

MPI_Reduce combines the operands stored in the memory referenced by operand using operation operator and stores the result in *result on process root. Both operand and result refer to count memory locations with type datatype. MPI_Reduce must be called by all processes in the communicator comm, and count, datatype, operator, and root must be the same on each process.

The parameter operator can take on one of the predefined values listed in Table 5.4. (It is also possible to define additional operations. See the MPI Standard for details [28].)

As an example, let's rewrite the last few lines of the trapezoidal rule program.

⋮

```
/* Add up the integrals calculated by each process */
MPI_Reduce(&integral, &total, 1, MPI_FLOAT,
    MPI_SUM, 0, MPI_COMM_WORLD);

/* Print the result */
```

⋮

Note that each processor calls MPI_Reduce with the same arguments. In particular, even though total only has significance on process 0, each process must supply an argument. This makes sense; otherwise, the syntax would be different on the root process, and this would create the impression that there were distinct function calls, rather than a single collective call.

It may be tempting to pass the same argument to both operand and result on the process with rank root. For example, we might try to call the function with

```
/* Attempt to store the result in the same
 * location as the operand.  Illegal call.
 */
MPI_Reduce(&integral, &integral, 1, MPI_FLOAT,
    MPI_SUM, 0, MPI_COMM_WORLD);
```

This is called **aliasing** of arguments, and it is illegal to alias out or in/out arguments in *any* MPI function. The main reason is that without the extra argument, an implementation may be forced to provide large temporary buffers. For an exploration of this problem, take a look at programming assignment 2.

5.5 Dot Product

As another example of the application of MPI_Reduce, let's write a function that calculates the dot product of two vectors.

Recall that if $\mathbf{x} = (x_0, x_1, \ldots, x_{n-1})^T$ and $\mathbf{y} = (y_0, y_1, \ldots, y_{n-1})^T$ are n-dimensional vectors of real numbers,[2] then their **dot product** is just

$$\mathbf{x} \cdot \mathbf{y} = x_0 y_0 + x_1 y_1 + \cdots + x_{n-1} y_{n-1}.$$

So on a conventional system, we can form the dot product as follows:

```
float Serial_dot(
            float  x[]  /* in */,
            float  y[]  /* in */,
            int    n    /* in */) {

    int    i;
    float  sum = 0.0;

    for (i = 0; i < n; i++)
        sum = sum + x[i]*y[i];
    return sum;
} /* Serial_dot */
```

If we have p processes, and n is divisible by p, it's natural to divide the vectors among the processes so that each process has $\bar{n} = n/p$ components

---

2   The transpose of $\mathbf{x}$ is denoted $\mathbf{x}^T$. We adhere to the convention that vectors are *column* vectors. We also use the C convention that arrays are indexed from 0 to $n - 1$, rather than the more common 1 to n.

Table 5.5 Block mapping of the vector **x** to the processes

Process	Components
0	$x_0, x_1, \ldots, x_{\bar{n}-1}$
1	$x_{\bar{n}}, x_{\bar{n}+1}, \ldots, x_{2\bar{n}-1}$
$\vdots$	$\vdots$
k	$x_{k\bar{n}}, x_{k\bar{n}+1}, \ldots, x_{(k+1)\bar{n}-1}$
$\vdots$	$\vdots$
$p-1$	$x_{(p-1)\bar{n}}, x_{(p-1)\bar{n}+1}, \ldots, x_{n-1}$

of each of the vectors. For the sake of explicitness, let's suppose that we use a **block** distribution of the data. Recall (from section 2.2.5) that this means that the vector **x** is distributed as indicated in Table 5.5. A similar distribution would be used for **y**.

With this distribution of the data, we can calculate a "local" dot product, by just calling `Serial_dot`, and then calling `MPI_Reduce` to get the "global" dot product.

```
float Parallel_dot(
            float   local_x[]   /* in */,
            float   local_y[]   /* in */,
            int     n_bar       /* in */) {

    float   local_dot;
    float   dot = 0.0;
    float   Serial_dot(float x[], float y[], int m);

    local_dot = Serial_dot(local_x, local_y, n_bar);
    MPI_Reduce(&local_dot, &dot, 1, MPI_FLOAT,
        MPI_SUM, 0, MPI_COMM_WORLD);
    return dot;
} /* Parallel_dot */
```

5.6 Allreduce

Note that in our `Parallel_dot` function only process 0 will return the dot product. The other processes will return 0. If we only wish, for example, to print the result, this won't be a problem. However, if we want to use the result in subsequent calculations, we may want each process to return the correct dot product. An obvious approach to doing this is to follow the call to `MPI_Reduce` with a call to `MPI_Bcast`. However, it may be possible to use a more efficient implementation.

Consider the following approach to calculating the sum that will store the

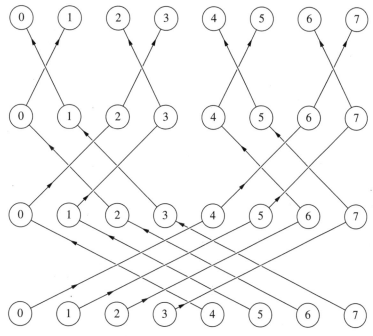

Figure 5.2   A butterfly

result on all the processes. Once again, for the sake of explicitness, let's assume that we have eight processes.

1. a. Processes 0 and 4 exchange their local results, processes 1 and 5 exchange theirs, processes 2 and 6 exchange, and processes 3 and 7 exchange.
   b. Each process adds its result to the result just received.
2. a. Processes 0 and 2 exchange their intermediate results, processes 1 and 3 exchange theirs, processes 4 and 6 exchange, and processes 5 and 7 exchange.
   b. Each process adds.
3. a. Processes 0 and 1 exchange, processes 2 and 3 exchange, processes 4 and 5 exchange, and processes 6 and 7 exchange.
   b. Each process adds.

What's happened? Essentially we've done a tree-structured reduce rooted at all the processes simultaneously! Figure 5.2 illustrates the process. This communication structure is frequently called a **butterfly**. If you add vertical lines joining processes of the same rank in adjacent rows, you'll see that it contains a tree rooted at each process.

Of course, we don't want to have to write this communication scheme ourselves, so let's let MPI take care of it.

```
int MPI_Allreduce(
         void*         operand     /* in  */,
         void*         result      /* out */,
         int           count       /* in  */,
         MPI_Datatype  datatype    /* in  */,
         MPI_Op        operator    /* in  */,
         MPI_Comm      comm        /* in  */)
```

It is used in exactly the same way as MPI_Reduce. The only difference is that
the result of the reduction is returned in result on *all* the processes. Hence
there is no root parameter.

In order to use it in Parallel_dot, we can simply replace the call to
MPI_Reduce with a call to MPI_Allreduce.

5.7 Gather and Scatter

Let's take a look at how we might implement another linear algebra operation:
matrix-vector product. Recall that if $A = (a_{ij})$ is an $m \times n$ matrix, and $\mathbf{x} = (x_0, \dots, x_{n-1})^{\mathrm{T}}$ is an n-dimensional vector, then we can form the matrix-vector
product $\mathbf{y} = A\mathbf{x}$ by taking the dot product of each row of A with $\mathbf{x}$. If A has m
rows, then we will form m dot products. So the product vector $\mathbf{y}$ will consist
of m entries: $\mathbf{y} = (y_0, y_1, \dots, y_{m-1})$ and

$$y_k = a_{k0}x_0 + a_{k1}x_1 + \cdots + a_{k,n-1}x_{n-1}.$$

Thus, a serial function for forming a matrix-vector product might look something like this:

```
/* MATRIX_T is a two-dimensional array of floats */
void Serial_matrix_vector_prod(
         MATRIX_T  A     /* in  */,
         int       m     /* in  */,
         int       n     /* in  */,
         float     x[]   /* in  */,
         float     y[]   /* out */) {

    int k, j;

    for (k = 0; k < m; k++) {
        y[k] = 0.0;
        for (j = 0; j < n; j++)
            y[k] = y[k] + A[k][j]*x[j];
    }
}  /* Serial_matrix_vector_prod */
```

In order to parallelize this, we must decide how the matrices and vectors
are to be distributed among the processes. One of the simplest matrix distributions is a **block-row** or **panel** distribution. In this distribution, we partition the

Table 5.6   Block-row distribution

Process	Elements of A			
0	a_{00}	a_{01}	a_{02}	a_{03}
	a_{10}	a_{11}	a_{12}	a_{13}
1	a_{20}	a_{21}	a_{22}	a_{23}
	a_{30}	a_{31}	a_{32}	a_{33}
2	a_{40}	a_{41}	a_{42}	a_{43}
	a_{50}	a_{51}	a_{52}	a_{53}
3	a_{60}	a_{61}	a_{62}	a_{63}
	a_{70}	a_{71}	a_{72}	a_{73}

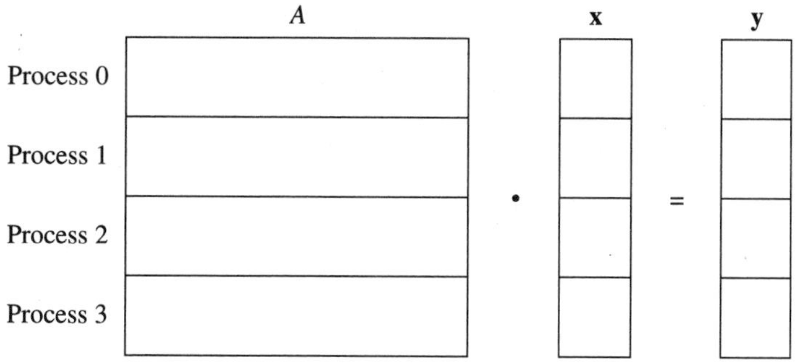

Figure 5.3   Mappings of A, $\mathbf{x}$, and $\mathbf{y}$ for matrix-vector product

matrix into blocks of consecutive rows or panels, and assign a panel to each process. For example, if $m = 8, n = 4$, and $p = 4$, the assignment of matrix elements to the processes is illustrated in Table 5.6. Let's use our familiar block distribution for the vectors (see Table 5.5). A schematic illustration of all the mappings (with four processes) is contained in Figure 5.3.

Now in order to form the dot product of each row of A with $\mathbf{x}$, we need to either **gather** all of $\mathbf{x}$ onto each process or **scatter** each row of A across the processes. For example, suppose, $m = n = p = 4$. Then, before we form the dot products, $a_{00}, a_{01}, a_{02}, a_{03}$, and x_0 are assigned to process 0, while x_1 is assigned to process 1, x_2 is assigned to process 2, and x_3 is assigned to process 3. So in order to form the dot product of the first row of A with $\mathbf{x}$, we can either send x_1, x_2, and x_3 to process 0, or we can send a_{01} to process 1, a_{02} to process 2, and a_{03} to process 3. The first collection of sends is called a gather. The second is called a scatter. See Figures 5.4 and 5.5.

In view of our previous discussion, it isn't surprising that MPI provides both a gather and a scatter function. For example, we can gather $\mathbf{x}$ onto process 0 with the call

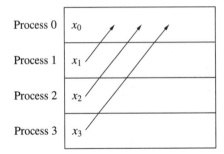

Figure 5.4   A gather

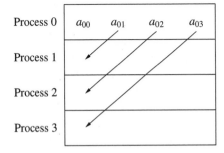

Figure 5.5   A scatter

```
/* Space allocated in calling program      */
float local_x[];  /* local storage for x  */
float global_x[]; /* storage for all of x */

/* Assumes n is divisible by p */
MPI_Gather(local_x, n/p, MPI_FLOAT,
           global_x, n/p, MPI_FLOAT,
           0, MPI_COMM_WORLD);
```

The exact syntax of MPI_Gather is

```
int MPI_Gather(
        void*        send_data    /* in  */,
        int          send_count   /* in  */,
        MPI_Datatype send_type    /* in  */,
        void*        recv_data    /* out */,
        int          recv_count   /* in  */,
        MPI_Datatype recv_type    /* in  */,
        int          root         /* in  */,
        MPI_Comm     comm         /* in  */)
```

MPI_Gather collects the data referenced by send_data from each process
in the communicator comm and stores the data in process rank order on the
process with rank root in the memory referenced by recv_data. Thus, the
data from process 0 is followed by the data from process 1, which is followed
by the data from process 2, etc. The parameters send_count and send_type
have their usual interpretation: the data referenced by send_data on each
process consists of send_count elements, each of which has type send_type.
The parameters recv_count and recv_type will, in most cases, be the same
as send_count and send_type, respectively. They specify the number of
elements and type of elements received from *each* process. They do not specify
the total amount of data received. The recv parameters are only significant
on the root process. The parameters root and comm must be identical on
all the processes in the communicator comm. In most cases, the parameters
send_count and send_type will be the same on all the processes.

We can scatter the first row of *A* among the processes using MPI_Scatter:

```
/* Both arrays allocated by calling program       */
LOCAL_MATRIX_T local_A; /* A 2-dimensional array  */
float          row_segment[];
                            /* An array containing    */
                            /* storage for n/p floats */

/* Assumes n is divisible by p */
MPI_Scatter(&(local_A[0][0]), n/p, MPI_FLOAT,
            row_segment, n/p, MPI_FLOAT,
            0, MPI_COMM_WORLD);
```

The syntax of MPI_Scatter is

```
int MPI_Scatter(
        void*         send_data      /* in  */,
        int           send_count     /* in  */,
        MPI_Datatype  send_type      /* in  */,
        void*         recv_data      /* out */,
        int           recv_count     /* in  */,
        MPI_Datatype  recv_type      /* in  */,
        int           root           /* in  */,
        MPI_Comm      comm           /* in  */)
```

MPI_Scatter splits the data referenced by send_data on the process with
rank root into *p* segments, each of which consists of send_count elements
of type send_type. The first segment is sent to process 0, the second to
process 1, etc. The send parameters are significant only on the process with
rank root. In most cases send_count will be the same as recv_count and
send_type will be the same as recv_type. The parameters root and comm
must be the same on all processes.

Table 5.7   Products of elements of first row with elements of **x** if first row is scattered

Process	Product
0	$a_{00}x_0$
1	$a_{01}x_1$
2	$a_{02}x_2$
3	$a_{03}x_3$

5.8 Allgather

We still need to decide how to carry out our parallel matrix-vector multiplication! Observe that if we gather **x** onto each process and form the dot product of each local row of A with **x**, no additional communication is needed. The kth element of **y** is assigned to the same process as the kth row of A, and the kth element of **y** is computed by forming the dot product of the kth row of A with x.

On the other hand, suppose we scatter each row of A, and, for the sake of explicitness, suppose $m = n = p = 4$. Then after the scatter of row 0 (for example), process q will compute $a_{0q}x_q$ (see Table 5.7). That is, the individual terms in the dot product will be assigned to different processes. Thus, we'll need to call MPI_Reduce in order to finish the dot product.

Thus, it appears that by scattering the rows of A, we'll have to do considerably more communication, and, as a consequence, we should gather **x** onto each process. The obvious approach to carrying this out would be to have each process call MPI_Gather p times: once to gather **x** onto 0, once to gather **x** onto 1, etc.:

```
for (root = 0; root < p; root++)
    MPI_Gather(local_x, n/p, MPI_FLOAT,
        global_x, n/p, MPI_FLOAT,
        root, MPI_COMM_WORLD);
```

However, a little thought will convince you that we can use the butterfly scheme to simultaneously gather all of **x** onto each process. Thus, MPI should provide a more efficient solution to the problem of gathering a distributed array to every process, and, not surprisingly, it does. The function is called MPI_Allgather:

```
int MPI_Allgather(
        void*          send_data    /* in  */,
        int            send_count   /* in  */,
        MPI_Datatype   send_type    /* in  */,
        void*          recv_data    /* out */,
        int            recv_count   /* in  */,
        MPI_Datatype   recv_type    /* in  */,
        MPI_Comm       comm         /* in  */)
```

It gathers the contents of each process's send_data into each process's recv_data.

At last, we can write the parallel matrix-vector product function.

```
/* All arrays are allocated in calling program */
void Parallel_matrix_vector_prod(
          LOCAL_MATRIX_T  local_A     /* in  */,
          int             m           /* in  */,
          int             n           /* in  */,
          float           local_x[]   /* in  */,
          float           global_x[]  /* in  */,
          float           local_y[]   /* out */,
          int             local_m     /* in  */,
          int             local_n     /* in  */) {

/* local_m = m/p, local_n = n/p */

    int i, j;

    MPI_Allgather(local_x, local_n, MPI_FLOAT,
                  global_x, local_n, MPI_FLOAT,
                  MPI_COMM_WORLD);
    for (i = 0; i < local_m; i++) {
        local_y[i] = 0.0;
        for (j = 0; j < n; j++)
            local_y[i] = local_y[i] +
                         local_A[i][j]*global_x[j];
    }
}   /* Parallel_matrix_vector_prod */
```

5.9 Summary

Collective communication is communication that involves all the processes in a communicator. It usually involves more than two processes. We looked at several different types of collective communication. In a *broadcast,* a single process sends the same data to all the other processes in a communicator. In a *reduction,* each process in a communicator contains an operand, and all of them are combined using a binary operator that is successively applied to each. The reduction operation that we studied was sum: the reduction adds a collection of numbers distributed across the processes. In a *gather,* a distributed data structure is collected onto a single process. In a *scatter,* a data structure that is stored on a single process is distributed across the processes.

We saw that the performance of both a broadcast and a reduce can be greatly improved if the processes are viewed as a tree, and the communication proceeds along the branches of the tree. Constructing an optimal tree depends on the topology of the parallel system, and, as a consequence, the internals of such commands should be system-dependent.

The MPI command for a broadcast is

```
int MPI_Bcast(
        void*         message    /* in/out */,
        int           count      /* in     */,
        MPI_Datatype  datatype   /* in     */,
        int           root       /* in     */,
        MPI_Comm      comm       /* in     */)
```

The process in the communicator with rank `root` broadcasts the contents of `message` to all the other processes in the communicator.

The MPI command for a reduce operation is

```
int MPI_Reduce(
        void*         operand    /* in  */,
        void*         result     /* out */,
        int           count      /* in  */,
        MPI_Datatype  datatype   /* in  */,
        MPI_Op        operator   /* in  */,
        int           root       /* in  */,
        MPI_Comm      comm       /* in  */)
```

The values stored in each process's `operand` are combined using `operator`. The result is stored in `result` on the process with rank `root`.

The MPI command for a gather operation is

```
int MPI_Gather(
        void*         send_data   /* in  */,
        int           send_count  /* in  */,
        MPI_Datatype  send_type   /* in  */,
        void*         recv_data   /* out */,
        int           recv_count  /* in  */,
        MPI_Datatype  recv_type   /* in  */,
        int           root        /* in  */,
        MPI_Comm      comm        /* in  */)
```

It gathers the data stored in each process's `send_data` into the memory referenced by `recv_data` on the process with rank `root`.

The MPI command for a scatter operation is

```
int MPI_Scatter(
        void*         send_data   /* in  */,
        int           send_count  /* in  */,
        MPI_Datatype  send_type   /* in  */,
        void*         recv_data   /* out */,
        int           recv_count  /* in  */,
        MPI_Datatype  recv_type   /* in  */,
        int           root        /* in  */,
        MPI_Comm      comm        /* in  */)
```

It distributes the memory referenced by send_data across the processes in comm.

None of the collective communication operations use tags. This is because they are supposed to behave, in terms of the data transmitted, as if they were *synchronous* operations. A communication operation is synchronous if it cannot complete on any one process until all the other processes involved have begun execution of the operation. The practical effect of the absence of tags is that if the processes in a communicator are executing a sequence of collective communication operations, they must all execute the same operations in the same order.

The use of the same argument for two distinct parameters is called *aliasing*. Aliasing of output or input/output parameters is illegal in MPI. In particular, it is illegal to use the same argument for both operand and result in MPI_Reduce, and it is illegal to use the same argument for send_data and recv_data in both MPI_Gather and MPI_Scatter.

Most parallel systems use *buffered* communication. This means that the data in a message that is being sent is put into temporary storage until the receiving process calls a receive function, at which point the data is transferred into regular storage. If a parallel system doesn't provide buffering, then all communication must be synchronous.

In MPI, a program that will run correctly with buffering but will fail without buffering is said to be *unsafe*. The most common reason for a program to fail when run without buffering is *deadlock*. This means that the processes are all waiting or hung, and the program will stop executing new commands.

We saw that it may be useful for the result of a reduce or a gather to be available to all the processes in the communicator. We also saw that implementations of these extended operations may be more efficient if they are not based on MPI_Reduce or MPI_Gather. For example, we can use a *butterfly-structured* communication pattern. MPI allows for this possibility by defining extended reduce and gather operations.

```
int MPI_Allreduce(
        void*           operand     /* in  */,
        void*           result      /* out */,
        int             count       /* in  */,
        MPI_Datatype    datatype    /* in  */,
        MPI_Op          operator    /* in  */,
        MPI_Comm        comm        /* in  */)
```

This function is used in exactly the same way as MPI_Reduce. The only difference is that after the function returns, all the processes in the communicator will have the result stored in the memory referenced by result.

The extended gather function is

```
int MPI_Allgather(
        void*           send_data   /* in  */,
```

```
      int             send_count   /* in  */,
      MPI_Datatype    send_type    /* in  */,
      void*           recv_data    /* out */,
      int             recv_count   /* in  */,
      MPI_Datatype    recv_type    /* in  */,
      MPI_Comm        comm         /* in  */)
```

This has the effect of gathering the contents of each process's `send_data` into each process's `recv_data`.

5.10 References

Definitions, discussions, and examples of MPI's collective communications are contained in the MPI Standard [28, 29]. Further discussion and examples are contained in [34] and [21]. For background material and detailed discussions of implementations of collective operations, see [26]. For an elementary discussion of parallel implementations of linear algebra operations, see [19].

5.11 Exercises

1. Study the two tree-structured broadcasts on a linear array of eight processors, a 2 × 4 mesh, and a three-dimensional hypercube. Is there any reason to prefer one of the broadcasts to the other on each topology? Can you devise a better pattern for the broadcast on any of the architectures?

2. Suppose that `MPI_COMM_WORLD` consists of the three processes 0, 1, and 2, and suppose the following code is executed:

```
int x, y, z;

switch (my_rank) {
    case 0: x = 0; y = 1; z = 2;
        MPI_Bcast(&x, 1, MPI_INT, 0, MPI_COMM_WORLD);
        MPI_Send(&y, 1, MPI_INT, 2, 43, MPI_COMM_WORLD);
        MPI_Bcast(&z, 1, MPI_INT, 1, MPI_COMM_WORLD);
        break;
    case 1: x = 3; y = 4; z = 5;
        MPI_Bcast(&x, 1, MPI_INT, 0, MPI_COMM_WORLD);
        MPI_Bcast(&y, 1, MPI_INT, 1, MPI_COMM_WORLD);
        break;
    case 2: x = 6; y = 7; z = 8;
        MPI_Bcast(&z, 1, MPI_INT, 0, MPI_COMM_WORLD);
        MPI_Recv(&x, 1, MPI_INT, 0, 43, MPI_COMM_WORLD,
            &status);
        MPI_Bcast(&y, 1, MPI_INT, 1, MPI_COMM_WORLD);
        break;
}
```

What are the values of x, y, and z on each process after the code has been executed?

3. Modify the trapezoidal rule program so that it uses Get_data1.

4. Modify the trapezoidal rule program so that it uses Get_data2.

5. Let's take a look at a simple special case of the scatter-reduce matrix-vector multiplication: $m = n = p = 2$. Illustrate the steps involved in multiplying a 2×2 matrix by a vector if we first scatter each row of the matrix, carry out the multiplication of the matrix entries by the elements of the vector, and then sum the results of the multiplications. Your illustration should show how the contents of each process's memory changes after each step of the process. Use arrows to indicate communication of data. Does this example suggest a distribution of the matrix that might produce a more efficient matrix-vector multiplication?

6. Illustrate the implementation of gather and scatter using a tree and the implementation of allgather using a butterfly. Use eight processes and arrays of order 16. Your diagram should show the memory referenced by send_data on each process at the beginning of the communication. It should also show the contents of recv_data at each stage of the process.

5.12 Programming Assignments

In each of the assignments, assume that the appropriate parameters are divisible by p. For example, if you are writing a matrix-vector multiply in which you use a block row distribution of the matrix and a block distribution of the vectors, then the number of rows and the number of columns of the matrix should both be divisible by p.

Be sure to write assignment 1 before working on the other assignments.

1. In order to avoid some of the problems that may occur with I/O on your system, you should only input the scalar parameters to your programs. For example, if you are multiplying a matrix by a vector, you should only input the order of the matrix. The program should generate the matrix and vector (e.g., a matrix of all ones and a vector of all ones). Of course, you won't be able to tell whether your program works unless you print the results of your computations. So you should write two output functions: a vector output function and a matrix output function for matrices distributed by block rows.

2. Write a subprogram that performs a "global sum" of a distributed collection of floats. The parameters to the subprogram should consist of a scalar operand provided by each process and a root process. The operand will be an in/out parameter on the root. That is, on the root, the result of the global sum will be returned in the operand. We're not aiming for efficiency here. So a simple loop of receives on the root process will suffice. Does

your subprogram have to create a temporary buffer on the root process? Modify your subprogram so that it performs a "global vector sum." Each process passes a vector of floats, the size of the vector, and a root process to the subprogram. The root process returns the result in its input vector. Does your subprogram have to create a temporary buffer on the root process? If so, can you come up with an approach to solving this problem so that the root process doesn't need to create a temporary buffer?

3. Recollect that a matrix-matrix product is formed by taking the dot product of each row of the left factor with each column of the right factor. More explicitly, suppose $A = (a_{ij})$ is an $m \times n$ matrix and $B = (b_{ij})$ is an $n \times r$ matrix. Then the product matrix, $AB = C = (c_{ij})$ is an $m \times r$ matrix, and c_{ij} is the dot product of the ith row of A with the jth column of B, or

$$c_{ij} = a_{i0}b_{0j} + a_{i1}b_{1j} + \cdots + a_{i,n-1}b_{n-1,j}.$$

If A and B have been distributed by block rows, then we can use our parallel matrix-vector product to compute a parallel matrix-matrix product as follows:

```
for each column x of B {
    Compute the parallel matrix-vector product Ax
}
```

Write a subprogram that will compute a parallel matrix-matrix product using this algorithm.

CHAPTER 6

Grouping Data for Communication

WE MENTIONED IN CHAPTER 3 that with the current generation of parallel systems, sending a message is an expensive operation. A natural consequence of this is that, as a rule of thumb, the fewer messages sent, the better the overall performance of the program. However, in each of our trapezoidal rule programs, when we distributed the input data, we sent a, b, and n in separate messages—whether we used MPI_Send and MPI_Recv or MPI_Bcast. So we should be able to improve the performance of our program by sending the three input values in a single message. MPI provides three mechanisms for grouping individual data items into a single message: the count parameter to the various communication routines, derived datatypes, and MPI_Pack/MPI_Unpack. We examine each of these options in turn.

6.1 The count Parameter

Recall that MPI_Send, MPI_Receive, MPI_Bcast, and MPI_Reduce all have a count and a datatype parameter. These two parameters allow the user to group data items having the same basic type into a single message. In order to use this, the grouped data items must be stored in *contiguous* memory locations. Since C guarantees that array elements are stored in contiguous memory locations, if we wish to send the elements of an array, or a subset of an array, we can do so in a single message. In fact, we've already done this in Chapter 3, when we sent an array of char.

As another example, suppose we wish to send the second half of a vector containing 100 floats from process 0 to process 1.

```
float vector[100];
MPI_Status status;
int p;
int my_rank;

        .
        .
        .

/*  Initialize vector and send */
if (my_rank == 0) {

        .
        .
        .

    MPI_Send(vector+50, 50, MPI_FLOAT, 1, 0,
        MPI_COMM_WORLD);
} else { /* my_rank == 1 */
    MPI_Recv(vector+50, 50, MPI_FLOAT, 0, 0,
        MPI_COMM_WORLD, &status);
}
```

Unfortunately, this doesn't help us with the trapezoidal rule program. The data we wish to distribute to the other processes, a, b, and n, are not stored in an array. So even if we declared them one after the other in our program,

```
float a;
float b;
int n;
```

C does not guarantee that they are stored in contiguous memory locations. One might be tempted to store n as a float and put the three values in an array, but this would be poor programming style. In order to solve our problem we need to use one of MPI's other facilities for grouping data.

6.2 Derived Types and `MPI_Type_struct`

It might seem that another option would be to store a, b, and n in a struct with three members—two floats and an int—since C does guarantee that the members of a struct are stored in contiguous memory locations. However, this solution introduces another problem. Suppose we included the type definition

```
typedef struct {
    float   a;
    float   b;
    int     n;
} INDATA_T;
```

and the variable definition

```
INDATA_T indata;
```

Now suppose we call `MPI_Bcast`

```
MPI_Bcast(&indata, 1, INDATA_T, 0, MPI_COMM_WORLD);
```

What happens? It won't work. The compiler should scream at you when you try to do this: arguments to functions must be *variables,* not defined types. What we need is a method of defining a type that can be used as a function argument—i.e., a type that can be stored in a variable. Yes, you guessed it, MPI provides just such a type: MPI_Datatype. The problem now is how do we define a variable of type MPI_Datatype that represents two floats and an int?

Let's suppose we've declared a, b, and n in our main program as follows:

```
float   a;
float   b;
int     n;
```

(We could use the struct indata, but it's not necessary.) Also suppose that the user has entered "0.0 1.0 1024" when prompted by the program for input and that on process 0, a, b, and n are stored as follows:

Variable	Address	Contents
a	24	0.0
b	40	1.0
n	48	1024

In order for the communications subsystem to send a, b, and n in a single message, the following information is required:

1. There are three elements to be transmitted.
2. a. The first element is a float.
   b. The second element is a float.
   c. The third element is an int.
3. a. The first element has address &a.
   b. The second element has address &b.
   c. The third element has address &n.

Looking at this in a somewhat different way, we can compute the **relative addresses** or **displacements** of b and n from a and only provide the address &a. According to our table, a has address &a = 24. The second float, b, is *displaced* $40 - 24 = 16$ bytes beyond a. The int, n, is *displaced* $48 - 24 = 24$ bytes beyond a. So, alternatively, in order for process 0 to specify completely the data to be transmitted, the following information can be provided to the communications subsystem:

1. There are three elements to be transmitted.
2. a. The first element is a float.

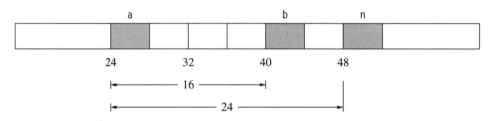

Figure 6.1 Memory layout with displacements

   b. The second element is a `float`.
   c. The third element is an `int`.
3. a. The first element is displaced 0 bytes from the beginning of the message.
   b. The second element is displaced 16 bytes from the beginning of the message.
   c. The third element is displaced 24 bytes from the beginning of the message.
4. The beginning of the message has address `&a`.

See Figure 6.1.

Note also that with this information (displacements computed according to local data layouts), each of the receiving processes can determine exactly where the data should be received. The principle behind MPI's derived datatypes is to provide all of the information *except* the address of the beginning of the message in a new *MPI* datatype. Then, when a program calls `MPI_Send`, `MPI_Recv`, etc., it simply provides the address of the first element, and the communications subsystem can determine exactly what needs to be sent or received. In effect, we are defining a struct during execution, rather than at compile time.

More precisely, a **general MPI datatype** or **derived datatype** is a sequence of pairs

$$\{(t_0, d_0), (t_1, d_1), \ldots, (t_{n-1}, d_{n-1})\},$$

where each t_i is a basic MPI datatype and each d_i is a displacement in bytes. Recall that the basic MPI datatypes correspond for the most part to the predefined types in C: `MPI_INT`, `MPI_CHAR`, `MPI_FLOAT`, etc.—see Table 3.1. A displacement d_i is the number of bytes the element of type t_i lies from the start of a message using the derived type. In order to send `a`, `b`, and `n` in a single message, we would like to build the following derived datatype.

$$\{(\texttt{MPI\_FLOAT}, 0), (\texttt{MPI\_FLOAT}, 16), (\texttt{MPI\_INT}, 24)\}$$

There are several mechanisms for building derived datatypes. Let's take a look at an example of one of them: this is how we might build a derived datatype that can be used to incorporate `a`, `b`, and `n` into a single message.

```c
void Build_derived_type(
        float*        a_ptr           /* in   */,
        float*        b_ptr           /* in   */,
        int*          n_ptr           /* in   */,
        MPI_Datatype* mesg_mpi_t_ptr  /* out  */) {
                                      /* pointer to new MPI type */

    /* The number of elements in each "block" of the   */
    /*      new type.  For us, 1 each.                  */
    int block_lengths[3];

    /* Displacement of each element from start of new   */
    /*      type.  The "d_i's."                         */
    /* MPI_Aint ("address int") is an MPI defined C     */
    /*      type.  Usually an int or a long int.        */
    MPI_Aint displacements[3];

    /* MPI types of the elements.  The "t_i's."         */
    MPI_Datatype typelist[3];

    /* Use for calculating displacements               */
    MPI_Aint start_address;
    MPI_Aint address;

    block_lengths[0] = block_lengths[1]
                     = block_lengths[2] = 1;

    /* Build a derived datatype consisting of  */
    /* two floats and an int                   */
    typelist[0] = MPI_FLOAT;
    typelist[1] = MPI_FLOAT;
    typelist[2] = MPI_INT;

    /* First element, a, is at displacement 0      */
    displacements[0] = 0;

    /* Calculate other displacements relative to a */
    MPI_Address(a_ptr, &start_address);

    /* Find address of b and displacement from a   */
    MPI_Address(b_ptr, &address);
    displacements[1] = address - start_address;

    /* Find address of n and displacement from a   */
    MPI_Address(n_ptr, &address);
    displacements[2] = address - start_address;

    /* Build the derived datatype */
    MPI_Type_struct(3, block_lengths, displacements,
        typelist, mesg_mpi_t_ptr);
```

```
        /* Commit it--tell system we'll be using it for */
        /* communication.                              */
        MPI_Type_commit(mesg_mpi_t_ptr);
} /* Build_derived_type */

void Get_data3(
         float*       a_ptr      /* out */,
         float*       b_ptr      /* out */,
         int*         n_ptr      /* in  */,
         int          my_rank  /* in  */) {
    MPI_Datatype  mesg_mpi_t;  /* MPI type corresponding */
                               /* to a, b, and n         */

    if (my_rank == 0){
        printf("Enter a, b, and n\n");
        scanf("%f %f %d", a_ptr, b_ptr, n_ptr);
    }

    Build_derived_type(a_ptr, b_ptr, n_ptr, &mesg_mpi_t);
    MPI_Bcast(a_ptr, 1, mesg_mpi_t, 0, MPI_COMM_WORLD);
} /* Get_data3 */
```

Observe that in the call to MPI_Type_struct we provide all but one of the items we listed as necessary for correct identification of the data to be sent (or received):

1. The first argument (3) is the number of elements (or more generally blocks of elements) in the new MPI type.

2. The fourth argument (typelist) contains a list of the types of the elements to be sent.

3. The third argument (displacements) contains a list of the displacements of the elements from the beginning of the message.

The beginning of the message (&a) is omitted to allow for the possibility that the derived datatype represents a data layout that occurs often in the program. For example, it might represent a frequently used user-defined struct. If this is the case, the derived type can be used for *any* variable having the frequently used type.

The remaining argument to MPI_Type_struct, block_lengths, allows for the possibility that an element is an array. For example, if the second element of the derived type consisted of ten floats rather than one, we would have initialized block_lengths as follows:

```
block_lengths[0] = block_lengths[2] = 1;
block_lengths[1] = 10;
```

Note that in this case, the first argument would still be 3 (not 12).

To summarize, then, we can build general derived datatypes by calling `MPI_Type_struct`. The syntax is

```
int MPI_Type_struct(
        int             count           /* in  */,
        int             block_lengths[] /* in  */,
        MPI_Aint        displacements[] /* in  */,
        MPI_Datatype    typelist[]      /* in  */,
        MPI_Datatype*   new_mpi_t       /* out */);
```

The parameter `count` is the number of blocks of elements in the derived type. It is also the size of the three arrays, `block_lengths`, `displacements`, and `typelist`. The array `block_lengths` contains the number of entries in each element of the type. So if an element of the type is an array of m values, then the corresponding entry in `block_lengths` is m. The array `displacements` contains the displacement of each element from the beginning of the message, and the array `typelist` contains the MPI datatype of each entry. The parameter `new_mpi_t` returns a pointer to the MPI datatype created by the call to `MPI_Type_struct`.

A few observations are in order. Note that the type of `displacements` is `MPI_Aint`—not int. This is a special C type in MPI. It allows for the possibility that addresses are too large to be stored in an int. Note also that `new_mpi_t` and the entries in `typelist` all have type `MPI_Datatype`. So `MPI_Type_struct` can be called recursively to build more complex derived datatypes.

In order to compute addresses, we used the function

```
MPI_Address(
    void*       location    /* in  */
    MPI_Aint*   address     /* out */)
```

It returns the byte address of `location` in `address`. We use it instead of C's & operator to insure portability. Although many implementations of C allow arithmetic on pointers, it is technically legal to do this only when the pointers refer to elements of the same array.

After the call to `MPI_Type_struct`, we can't use `new_mpi_t` in communication functions until we call `MPI_Type_commit`. Its syntax is simply

```
int MPI_Type_commit(
        MPI_Datatype*   new_mpi_t   /* in/out */)
```

This is a mechanism for the system to make internal changes in the representation of `new_mpi_t` that may improve the communication performance. These changes won't be needed if the new type is only going to be used as a building block for another, more complex type. Hence MPI makes it a separate function.

6.3 Other Derived Datatype Constructors

MPI_Type_struct is the most general datatype constructor in MPI, and as
a consequence, the user must provide a *complete* description of each element of the type. If the data to be transmitted consists of a subset of the
entries in an array, we shouldn't need to provide such detailed information
since all the elements have the same basic type. MPI provides three derived
datatype constructors for dealing with this situation: MPI_Type_contiguous,
MPI_Type_vector, and MPI_Type_indexed. The first constructor builds a
derived type whose elements are contiguous entries in an array. The second
builds a type whose elements are equally spaced entries of an array, and the
third builds a type whose elements are arbitrary entries of an array.

As an example, we'll use MPI_Type_vector to send a column of a two-
dimensional array. So suppose that a program contains the following definition:

```
float A[10][10];
```

Recall that C stores two-dimensional arrays in *row-major* order. This means,
for example, that in memory A[2][3] is preceded by A[2][2] and followed
by A[2][4].[1] So if we wish to send, say, the third row of A from process 0 to
process 1, we can simply use the following code:

```
if (my_rank == 0) {
    MPI_Send(&(A[2][0]), 10, MPI_FLOAT, 1, 0,
        MPI_COMM_WORLD);
} else { /* my_rank = 1 */
    MPI_Recv(&(A[2][0]), 10, MPI_FLOAT, 0, 0,
        MPI_COMM_WORLD, &status);
}
```

The reason this works is that the 10 memory locations starting at A[2][0] are
A[2][0], A[2][1], A[2][2], ... , A[2][9]—the third row of A.

If we wish to send the third column of A, this won't work, since A[0][2],
A[1][2], ... , A[9][2] aren't stored in contiguous memory locations. However, we can use MPI_Type_vector to create a derived datatype, since the
displacement of successive elements of the derived type is constant—A[1][2]
is displaced 10 floats beyond A[0][2], A[2][2] is 10 floats beyond A[1][2],
etc. The syntax is

```
int MPI_Type_vector(
            int              count           /* in */,
```

---

[1] Fortran stores two-dimensional arrays in *column-major* order. So A(2,3) is preceded by
A(1,3) and followed by A(3,3). Thus, an equivalent problem in Fortran would be sending
a *row* of A.

```
int             block_length   /* in  */,
int             stride         /* in  */,
MPI_Datatype    element_type   /* in  */,
MPI_Datatype*   new_mpi_t      /* out */)
```

The parameter `count` is the number of elements in the type. `Block_length` is the number of entries in each element. `Stride` is the number of elements of type `element_type` between successive elements of `new_mpi_t`. `Element_type` is the type of the elements composing the derived type, and `new_mpi_t` is the MPI type of the new derived type.

So in order to send the third column of A from process 0 to process 1, we can use the following code:

```
/* column_mpi_t is declared to have type */
/* MPI_Datatype                          */
MPI_Type_vector(10, 1, 10, MPI_FLOAT, &column_mpi_t);
MPI_Type_commit(&column_mpi_t);
if (my_rank == 0)
    MPI_Send(&(A[0][2]), 1, column_mpi_t, 1, 0,
        MPI_COMM_WORLD);
else
    MPI_Recv(&(A[0][2]), 1, column_mpi_t, 0, 0,
        MPI_COMM_WORLD, &status);
```

Note that `column_mpi_t` can be used to send any column of A. If we want to send the jth column of A, $j = 0, 1, \ldots, 9$, we simply call the communication routine with first argument `&(A[0][j])`. Also note that in fact `column_mpi_t` can be used to send any column of any 10×10 matrix of floats, since the stride and element type will be the same.

This last point is important. In general, it is fairly expensive to build a derived datatype. So applications that make use of derived datatypes typically use the types many times.

The syntax for the other two constructors is

```
int MPI_Type_contiguous(
        int             count       /* in  */,
        MPI_Datatype    old_type    /* in  */,
        MPI_Datatype*   new_mpi_t   /* out */)

int MPI_Type_indexed(
        int             count,
        int             block_lengths[],
        int             displacements[],
        MPI_Datatype    old_type,
        MPI_Datatype*   new_mpi_t)
```

In `MPI_Type_contiguous`, one simply specifies that the derived type `new_mpi_t` will consist of `count` contiguous elements, each of which has type `old_type`. In `MPI_Type_indexed`, the derived type consists of `count` elements of type `old_type`. The *i*th element consists of `block_lengths[i]` entries, and it is displaced `displacements[i]` units of `old_type` from the beginning (displacement 0) of the type. Note that displacements are not measured in bytes.[2]

As an example of the use of `MPI_Type_indexed`, let's send the upper triangular portion of a square matrix stored on process 0 to process 1:

```
float         A[n][n];          /* Complete Matrix */
float         T[n][n];          /* Upper Triangle  */
int           displacements[n];
int           block_lengths[n];
MPI_Datatype  index_mpi_t;

for (i = 0; i < n; i++) {
    block_lengths[i] = n-i;
    displacements[i] = (n+1)*i;
}

MPI_Type_indexed(n, block_lengths, displacements,
    MPI_FLOAT, &index_mpi_t);
MPI_Type_commit(&index_mpi_t);

if (my_rank == 0)
    MPI_Send(A, 1, index_mpi_t, 1, 0, MPI_COMM_WORLD);
else /* my_rank == 1 */
    MPI_Recv(T, 1, index_mpi_t, 0, 0, MPI_COMM_WORLD,
        &status);
```

Note that even though the blocks are uniformly spaced in memory ($n + 1$ floats apart), we couldn't use `MPI_Type_vector` here because the block lengths are different for each row.

6.4 Type Matching

At this point it is natural to ask, What are the rules for matching MPI datatypes? For example, suppose a program contains the following code:

```
if (my_rank == 0)
    MPI_Send(message, send_count, send_mpi_t, 1, 0,
            MPI_COMM_WORLD);
else if (my_rank == 1)
    MPI_Recv(message, recv_count, recv_mpi_t, 0, 0,
            MPI_COMM_WORLD, &status);
```

---

2 MPI does provide functions where the stride or displacements are measured in bytes: `MPI_Type_hvector` and `MPI_Type_hindexed`. For details see [28, 29].

Must `send_mpi_t` be identical to `recv_mpi_t`? What about `send_count` and `recv_count`?

In order to answer this question, recall that a derived datatype is a sequence of pairs. The first element of a pair is a basic MPI type; the second, a displacement. That is, a general datatype has the form

$$\{(t_0, d_0), (t_1, d_1), \ldots, (t_{n-1}, d_{n-1})\},$$

where each t_i is a basic MPI type and each d_i is a displacement in bytes. The sequence of basic types,

$$\{t_0, t_1, \ldots, t_{n-1}\},$$

is called the **type signature** of the type. The fundamental rule for type matching in MPI is that the type signatures specified by the sender and the receiver must be compatible. That is, suppose the type signature specified by the arguments passed to `MPI_Send` is

$$\{t_0, t_1, \ldots, t_{n-1}\},$$

and the type signature specified by the arguments to `MPI_Recv` is

$$\{u_0, u_1, \ldots, u_{m-1}\}.$$

Then n must be less than or equal to m and t_i must equal u_i for $i = 0, \ldots, n - 1$. So displacements do not affect type matching.

In order to fully understand this rule, keep in mind that if, for example, `send_count` is greater than 1, then the type signature is obtained by simply concatenating `send_count` copies of the type signature of `send_mpi_t`.

Also keep in mind that for collective communication functions (unlike `MPI_Send` and `MPI_Recv`), the type signatures specified by all the processes must be *identical*.

Let's take a look at a short example. Recall that in section 6.3 we created a type `column_mpi_t` that corresponded to a column of a 10×10 array of floats. Thus the type is

```
{(MPI_FLOAT, 0), (MPI_FLOAT, 10*sizeof(float)),
     (MPI_FLOAT,20*sizeof(float)), . . . ,
     (MPI_FLOAT,90*sizeof(float))}
```

and its type signature is

```
{MPI_FLOAT, MPI_FLOAT, . . . , MPI_FLOAT}
```

(repeated 10 times). So if we use `MPI_Send` to send a message consisting of one copy of `column_mpi_t`, it can be received by a call to `MPI_Recv` provided the type signature specified by the receive consists of at least 10 floats. Thus, we can receive a column of a 10×10 matrix into a row of a 10×10 matrix as follows:

```
        float A[10][10];

        if (my_rank == 0)
            MPI_Send(&(A[0][0]), 1, column_mpi_t, 1, 0,
                    MPI_COMM_WORLD);
        else if (my_rank == 1)
            MPI_Recv(&(A[0][0]), 10, MPI_FLOAT, 0, 0,
                    MPI_COMM_WORLD, &status);
```

This will send the first column of the matrix A on process 0 to the first row of the matrix A on process 1.

6.5 Pack/Unpack

An alternative approach to grouping data is provided by the MPI functions MPI_Pack and MPI_Unpack. MPI_Pack allows one to explicitly store noncontiguous data in contiguous memory locations, and MPI_Unpack can be used to copy data from a contiguous buffer into noncontiguous memory locations. In order to see how they are used, let's rewrite Get_data one last time.

```
void Get_data4(
            float*   a_ptr     /* out */,
            float*   b_ptr     /* out */,
            int*     n_ptr     /* out */,
            int      my_rank   /* in  */) {

        char  buffer[100];  /* Store data in buffer       */
        int   position;     /* Keep track of where data is */
                            /*     in the buffer          */

        if (my_rank == 0){
            printf("Enter a, b, and n\n");
            scanf("%f %f %d", a_ptr, b_ptr, n_ptr);

            /* Now pack the data into buffer.  Position = 0 */
            /* says start at beginning of buffer.           */
            position = 0;

            /* Position is in/out */
            MPI_Pack(a_ptr, 1, MPI_FLOAT, buffer, 100,
                &position, MPI_COMM_WORLD);
            /* Position has been incremented: it now refer- */
            /* ences the first free location in buffer.     */

            MPI_Pack(b_ptr, 1, MPI_FLOAT, buffer, 100,
                &position, MPI_COMM_WORLD);
            /* Position has been incremented again. */
```

```
          MPI_Pack(n_ptr, 1, MPI_INT, buffer, 100,
              &position, MPI_COMM_WORLD);
          /* Position has been incremented again. */

          /* Now broadcast contents of buffer */
          MPI_Bcast(buffer, 100, MPI_PACKED, 0,
              MPI_COMM_WORLD);
      } else {
          MPI_Bcast(buffer, 100, MPI_PACKED, 0,
              MPI_COMM_WORLD);

          /* Now unpack the contents of buffer */
          position = 0;
          MPI_Unpack(buffer, 100, &position, a_ptr, 1,
              MPI_FLOAT, MPI_COMM_WORLD);
          /* Once again position has been incremented: */
          /* it now references the beginning of b.      */

          MPI_Unpack(buffer, 100, &position, b_ptr, 1,
              MPI_FLOAT, MPI_COMM_WORLD);
          MPI_Unpack(buffer, 100, &position, n_ptr, 1,
              MPI_INT, MPI_COMM_WORLD);
      }
  } /* Get_data4 */
```

In this version of Get_data, process 0 uses MPI_Pack to copy a to buffer
and then successively append b and n. After the broadcast of buffer, the
remaining processes use MPI_Unpack to successively extract a, b, and n from
buffer. Note that the datatype for the calls to MPI_Bcast is MPI_PACKED.

The syntax of MPI_Pack is

```
int MPI_Pack(
          void*          pack_data      /* in     */,
          int            in_count       /* in     */,
          MPI_Datatype   datatype       /* in     */,
          void*          buffer         /* out    */,
          int            buffer_size    /* in     */,
          int*           position       /* in/out */,
          MPI_Comm       comm           /* in     */)
```

The parameter pack_data references the data to be buffered. It should consist
of in_count elements, each having type datatype. The parameter position
is an in/out parameter. On input, the data referenced by pack_data is copied
into memory starting at address buffer + *position. On return, *position references the first location in buffer *after* the data that was copied.
The parameter buffer_size contains the size in bytes of the memory referenced by buffer, and comm is the communicator that will be using buffer.
See Figure 6.2.

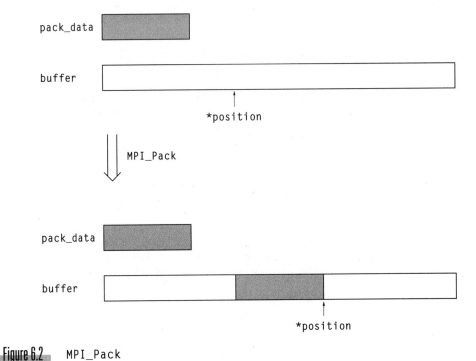

Figure 6.2   `MPI_Pack`

The syntax of `MPI_Unpack` is

```
int MPI_Unpack(
        void*        buffer       /* in     */,
        int          size         /* in     */,
        int*         position     /* in/out */,
        void*        unpack_data  /* out    */,
        int          count        /* in     */,
        MPI_Datatype datatype     /* in     */,
        MPI_Comm     comm         /* in     */)
```

The parameter `buffer` references the data to be unpacked. It consists of `size` bytes. The parameter `position` is once again an `in/out` parameter. When `MPI_Unpack` is called, the data starting at address `buffer + *position` is copied into the memory referenced by `unpack_data`. On return, `*position` references the first location in `buffer` after the data that was just copied. `MPI_Unpack` will copy `count` elements having type `datatype` into `unpack_data`. The communicator associated with `buffer` is `comm`. See Figure 6.3.

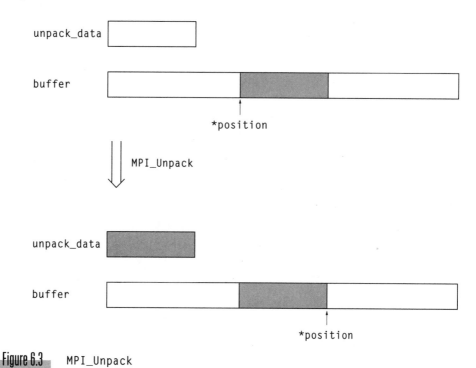

Figure 6.3   MPI_Unpack

6.6 Deciding Which Method to Use

If the data to be sent is stored in consecutive entries of an array, then one should simply use the count and datatype parameters to the communication function(s). This approach involves no additional overhead in the form of calls to derived datatype creation functions or calls to MPI_Pack/MPI_Unpack.

If there are a large number of elements that are not in contiguous memory locations, then building a derived type will probably involve less overhead than a large number of calls to MPI_Pack/MPI_Unpack.

If the data all have the same type and are stored at regular intervals in memory (e.g., a column of a matrix), then it will almost certainly be much easier and faster to use a derived datatype than it will be to use MPI_Pack/ MPI_Unpack. Furthermore, if the data all have the same type, but are stored in irregularly spaced locations in memory, it will still probably be easier and more efficient to create a derived type using MPI_Type_indexed. Finally, if the data are heterogeneous and you are repeatedly sending the same collection of data (e.g., row number, column number, matrix entry), then it will be better to use a derived type, since the overhead of creating the derived type is incurred only once, while the overhead of calling MPI_Pack/MPI_Unpack must be incurred every time the data is communicated.

This leaves the case where you are sending heterogeneous data only once,

or very few times. In this case, it may be a good idea to collect some data on
the cost of derived type creation and packing/unpacking the data. For example,
on an nCUBE 2 running the mpich implementation of MPI, it takes about 12
milliseconds to create the derived type used in Get_data3, while it only takes
about 2 milliseconds to pack or unpack the data in Get_data4. Of course, the
saving isn't as great as it seems because of the asymmetry in the pack/unpack
procedure. That is, while process 0 packs the data, the other processes are
idle, and the entire function won't complete until both the pack and unpack
are executed. So the cost ratio is probably more like 3:1 than 6:1.

There are also a couple of situations in which the use of MPI_Pack/
MPI_Unpack is preferred. Note first that it may be possible to avoid the use of
system buffering with pack, since the data is explicitly stored in a user-defined
buffer. The system can exploit this by noting that the message datatype is
MPI_PACKED. Also note that the user can send "variable length" messages by
packing the number of elements at the beginning of the buffer. For example,
suppose we want to send rows of a sparse matrix. If we have stored each row
as a pair of arrays—one containing the column subscripts, and one containing the corresponding matrix entries—we could send a row from process 0 to
process 1 as follows:

```
float*      entries;
int*        column_subscripts;
int         nonzeroes;
int         position;
int         row_number;
char        buffer[HUGE]; /* HUGE is a constant    */
                          /* defined in the program */
MPI_Status  status;
    .
    .
    .
if (my_rank == 0) {
    /* Get the number of nonzeroes in the row.   */
    /* Allocate storage for the row.             */
    /* Initialize entries and column_subscripts */
        .
        .
        .
    /* Now pack the data and send */
    position = 0;
    MPI_Pack(&nonzeroes, 1, MPI_INT, buffer, HUGE,
        &position, MPI_COMM_WORLD);
    MPI_Pack(&row_number, 1, MPI_INT, buffer, HUGE,
        &position, MPI_COMM_WORLD);
    MPI_Pack(entries, nonzeroes, MPI_FLOAT, buffer,
        HUGE, &position, MPI_COMM_WORLD);
    MPI_Pack(column_subscripts, nonzeroes, MPI_INT,
        buffer, HUGE, &position, MPI_COMM_WORLD);
    MPI_Send(buffer, position, MPI_PACKED, 1, 0,
        MPI_COMM_WORLD);
} else { /* my_rank == 1 */
```

```
          MPI_Recv(buffer, HUGE, MPI_PACKED, 0, 0,
              MPI_COMM_WORLD, &status);
          position = 0;
          MPI_Unpack(buffer, HUGE, &position, &nonzeroes,
              1, MPI_INT, MPI_COMM_WORLD);
          MPI_Unpack(buffer, HUGE, &position, &row_number,
              1, MPI_INT, MPI_COMM_WORLD);
          /* Allocate storage for entries */
          /* and column_subscripts        */
          entries = (float *) malloc(nonzeroes*sizeof(float));
          column_subscripts =
              (int *) malloc(nonzeroes*sizeof(int));
          MPI_Unpack(buffer,HUGE, &position, entries,
              nonzeroes, MPI_FLOAT, MPI_COMM_WORLD);
          MPI_Unpack(buffer, HUGE, &position,
              column_subscripts, nonzeroes, MPI_INT,
              MPI_COMM_WORLD);
      }
```

6.7 Summary

MPI provides three methods for sending messages consisting of more than one
scalar element. The simplest method can be used for sending consecutive
entries in arrays: call the appropriate communication function with the count
parameter set equal to the number of entries to be sent and the datatype
parameter set equal to the basic type of the array elements. For more complex
messages, one can either build a *derived* datatype, or one can use the two
functions MPI_Pack and MPI_Unpack.

A derived datatype is essentially a struct that is built *during execution* of
the program and can be passed as the datatype argument to MPI communication functions. In order to build one, the user must specify

1. the number of elements in the type
2. the types of the elements
3. the relative locations, or *displacements*, of the elements in memory

MPI provides a number of functions for building derived types. The simplest
to use are MPI_Type_contiguous and MPI_Type_vector. The first can be
used to construct a type containing a subset of consecutive entries in an array.
The second can be used to construct a type consisting of array elements that are
uniformly spaced in memory. MPI_Type_indexed can be used to construct a
type consisting of array elements that may not be uniformly spaced in memory.
The most general constructor is MPI_Type_struct. It can be used to build
derived types whose elements have different types and arbitrary locations in
memory. Their syntax is

```
int MPI_Type_contiguous(
        int           count            /* in  */,
        MPI_Datatype  old_type         /* in  */,
        MPI_Datatype* new_mpi_t        /* out */)

int MPI_Type_vector(
        int           count            /* in  */,
        int           block_length     /* in  */,
        int           stride           /* in  */,
        MPI_Datatype  element_type     /* in  */,
        MPI_Datatype* new_mpi_t        /* out */)

int MPI_Type_indexed(
        int           count            /* in  */,
        int           block_lengths[]  /* in  */,
        int           displacements[]  /* in  */,
        MPI_Datatype  old_type         /* in  */,
        MPI_Datatype* new_mpi_t        /* out */)

int MPI_Type_struct(
        int           count            /* in  */,
        int           block_lengths[]  /* in  */,
        MPI_Aint      displacements[]  /* in  */,
        MPI_Datatype  typelist[]       /* in  */,
        MPI_Datatype* new_mpi_t        /* out */);
```

Before a derived type can be used by a comunication function, it must be *committed* with a call to MPI_Type_commit. Its syntax is simply

```
int MPI_Type_commit(
        MPI_Datatype* new_mpi_t  /* in/out */)
```

Formally, a derived datatype is a sequence of pairs:

$$\{(t_0, d_0), (t_1, d_1), \dots, (t_{n-1}, d_{n-1})\}.$$

The first element of each pair is a basic MPI datatype—MPI_INT, MPI_CHAR, etc. The second element is a displacement in bytes. The *type signature* is just the sequence of types specified by a derived datatype:

$$\{t_0, t_1, \dots, t_{n-1}\}.$$

In order for a message to be received, the type signatures specified by the sender and the receiver must be compatible. Suppose the type signature specified by the sender is

$$\{s_0, s_1, \dots, s_{m-1}\}.$$

and the type signature specified by the receiver is

$$\{t_0, t_1, \dots, t_{n-1}\}.$$

Then if the communication is carried out using MPI_Send and MPI_Recv, m must be less than or equal to n, and s_i must be the same as t_i for $i = 0, 1, \ldots ,$ $m - 1$. If the communication is carried out using a collective communication function (MPI_Bcast, MPI_Reduce, etc.), then the type signatures must be identical.

MPI_Pack can be used to explicitly store data in a *user-defined* buffer. MPI_Unpack can be used to extract data from a buffer that was constructed using MPI_Pack. Messages that have been constructed using MPI_Pack should be communicated with datatype argument MPI_PACKED. Their syntax is

```
int MPI_Pack(
        void*         pack_data     /* in     */,
        int           in_count      /* in     */,
        MPI_Datatype  datatype      /* in     */,
        void*         buffer        /* out    */,
        int           buffer_size   /* in     */,
        int*          position      /* in/out */,
        MPI_Comm      comm          /* in     */)

int MPI_Unpack(
        void*         buffer        /* in     */,
        int           size          /* in     */,
        int*          position      /* in/out */,
        void*         unpack_data   /* out    */,
        int           count         /* in     */,
        MPI_Datatype  datatype      /* in     */,
        MPI_comm      comm          /* in     */)
```

In general, if a message consists of an array of scalar types, it's a good idea to just use the count and datatype parameters to the communications routines. For more complicated messages, it's usually better to use derived types. The most important exceptions are the following:

1. The type would only be used a very few times, and the overhead associated with building the derived type is greater than the overhead associated with using pack and unpack.

2. You wish to buffer messages in user memory instead of system memory.

3. You wish to specify *in the message* the number of items it contains.

6.8 References

Details on rules for using derived datatypes and MPI_Pack/MPI_Unpack can be found in both the MPI Standard [28, 29] and [34]. Examples of their use can be found in these references and [21]. A discussion of legal operations on pointers can be found in [24].

6.9 Exercises

1. Edit the trapezoidal rule program so that it uses `Get_data3`.

2. Edit the trapezoidal rule program so that it uses `Get_data4`.

3. Write a function that creates a derived type representing a sparse matrix entry. A matrix entry is a struct consisting of a float and two ints. The ints represent the row and column number of an entry whose value is given by the float. Test your derived type by using it in a short program that sends a matrix entry from one process to another.

4. In view of the type matching rule (section 6.4), it's possible to have many different types specified by a sender correspond to a given type specified · by the receiver. Consider the following definitions:

```
float           B[5][5];
float           x[5];
MPI_Datatype    first_mpi_t;
MPI_Datatype    second_mpi_t;
MPI_Datatype    third_mpi_t;
int             blocklengths[5] = {1,1,1,1,1};
int             displacements[5];

MPI_Type_contiguous(5, MPI_FLOAT, &first_mpi_t);
MPI_Type_vector(5, 1, 5, MPI_FLOAT,
                &second_mpi_t);
for (i = 0; i < 5; i++)
    displacements[i] = 6*i;
MPI_Type_indexed(5, block_lengths, displacements,
                MPI_FLOAT, &third_mpi_t);
```

Suppose a program contains these definitions, and the following sends and receives (in no particular order):

```
Process 0:
    MPI_Send(x, 5, MPI_FLOAT, 1, 0,
            MPI_COMM_WORLD);
    MPI_Send(&(B[1][0]), 5, MPI_FLOAT, 1, 0,
            MPI_COMM_WORLD);
    MPI_Send(x, 1, first_mpi_t, 1, 0,
            MPI_COMM_WORLD);
    MPI_Send(&(B[0][3]), 1, second_mpi_t, 1, 0,
            MPI_COMM_WORLD);
    MPI_Send(&(B[0][0]), 1, third_mpi_t, 1, 0,
            MPI_COMM_WORLD);
Process 1:
    MPI_Recv(x, 5, MPI_FLOAT, 0, 0,
            MPI_COMM_WORLD, &status);
```

```
MPI_Recv(&(B[1][0]), 5, MPI_FLOAT, 0, 0,
        MPI_COMM_WORLD, &status);
MPI_Recv(x, 1, first_mpi_t, 0, 0,
        MPI_COMM_WORLD, &status);
MPI_Recv(&(B[0][1]), 1, second_mpi_t, 0, 0,
        MPI_COMM_WORLD, &status);
MPI_Recv(&(B[0][0]), 1, third_mpi_t, 0, 0,
        MPI_COMM_WORLD, &status);
```

Briefly describe the memory on process 0 and process 1 referenced by
each send/receive (e.g., "first row of B, second column of B, x"). Which
receives could match which sends?

6.10 Programming Assignments

1. We can use derived datatypes to write functions for (dense) matrix I/O
   when we store the matrix by block *columns*.

   a. Write a function that prints a square matrix distributed by block
      columns among the processes. Suppose that the order of the matrix is n
      and the number of processes is p, and assume that n is evenly divisible
      by p. The function should successively gather blocks of n/p rows to
      process 0, and process 0 should print each block of n/p rows immedi-
      ately after it has been received. For each gather of n/p rows, each pro-
      cess should send (using MPI_Send) a block of order $n/p \times n/p$ to pro-
      cess 0. Process 0 should carry out the gather using a sequence of calls
      to MPI_Recv. The datatype argument should be a derived datatype
      created with MPI_Type_vector. (Although it may be tempting to use
      MPI_Gather for this function, there are some technical problems this
      introduces that we aren't quite ready to deal with. See section 8.4 for
      details.)

   b. Write a function that reads in a square matrix stored in row-major or-
      der in a single file. Process 0 should read in the number of rows and
      broadcast this information to the other processes. Assume that n, the
      number of rows, is evenly divisible by p, the number of processes. Pro-
      cess 0 should then read in a block of n/p rows and distribute blocks
      of n/p columns to each of the processes: the first n/p columns go
      to 0, the next n/p to 1, etc. Process 0 should then repeat this pro-
      cess for each block of n/p rows. Use a derived type created with
      MPI_Type_vector so that the data sent to each process can be sent
      with a single call to MPI_Send. (Use MPI_Send and MPI_Recv rather
      than MPI_Scatter. See section 8.4 for details.)

2. Use your matrix I/O functions in a matrix-vector multiplication program.
   Read and distribute the coefficient matrix and the vector. Multiply them
   and print the result.

3. Write a dense matrix transpose function: Suppose a dense $n \times n$ matrix A is stored on process 0. Create a derived datatype representing a single column of A. Send each column of A to process 1, but have process 1 receive each column into a row. When the function returns, A should be stored on process 0 and A^T on process 1.

4. Repeat the preceding exercise for a sparse matrix. Suppose that a sparse matrix has been stored as an array of rows. Each row is represented by a struct consisting of three members: the number of nonzero entries in the row, the entries in the row, and the column numbers of the entries in the row. Write a function that identifies the entries in a column of the matrix. Also write a function that uses MPI_Pack to store the entries in a user-defined buffer, and a function that uses MPI_Unpack to extract the entries from the buffer and store them in the same fashion as a row.

   Use your functions in a program that stores the matrix A on process 0 and its transpose on process 1.

CHAPTER 7

Communicators and Topologies

THE USE OF COMMUNICATORS AND TOPOLOGIES makes MPI different from most other message-passing systems. Recollect that, loosely speaking, a communicator is a collection of processes that can send messages to each other. A topology is a structure imposed on the processes in a communicator that allows the processes to be addressed in different ways. In order to illustrate these ideas, we will develop code to implement Fox's algorithm for multiplying two square matrices.

7.1 Matrix Multiplication

Recall that if $A = (a_{ij})$ and $B = (b_{ij})$ are square matrices of order n, then $C = (c_{ij}) = AB$ is also a square matrix of order n, and c_{ij} is obtained by taking the dot product of the ith row of A with the jth column of B. That is,

$$c_{ij} = a_{i0}b_{0j} + a_{i1}b_{1j} + \cdots + a_{i,n-1}b_{n-1,j}.$$

See Figure 7.1. Here's a simple algorithm for matrix multiplication:

```
for each row of C
    for each column of C {
        C[row][column] = 0.0;
        for each element of this row of A
            Add A[row][element]*B[element][column]
                to C[row][column]
    }
```

This can be readily implemented in C as follows:

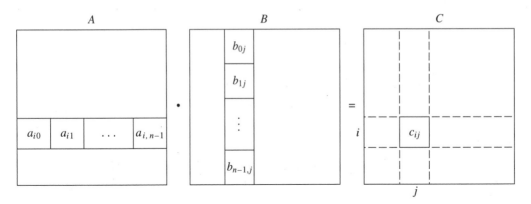

Figure 7.1   Matrix multiplication

```
/* MATRIX_T is a two-dimensional array of floats */
void Serial_matrix_mult(
        MATRIX_T    A    /* in  */,
        MATRIX_T    B    /* in  */,
        MATRIX_T    C    /* out */,
        int         n    /* in  */) {
    int i, j, k;

    for (i = 0; i < n; i++)
        for (j = 0; j < n; j++) {
            C[i][j] = 0.0;
            for (k = 0; k < n; k++)
                C[i][j] = C[i][j] + A[i][k]*B[k][j];
        }
} /* Serial_matrix_mult */
```

Observe that a straightforward parallel implementation will be quite costly. For example, suppose (for the sake of simplicity) that the number of processes is the same as the order of the matrices; i.e., $p = n$, and suppose that we have distributed the matrices by rows. So process 0 is assigned row 0 of $A, B,$ and C; process 1 is assigned row 1 of $A, B,$ and C; etc. Then in order to form the dot product of the ith row of A with the jth column of B, we will need to gather the jth column of B onto process i. But we will need to form the dot product of the jth column with *every* row of A. So we'll have to carry out an allgather rather than a gather, and we'll have to do this for *every* column of B. If we assume that there is insufficient storage for each process to store all of B, our parallel matrix-matrix multiply might be something like this:

```
for each column of B {
    Allgather(column);
    Compute dot product of my row of A with
        column;
}
```

Process 0		Process 1	
a_{00}	a_{01}	a_{02}	a_{03}
a_{10}	a_{11}	a_{12}	a_{13}
Process 2		Process 3	
a_{20}	a_{21}	a_{22}	a_{23}
a_{30}	a_{31}	a_{32}	a_{33}

Figure 7.2   Checkerboard mapping of a 4 × 4 matrix to four processes

Even with an efficient implementation of allgather, this will involve quite a lot
of (expensive) communication. Similar reasoning shows that an algorithm that
distributes the matrices by columns will also involve large amounts of communication. In view of these considerations, most parallel matrix multiplication
functions use a **checkerboard** distribution of the matrices. This means that
the processes are viewed as a grid, and, rather than assigning entire rows or
entire columns to each process, we assign small submatrices. For example, if
we have four processes, we might assign the elements of a 4 × 4 matrix as
shown in Figure 7.2. In the next section we'll take a look at one algorithm that
uses checkerboard mappings of the matrices.

7.2 Fox's Algorithm

In order to simplify the discussion, let's assume (for the time being) that the
matrices have order n, and the number of processes, p, equals n^2. Then a
checkerboard mapping assigns a_{ij}, b_{ij}, and c_{ij} to process $i * n + j$, or, loosely,
process (i, j). Fox's algorithm for matrix multiplication proceeds in n stages:
one stage for each term $a_{ik}b_{kj}$ in the dot product

$$c_{ij} = a_{i0}b_{0j} + a_{i1}b_{1j} + \cdots + a_{i,n-1}b_{n-1,j}.$$

During the initial stage, each process multiplies the diagonal entry of A in its
process row by its element of B:

Stage 0 on process (i, j): $c_{ij} = a_{ii}b_{ij}$.

During the next stage, each process multiplies the element immediately to the
right of the diagonal of A (in its process row) by the element of B directly
beneath its own element of B:

Stage 1 on process (i, j): $c_{ij} = c_{ij} + a_{i,i+1}b_{i+1,j}$.

In general, during the kth stage, each process multiplies the element k columns
to the right of the diagonal of A by the element k rows below its own element
of B:

Stage k on process (i, j): $c_{ij} = c_{ij} + a_{i,i+k}b_{i+k,j}$.

	i	ii	iii
Stage 0	a_{00} → ←a_{11}→ →a_{22}	$c_{00} += a_{00}b_{00}$ $\quad c_{01} += a_{00}b_{01}$ $\quad c_{02} += a_{00}b_{02}$ $c_{10} += a_{11}b_{10}$ $\quad c_{11} += a_{11}b_{11}$ $\quad c_{12} += a_{11}b_{12}$ $c_{20} += a_{22}b_{20}$ $\quad c_{21} += a_{22}b_{21}$ $\quad c_{22} += a_{22}b_{22}$	$\begin{pmatrix} b_{00} & b_{01} & b_{02} \\ b_{10} & b_{11} & b_{12} \\ b_{20} & b_{21} & b_{22} \end{pmatrix}$
Stage 1	←a_{01}→ →a_{12} a_{20} →	$c_{00} += a_{01}b_{10}$ $\quad c_{01} += a_{01}b_{11}$ $\quad c_{02} += a_{01}b_{12}$ $c_{10} += a_{12}b_{20}$ $\quad c_{11} += a_{12}b_{21}$ $\quad c_{12} += a_{12}b_{22}$ $c_{20} += a_{20}b_{00}$ $\quad c_{21} += a_{20}b_{01}$ $\quad c_{22} += a_{20}b_{02}$	$\begin{pmatrix} b_{10} & b_{11} & b_{12} \\ b_{20} & b_{21} & b_{22} \\ b_{00} & b_{01} & b_{02} \end{pmatrix}$
Stage 2	→a_{02} a_{10} → ←a_{21}→	$c_{00} += a_{02}b_{20}$ $\quad c_{01} += a_{02}b_{21}$ $\quad c_{02} += a_{02}b_{22}$ $c_{10} += a_{10}b_{00}$ $\quad c_{11} += a_{10}b_{01}$ $\quad c_{12} += a_{10}b_{02}$ $c_{20} += a_{21}b_{10}$ $\quad c_{21} += a_{21}b_{11}$ $\quad c_{22} += a_{21}b_{12}$	$\begin{pmatrix} b_{20} & b_{21} & b_{22} \\ b_{00} & b_{01} & b_{02} \\ b_{10} & b_{11} & b_{12} \end{pmatrix}$

Figure 7.3   Fox's algorithm

Of course, we can't just add k to a row or column subscript and expect to always get a valid row or column number. For example, if $i = j = n - 1$, then any positive value added to i or j will result in an out-of-range subscript. One possible solution is to use subscripts modulo n. That is, rather than use $i + k$ for a row or column subscript, use $i + k$ mod n. Then, we will get a valid pair of subscripts:

Stage k on process (i,j): $\bar{k} = (i + k)$ mod n; $c_{ij} = c_{ij} + a_{i,\bar{k}}b_{\bar{k},j}$.

Also observe that we'll compute c_{ij} as follows:

$$c_{ij} = a_{ii}b_{ij} + a_{i,i+1}b_{i+1,j} + \cdots + a_{i,n-1}b_{n-1,j} + a_{i0}b_{0j} + \cdots$$
$$+ a_{i,i-1}b_{i-1,j}.$$

In other words, if we compute the subscripts modulo n, the algorithm is correct.

Perhaps we should say that the *incomplete* algorithm is correct. We still haven't said how we arrange that each process gets the appropriate values $a_{i,\bar{k}}$ and $b_{\bar{k},i}$. Since the algorithm computes the correct element-wise products, we know that process (i,j) will get the correct element of A from its *process* row and the correct element of B from its *process* column. Also observe that during the initial stage each process in the ith row uses a_{ii}. In general, during the kth stage, each process in the ith row uses $a_{i\bar{k}}$, where $\bar{k} = i + k$ mod n. Thus, we need to broadcast $a_{i\bar{k}}$ across the ith row before each multiplication. Finally observe that during the initial stage, each process uses its own element, b_{ij}, of B. During subsequent stages, process (i,j) will use $b_{\bar{k}j}$. Thus, *after* each multiplication is completed, the elements of B should be "shifted" up one row, and elements in the top row should be sent to the bottom row. Figure 7.3 illustrates the stages in Fox's algorithm for multiplying two 3×3 matrices distributed across nine processes.

It's not obvious that Fox's algorithm is superior to the basic parallel matrix multiplication we discussed in the preceding section. So we'll return to this problem when we discuss parallel program performance in Chapter 11. It is obvious, however, that we're unlikely to have access to n^2 processors even for relatively small (e.g., 100×100) matrices. So how can we modify our algorithm so that it uses fewer than n^2 processes?

A natural solution would seem to be to store submatrices rather than matrix elements on each process, and try carrying out the algorithm we have just outlined using submatrices. It turns out that this idea works, provided the submatrices can be multiplied together as needed. One way we can insure that this is the case is to use a square grid of processes, where the number of process rows or process columns, $\sqrt{p}$, evenly divides n. With this assumption, each process is assigned a square $n/\sqrt{p} \times n/\sqrt{p}$ submatrix of each of the three matrices. Specifically, let $\bar{n} = n/\sqrt{p}$ and define A_{ij} to be the $\bar{n} \times \bar{n}$ submatrix of A whose first entry is $a_{i*\bar{n}, j*\bar{n}}$. For example, if $n = p = 4$, then $\bar{n} = 4/\sqrt{4} = 2$, and

$$A_{00} = \begin{pmatrix} a_{00} & a_{01} \\ a_{10} & a_{11} \end{pmatrix}, \quad A_{01} = \begin{pmatrix} a_{02} & a_{03} \\ a_{12} & a_{13} \end{pmatrix},$$

$$A_{10} = \begin{pmatrix} a_{20} & a_{21} \\ a_{30} & a_{31} \end{pmatrix}, \quad A_{11} = \begin{pmatrix} a_{22} & a_{23} \\ a_{32} & a_{33} \end{pmatrix}.$$

If we make similar definitions of B_{ij} and C_{ij}, assign A_{ij}, B_{ij}, and C_{ij} to process (i, j), and we define $q = \sqrt{p}$, then our algorithm will compute

$$C_{ij} = A_{ii}B_{ij} + A_{i,i+1}B_{i+1,j} + \cdots + A_{i,q-1}B_{q-1,j} + A_{i0}B_{0j} + \cdots$$
$$+ A_{i,i-1}B_{i-1,j}.$$

If we multiply out each submatrix product, we can verify that this does in fact compute the correct values for each c_{ij}.

To summarize then, if we denote the submatrices A_{ij}, B_{ij}, and C_{ij} by A[i,j], B[i,j], and C[i,j], respectively, we can outline Fox's algorithm as follows:

```
/* my process row = i, my process column = j */
q = sqrt(p);
dest = ((i-1) mod q, j);
source = ((i+1) mod q, j);
for (stage = 0; stage < q; stage++) {
      k_bar = (i + stage) mod q;
(a)   Broadcast A[i,k_bar] across process row i;
(b)   C[i,j] = C[i,j] + A[i,k_bar]*B[k_bar,j];
(c)   Send B[k_bar,j] to dest;  Receive
      B[(k_bar+1) mod q ,j] from source;
   }
```

7.3 Communicators

If we start working on coding Fox's algorithm, it becomes apparent that implementation will be greatly facilitated if we can treat certain subsets of processes as a "communication universe"—at least on a temporary basis. For example, in statement (a),

```
(a)   Broadcast A[i,k_bar] across process row i
```

it would be useful to treat each row of processes as a communication universe, while in statement (c),

```
(c)   Send B[k_bar,j] to dest;  Receive
      B[(k_bar+1) mod q ,j] from source;
```

it would be useful to treat each column of processes as a communication universe.

The mechanism that MPI provides for treating a subset of processes as a communication universe is the *communicator*. Up to now, we've been loosely defining a communicator as a collection of processes that can send messages to each other. However, now that we want to construct our own communicators, we will need a more careful discussion.

In MPI, there are two types of communicators: **intra-communicators** and **inter-communicators**. Intra-communicators are essentially a collection of processes that can send messages to each other *and* engage in collective communication operations. Inter-communicators, as the name implies, are used for sending messages between processes belonging to *disjoint* intra-communicators. We'll focus on intra-communicators now and briefly touch on inter-communicators in programming assignment 2.

A minimal (intra-)communicator is composed of

- a group
- a context

A **group** is an ordered collection of processes. If a group consists of p processes, each process in the group is assigned a unique **rank**, which is just a nonnegative integer in the range $0, 1, \ldots, p-1$. A **context** is a system-defined object that uniquely identifies a communicator. Two distinct communicators will have different contexts, even if they have identical underlying groups. A context can be thought of as a system-defined tag that is associated with a group in a communicator. Contexts are used to insure that messages are received correctly. Recall that no message can be received by any process unless the communicator used by the sending process is identical to the communicator used by the receiving process: this is true for both point-to-point (e.g., MPI_Send/Recv) and collective communications. Since distinct communicators use distinct contexts, the system can check whether two communicators are identical by simply checking whether the contexts are identical.

In order to understand contexts better, let's speculate for a moment about how a system developer might implement communicators. She might define a group to be an array, group, and the rank of process i in the group would correspond to rank group[i] in MPI_COMM_WORLD.

For example, suppose we've coded Fox's algorithm, and we're running it with nine processes; i.e., MPI_COMM_WORLD consists of nine processes. As we've already observed, it is convenient for us to view our nine processes as a 3×3 grid. So we might create a communicator for each row of the grid. In particular, the group for the "second row communicator" might be composed of processes 3, 4, and 5 from MPI_COMM_WORLD. Thus

```
group[0] = 3;
group[1] = 4;
group[2] = 5;
```

and process 0 in the second row communicator would be the same as process 3 in MPI_COMM_WORLD, process 1 the same as process 4, and process 2 the same as process 5.

She might also define a context to be an int. Each process could keep a list of available contexts. When a new communicator is created, the processes participating in the creation could "negotiate" the choice of a context that is available to each process. Then, in communication functions, rather than sending the entire communicator every time a message is sent, just the context can be sent.

Keep in mind that these constructions of communicators, groups, and contexts are purely hypothetical. The implementation of each object is system dependent, and it's entirely possible that your system uses something very different.

This pairing of a group with a context is the most basic form of a communicator. Other data can be associated with a communicator. In particular, a structure or topology can be imposed on the processes in a communicator, allowing a more natural addressing scheme. We'll discuss topologies in section 7.6.

7.4 Working with Groups, Contexts, and Communicators

To illustrate the basics of working with communicators, let's create a communicator whose underlying group consists of the processes in the first row of our virtual grid. Suppose that MPI_COMM_WORLD consists of p processes, where $q^2 = p$. Let's also suppose that our first row of processes consists of the processes with ranks $0, 1, \ldots, q - 1$. (Here, the ranks are in MPI_COMM_WORLD.) In order to create the group of our new communicator, we can execute the following code:

```
MPI_Group  group_world;
MPI_Group  first_row_group;
MPI_Comm   first_row_comm;
int*       process_ranks;

/* Make a list of the processes in the new
 * communicator */
process_ranks = (int*) malloc(q*sizeof(int));
for (proc = 0; proc < q; proc++)
    process_ranks[proc] = proc;

/* Get the group underlying MPI_COMM_WORLD */
MPI_Comm_group(MPI_COMM_WORLD, &group_world);

/* Create the new group */
MPI_Group_incl(group_world, q, process_ranks,
    &first_row_group);

/* Create the new communicator */
MPI_Comm_create(MPI_COMM_WORLD, first_row_group,
    &first_row_comm);
```

This code proceeds in a fairly straightforward fashion to build the new communicator. First it creates a list of the processes to be assigned to the new communicator. Then it creates a group consisting of these processes. This requires two commands: first get the group associated with MPI_COMM_WORLD, since this is the group from which the processes in the new group will be taken; then create the group with MPI_Group_incl. Finally, the actual communicator is created with a call to MPI_Comm_create. The call to MPI_Comm_create associates a context with the new group. The result is the communicator first_row_comm. Now the processes in first_row_comm can perform collective communication operations. For example, process 0 (in first_row_group) can broadcast A_{00} to the other processes in first_row_group.

```
int my_rank_in_first_row;
float* A_00;

/* my_rank is process rank in group_world */
if (my_rank < q) {
    MPI_Comm_rank(first_row_comm,
        &my_rank_in_first_row);
    /* Allocate space for A_00 */
    A_00 = (float*) malloc (n_bar*n_bar*sizeof(float));
    if (my_rank_in_first_row == 0) {
        /* Initialize A_00 */

        ⋮

    }
}
```

```
            MPI_Bcast(A_00, n_bar*n_bar, MPI_FLOAT, 0,
                first_row_comm);
    }
```

Groups and communicators are **opaque objects**. From a practical stand-point, this means that the details of their internal representation depend on the particular implementation, and, as a consequence, they cannot be directly accessed by the user. Rather, the user accesses a **handle** that references the opaque object, and the opaque objects are manipulated by special MPI functions, for example, MPI_Comm_create, MPI_Group_incl, and MPI_Comm_group.

Contexts are not explicitly used in any MPI functions. Rather they are implicitly associated with groups when communicators are created.

The syntax of the commands we used to create first_row_comm is fairly self-explanatory. The first command

```
int MPI_Comm_group(
        MPI_Comm    comm    /* in  */,
        MPI_Group*  group   /* out */)
```

simply returns the group underlying the communicator comm.

The second command

```
int MPI_Group_incl(
        MPI_Group    old_group               /* in  */,
        int          new_group_size          /* in  */,
        int          ranks_in_old_group[]    /* in  */,
        MPI_Group*   new_group               /* out */)
```

creates a new group from a list of processes in the existing group, old_group. The number of processes in the new group is new_group_size, and the processes to be included are listed in ranks_in_old_group. Process 0 in new_group has rank ranks_in_old_group[0] in old_group, process 1 in new_group has rank ranks_in_old_group[1] in old_group, etc.

The final command

```
int MPI_Comm_create(
        MPI_Comm    old_comm     /* in  */,
        MPI_Group   new_group    /* in  */,
        MPI_Comm*   new_comm     /* out */)
```

associates a context with the group new_group and creates the communicator new_comm. All of the processes in new_group belong to the group underlying old_comm.

There is an extremely important distinction between the first two functions and the third. MPI_Comm_group and MPI_Group_incl are both **local** operations. That is, there is no communication among processes involved in their execution. However, MPI_Comm_create is a collective operation. *All* the processes in old_comm—including those not joining new_comm—must call MPI_Comm_create with the same arguments. The main reason for this was noted in the preceding section: it provides a means for the processes to choose a single context for the new communicator. Note that since MPI_Comm_create is collective, it will behave, in terms of the data transmitted, as if it synchronizes. In particular, if several communicators are being created, they must be created in the same order on all the processes.

7.5 MPI_Comm_split

In our matrix multiplication program we need to create multiple communicators—one for each row of processes and one for each column. This would be an extremely tedious process if the number of processes, p, were large, and we had to create each communicator using the three functions discussed in the previous section. Fortunately, MPI provides a function, MPI_Comm_split, that can create several communicators simultaneously. As an example of its use, we'll create one communicator for each row of processes.

```
MPI_Comm   my_row_comm;
int        my_row;

/* my_rank is rank in MPI_COMM_WORLD.
 * q*q = p */
my_row = my_rank/q;
MPI_Comm_split(MPI_COMM_WORLD, my_row, my_rank,
    &my_row_comm);
```

The single call to MPI_Comm_split creates q new communicators, all of them having the same name, my_row_comm. For example, if $p = 9$, the group underlying my_row_comm will consist of the processes $\{0, 1, 2\}$ on processes 0, 1, and 2. On processes 3, 4, and 5, the group underlying my_row_comm will consist of the processes $\{3, 4, 5\}$, and on processes 6, 7, and 8, it will consist of processes $\{6, 7, 8\}$.

The syntax of MPI_Comm_split is

```
int MPI_Comm_split(
        MPI_Comm   old_comm    /* in  */,
        int        split_key   /* in  */,
        int        rank_key    /* in  */,
        MPI_Comm*  new_comm    /* out */)
```

It creates a new communicator for each value of split_key. Processes with the same value of split_key form a new group. The rank in the new group is determined by the value of rank_key. If process *A* and process *B* call MPI_Comm_split with the same value of split_key, and the rank_key argument passed by process *A* is less than that passed by process *B*, then the rank of *A* in the group underlying new_comm will be less than the rank of process *B*. If they call the function with the same value of rank_key, the system will arbitrarily assign one of the processes a lower rank.

MPI_Comm_split is a collective call, and it must be called by all the processes in old_comm. The function can be used even if the user doesn't wish to assign every process to a new communicator. This can be accomplished by passing the predefined constant MPI_UNDEFINED as the split_key argument. Processes doing this will have the predefined value MPI_COMM_NULL returned in new_comm.

7.6 Topologies

Recollect that it is possible to associate additional information—information beyond the group and context—with a communicator. Such information is said to be **cached** with the communicator. One of the most important possibilities for cached information, or **attributes**, is a topology. In MPI, a **topology** is just a mechanism for associating different addressing schemes with the processes belonging to a group. Note that MPI topologies are *virtual* topologies—there may be no simple relation between the process structure implicit in a virtual topology and the actual underlying physical structure of the parallel system.

There are essentially two types of virtual topologies that can be created in MPI—a Cartesian or grid topology and a graph topology. Conceptually, Cartesian topologies form a special case of graph topologies. However, because of the importance of grids in applications, there is a separate collection of functions in MPI whose purpose is the manipulation of virtual grids.

In Fox's algorithm we wish to identify the processes in MPI_COMM_WORLD with the coordinates of a square grid, and each row and each column of the grid needs to form its own communicator. Let's look at one method for building this structure.

We begin by associating a square grid structure with MPI_COMM_WORLD. In order to do this, we need to specify the following information:

1. The number of dimensions in the grid. We have two.

2. The size of each dimension. In our case, this is just the number of rows and the number of columns. We have q rows and q columns.

3. Periodicity of each dimension. In our case, this information specifies whether the first entry in each row or column is "adjacent" to the last entry in that row or column, respectively. Since we want a "circular" shift of the submatrices in each column, we want the second dimension to be periodic. It's unimportant whether the first dimension is periodic.

4. Finally, MPI gives the user the option of allowing the system to optimize the mapping of the grid of processes to the underlying physical processors

by possibly reordering the processes in the group underlying the communicator. Since we don't need to preserve the ordering of the processes in MPI_COMM_WORLD, we should allow the system to reorder.

Having made all these decisions, we simply execute the following code:

```
MPI_Comm  grid_comm;
int       dim_sizes[2];
int       wrap_around[2];
int       reorder = 1;

dim_sizes[0] = dim_sizes[1] = q;
wrap_around[0] = wrap_around[1] = 1;
MPI_Cart_create(MPI_COMM_WORLD, 2, dim_sizes,
    wrap_around, reorder, &grid_comm);
```

After executing this code, the communicator grid_comm will contain all the processes in MPI_COMM_WORLD (possibly reordered), and a two-dimensional Cartesian coordinate system will be associated with it. In order for a process to determine its coordinates, it simply calls the function MPI_Cart_coords:

```
int  coordinates[2];
int  my_grid_rank;

MPI_Comm_rank(grid_comm, &my_grid_rank);
MPI_Cart_coords(grid_comm, my_grid_rank, 2,
    coordinates);
```

Notice that we needed to call MPI_Comm_rank in order to get the process rank in grid_comm. This was necessary because in our call to MPI_Cart_create we set the reorder flag to 1, and hence the original process ranking in MPI_COMM_WORLD may have changed.

The "inverse" to MPI_Cart_coords is MPI_Cart_rank.

```
MPI_Cart_rank(grid_comm, coordinates,
    &grid_rank);
```

Given the coordinates of a process, MPI_Cart_rank returns the rank of the process in its third parameter grid_rank.

The syntax of MPI_Cart_create is

```
int MPI_Cart_create(
        MPI_Comm    old_comm         /* in  */,
        int         number_of_dims   /* in  */,
        int         dim_sizes[]      /* in  */,
        int         wrap_around[]    /* in  */,
        int         reorder          /* in  */,
        MPI_Comm*   cart_comm        /* out */)
```

MPI_Cart_create creates a new communicator, cart_comm, by caching a Cartesian topology with old_comm. Information on the structure of the Cartesian topology is contained in the parameters number_of_dims, dim_sizes, and wrap_around. The first of these, number_of_dims, contains the number of dimensions in the Cartesian coordinate system. The next two, dim_sizes and wrap_around, are arrays with order equal to number_of_dims. The array dim_sizes specifies the order of each dimension, and wrap_around specifies whether each dimension is circular, wrap_around[i] = 1, or linear, wrap_around[i] = 0.

The processes in cart_comm are ranked in *row-major* order. If there are two dimensions, then the first row consists of processes 0, 1, ..., dim_sizes[1] − 1; the second row consists of processes dim_sizes[1], dim_sizes[1] + 1, ..., 2*dim_sizes[1] − 1; etc. Thus it may be advantageous to change the relative ranking of the processes in old_comm. For example, suppose the physical topology is a 3 × 3 grid, and the processes (numbers) in old_comm are assigned to the processors (grid squares) as follows:

3	4	5
0	1	2
6	7	8

Clearly, the performance of Fox's algorithm would be improved if we renumbered the processes. However, since the user doesn't know what the exact mapping of processes to processors is, we must let the system do it by setting the reorder parameter to 1.

Since MPI_Cart_create constructs a new communicator, it is a collective operation.

The syntax of the address information functions is

```
int MPI_Cart_rank(
        MPI_Comm    comm            /* in  */,
        int         coordinates[]   /* in  */,
        int*        rank            /* out */);

int MPI_Cart_coords(
        MPI_Comm    comm            /* in  */,
        int         rank            /* in  */,
        int         number_of_dims  /* in  */,
        int         coordinates[]   /* out */)
```

MPI_Cart_rank returns the rank in the Cartesian communicator comm of the process with Cartesian coordinates coordinates. So coordinates is an array with order equal to the number of dimensions in the Cartesian topology associated with comm. MPI_Cart_coords is the inverse to MPI_Cart_rank: it returns the coordinates of the process with rank rank in the Cartesian communicator comm. Note that both of these functions are local.

7.7 MPI_Cart_sub

We can also partition a grid into grids of lower dimension. For example, we can create a communicator for each row of the grid as follows:

```
int         free_coords[2];
MPI_Comm  row_comm;

free_coords[0] = 0;
free_coords[1] = 1;
MPI_Cart_sub(grid_comm, free_coords, &row_comm);
```

The call to MPI_Cart_sub creates q new communicators. The free_coords parameter is an array of boolean. It specifies whether each dimension "belongs" to the new communicator. Since we're creating communicators for the rows of the grid, each new communicator consists of the processes obtained by fixing the row coordinate and letting the column coordinate vary; i.e., the row coordinate is fixed and the column coordinate is free. Hence we assigned free_coords[0] the value 0—the first coordinate isn't free—and we assigned free_coords[1] the value 1—the second coordinate is free or varies. On each process, the new communicator is returned in row_comm. In order to create the communicators for the columns, we simply reverse the assignments to the entries in free_coords.

```
MPI_Comm col_comm;

free_coords[0] = 1;
free_coords[1] = 0;
MPI_Cart_sub(grid_comm, free_coords, &col_comm);
```

Note the similarity of MPI_Cart_sub to MPI_Comm_split. They perform similar functions—they both partition a communicator into a collection of new communicators. However, MPI_Cart_sub can only be used with a communicator that has an associated Cartesian topology, and the new communicators can only be created by fixing one or more dimensions of the old communicators and letting the other dimensions vary. Also note that MPI_Cart_sub is, like MPI_Comm_split, a collective operation.

The syntax of MPI_Cart_sub is

```
int MPI_Cart_sub(
        MPI_Comm    cart_comm       /* in  */,
        int         free_coords[]   /* in  */,
        MPI_Comm*   new_comm        /* out */)
```

It partitions the processes in cart_comm into a collection of disjoint communicators whose union is cart_comm. Both cart_comm and each new_comm have associated Cartesian topologies. If cart_comm has dimensions

$d_0 \times d_1 \times \cdots \times d_{n-1}$, then the dimension of free_coords is n. If free_coords[i] is 0 (or false), then the ith coordinate is fixed for the construction of the new communicators. If free_coords[j] is 1 (or true), then the jth coordinate is free or allowed to vary. Thus, if free_coords[i] is 0, for $i = i_0, i_1, \ldots, i_{k-1}$, then the call to MPI_Cart_sub will create $d_{i_0} d_{i_1} \cdots d_{i_{k-1}}$ new communicators. Each new communicator will be obtained by letting the remaining dimensions (i.e., those for which free_coords is 1) vary over their ranges.

7.8 Implementation of Fox's Algorithm

To complete our discussion, let's write the code to implement Fox's algorithm. First, we'll write a function that creates the various communicators and associated information. Since this requires a large number of variables, and we'll be using this information in other functions, we'll put it into a struct to facilitate passing it.

```
typedef struct {
    int         p;          /* Total number of processes    */
    MPI_Comm    comm;       /* Communicator for entire grid */
    MPI_Comm    row_comm;   /* Communicator for my row      */
    MPI_Comm    col_comm;   /* Communicator for my col      */
    int         q;          /* Order of grid                */
    int         my_row;     /* My row number                */
    int         my_col;     /* My column number             */
    int         my_rank;    /* My rank in the grid comm     */
} GRID_INFO_T;

/* We assume space for grid has been allocated in the
 * calling routine.
 */
void Setup_grid(
        GRID_INFO_T*  grid  /* out */) {
    int old_rank;
    int dimensions[2];
    int wrap_around[2];
    int coordinates[2];
    int free_coords[2];

    /* Set up Global Grid Information */
    MPI_Comm_size(MPI_COMM_WORLD, &(grid->p));
    MPI_Comm_rank(MPI_COMM_WORLD, &old_rank);

    /* We assume p is a perfect square */
    grid->q = (int) sqrt((double) grid->p);
    dimensions[0] = dimensions[1] = grid->q;
```

```
    /* We want a circular shift in second dimension. */
    /* Don't care about first                        */
    wrap_around[0] = wrap_around[1] = 1;
    MPI_Cart_create(MPI_COMM_WORLD, 2, dimensions,
        wrap_around, 1, &(grid->comm));
    MPI_Comm_rank(grid->comm, &(grid->my_rank));
    MPI_Cart_coords(grid->comm, grid->my_rank, 2,
        coordinates);
    grid->my_row = coordinates[0];
    grid->my_col = coordinates[1];

    /* Set up row communicators */
    free_coords[0] = 0;
    free_coords[1] = 1;
    MPI_Cart_sub(grid->comm, free_coords,
        &(grid->row_comm));

    /* Set up column communicators */
    free_coords[0] = 1;
    free_coords[1] = 0;
    MPI_Cart_sub(grid->comm, free_coords,
        &(grid->col_comm));
} /* Setup_grid */
```

Notice that since each of our communicators has an associated topology, we constructed them using the topology construction functions—MPI_Cart_ create and MPI_Cart_sub—rather than the more general communicator construction functions MPI_Comm_create and MPI_Comm_split.

Now let's write the function that does the actual multiplication. We'll assume that the user has supplied the type definitions and functions for the local matrices. Specifically, we'll assume she has supplied a type definition for LOCAL_MATRIX_T, a corresponding derived type, local_matrix_mpi_t, and three functions: Local_matrix_multiply, Local_matrix_allocate, and Set_to_zero. We also assume that storage for the parameters has been allocated in the calling function, and all the parameters, except the product matrix local_C, have been initialized.

```
void Fox(
        int            n           /* in  */,
        GRID_INFO_T*   grid        /* in  */,
        LOCAL_MATRIX_T*  local_A   /* in  */,
        LOCAL_MATRIX_T*  local_B   /* in  */,
        LOCAL_MATRIX_T*  local_C   /* out */) {

    LOCAL_MATRIX_T* temp_A; /* Storage for the sub-    */
                            /* matrix of A used during */
                            /* the current stage       */
```

```
        int                 stage;
        int                 bcast_root;
        int                 n_bar;  /* n/sqrt(p)              */
        int                 source;
        int                 dest;
        MPI_Status          status;

        n_bar = n/grid->q;
        Set_to_zero(local_C);

        /* Calculate addresses for circular shift of B */
        source = (grid->my_row + 1) % grid->q;
        dest = (grid->my_row + grid->q - 1) % grid->q;

        /* Set aside storage for the broadcast block of A */
        temp_A = Local_matrix_allocate(n_bar);

        for (stage = 0; stage < grid->q; stage++) {
            bcast_root = (grid->my_row + stage) % grid->q;
            if (bcast_root == grid->my_col) {
                MPI_Bcast(local_A, 1, local_matrix_mpi_t,
                    bcast_root, grid->row_comm);
                Local_matrix_multiply(local_A, local_B,
                    local_C);
            } else {
                MPI_Bcast(temp_A, 1, local_matrix_mpi_t,
                    bcast_root, grid->row_comm);
                Local_matrix_multiply(temp_A, local_B,
                    local_C);
            }
            MPI_Sendrecv_replace(local_B, 1, local_matrix_mpi_t,
                dest, 0, source, 0, grid->col_comm, &status);
        } /* for */

} /* Fox */
```

In the last function call, we have used a new MPI function, MPI_Sendrecv_replace. It performs both the send and the receive required for the circular shift of local_B: it sends the current copy of local_B to the process in col_comm with rank dest, and then receives the copy of local_B residing on the process in col_comm with rank source. Its syntax is

```
int MPI_Sendrecv_replace(
        void*           buffer      /* in/out */,
        int             count       /* in     */,
        MPI_Datatype    datatype    /* in     */,
        int             dest        /* in     */,
        int             send_tag    /* in     */,
        int             source      /* in     */,
```

```
int             recv_tag   /* in     */,
MPI_Comm        comm       /* in     */,
MPI_Status*     status     /* out    */)
```

It sends the contents of `buffer` to the process in `comm` with rank `dest` and receives in `buffer` data sent from the process with rank `source`. The send uses the tag `send_tag`, and the receive uses the tag `recv_tag`. The processes involved in the send and the receive don't have to be distinct. The process `dest` can receive the contents of `buffer` with a call to `MPI_Recv`, and the process `source` can send with a call to `MPI_Send`. The function is called `MPI_Sendrecv_replace` to distinguish it from the function `MPI_Sendrecv`, which also performs a send and a receive, but it uses different buffers for the send and the receive.

7.9 Summary

We covered a lot of ground in this chapter. We studied two algorithms for parallel matrix multiplication, and we learned about two new ideas in MPI: communicators and topologies.

We started the chapter with a discussion of matrix multiplication and a simple algorithm for parallel matrix multiplication. The parallel algorithm mapped rows of the matrices to the processes, and we saw that this mapping would require a large amount of communication. So we explored alternative mappings. The alternative mapping we used in our second matrix multiplication function is called a *checkerboard* mapping. It mapped square submatrices to the processes rather than rows or columns.

Our initial development of Fox's algorithm made the assumption that each process stored a single element of the matrix rather than an entire submatrix. Although this is an unrealistic assumption, it is a common design technique in parallel programming, since it reduces the complexity of the initial design by reducing the number of parameters we need to work with. Care must be taken in moving from the simplified design to the final, general design: it's easy to make mistakes in computing the extra parameters. In our case, the extra parameters were the order of the submatrices and the order of the process grid.

Fox's algorithm views the processes as a virtual grid, and in order to carry out several operations in Fox's algorithm, it is convenient to view certain subgrids as communication universes. MPI provides mechanisms for the construction and manipulation of both virtual grids and communication universes. Communication universes correspond to MPI **communicators**, and virtual grids correspond to a type of MPI process topology.

There are two types of MPI communicator: intra-communicators and inter-communicators. Intra-communicators can be used in `MPI_Send/Recv` and in collective communication functions. Inter-communicators are used for communication between processes belonging to disjoint communicators. We discussed intra-communicators.

Basic intra-communicators consist of a **group** and a **context**. A group is an ordered collection of processes. A context is a unique, system-defined label that is associated with a group when a communicator is created. It can be viewed as a system-defined tag that is used by the system to check the communicator arguments to communication functions: a message can only be received if the context of the communicator argument used by the receiving process equals the context of the communicator argument used by the sending process. The key distinction between contexts and tags is that contexts are system defined, and hence guaranteed to be unique, even across subprograms written by different programmers.

Groups and communicators are **opaque objects**. From a practical standpoint, this means that the details of their internal representation depend on the particular implementation, and, as a consequence, they cannot be directly accessed by the user. Rather, the user accesses a **handle** that references the opaque object, and the opaque objects are manipulated by special MPI functions, for example, MPI_Comm_create, MPI_Group_incl, and MPI_Comm_group. Contexts are not accessed at all by MPI functions: they are implicitly defined by the system when a communicator is created.

We discussed several methods for building user-defined communicators. Our most basic approach consisted in building a group, and then having the system associate a context with the group. This proceeded in three stages. First we get the group underlying a communicator that contains the processes we want in our new communicator with

```
int MPI_Comm_group(
        MPI_Comm    comm        /* in  */,
        MPI_Group*  old_group   /* out */)
```

Then we create an array, ranks_in_old_group, listing the process ranks in the old group of the processes we want from our old group. That is, ranks_in_old_group[i] is the rank in old_group of the *i*th process in new_group. In order to create the new group, we call

```
int MPI_Group_incl(
        MPI_Group   old_group                /* in  */,
        int         new_group_size           /* in  */,
        int         .ranks_in_old_group[]    /* in  */,
        MPI_Group*  new_group                /* out */)
```

Once we have our new group, we can associate a context with it by calling

```
int MPI_Comm_create(
        MPI_Comm    old_comm    /* in  */,
        MPI_Group   new_group   /* in  */,
        MPI_Comm*   new_comm    /* out */)
```

There is an important distinction between the first two functions and the third: the first two are completely local functions—they involve no communication— while the third function, `MPI_Comm_create`, is a collective communication function: it involves all the processes in `old_comm`.

Once we have built our communicator, we can use it as an argument to `MPI_Send/ Recv` or a collective communication function just as we've been using `MPI_COMM_WORLD`.

If we want to simply split the communicator into a collection of disjoint subcommunicators, we can use a single call to

```
int MPI_Comm_split(
        MPI_Comm   old_comm    /* in  */,
        int        split_key   /* in  */,
        int        rank_key    /* in  */,
        MPI_Comm*  new_comm    /* out */)
```

It creates a new communicator for each value of `split_key`. If two processes have the same value of `split_key`, they will be assigned to the same communicator. If two processes are assigned to the same new communicator by `MPI_Comm_split`, their relative ranks in the new communicator are determined by the value of `rank_key`: the process with the smaller value of `rank_key` will be assigned a lower rank in the communicator. This is a collective operation.

Process topologies allow us to address processes in ways that are more natural to our application. MPI provides two types of process topologies: graphs and grids. We discussed grids. In a grid topology we identify the processes with vertices in a regular rectangular grid of any dimension. For example, in a two-dimensional grid, we can associate a row and column with each process.

MPI allows user programs to associate information, or **attributes**, with communicators by a process called **caching**. Process topologies are one of the most important examples of cached attributes. In order to create a communicator with a cached grid topology, we can call

```
int MPI_Cart_create(
        MPI_Comm   old_comm          /* in  */,
        int        number_of_dims    /* in  */,
        int        dim_sizes[]       /* in  */,
        int        wrap_around[]     /* in  */,
        int        reorder           /* in  */,
        MPI_Comm*  cart_comm         /* out */)
```

This will create a new communicator, `cart_comm`, and is a collective operation. In addition to the group and context, `cart_comm` has cached information that associates a `number_of_dims`-dimensional coordinate system with the processes in `cart_comm`. In order to access this coordinate system, we can use the functions

```
int MPI_Cart_coords(
        MPI_Comm    cart_comm        /* in  */,
        int         rank             /* in  */,
        int         number_of_dims   /* in  */,
        int         coordinates[]    /* out */)

int MPI_Cart_rank(
        MPI_Comm    cart_comm        /* in  */,
        int         coordinates[]    /* in  */,
        int*        rank             /* out */);
```

The first function takes the rank of a process in cart_comm and returns its coordinates in the grid. The second returns a process's rank given its coordinates.

Since we frequently wish to partition a grid into subgrids (e.g., rows or columns in a two-dimensional grid), MPI provides a function analogous to MPI_Comm_split that can be used for creating subgrids:

```
int MPI_Cart_sub(
        MPI_Comm    cart_comm        /* in  */,
        int         free_coords[]    /* in  */,
        MPI_Comm*   new_comm         /* out */)
```

The array free_coords has order equal to the dimension of cart_comm. The new communicators new_comm are determined by free_coords. If free_coords[i] is 0, the ith coordinate is fixed; if it's 1, the ith coordinate is allowed to vary. For example, in a two-dimensional grid, if free_coords[0] is 0 and free_coords[1] is 1, the zeroth coordinate is fixed and the first coordinate varies. So MPI_Cart_sub will create a new communicator for each row of cart_comm. MPI_Cart_sub is a collective operation.

Our last MPI function in this chapter was the point-to-point communication function

```
int MPI_Sendrecv_replace(
        void*         buffer      /* in/out */,
        int           count       /* in     */,
        MPI_Datatype  datatype    /* in     */,
        int           dest        /* in     */,
        int           send_tag    /* in     */,
        int           source      /* in     */,
        int           recv_tag    /* in     */,
        MPI_Comm      comm        /* in     */,
        MPI_Status*   status      /* out    */)
```

It performs both a send and a receive, and buffer is used both for the outgoing and incoming messages. It is very convenient to use this function if we have to carry out an operation such as a circular shift of data across a group of processes.

7.10 References

Fox's algorithm is discussed in both [18] and [26]. [26] also discusses several other approaches to parallel matrix multiplication.

Communicators and topologies are discussed in detail in both the MPI Standard [28, 29] and [34]. [21] has several examples of the use of both intra- and inter-communicators. See [28, 29] for a discussion of graph topologies.

7.11 Exercises

1. Suppose that MPI_COMM_WORLD consists of $p = mn$ processes. Even if we don't associate a topology with this communicator, we can view it as a virtual grid with m rows and n columns by considering the first row to consist of processes $\{0, 1, \ldots, n-1\}$, the second row to consist of processes $\{n, n+1, \ldots, 2n-1\}$, etc.

   a. Use MPI_Comm_group, MPI_Group_incl, and MPI_Comm_create to create a communicator consisting of the processes belonging to the first column of the virtual grid.

   b. Use MPI_Comm_split to create n communicators. Each communicator should consist of the processes belonging to a column of the virtual grid.

   c. If you wrote a program that contained the code in both parts (a) and (b), would the two communicators containing the processes belonging to the first column of the grid be identical?

2. We suggested that we might implement communicators as follows. Groups would be arrays whose entries are the ranks of the processes in MPI_COMM_WORLD. Contexts would be integers, and each process would keep a list of available contexts. An actual implementation will probably store considerably more information in a communicator, but we can use this to get a feel for some of the issues involved in the use of communicators.

   a. Using the basic implementation as your starting point, suggest an implementation of MPI_Comm_create.

   b. Suggest an implementation of MPI_Comm_split.

3. When we discussed Fox's algorithm, we observed that it would be unrealistic to expect the system to provide n^2 physical processors. So we modified our original algorithm so that each process stored submatrices of order $n/\sqrt{p}$. Our basic algorithm, in which we store a single row on each process, is also unrealistic. Outline a modification to the basic algorithm so that it stores a block of n/p rows on each process and, at each stage, gathers n/p columns of B onto each process. Compare the storage requirements of the modified Fox algorithm and the modified basic algorithm.

4. A program is using a three-dimensional process topology. If the dimension sizes are l, m, and n, respectively, use MPI_Cart_sub to create the following sets of Cartesian communicators:

   a. m two-dimensional communicators, each consisting of ln processes
   b. lm one-dimensional communicators, each consisting of n processes
   c. lmn zero-dimensional communicators, each consisting of one process

   In addition to MPI_COMM_WORLD, MPI provides one predefined communicator for each process: MPI_COMM_SELF. Is the communicator you defined in part (c) on process 0 the same as the communicator MPI_COMM_SELF on process 0?

5. One reason that it is convenient to use MPI_Sendrecv_replace is that it takes care of buffering for us. Can you devise a "safe" implementation of our circular shift that only uses MPI_Send and MPI_Recv? Recall that a program is safe if it will run correctly even if the system provides no buffering. (Hint: split the processes into two sets; one set sends first, the other set receives first.)

7.12 Programming Assignments

1. Write the additional functions necessary to completely implement a program that uses Fox's algorithm to multiply two square matrices. Have each process generate its local submatrices (rather than reading them in). For output, have each process send its result submatrix to process 0, and have process 0 print out the submatrix. Don't try to print out a "unified" matrix.

2. Recollect that inter-communicators can be used for communication between processes belonging to disjoint intra-communicators. This ability is especially useful in a **client-server** type of program: one or more processes (the server processes) have resources that other processes (the client processes) need access to. A simple example is provided by automatic teller machines (the clients) and a bank's central database system (the server). Probably their most important use will be in *future* versions of MPI that allow for the dynamic creation of processes: inter-communicators will provide a means for newly created processes to communicate with already existing processes.

   Suppose that we wish to send messages from processes in comm_1 to processes in comm_2, and comm_1 and comm_2 are disjoint: no process belongs to both of them. In order to do this using inter-communicators, we first need to identify a process in comm_1 and a process in comm_2 that both belong to a "parent" communicator comm_0. Then we can build the inter-communicator using MPI_Intercomm_create:

```
if (I belong to comm_1) {
    local_leader = rank in comm_1 of process
        belonging to both comm_0 and comm_1;
    remote_leader =  rank in comm_0 of
        local_leader of comm_2;
    MPI_Intercomm_create(comm_1, local_leader,
        comm_0, remote_leader, 0, &inter_comm);
} else /* I belong to comm_2 */ {
    local_leader = rank in comm_2 of process
        belonging to both comm_0 and comm_2;
    remote_leader =  rank in comm_0 of
        local_leader of comm_1;
    MPI_Intercomm_create(comm_2, local_leader,
        comm_0, remote_leader, 0, &inter_comm);
}
```

Now processes belonging to comm_1 can send messages to processes belonging to comm_2 using *point-to-point* communication functions. For example, process 0 (rank in comm_1) can send a message to process 0 (rank in comm_2) as follows:

```
char message[100];

if (my_rank in comm_1 == 0) {
    sprintf(message,"Greetings from comm_1!");
    MPI_Send(message, strlen(message)+1, MPI_CHAR,
        0, 0, inter_comm);
} else if (my_rank in comm_2 == 0) {
    MPI_Recv(message, 100, MPI_CHAR, 0, 0,
        inter_comm, &status);
}
```

The source and destination ranks are the ranks in the *remote* communicator. Inter-communicators cannot be used for collective communication.

The syntax of MPI_Intercomm_create is

```
int MPI_Intercomm_create(
        MPI_Comm    local_comm      /* in  */,
        int         local_leader    /* in  */,
        MPI_Comm    parent_comm     /* in  */,
        int         remote_leader   /* in  */,
        int         tag             /* in  */,
        MPI_Comm*   inter_comm      /* out */)
```

Note that the type of inter-communicators is the same as the type of intra-communicators. Also note that all the processes in the first communicator should use the same arguments, and all the processes in the second communicator should use the same arguments. The function call is collective across the union of the two communicators.

Write a short program that splits the processes in MPI_COMM_WORLD into two communicators: the processes with even ranks and the processes with odd ranks. Create an inter-communicator from these two communicators and have each process in the odd-ranked communicator send a message to a process in the even-ranked communicator. Be sure you can handle the case where there's an odd number of processes in MPI_COMM_WORLD.

CHAPTER 8

Dealing with I/O

ON SEVERAL OCCASIONS, we've run across the problem of I/O on parallel systems. For example, in Chapter 4 we briefly discussed some of the problems involved with using functions as fundamental as `printf` and `scanf`. Recall that if a parallel program executes a statement such as

```
printf("x = %d\n", x);
```

it isn't immediately clear what should appear on the user's terminal screen. Should there be one value printed from each process? Should only one value appear? If multiple values are printed, how should they be ordered? How will we know which value comes from which process? Similar problems occur with the use of `scanf`. Of course, the problem becomes even more complex when we want to read or print the elements of a composite type.

The problem is that C's I/O functions were not written with parallel systems in mind, and, unfortunately, there isn't a clear consensus about how to carry out I/O on a parallel system. In view of this lack of consensus, the MPI Forum avoided the issue of I/O: the MPI Standard imposes no requirements on the I/O capabilities of an MPI implementation. In spite of this, all implementations of MPI provide *some* support for I/O, and in this chapter we'll take a look at how we can use MPI to leverage very limited support for I/O to the point where we can develop general and powerful programs.

Our main purpose in writing these functions is to provide tools for program development. We are not attempting to develop a high-performance parallel I/O library. As a consequence, we will favor simplicity and reliability over performance.

In the course of developing the I/O functions, we'll learn a lot about MPI and parallel programming. In particular, we'll learn more about attribute caching, derived datatypes, and data distributions. So even if your system provides very good I/O facilities, you will probably find a lot of useful information in this chapter.

8.1 Dealing with `stdin`, `stdout`, and `stderr`

Since the MPI standard imposes no requirements on the I/O capabilities of an MPI implementation, users have no way of knowing, a priori, what the I/O capabilities of the processes will be. For example, there are many systems that allow each process full access to `stdin`, `stdout`, and `stderr`, while other systems only allow process 0 in `MPI_COMM_WORLD` access to `stdout` and `stderr`. Of course, this creates serious difficulties for the user wishing to write portable programs, since there are few useful programs that do no I/O. This is especially problematic during the coding and debugging phases of program development—it can be very difficult to determine whether a program is functioning correctly, and, if it isn't, what the precise nature of the problem is.

In order to address this problem, we'll develop some functions that will allow programs access to `stdin`, `stdout`, and `stderr` on most systems running MPI. We'll write routines that assume that at least one process has access to `stdin`, `stdout`, and `stderr`. All the implementations with which we are acquainted allow at least one process access to `stdout` and `stderr`. If your implementation doesn't allow access to `stdin`, we'll discuss a few alternatives that may be available to you.

Since our main purpose in writing these functions is to provide ourselves with program development tools, we'll want to use these functions to monitor the state of our programs. As a consequence, we'll want to see output from all the processes, and our I/O functions will turn I/O operations into collective operations with one process designated as the "I/O process." For output, the I/O process will collect data from all the other processes and print it out, and for input, it will read in data and broadcast it to the other processes. Since these are collective operations, each I/O function will take a communicator argument.

Note that making our output functions collective will allow us to organize our output by process rank. Even MPI implementations that allow full access to all of C's I/O functions usually don't organize output very well. For example, if each process executes, more or less simultaneously, the statement

```
printf("Process %d > x = %d\n", my_rank, x);
```

we're liable to get output that looks like this:

```
Process 3 > x = 3
Process 1 > x = 1
Process 0 > x = 2
Process 2 > x = 4
```

and most of us would prefer

```
Process 0 > x = 2
Process 1 > x = 1
Process 2 > x = 4
Process 3 > x = 3
```

So you may want to use our output functions instead of simple `printf`s.

Since each communicator used by the I/O functions should have a designated I/O process, and the rank of the I/O process will depend on the communicator, it will be convenient for us to use MPI's attribute caching facility to store the rank of the I/O process *with the communicator.* So let's begin by discussing attribute caching in MPI.

8.1.1 Attribute Caching

Recall from Chapter 7 that although a basic communicator consists of a group and a context, additional information can be associated with any communicator by a process called *attribute caching.* In that chapter, we were interested in caching topologies with communicators. Since topologies are so important and so generally useful, the functions that are used to create, access, and modify them are specific to topologies. However, MPI provides a completely general interface to attribute caching, so that we can cache attributes of our own with communicators. In particular, we can cache the rank of a process that can carry out I/O.

The content of an attribute in MPI can be a simple scalar or a complex composite datatype. We want our attribute to be a process rank. However, it's not difficult to imagine useful attributes that are much more complex. For example, suppose we want to write our own broadcast function. Recollect (from Chapter 5) that an efficient broadcast will probably use a tree-structured communication pattern, and that the exact characteristics of the optimal tree structure will depend on the underlying parallel system. Thus, we might store with each communicator a composite attribute that provides a readily accessible description of the tree on the system we're using. The content of the attribute might be a struct or array indicating the pairing of processes during the stages of the broadcast, or it might be a function that computes this information.

In order to accommodate this diversity of possible attribute values, an attribute in MPI is a pointer of type `void*`, and we distinguish between an *attribute*, which is a pointer, and the *attribute content*, which is the data referenced by the attribute.

Since any communicator can have multiple different cached attributes, each attribute is identified to the system by a key, which is just a system-defined int. Thus, when we create a new attribute, we call the function `MPI_ Keyval_create`, which will generate a new attribute key. Of course, once we've created an attribute and its identifying key, we still need to be able to

access it. For the most part, attributes are accessed with the two functions
`MPI_Attr_put` and `MPI_Attr_get`. The first assigns a value to an attribute.
The second returns a pointer to an attribute.[1]

Here's a short example that makes a copy of `MPI_COMM_WORLD` and creates
an attribute key we can use to identify our I/O process rank attribute. It then
caches process rank 0 with the I/O process rank attribute.

```
MPI_Comm  io_comm;      /* Communicator for I/O      */
int       IO_KEY;       /* I/O process attribute key */
int*      io_rank_ptr;  /* Attributes are pointers   */
void*     extra_arg;    /* Unused                    */

/* Get a separate communicator for I/O functions by */
/*     duplicating MPI_COMM_WORLD                    */
MPI_Comm_dup(MPI_COMM_WORLD, &io_comm);

/* Create the attribute key */
MPI_Keyval_create(MPI_DUP_FN, MPI_NULL_DELETE_FN,
    &IO_KEY, extra_arg);

/* Allocate storage for the attribute content */
io_rank_ptr = (int*) malloc(sizeof(int));

/* Set the attribute content */
*io_rank_ptr = 0;

/* Cache the attribute with io_comm */
MPI_Attr_put(io_comm, IO_KEY, io_rank_ptr);
```

The call to `MPI_Comm_dup` creates a new communicator with the same underlying group as `MPI_COMM_WORLD`, but a different context. We do this so that
the communication in the I/O functions can't be mixed up with the communication in the rest of the program.

Any time we want to print data, we can retrieve the rank we cached with
`io_comm` as follows:

```
int    flag;
int*   io_rank_attr;

/* Retrieve the I/O process rank  */
MPI_Attr_get(io_comm, IO_KEY, &io_rank_attr, &flag);
```

---

1   The syntax of `MPI_Attr_get` was changed in version 1.1 of the MPI Standard [29]. The
    `attribute` parameter formerly had type `void**`. It now has type `void*`. This doesn't
    change its functionality; it simply makes it possible to call the function without casting the
    corresponding argument.

```
/* If flag == 0, something went wrong: */
/*     there's no attribute cached.    */
if ((flag != 0) && (my_rank == *io_rank_attr))
    printf("Greetings from the I/O Process!\n");
```

Attributes and attribute keys in MPI are process local, as are the functions MPI_Keyval_create, MPI_Attr_put, and MPI_Attr_get. In particular, it's entirely possible that different processes can cache different attributes with the same communicator. Thus, if we wish to create an attribute that has the same content across all the processes in a communicator (as with our I/O process rank), it's up to us to insure that this is the case.

This brief discussion should provide us with enough information about attribute caching so that we can understand how the I/O functions work. So on a first reading, you might want to skip the following subsection.

8.1.2 Callback Functions

Of course, you're wondering about those arguments we used in our call to MPI_Keyval_create: MPI_DUP_FN, MPI_NULL_DELETE_FN, and extra_arg. The syntax of MPI_Keyval_create is

```
int MPI_Keyval_create(
        MPI_Copy_function*    copy_fn     /* in  */,
        MPI_Delete_function*  delete_fn   /* in  */,
        int*                  key_ptr     /* out */,
        void*                 extra_arg   /* in  */)
```

As we already know, the third parameter returns a pointer to a key that we can use to identify a new attribute. The remaining three parameters all have to do with the management of attributes when we create or free communicators.

If we create a communicator with MPI_Comm_dup:

```
MPI_Comm  old_comm;
MPI_Comm  new_comm;

MPI_Comm_dup(old_comm, &new_comm);
```

each attribute cached with old_comm is "copied" to new_comm. For a given attribute key, the function that does the actual copying is specified by the copy_fn parameter of MPI_Keyval_create. In our example, we just used the predefined MPI function, MPI_DUP_FN. It simply copies the attribute (a pointer) in old_comm to the corresponding attribute in new_comm. In general, however, we may want to do something else. So MPI allows for us to define our own functions. For example, we might want to duplicate the memory referenced by the attribute old_comm and make the corresponding attribute in new_comm reference this new block of memory. This, of course, can't be accomplished by just copying a pointer, and we need to define a function to do this.

Similarly, the second parameter to MPI_Keyval_create, delete_fn, is used by the system when we free a communicator or delete an attribute. We can free a communicator with the collective function MPI_Comm_free, and we can delete an attribute with the function MPI_Attr_delete. So, for example, if we call

```
MPI_Comm_free(&comm);
```

each attribute cached with comm will be "deleted." For each attribute, the actual deletion will be carried out by the delete_fn function specified in the call to MPI_Keyval_create. In our example, we just used the predefined function MPI_NULL_DELETE_FN, which does nothing. However, it's not difficult to imagine cases where we would want to do something more complex. If an attribute references a large block of dynamically allocated memory, we will probably want the delete function to systematically free the block.

In MPI, these attribute copy and delete functions are called **callback** functions. Their type definitions are

```
typedef int MPI_Copy_function(
                MPI_Comm  old_comm       /* in  */,
                int       keyval         /* in  */,
                void*     extra_arg      /* in  */,
                void*     attribute_in   /* in  */,
                void*     attribute_out  /* out */,
                int*      flag           /* out */)

typedef int MPI_Delete_function(
                MPI_Comm  comm           /* in  */,
                int       keyval         /* in  */,
                void*     attribute      /* in  */,
                void*     extra_arg      /* in  */)
```

Our example of a copy_fn that copies the block of memory referenced by an attribute can be used to explain the purpose of the mysterious extra_arg parameter in both MPI_Keyval_create and the type definitions of the copy and delete functions: suppose that the content of the attribute is a struct with one or more dynamically allocated array members. Then, unless the sizes of the arrays are stored in the struct itself, the copy_fn won't have any way of knowing how much memory to allocate for them. The extra_arg can be used for this by passing in the sizes of the arrays when the attribute key is created.

8.1.3 Identifying the I/O Process Rank

We still don't know how to identify a process that can carry out I/O. In our example, we just used process 0 in MPI_COMM_WORLD. While this is probably

a safe bet, there may be an alternative. Each implementation of MPI is supposed to provide several predefined attributes cached with `MPI_COMM_WORLD`.
Among these is the attribute with key `MPI_IO`. The content of this attribute is
the rank of a process that can carry out language standard I/O (e.g., `fopen`,
`fprintf`). However, there are numerous caveats:

1. If no process can carry out I/O, the attribute content will be the predefined
   constant `MPI_PROC_NULL`.
2. If every process can carry out I/O, the attribute content will be the predefined constant `MPI_ANY_SOURCE`.
3. If some processes can carry out I/O, but others cannot, different processes
   may have different attribute content. Processes that can carry out I/O
   are required to have attribute content equal to their rank. Processes that
   cannot should have attribute content equal to the rank of some process
   that can.
4. The `MPI_IO` attribute does not indicate which processes can provide input.
   So even if the content of the `MPI_IO` attribute is `MPI_ANY_SOURCE`, it may
   be the case that the implementation doesn't provide any access to `stdin`.

Thus, we cannot rely on the `MPI_IO` attribute to provide a unique process rank,
nor can we be sure that it will provide information about input. However, we
can use it to try to define a unique I/O process rank as follows:

```
int* mpi_io_ptr;
int  io_rank;
int  flag;

MPI_Attr_get(MPI_COMM_WORLD, MPI_IO, &mpi_io_ptr,
    &flag);

if (flag == 0) {
    /* Attribute not cached.  Not MPI compliant */
    io_rank = MPI_PROC_NULL;
} else if (*mpi_io_ptr == MPI_PROC_NULL) {
    io_rank = MPI_PROC_NULL;
} else if (*mpi_io_ptr == MPI_ANY_SOURCE) {
    /* Any process can carry out I/O.  */
    /* Use process 0 */
    io_rank = 0;
} else {
    /* Different ranks may have been returned */
    /* on different processes.  Get min        */
    MPI_Allreduce(mpi_io_ptr, &io_rank, 1, MPI_INT,
        MPI_MIN, MPI_COMM_WORLD);
}
```

The code attempts to retrieve the attribute corresponding to `MPI_IO` and copy
its contents into `io_rank`. If the `flag` argument is 0, the `MPI_IO` attribute

hasn't been cached. Otherwise, we consider the first three possibilities enumerated above. If the attribute content is neither `MPI_PROC_NULL` nor `MPI_ANY_SOURCE`, we must perform some global operation in order to insure a unique rank across all the processes: we chose to take the minimum rank.

8.1.4   Caching an I/O Process Rank

Armed with this information on attributes, we can build a communicator for use in our I/O functions and attempt to cache the rank of a process with it. We should build a separate communicator so that the communication we do in the I/O functions can't be confused with other communication. In order to build it, we can use any of the communicator construction functions; e.g., `MPI_Comm_split` or `MPI_Comm_dup`. Then we can call the first function in our "I/O library," `Cache_io_rank`, to try to cache an I/O process rank with the new communicator.

In an external definition, we define the key that we'll use to identify the I/O process rank attribute: `IO_KEY`. It is initialized with `MPI_KEYVAL_INVALID`, a predefined MPI identifier. We also define a constant, `NO_IO_ATTR`, which we'll use as a return value for the functions in the I/O library if they were unable to find an I/O process rank attribute. In the actual source code this constant will go into a header file.

The function takes two parameters: the original communicator from which the I/O communicator was created, and the I/O communicator, `io_comm`. It begins by checking to see whether `IO_KEY` has been initialized by MPI; i.e., whether it no longer has the value `MPI_KEYVAL_INVALID`. If it hasn't been initialized by MPI, the function calls `MPI_Keyval_create`, as discussed above.

Once we're sure `IO_KEY` has been initialized, we first check to see whether either `orig_comm` or `io_comm` already has an I/O process rank attribute cached. If so, we use this rank. If not, we see if an `MPI_IO` attribute has been cached with either communicator, and use the method outlined above to try determine an I/O process rank from the value of the `MPI_IO` attribute. If all the attempts to find a valid process rank fail, we cache `MPI_PROC_NULL` as the content of the I/O process rank attribute and return `NO_IO_ATTR`.

The work of actually retrieving attributes and caching values is done by the function `Copy_attr`.

```
/* Key identifying I/O process rank attribute */
int    IO_KEY = MPI_KEYVAL_INVALID;

/* Unused */
void*  extra_arg;

#define NO_IO_ATTR -1
```

```
int Cache_io_rank(
        MPI_Comm    orig_comm          /* in      */,
        MPI_Comm    io_comm            /* in/out */) {

    int retval;    /* 0 or NO_IO_ATTR */

    /* Check whether IO_KEY is defined.  If not, define */
    if (IO_KEY == MPI_KEYVAL_INVALID) {
        MPI_Keyval_create(MPI_DUP_FN,
            MPI_NULL_DELETE_FN, &IO_KEY, extra_arg);
    } else if ((retval = Copy_attr(io_comm, io_comm,
                IO_KEY)) != NO_IO_ATTR) {
        /* Value cached */
        return retval;
    } else if ((retval = Copy_attr(orig_comm, io_comm,
                IO_KEY)) != NO_IO_ATTR) {
        /* Value cached */
        return retval;
    }

    /* Now see if we can find a value cached for MPI_IO */
    if ((retval = Copy_attr(orig_comm, io_comm,
                MPI_IO)) != NO_IO_ATTR) {
        /* Value cached */
        return retval;
    } else if ((retval = Copy_attr(io_comm, io_comm,
                MPI_IO)) != NO_IO_ATTR) {
        /* Value cached */
        return retval;
    }

    /* Couldn't find process that could carry out I/O */
    /* Copy_attr has cached MPI_PROC_NULL             */
    return NO_IO_ATTR;

}    /* Cache_io_rank */
```

The function Copy_attr attempts to retrieve the contents of the attribute identified by the parameter KEY from the communicator comm1 and cache it with the IO_KEY attribute on comm2. KEY can be either MPI_IO or IO_KEY. If it finds a valid process rank to cache, it returns 0. Otherwise, it caches MPI_PROC_NULL and returns NO_IO_ATTR.

Copy_attr uses a new MPI function, MPI_Comm_compare. This can be used to determine whether two communicators are identical (same group and context), whether they are congruent (same group, different contexts), or whether they are similar (underlying process sets are the same, but ranks are different). In the first case it returns MPI_IDENT, in the second it returns

MPI_CONGRUENT, and in the third it returns MPI_SIMILAR. If the communicators are neither identical, similar, nor congruent, it returns MPI_UNEQUAL.

Copy_attr also calls a function in our I/O library, Get_corresp_rank. If comm1 and comm2 are distinct communicators, Get_corresp_rank attempts to determine whether a process in comm1 also belongs to comm2. If it does, it returns the rank in comm2. If it doesn't, it returns MPI_UNDEFINED, a predefined MPI constant. Get_corresp_rank also uses a new MPI function, MPI_Group_translate_ranks, which takes a list of process ranks in one group and attempts to determine the corresponding ranks in a second group. If a process in the first group doesn't belong to the second, the corresponding rank is MPI_UNDEFINED.

```
/* All process ranks are < HUGE */
#define HUGE 32768

int Copy_attr(
        MPI_Comm    comm1    /* in      */,
        MPI_Comm    comm2    /* in/out */,
        int         KEY      /* in      */) {

    int    io_rank;
    int    temp_rank;
    int*   io_rank_ptr;
    int    equal_comm;
    int    flag;

    MPI_Attr_get(comm1, KEY, &io_rank_ptr, &flag);

    if (flag == 0) {
        /* Attribute not cached with comm1 */
        io_rank_ptr = (int*) malloc(sizeof(int));
        *io_rank_ptr = MPI_PROC_NULL;
        MPI_Attr_put(comm2, IO_KEY, io_rank_ptr);
        return NO_IO_ATTR;
    } else if (*io_rank_ptr == MPI_PROC_NULL) {
        MPI_Attr_put(comm2, IO_KEY, io_rank_ptr);
        return NO_IO_ATTR;
    } else if (*io_rank_ptr == MPI_ANY_SOURCE) {
        /* Any process can carry out I/O.  Use */
        /* process 0                           */
        io_rank_ptr = (int*) malloc(sizeof(int));
        *io_rank_ptr = 0;
        MPI_Attr_put(comm2, IO_KEY, io_rank_ptr);
        return 0;
    }
```

```
                    /* Value in *io_rank_ptr is a valid process  */
                    /* rank in comm1.  Action depends on whether */
                    /* comm1 == comm2.                           */
                    MPI_Comm_compare(comm1, comm2, &equal_comm);

                    if (equal_comm == MPI_IDENT) {
                        /* comm1 == comm2.  Valid value already */
                        /* cached.  Do nothing.                */
                        return 0;
                    } else {
                        /* Check whether rank returned is valid */
                        /* process rank in comm2               */
                        Get_corresp_rank(comm1, *io_rank_ptr,
                            comm2, &temp_rank);

                        /* Different ranks may have been returned */
                        /* on different processes.  Get min      */
                        if (temp_rank == MPI_UNDEFINED) temp_rank = HUGE;
                        MPI_Allreduce(&temp_rank, &io_rank, 1, MPI_INT,
                            MPI_MIN, comm2);

                        io_rank_ptr = (int*) malloc(sizeof(int));
                        if (io_rank < HUGE) {
                            *io_rank_ptr = io_rank;
                            MPI_Attr_put(comm2, IO_KEY, io_rank_ptr);
                            return 0;
                        } else {
                            /* No process got a valid rank in comm2 */
                            /* from Get_corresp_rank               */
                            *io_rank_ptr = MPI_PROC_NULL;
                            MPI_Attr_put(comm2, IO_KEY, io_rank_ptr);
                            return NO_IO_ATTR;
                        }
                    }
                }
            } /* Copy_attr */


            /**********************************************************/
            void Get_corresp_rank(
                    MPI_Comm   comm1        /* in  */,
                    int        rank1        /* in  */,
                    MPI_Comm   comm2        /* in  */,
                    int*       rank2_ptr    /* out */) {

                MPI_Group  group1;
                MPI_Group  group2;

                MPI_Comm_group(comm1, &group1);
                MPI_Comm_group(comm2, &group2);
```

```
MPI_Group_translate_ranks(group1, 1,
        &rank1, group2, rank2_ptr);

}   /* Get_corresp_rank */
```

Note that `Copy_attr` is a collective function since it may call `MPI_Allreduce`, and since `Copy_attr` is collective, `Cache_io_rank` is also collective.

8.1.5 Retrieving the I/O Process Rank

Before writing the actual I/O functions, we need one more attribute management function: a function that will retrieve the rank of the I/O process. If we were sure that a valid rank had been cached, we could simply call `MPI_Attr_get`:

```
int* io_rank_ptr;
int  flag;

MPI_Attr_get(io_comm, IO_KEY, &io_rank_ptr, &flag);
```

However, if our program has mistakenly failed to cache an attribute or if the attribute content is `MPI_PROC_NULL`, we won't be able to carry out any I/O. So let's try to add a little security by having the attribute retrieval function do a little checking. First it will check to see if `IO_KEY` has been initialized by MPI. If it isn't, it will try to initialize it. If it is, it will try to retrieve the I/O process rank attribute from `io_comm`. If this fails, either because the attribute hasn't been cached or because it's `MPI_PROC_NULL`, the function will try to get an I/O process rank from `MPI_COMM_WORLD` by calling `Copy_attr`. The return values are 0 if a valid rank has been found, and `NO_IO_ATTR` otherwise. Because it may call `Copy_attr`, `Get_io_rank` is also a collective function.

```
int Get_io_rank(
        MPI_Comm io_comm      /* in  */,
        int*     io_rank_ptr  /* out */) {

        void*    extra_arg;
        int*     temp_ptr;
        int      flag;

    if (IO_KEY == MPI_KEYVAL_INVALID) {
        MPI_Keyval_create(MPI_DUP_FN,
            MPI_NULL_DELETE_FN, &IO_KEY, extra_arg);
    } else {
        MPI_Attr_get(io_comm, IO_KEY, &temp_ptr, &flag);
        if ((flag != 0) && (*temp_ptr != MPI_PROC_NULL)) {
            *io_rank_ptr = *temp_ptr;
```

```
                        return 0;
                    }
                }
                if (Copy_attr(MPI_COMM_WORLD, io_comm, MPI_IO)
                        == NO_IO_ATTR) {
                    return NO_IO_ATTR;
                } else {
                    MPI_Attr_get(io_comm, IO_KEY, &temp_ptr, &flag);
                    *io_rank_ptr = *temp_ptr;
                    return 0;
                }

            }  /* Get_io_rank */
```

8.1.6 Reading from stdin

As you've probably already seen, any time we try to design an I/O routine
for parallel processors, we need to make some decisions about where the data
is going to or coming from. For example, in an input routine, do we want
every process to receive all the input data? Or would we prefer to distribute
different parts of the data to different processes? For our input routine, we're
going to assume that all the data is needed on all the processes, or else that
the amount of data is so small that it will not be terribly expensive to send
it to all the processes even if they don't need it. The I/O process will just
read in a line of data as a string and broadcast it to all the processes. Each
process will then make use of the stdarg macros to parse the input line. Some
implementations of C provide a function, vsscanf, that can read data from a
string into a variable length argument list. However, this is not standard, and
it may be necessary to write your own. In our code, we assume the existence
of this function.

Since all of our I/O functions are collective, we'll use the familiar C names
printf and scanf with a "C" prefix. The Cscanf function will be similar
to the scanf function: it will take a format string and a list of variables in
its parameter list. However, it will also take a communicator (io_comm) and
a string that can be used to prompt the user for input. Like the other I/O
functions, its return values will be 0 and NO_IO_ATTR.

```
/* Used by all the I/O functions.  BUFSIZ is defined  */
/*     in stdio.h                                      */
char io_buf[BUFSIZ];

int Cscanf(
        MPI_Comm  io_comm  /* in  */,
        char*     prompt   /* in  */,
        char*     format   /* in  */,
        ...                /* out */) {
```

```
va_list  args;         /* Must include stdarg.h */
int      my_io_rank;   /* My_rank in io_comm    */
int      root;         /* The I/O process       */

/* Try to get the rank of a process that can carry */
/*     out I/O                                      */
if (Get_io_rank(io_comm, &root) == NO_IO_ATTR)
    return NO_IO_ATTR;
MPI_Comm_rank(io_comm, &my_io_rank);

/* Read in data on root */
if (my_io_rank == root) {
    printf("%s\n", prompt);
    gets(io_buf);
}   /* my_io_rank == root */

/* Broadcast the input data */
MPI_Bcast(io_buf, BUFSIZ, MPI_CHAR, root, io_comm);

/* Copy the input data into the parameters */
va_start(args, format);
vsscanf(io_buf, format, args);
va_end(args);

    return 0;
} /* Cscanf */
```

8.1.7 Writing to stdout

Writing to stdout reverses the steps of reading from stdin: we copy the output data into a string and gather each process's string onto the I/O process, which prints them. Once again we use the stdarg package, since we don't know what data will be printed. The parameter list includes the same format string and variable list we use with printf. However, it also contains a communicator and a title. The analog of vsscanf, vsprintf, is a standard C function. So we don't need to worry about writing our own function to copy the data into the string.

In order to gather the data onto the I/O process, we can either use MPI_Gather or a loop of receives. If we use MPI_Gather, we'll have to allocate a very long array on the I/O process in which to collect the data. As a consequence, we've opted to use the simple loop of receives.

As usual, the return value is either 0 or NO_IO_ATTR.

```
int Cprintf(
        MPI_Comm  io_comm  /* in */,
        char*     title    /* in */,
        char*     format   /* in */,
        ...                /* in */) {
```

```
int        q;
int        my_io_rank;
int        io_p;
int        root;
MPI_Status status;
va_list    args;

if (Get_io_rank(io_comm, &root) == NO_IO_ATTR)
    return NO_IO_ATTR;
MPI_Comm_rank(io_comm, &my_io_rank);
MPI_Comm_size(io_comm, &io_p);

/* Send output data to root */
if (my_io_rank != root) {
    /* Copy the output data into io_buf */
    va_start(args, format);
    vsprintf(io_buf, format, args);
    va_end(args);

    MPI_Send(io_buf, strlen(io_buf) + 1, MPI_CHAR,
        root, 0, io_comm);
} else { /* my_io_rank == root */
    printf("%s\n",title);
    fflush(stdout);
    for (q = 0; q < root; q++) {
        MPI_Recv(io_buf, BUFSIZ, MPI_CHAR, q,
            0, io_comm, &status);
        printf("Process %d > %s\n",q, io_buf);
        fflush(stdout);
    }

    /* Copy the output data into io_buf */
    va_start(args, format);
    vsprintf(io_buf, format, args);
    va_end(args);
    printf("Process %d > %s\n",root, io_buf);
    fflush(stdout);

    for (q = root+1; q < io_p; q++) {
        MPI_Recv(io_buf, BUFSIZ, MPI_CHAR, q,
            0, io_comm, &status);
        printf("Process %d > %s\n",q, io_buf);
        fflush(stdout);
    }
    printf("\n");
    fflush(stdout);
}
```

```
        return 0;
} /* Cprintf */
```

8.1.8 Writing to stderr and Error Checking

We want to write to stderr and end execution if we detect an error in our
program. For example, if we attempt to allocate a large array and the call to
malloc fails, we would like to inform the user and shut the program down. It
would seem that a "natural" way to do this would be for the process on which
the malloc failed to print a message and shut down the other processes.
However, given the restrictions on which processes can carry out I/O, unless
the malloc fails on the I/O process, we won't be able to print a message.
Alternatively, we might like to interrupt the I/O process and have it print a
message, but the current version of MPI provides no mechanism for us to do
this.

Thus, it seems that we have two options: we can dedicate the I/O process
to I/O exclusively (i.e., it spends all its time waiting for and printing messages
from other processes) or we can make error checking a collective operation.
We're probably reluctant to just give up a process so that we can print error
messages. So let's take a look at setting up a collective operation.

The idea is that we're running an SPMD-style program, and every process
is doing more or less the same thing. For example, in order to check whether a
malloc failed, we assume that every process called malloc at about the same
point in the program. We can then carry out a collective operation to check
whether any process encountered an error. So if each process is executing a
completely different sequence of statements, this approach won't work.

In this setting we can check for an error by performing an allgather on the
error code generated on each process. Then each process can check the list of
error codes; the I/O process can print a list of the processes that failed, and, if
this list is nonempty, we can stop the program. We'll use negative error codes
to indicate that the program should be stopped.

MPI provides a function, MPI_Abort, that can be called to terminate
execution. Its syntax is

```
int MPI_Abort(
        MPI_Comm    comm        /* in */,
        int         error_code  /* in */)
```

It tries to shut down all the processes in comm. However, its behavior is implementation dependent, and an implementation is only required to try to shut
down all the processes in MPI_COMM_WORLD. In a UNIX environment, the
error code is returned as if the main program returned with

```
        return error_code;
```

As usual the return value of Cerror_test is either 0 or NO_IO_ATTR.

```
            char* error_buf;
            int   error_bufsiz = 0;

            int Cerror_test(
                    MPI_Comm   io_comm       /* in */,
                    char*      routine_name  /* in */,
                    int        error         /* in */) {

                int q;
                int io_p;
                int error_count = 0;
                int io_process;
                int my_io_rank;

                if (Get_io_rank(io_comm, &io_process) == NO_IO_ATTR)
                    return NO_IO_ATTR;
                MPI_Comm_size(io_comm, &io_p);
                MPI_Comm_rank(io_comm, &my_io_rank);

                /*  If necessary increase the size of error_buf */
                if (error_bufsiz == 0) {
                    error_buf = (int*) malloc(io_p*sizeof(int));
                    error_bufsiz = io_p;
                } else if (error_bufsiz < io_p) {
                    realloc(error_buf, io_p);
                    error_bufsiz = io_p;
                }

                MPI_Allgather(&error, 1, MPI_INT, error_buf, 1,
                    MPI_INT, io_comm);
                for (q = 0; q < io_p; q++) {
                    if (error_buf[q] < 0) {
                        error_count++;
                        if (my_io_rank == io_process) {
                            fprintf(stderr,"Error in %s on process %d\n",
                                routine_name, q);
                            fflush(stderr);
                        }
                    }
                }
                if (error_count > 0)
                    MPI_Abort(MPI_COMM_WORLD, -1);
                return 0;
            } /* Cerror_test */
```

We can use this function to check for errors in both MPI and non-MPI functions. However, in order to use it with MPI functions, we need to change MPI's default behavior when it encounters an error. See section 9.6 for a discussion of how to do this.

8.2 **Limited Access to** stdin

As we mentioned earlier, there are MPI implementations that provide no access
to stdin, and the MPI_IO attribute says nothing about whether processes can
read input. Thus, before you can safely use any input functions, you need to
test your implementation of MPI. Fortunately, this should be pretty simple. If
you run the following program on one process, you should be able to determine
whether your implementation allows any process access to stdin.

```
#include <stdio.h>
#include "mpi.h"

main(int argc, char* argv[]) {
    int x;

    MPI_Init(&argc, &argv);

    printf("Enter an integer\n");
    fflush(stdout);
    scanf("%d", &x);
    printf("We read x = %d\n", x);
    fflush(stdout);

    MPI_Finalize();
}
```

If the program hangs or crashes after "Enter an integer," you can be fairly sure
that your implementation won't let you read from stdin. Don't despair. We
have several options: we may be able to use command line arguments, self-
initialization, or files other than stdin. We'll discuss command line arguments
and self-initialization in this section. We'll discuss file I/O in the next section.

   Many implementations of MPI allow each process full access to any command line arguments the user may have typed. This can be quite useful if
your program doesn't take much input. In order to determine what the capabilities of your implementation are, try running the following program with
two processes.

```
#include <stdio.h>
#include "mpi.h"

/* Header file for our I/O library */
#include "cio.h"

main(int argc, char* argv[]) {
    MPI_Comm  io_comm;
    int       i;

    MPI_Init(&argc, &argv);
```

```
              /* Set up communicator for I/O */
              MPI_Comm_dup(MPI_COMM_WORLD, &io_comm);
              Cache_io_rank(MPI_COMM_WORLD, io_comm);

              for (i = 0; i < argc; i++)
                  Cprintf(io_comm,"","argv[%d] = %s", i, argv[i]);

              MPI_Finalize();
          }
```

If we run this program with some command line arguments, it should print the arguments available to each process. For example, if we run the program with two processes on a network of workstations using the mpich implementation of MPI, we get

```
% mpirun -np 2 argtest hello, world
Process 0 > argv[0] = /home/peter/argtest
Process 1 > argv[0] = /home/peter/argtest

Process 0 > argv[1] = hello,
Process 1 > argv[1] = hello,

Process 0 > argv[2] = world
Process 1 > argv[2] = world
```

Beware that if your implementation doesn't give each process access to the command line arguments, the program may crash or hang. If this is the case, you may want to try running the program with only one process to see if process 0 is passed the command line arguments. If it is, you can have it broadcast them to the other processes.

Our second alternative, self-initialization, is really quite simple. Just create a C source file with the necessary data stored in static variables, and write a short function that assigns the values in the static variables to parameters. For example, suppose we are writing a program that reads in the order of two vectors, and then reads in the two vectors.

```
/* data.c
 * A separate file containing the input data.
 */

static int n = 4;

static float a[] = {1.0, 2.0, 3.0, 4.0};

static float b[] = {4.0, 3.0, 2.0, 1.0};
```

```
void Initialize(
        int*    n_ptr,
        float   vector_a[],
        float   vector_b[]) {
    int i;

    *n_ptr = n;

    for (i = 0; i < n; i++) {
        vector_a[i] = a[i];
        vector_b[i] = b[i];
    }
} /* Initialize */
```

Now, if you want to run your program with different input data, you simply edit the file data.c, recompile it, and link it with your already compiled source code. This approach has the virtue that it is guaranteed to work. However, it has the liability that you do need to recompile every time you want to change the input.

8.3 File I/O

Thus far all of our attention has been focussed on stdin, stdout, and stderr. While the use of these streams is adequate for many applications, access to only these streams can be a severe limitation in others. Fortunately, many implementations of MPI allow all processes to read and write files other than stdin, stdout, and stderr. So we may have more flexibility in dealing with file I/O than with stdin, stdout, and stderr.

Of course, increased flexibility usually implies increased complexity, and dealing with file I/O is definitely more complex than dealing with stdin, stdout, and stderr. The reason for this is that when we deal with stdin, stdout, and stderr, we have essentially a single input stream and a single output stream, while with file I/O, we have the possibility of multiple input and multiple output streams. Furthermore, in a parallel system, the underlying hardware may make it possible to access multiple streams simultaneously. Thus, a key issue in parallel I/O is data mapping. For example, suppose a large array has been distributed across d disks, and we wish to access this array in a program with p processes. In general, p won't be the same as d, and we'll have to redistribute the data when we read it in. The details of implementing such a mapping and the design of language interface continue to be the subject of intensive research. As a consequence we'll limit ourselves to the simplest cases: $d = 1$ and $d = p$.

In the case where $d = 1$, we can simply modify our collective I/O functions so that they take a file parameter. For example, the Cprintf function might become Cfprintf and its declaration might be

```
int Cfprintf(
        FILE*      fp          /* in/out */,
        MPI_Comm   io_comm     /* in     */,
        char*      title       /* in     */,
        char*      format      /* in     */,
        ...                    /* in     */)
```

Of course, we'll need to define open and close functions analogous to the C functions. For example, to open a file, we might use the following function.

```
FILE* Cfopen(
        char*      filename    /* in */,
        char*      mode        /* in */,
        MPI_Comm   io_comm     /* in */) {

    int    root;
    int    my_io_rank;
    FILE*  fp;

    Get_io_rank(io_comm, &root);

    MPI_Comm_rank(io_comm, &my_io_rank);

    if (my_io_rank == root) {
        fp = fopen(filename, mode);
        return fp;
    } else {
        return NULL;
    }
}   /* Cfopen */
```

This function simply has the I/O process open the file and return a pointer to it, while the other processes return NULL.

Note that if all our processes can read files other than stdin, we can avoid the problems we discussed in the previous section by arbitrarily designating a process to be the I/O process (e.g., process 0), caching this rank with io_comm, putting the input data into a file, and using Cfscanf instead of Cscanf.

If each process is reading or writing a file, we can simply use the standard C file manipulation functions. For example, if each process is writing to a separate file, we might include something like this:

```
    FILE*  my_fp;
    int    my_rank;
    char   filename[100];

    MPI_Init(&argc, &argv);
    MPI_Comm_rank(MPI_COMM_WORLD, &my_rank);
    sprintf(filename,"file.%d", my_rank);
    my_fp = fopen(filename, "w");
```

```
         ⋮
fprintf(my_fp, "Greetings from Process %d!\n",
    my_rank);
         ⋮
fclose(my_fp);
MPI_Finalize();
```

A couple of points should be mentioned here. First, we were careful to make sure that each process opened a file with a different filename. We did this by appending the process rank to the filename. The reason for this is that although it may appear to us that each process is accessing a different disk, the I/O subsystem may in fact be directing all I/O to a single disk. For example, if we're using a network of workstations, it's highly likely that our home directory resides on a single disk that is NFS mounted on the other systems.

Second, `MPI_Init` and `MPI_Finalize` may change the program's view of the file system. For example, on a network of workstations, the pathname of the current working directory may be changed. Hence, files shouldn't be opened until after calling `MPI_Init`, and they should be closed before calling `MPI_Finalize`.

8.4 Array I/O

Unfortunately, our simple, collective I/O functions don't generalize to arrays very well. For example, suppose we have a distributed linear array of floats that we would like to print. Say each process has 100 floats, and the first 100 are on process 0, the next on process 1, etc. Since the `Cprintf` function expects to receive data from all the processes, together with a format string, it would be necessary to copy the 100 floats into a string using `sprintf` and send the string to `Cprintf`. If the floats are distributed in "cyclic" order—the first float in the global ordering is on process 0, the next on process 1, etc.— then it would be necessary to call `Cprintf` 100 times from each process, and it could be a *long* time before the data were printed. Finally, the data would be printed with the ordinarily useful, but in this case probably useless and probably annoying, information on the process from which the data came. So we would like to develop some more useful functions for array I/O.

Before proceeding, note that the key issue here, data distribution or mapping, has been encountered many times already. For example, we devoted section 2.2.5 to a brief discussion, and we discussed it in several connections in Chapters 4, 5, and 7. Thus, this is not simply an I/O issue: the problem of distributing composite data among processes is a central one in parallel computing. We're returning to it in this chapter because this is the first application we've discussed in which it's necessary to give it a somewhat more comprehensive treatment.

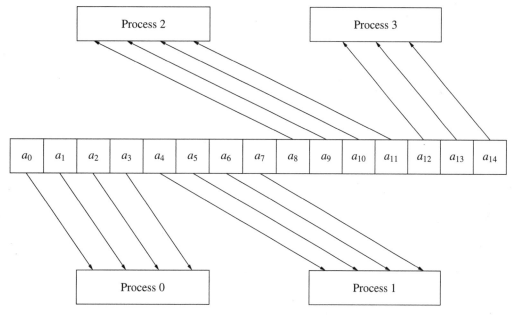

Figure 8.1 Block distribution of 15 elements among four processes

8.4.1 Data Distributions

Suppose that the array contains n elements, and we're running our program with p processes. For the sake of explicitness, suppose that the array is $A = (a_0, a_1, \ldots, a_{n-1})$. Since one of the goals of a well-designed parallel program is to equalize the amount of work done by the processes, we'll usually want to distribute the arrays so that the number of elements is the same (or nearly the same) on each process. That is, we would like to have approximately n/p elements assigned to each process. There are three basic methods that are commonly used for doing this. Here's a brief description.

1. **Block distribution.** If p evenly divides n, then the first n/p elements are assigned to process 0, the next n/p to process 1, etc. If p doesn't divide n evenly, suppose that $n = qp + r$, where $0 \le r < p$. Then we can assign $\lceil n/p \rceil$ elements to the first r processes, and $\lfloor n/p \rfloor$ elements to the remaining $p - r$ processes.[2] See Figure 8.1.

2. **Cyclic distribution.** The first element is assigned to process 0, the next to process 1, etc., until we've assigned one element to each process. Then we assign the pth element to process 0, the $(p + 1)$st to process 1, etc.

---

2 Recall that $\lceil x \rceil$ is the smallest integer greater than or equal to x, and $\lfloor x \rfloor$ is the largest integer less than or equal to x.

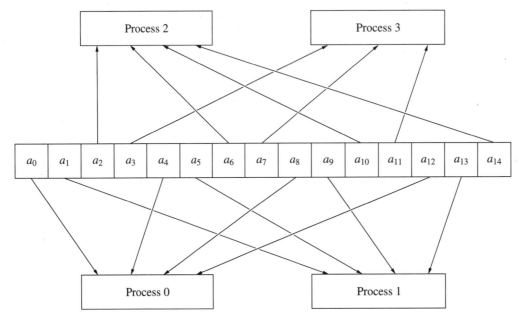

Figure 8.2 Cyclic distribution of 15 elements among four processes

If p doesn't divide n, and, as before, the remainder is r, we will have assigned $\lceil n/p \rceil$ elements to the first r processes and $\lfloor n/p \rfloor$ elements to the remaining $p - r$ processes. See Figure 8.2.

3. **Block-cyclic distribution.** In a block-cyclic distribution, there is a third parameter, the blocksize, b. The idea is to form a hybrid between the block and the cyclic distributions. We assign the first block of b elements to process 0, the next b elements to process 1, etc. If $pb < n$, we won't have exhausted all the elements after we've assigned b elements to process $p - 1$. So, as with the cyclic distribution, we go back to process 0, and continue. See Figure 8.3.

Clearly the cyclic distribution is a special case of the block-cyclic distribution: it is the block-cyclic distribution with blocksize 1. However, whether the block distribution is a special case of the block-cyclic depends on how the block-cyclic deals with remainders. We'll explore this issue further in the exercises.

As far as code goes, it would seem that we should develop functions for block-cyclic I/O. However, the complexity of these functions tends to obscure the main issues. On the other hand, coding of block I/O tends to miss some of the subtleties. So let's develop some functions for cyclic I/O.

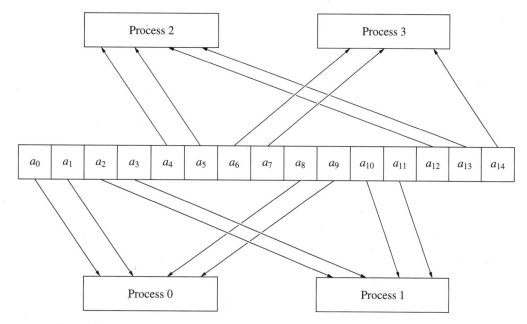

Figure 8.3 Block cyclic distribution of 15 elements among four processes with a blocksize of 2

8.4.2 Model Problem

In the process of designing the input and output functions, it will help to have a model problem in mind. With such a model in mind, it usually won't be too difficult to decide between several alternative solutions to subproblems we encounter in the process of developing our functions. Of course, the choices we make based on the model problem won't be suitable for all applications. However, if we review the design process we used, it shouldn't be too difficult to choose other alternatives and construct more suitable functions.

For our model problem, let's suppose our functions will be used in the solution of a linear system by an iterative method. Jacobi's method, which we'll discuss in Chapter 10, is an especially simple form of such a method. In this setting, we can think of our input array as the right-hand side of the linear system, $A\mathbf{x} = \mathbf{b}$, and the output array as the solution. Typical iterative methods for solving linear systems involve repeated use of the following operations:

1. Scalar multiplication and vector addition
2. Dot product
3. Matrix-vector multiplication

If we distribute the matrix of coefficients by rows among the processes and distribute the corresponding entries of the arrays in the same way, then the first operation is perfectly parallel and the second (as we've already seen) will require a local dot product followed by an `MPI_Allreduce`. Recollect that for the third operation we form the dot product of each row of the matrix with the vector. Thus, if the vector is distributed, it will be necessary to perform an `MPI_Allgather` before we form the dot products of the rows of the matrix with the vector.

8.4.3 Distribution of the Input

We'll assume that the input will be stored in a single file that can be read by the I/O process. We'll also assume that the input array is preceded by n, the order of the array, and the actual array entries are floats. The I/O process will read in n and broadcast it to the other processes—we can use `Cscanf` to do this. We'll also read in the array entries on the I/O process. In order to distribute them, we encounter the usual "speed vs. memory usage" trade-off. We can read all the entries into a single array and use `MPI_Scatter` to distribute them, or we can read a block of, say, p entries, scatter them, read a second block, scatter, etc. Since we cannot use the same argument as both the input and output buffer to `MPI_Scatter`, in order to use the first approach we'll need two arrays on process 0, while we'll only need one array and a scalar if we use the second approach. However, in our model problem, we will want to gather the entire array onto each process in order to carry out a matrix-vector multiplication. So we will need the extra storage anyway, and we might as well use the faster first approach.

8.4.4 Derived Datatypes

Note that since the elements to be sent to a single process are not stored in contiguous entries after we read in the data on process 0, we'll need to use a derived datatype when we use `MPI_Scatter`. For example, if $p = 3, n = 12$, and our input array is

$$(1, 2, 3, 4, 5, 6, 7, 8, 9, 10, 11, 12),$$

we'll send

$$(1, 4, 7, 10) \longrightarrow \text{process 0,}$$
$$(2, 5, 8, 11) \longrightarrow \text{process 1, and}$$
$$(3, 6, 9, 12) \longrightarrow \text{process 2.}$$

So the elements going to a single process are spaced a constant number of components apart, and for this array we could build a derived datatype using `MPI_Type_vector`. Recall its syntax:

```
int MPI_Type_vector(
        int             count         /* in  */,
        int             block_length  /* in  */,
        int             stride        /* in  */,
        MPI_Datatype    old_type      /* in  */,
        MPI_Datatype*   new_type      /* out */)
```

The parameter count is the number of blocks of elements in the type. In our example, it would be 4. The parameter blocklength is the number of contiguous elements in each block. In any cyclic mapping it should just be 1. The stride is the number of elements between the start of consecutive blocks. In our example, it's 3. Thus, we could build the derived type for our example with

```
MPI_Type_vector(4, 1, 3, MPI_FLOAT, &vector_mpi_t);
```

More generally, it would seem that the following code could be used to build the type:

```
count = n/p;
stride = p;

MPI_Type_vector(count, 1, stride, MPI_FLOAT,
    &vector_mpi_t);
```

However, you're probably wondering what happens if n doesn't evenly divide p. For example, suppose $n = 14$ and $p = 3$. Then if we're distributing the array

$$(1, 2, 3, 4, 5, 6, 7, 8, 9, 10, 11, 12, 13, 14),$$

we should send

$$(1, 4, 7, 10, 13) \longrightarrow \text{process } 0,$$
$$(2, 5, 8, 11, 14) \longrightarrow \text{process } 1, \text{ and}$$
$$(3, 6, 9, 12) \longrightarrow \text{process } 2.$$

But now the count parameter for the data sent to process 0 and process 1 should be 5, while it's still 4 for the data sent to process 3. If you recall that a derived datatype is a sequence of basic datatypes together with displacements, it becomes apparent that a single derived datatype cannot be used to represent both four floats and five floats. Thus, we either need to pad our arrays with fake data, or we need to reconsider our approach to data distribution. Since padding the arrays will increase their size by at most $p - 1$, and we expect n to be much larger than p in most cases of interest, let's take the easy alternative of padding the arrays.

The next subsection probes rather deeply into the details of MPI derived datatypes, so you may want to skip it on a first reading. However, since it contains some very important methods for dealing with derived datatypes that contain noncontiguous data, you should return to it before continuing with the rest of the book.

8.4.5 The Extent of a Derived Datatype

OK, so let's take a look at the call to `MPI_Scatter`. Recall its syntax:

```
int MPI_Scatter(
        void*         send_buf     /* in  */,
        int           send_count   /* in  */,
        MPI_Datatype  send_type    /* in  */,
        void*         recv_buf     /* out */,
        int           recv_count   /* in  */,
        MPI_Datatype  recv_type    /* in  */,
        int           root         /* in  */,
        MPI_Comm      comm         /* in  */)
```

In our input function we would call it as follows:

```
MPI_Scatter(input_data, 1, vector_mpi_t,
    local_data, padded_size/p, MPI_FLOAT,
    io_process, io_comm);
```

It might seem that there could be a problem with receiving noncontiguous data into contiguous locations, but this isn't a problem. Recall that we can receive data as long as the type signatures match, and that a derived datatype is just a list of pairs: the first element of each pair is a basic MPI type, the second is a displacement in bytes. So if we have 4-byte floats, `vector_mpi_t` can be represented as

$$\{(\mathtt{MPI\_FLOAT}, 0), (\mathtt{MPI\_FLOAT}, 4p), \dots, (\mathtt{MPI\_FLOAT}, 4(\mathtt{padded\_size}/p - 1))\}.$$

A type signature is just a list of the basic types in a derived datatype, and hence the type signature of `vector_mpi_t` is just a list of `padded_size/p` `MPI_FLOAT`s.

Unfortunately, we've still got problems. The problem isn't at all obvious, but a careful reading of the MPI Standard shows that the data sent to process q in our example will begin

$$q * \mathtt{extent}(\mathtt{vector\_mpi\_t})$$

bytes beyond the beginning of the `input_data` array. For example, the data going to process 1 will begin `extent(vector_mpi_t)` bytes beyond the beginning of the array. So if `extent(vector_mpi_t)` is different from `sizeof(float)`, we're in trouble. The **extent** of a derived datatype is, roughly speaking, the distance, in bytes, from the beginning to the end of the type. So in our

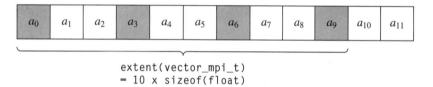

$$\text{extent(vector\_mpi\_t)}$$
$$= 10 \times \text{sizeof(float)}$$

Figure 8.4   Extent of `vector_mpi_t`

example of distributing an array of order 12 among three processes, if floats are 4 bytes long, our derived datatype consists of four equally spaced floats:

$$\{(\mathtt{MPI\_FLOAT}, 0), (\mathtt{MPI\_FLOAT}, 12), (\mathtt{MPI\_FLOAT}, 24), (\mathtt{MPI\_FLOAT}, 36)\}.$$

So the extent of our type isn't 4 bytes; it's 40 bytes! See Figure 8.4. Thus, the first four floats should arrive on process 0, but the floats going to process 1 will start with the 10th element of the input array, and we'll run past the end of the array when we try to send the data to processes 1 and 2.

All is not lost, however. MPI provides a method for us to artificially change the extent of a type. The basic idea is that we add an "upper bound" marker to the type. This marker overrides the natural extent calculation, and when the system calculates the extent of the type, instead of computing the distance from the beginning to the end of the entire type, it only computes the distance from the beginning of the type to the marker. All the other properties of the type are unchanged. In particular, the actual content—`padded_size`/p floats—is unchanged. In order to do this, we need to use `MPI_Type_struct`.

```
int          block_lengths[2];
MPI_Aint     displacements[2];
MPI_Datatype types[2];
MPI_Datatype vector_mpi_t;
MPI_Datatype ub_mpi_t;

/* First create vector_mpi_t                  */
count = padded_size/p;
stride = p;
MPI_Type_vector(count, 1, stride, MPI_FLOAT,
    &vector_mpi_t);

/* The first type is vector_mpi_t             */
types[0] = vector_mpi_t;

/* The second type is MPI_UB                  */
types[1] = MPI_UB;

/* vector_mpi_t starts at displacement 0      */
displacements[0] = 0;
```

```
/* MPI_UB starts at displacement sizeof(float)  */
displacements[1] = sizeof(float);

/* The derived type will have 1 element of type */
/*     vector_mpi_t and 1 element of type       */
/*     MPI_UB                                    */
block_lengths[0] = block_lengths[1] = 1;

/* Now create the full type */
MPI_Type_struct(2, block_lengths, displacements,
     types, &ub_mpi_t);
MPI_Type_commit(&ub_mpi_t);
```

A nontrivial exercise, but an extremely useful one!

Now ub_mpi_t is the same as the original vector_mpi_type, except for the MPI_UB marker. Thus, if floats are 4 bytes, our type is

$$\{(\texttt{MPI\_FLOAT}, 0), (\texttt{MPI\_UB}, 4), (\texttt{MPI\_FLOAT}, 4p), \ldots ,$$
$$(\texttt{MPI\_FLOAT}, 4(\texttt{padded\_size}/p - 1))\},$$

and its extent is computed by taking the difference between the displacement of the MPI_UB and the start of the type; i.e, $4 - 0 = 4$ bytes.

8.4.6 The Input Code

OK. Now we're ready to write some of the code. A program that uses the input function should first read in n using Cscanf. Before reading in the array entries, we'll build a data structure that can be used for storing the array. Rather than just storing the entries in an array, it will be extremely useful to group such information as the global array size, the padded array size, the local array size, etc., with the array itself. Thus, a header file might include the following definitions:

```
typedef struct {
    MPI_Comm* comm;         /* Comm for collective ops */
    #define Comm_ptr(array)  ((array)->comm)
    #define Comm(array)      (*((array)->comm))

    int      p;             /* Size of array_comm       */
    #define Comm_size(array) ((array)->p)

    int      my_rank;       /* My rank in array_comm    */
    #define Comm_rank(array) ((array)->my_rank)

    int      global_order;  /* Global size of array     */
    #define Order(array)     ((array)->global_order)
```

```
        int        padded_size;   /* Padded array size      */
        #define Padded_size(array) ((array)->padded_size)

        float      entries[MAX];   /* Elements of the array  */
        #define Entries(array)   ((array)->entries)
        #define Entry(array,i)   ((array)->entries[i])

        int        local_size;     /* = n/p or n/p+1         */
        #define Local_size(array) ((array)->local_size)

        float      local_entries[LOCAL_MAX];
                                   /* Local entries of array */
        #define Local_entries(array) ((array)->local_entries)
        #define Local_entry(array,i) ((array)->local_entries[i])

        MPI_Datatype ub_mpi_t;     /* The derived datatype   */
        #define Type(array)        ((array)->ub_mpi_t)
} CYCLIC_ARRAY_STRUCT;

typedef CYCLIC_ARRAY_STRUCT* CYCLIC_ARRAY_T;
```

The macros are defined for member access. Although this muddies up the type
definition, it has a couple of advantages that make it well worthwhile. First
it makes the rest of the code more readable: `Entry(A,i)` is almost certainly
easier to understand than `A->entries[i]` or `*(A->(entries+i))`. It also
makes it easy to change the member definition. If, for example, we decide to
group the scalars in a substructure, we can simply change the definition of the
macro, and the rest of the program won't need modification.

Assigning values to the scalar entries in the struct is straightforward. We'll
also need to use the code from section 8.4.5 to define `ub_mpi_t`. But after
we have taken care of these matters, the actual input function is surprisingly
simple. First get the I/O process rank cached with the communicator member
of the array struct, and have the I/O process read the entire array into its
global entries member. After reading in the array, the "fake" entries should be
assigned some value—e.g., 0. Then we can call `MPI_Scatter`. For the scatter,
we'll use our derived type on the I/O process, but we'll receive the local entries
into a contiguous block. So we'll just use `recv_count = padded_size/p`
and `recv_type = MPI_FLOAT`.

```
void Read_entries(
        char*          prompt /* in     */,
        CYCLIC_ARRAY_T array  /* in/out */) {

    int root;
    int i;
    int c;
    int recv_count;
```

```
        Get_io_rank(Comm(array), &root);

        if (Comm_rank(array) == root) {
            printf("%s\n",prompt);
            for (i = 0; i < Order(array); i++)
                scanf("%f", &Entry(array,i));
            /* Skip to end of line */
            while ((c = getchar()) != '\n');

            /* Fill padding with 0's */
            for (i = Order(array); i < Padded_size(array); i++)
                Entry(array,i) = 0.0;
        }

        /* Receive array element into contiguous block of */
        /*      Local_entries(array)                       */
        recv_count = Padded_size(array)/Comm_size(array);
        MPI_Scatter(Entries(array), 1, Type(array),
            Local_entries(array), recv_count,
            MPI_FLOAT, root, Comm(array));

    } /* Read_entries */
```

8.4.7 Printing the Array

Printing the array is also quite easy. We can simply get the I/O process rank of the array communicator, gather the array onto the I/O process, and have the I/O process print the entries. The only complexity occurs if we want a clear indication of which entries belong to which process and, at the same time, a clear picture of the sequential structure of the array. We can arrange for this by printing p entries of the array in each line of output. When we do this, a single column of output will contain the entries assigned to a single process, but the sequential structure of the array will be preserved as we read from left to right and from top to bottom. For example, if the array

$$(1, 2, 3, 4, 5, 6, 7, 8, 9, 10, 11, 12, 13, 14)$$

is scattered among three processes, we might print it as follows:

```
        Processes
        0         1         2
        -----------------------------
        1.0       2.0       3.0
        4.0       5.0       6.0
        7.0       8.0       9.0
       10.0      11.0      12.0
       13.0      14.0
```

In order to do this, we can compute the integer quotient $q = n/p$, and the remainder $r = n \bmod p$. Then we should print q lines consisting of p entries and 1 line consisting of r entries.

```
void Print_entries(
          char*              title   /* in */,
          CYCLIC_ARRAY_T     array   /* in */) {
    int root;
    int q;
    int quotient;
    int remainder;
    int i, j, k;
    int send_count;

    Get_io_rank(Comm(array), &root);

    send_count = Padded_size(array)/Comm_size(array);
    MPI_Gather(Local_entries(array), send_count, MPI_FLOAT,
          Entries(array), 1, Type(array), root, Comm(array));

    if (Comm_rank(array) == root) {
        printf("%s\n", title);
        printf("      Processes\n");
        for (q = 0; q < Comm_size(array); q++)
            printf("%4d    ",q);
        printf("\n");
        for (q = 0; q < Comm_size(array); q++)
            printf("--------");
        printf("\n");

        quotient = Order(array)/Comm_size(array);
        remainder = Order(array) % Comm_size(array);
        k = 0;
        for (i = 0; i < quotient; i++) {
            for (j = 0; j < Comm_size(array); j++) {
                printf("%7.3f ",  Entry(array,k));
                k++;
            }
            printf("\n");
            fflush(stdout);
        }
        for (j = 0; j < remainder; j++) {
            printf("%7.3f ",  Entry(array,k));
            k++;
        }
        printf("\n");
        fflush(stdout);
    }
} /* Print_entries */
```

8.4.8 An Example

In order to clarify the ideas, let's write a short program that uses our various I/O functions. It will simply read in two vectors (*x* and *y*), distribute them among the processes, find their sum (*z*), and print the result.

```c
#include <stdio.h>
#include "mpi.h"

/* Header file for the basic I/O functions */
#include "cio.h"

/* Header file for the cyclic array I/O functions */
#include "cyclic_io.h"

main(int argc, char* argv[]) {
    CYCLIC_ARRAY_STRUCT   x;
    CYCLIC_ARRAY_STRUCT   y;
    CYCLIC_ARRAY_STRUCT   z;
    int                   n;
    MPI_Comm              io_comm;
    int                   i;

    MPI_Init(&argc, &argv);

    /* Build communicator for I/O */
    MPI_Comm_dup(MPI_COMM_WORLD, &io_comm);
    if (Cache_io_rank(MPI_COMM_WORLD, io_comm) ==
            NO_IO_ATTR)
        MPI_Abort(MPI_COMM_WORLD, -1);

    /* Get n */
    Cscanf(io_comm, "Enter the array order", "%d", &n);

    /* Allocate storage and initialize scalar    */
    /*    members.  Calls function for building   */
    /*    derived type                            */
    Initialize_params(&io_comm, n, &x);
    Initialize_params(&io_comm, n, &y);
    Initialize_params(&io_comm, n, &z);

    /* Get vector elements */
    Read_entries("Enter elements of x", &x);
    Read_entries("Enter elements of y", &y);

    /* Add local entries */
    for (i = 0; i < Local_size(&x); i++)
        Local_entry(&z,i) =
            Local_entry(&x,i) + Local_entry(&y,i);
```

```
            /* Print z */
            Print_entries("x + y =", &z);

            MPI_Finalize();
}
```

If we run this with four processes and input

```
14
1 2 3 4 5 6 7 8 9 10 11 12 13 14
14 13 12 11 10 9 8 7 6 5 4 3 2 1
```

the output will be

```
Enter the array order
Enter elements of x
Enter elements of y
x + y =
    Processes
    0            1           2           3
- - - - - - - - - - - - - - - - - - - - - - - - - - -
    15.0        15.0        15.0        15.0
    15.0        15.0        15.0        15.0
    15.0        15.0        15.0        15.0
    15.0        15.0
```

8.5 Summary

We've covered a lot of ground in this chapter. Our goal was to write some functions that we can use for convenient I/O on parallel systems. However, in order to write these functions, we learned a lot about MPI and took a brief look at data distributions and a few of the issues involved in parallel I/O.

We started the chapter with a discussion of the problem of I/O on parallel systems. The most important point was that since there isn't a consensus on the mechanics of I/O on parallel systems, the MPI Standard imposes no requirements on the I/O capabilities of an MPI implementation. An unfortunate consequence of this is that programmers have no guaranteed I/O interface, and the main purpose of this chapter was to develop some simple I/O functions. We assume that there is at least one process that can carry out basic I/O—e.g., printf and scanf—and turn our I/O functions into *collective* operations: data to be read is read in by the process with I/O capabilities and distributed to the other processes, and data to be printed is collected onto the I/O process and printed.

Since I/O is collective, our I/O functions all take a communicator argument. Since the rank of the process with I/O capabilities is communicator dependent, it would be convenient if we could somehow attach this information to a communicator. MPI provides just such a facility: it's called *attribute caching.* Since, in general, we may want to attach much more complex sets of information with communicators, attributes in MPI are just pointers. So we distinguish between the attribute and the *attribute content.* For our I/O functions the attribute was a pointer to an int, and the attribute content was the rank of the process that can carry out I/O. Since a communicator may have many attributes cached, each attribute has a system-defined *key.*

Attributes and keys are process local: each process in a communicator may have different keys identifying an attribute and different attribute content associated with the key. Indeed, all the attribute access functions are purely local operations, so it's entirely possible that one process may have a given attribute defined while another doesn't.

We can create a key with the MPI function `MPI_Keyval_create`:

```
int MPI_Keyval_create(
        MPI_Copy_function*    copy_fn     /* in  */,
        MPI_Delete_function*  delete_fn   /* in  */,
        int*                  key_ptr     /* out */,
        void*                 extra_arg   /* in  */)
```

The main significance of this function for our purposes was that it returned a pointer to a key that we could use to identify our I/O process rank attribute. The parameters `copy_fn` and `delete_fn` are called *callback* functions. The `copy_fn` parameter tells MPI what should be done with the attribute when a communicator is duplicated with `MPI_Comm_dup`,

```
int MPI_Comm_dup(
        MPI_Comm   old_comm   /* in  */,
        MPI_Comm*  new_comm   /* out */)
```

The `delete_fn` parameter tells MPI what should be done when a communicator is freed with the collective function

```
int MPI_Comm_free(
        MPI_Comm*   comm   /* in/out */)
```

or when an attribute is deleted with

```
int MPI_Attr_delete(
        MPI_Comm    comm     /* in */
        int         keyval   /* in */)
```

Both `copy_fn` and `delete_fn` can, in general, be user defined. However, for our I/O process rank attribute, we just used the predefined MPI functions, `MPI_DUP_FN` and `MPI_NULL_DELETE_FN`. The first simply copies the attribute (pointer) from the old communicator to the new communicator, and the second does nothing. The purpose of the extra_arg parameter is to provide additional information to the copy_fn and the delete_fn; we made no use of it.

After creating a key for the I/O process rank attribute, we needed to devise a method for determining the rank of a process that could carry out I/O. We did this by accessing the predefined MPI attribute with key, MPI_IO. This attribute should be cached with MPI_COMM_WORLD in all MPI implementations. Its content can either be MPI_PROC_NULL (no process can carry out I/O), MPI_ANY_SOURCE (all processes can carry out I/O), or a process rank. We can determine the value of this and any other attribute by calling

```
int MPI_Attr_get(
        MPI_Comm   comm       /* in  */,
        int        key        /* in  */,
        void*      attr_ptr   /* out */,
        int*       flag       /* out */)
```

If the attribute identified by key has been cached with comm, on return the value referenced by flag will be nonzero, and attr_ptr will reference the attribute. Be careful here: attr_ptr points to the actual attribute, which in turn points to the content of the attribute.

Once we determine the rank of a process that can carry out I/O, we can cache with the communicator by calling

```
int MPI_Attr_put(
        MPI_comm   comm        /* in */,
        int        key         /* in */,
        void*      attribute   /* in */)
```

This will cache attribute with comm. The attribute is identified by key. Note that unlike MPI_Attr_get we pass the actual attribute to MPI_Attr_put. This distinction is natural: in MPI_Attr_put, the system copies the address of the attribute content to system-defined memory, while in MPI_Attr_get we want to *return* the attribute, and the only way we can do this in C is to return a pointer to the attribute. The confusion arises because both parameters have the same type—void*—and the reason for this is that void* indicates a pointer to anything, including another pointer.

We created a separate communicator for I/O so that the communications in the I/O functions couldn't be confused with other communication. However, this meant that after the new I/O communicator was created, we might need to get the I/O rank from another communicator. This led to our using two new MPI functions:

```
int MPI_Comm_compare(
        MPI_Comm   comm1    /* in  */,
        MPI_Comm   comm2    /* in  */,
        int*       result   /* out */)
```

```
int MPI_Group_translate_ranks(
        MPI_Group   group1        /* in  */,
        int         array_size    /* in  */,
        int         ranks_in_1[]  /* in  */,
        MPI_Group   group2        /* in  */,
        int         ranks_in_2[]  /* out */)
```

The first function compares the groups and contexts of comm1 and comm2. If
they're both identical, it returns MPI_IDENT. If the groups are identical but
the contexts are different, it returns MPI_CONGRUENT. If the groups contain
the same processes but the order of the processes is different, it returns MPI_
SIMILAR. Otherwise it returns MPI_UNEQUAL.

The second function, MPI_Group_translate_ranks, takes two arrays
of size array_size. The array ranks_in_1 contains a list of process ranks
in group1. The second array returns the corresponding process ranks in
group2—if they exist. If a process listed in ranks_in_1 doesn't belong to
group2, the corresponding entry in ranks_in_2 will be MPI_UNDEFINED.

Most of our work in section 8.1 was spent on learning about attributes and
communicators. Once we had this material, our actual communicator access
functions and our I/O functions were fairly simple to write. The input function
Cscanf gets the rank of the I/O process, reads in the data on this process, and
broadcasts it to the other processes. The output function Cprintf reverses
the sequence: after getting the rank of the I/O process, it gathers the data
from all the processes onto process 0 and prints the data from each. Probably
the most complicated of the functions was our Cerror_test function. In
it we gathered error codes from all the processes onto *all* the processes, and
then each process systematically checked the codes to see if any process had
encountered a problem. If this was the case, the I/O process printed the ranks
of the processes that had encountered errors, and all the processes called

```
MPI_Abort(
        MPI_Comm   comm        /* in */
        int        error_code  /* in */)
```

It tries to shut down all the processes in comm. However, its behavior is implementation dependent, and an implementation is only required to try to shut
down all the processes in MPI_COMM_WORLD. In a UNIX environment, the error
code is returned as if the main program returned with

```
return error_code;
```

After writing the basic I/O functions we considered some problems users
might encounter and possible solutions. The main issue here was access to
stdin. All MPI implementations with which we're familiar allow at least one
process access to stdout and stderr. However, it is not unusual for an
implementation to provide no access to stdin. If this is the case, there are

basically three additional options. The simplest may be to use command line arguments. If there isn't much input to our program, we can type the input on the command line, and many MPI implementations send the command line arguments to all the processes. A second alternative is to put the input in a separate C source file. Then changing input will involve recompiling the separate source file and relinking it with the rest of the code. The final option was to get input from a file other than stdin.

This last option brought up the more general problem of I/O to files other than stdin, stdout, and stderr. In general parallel systems there may be multiple I/O devices attached to multiple processes. So general parallel I/O can be extremely complex. We only briefly considered the case of a single input or output file, and the case where each process opens its own input or output file. In the first case, we saw that we could modify our functions for accessing stdin, stdout, and stderr so that they take file parameters. In the second case, we can simply use C's file I/O functions. The main problem here is to make sure that each process is writing a different file from the other processes.

The functions we developed in the first part of the chapter were designed for the I/O of small amounts of data. For large amounts of data they will be extremely slow and cumbersome. So the last section of the chapter dealt with array I/O. In order to design array I/O functions, it was necessary to consider how the arrays would be distributed among the processes. So we briefly recalled the three most common distributions: block, cyclic, and block-cyclic. We decided to develop functions for the I/O of cyclic arrays. The functions used the same model that we used for I/O of scalar data: a single process carried out the actual I/O, and the I/O functions were collective operations. Thus, the input function, Read_entries, retrieved the rank of the I/O process, had it read in the data into a single array, and scattered the data among the processes using MPI_Scatter. The output function, Print_entries, retrieved the I/O rank and gathered the data onto the I/O process, which printed the array.

Since we were using a cyclic distribution of the data, the data sent to a single process by Read_entries came from noncontiguous locations in the array used by the I/O process. So we had to use MPI_Type_vector to create a derived datatype, vector_mpi_t, for the distribution. However, we discovered that MPI_Scatter doesn't choose the data being sent to the different processes the way we wanted it to. For example, in our distribution, the data being sent to process 1 should begin one float past the point where the data sent to process 0 begins. However, MPI_Scatter will send the data beginning extent(vector_mpi_type) bytes past the point where the data sent to process 0 begins, and the extent of vector_mpi_type was much larger than a single float. This led to a discussion of the extent of an MPI datatype, and a method for artificially redefining a type's extent.

Roughly speaking, the extent of an MPI datatype is the distance in bytes from the beginning to the end of the type. So if the input array consisted of n

floats and we were using p processes, the extent of `vector_mpi_t` was

$$(n - p + 1) \ * \ \texttt{sizeof(float)}$$

bytes. However, MPI provides a special type, `MPI_UB`, that can be used to artificially change the extent of a type. We did this by first building `vector_mpi_t`
using `MPI_Type_vector` as before, but then we used
`MPI_Type_struct` to build a type from `vector_mpi_t` starting at displacement 0, and `MPI_UB` starting at displacement `sizeof(float)` bytes.

8.6 References

The main reference for this chapter is, as usual, the MPI Standard [28, 29].
Further discussion of attributes and derived datatypes can be found in both
[21] and [34].

Kernighan and Ritchie [24] discuss the use of the `stdarg` package. They
also provide a small example of how to write a "minimal" `printf` function.
This can be used as a model for writing your own `vsscanf` function. For
detailed discussions of issues in general parallel I/O, see [9] and [10].

8.7 Exercises

1. Create two files `cio.h` and `cio.c`. The first file should contain the declarations, definitions, etc., needed so that when a source program includes
   it, it can use our collective I/O functions. The second should contain the
   actual source code for the collective I/O functions. Make sure that you've
   set things up correctly by writing a short program that reads in different
   types of data, modifies them, and prints out the modified data.

2. Modify the functions in `cio.c` so that they take a file argument. Create
   analogs of `fopen` and `fclose`.

3. Repeat exercise 1 for the cyclic array I/O functions. In this case you'll have
   to write some of the functions yourself—e.g., `Initialize_params`. Name
   your files `cyclic_io.h` and `cyclic_io.c`. Be sure to test them. In order to reduce memory usage, you may want to delete the `entries` member and use local storage instead.

4. Modify the array I/O functions so that they take a file parameter.

5. Modify the array I/O functions so that the processes store the local array
   data in the same form in which it is stored globally. For example, if $p = 3$
   and the input array is

$$(1, 2, 3, 4, 5, 6, 7, 8, 9, 10)$$

then the local arrays should look something like this:

$$\text{Process 0: } (1, -, -, 4, -, -, 7, -, -, 10)$$
$$\text{Process 1: } (-, 2, -, -, 5, -, -, 8, -, -)$$
$$\text{Process 2: } (-, -, 3, -, -, 6, -, -, 9, -)$$

The "$-$" indicates an undefined entry. Modify the vector sum program so that it uses this new format.

6. If you store a matrix as a linear array, then a block-row distribution of the matrix corresponds to a block distribution of the array, while a block-column distribution corresponds to a block-cyclic distribution of the array. Discuss the MPI derived datatype declarations that would be needed for the I/O of a matrix that uses a block-column distribution. Can you devise MPI derived datatypes that could be used for other distributions? Consider cyclic row distributions, cyclic column distributions, and block-checkerboard distributions.

7. Programs whose performance is limited by I/O speed rather than processor speed are said to be **I/O bound.** List some application programs that are probably I/O bound.

8.8 Programming Assignments

1. Write a function that will broadcast an int from process 0 in MPI_COMM_WORLD to the other processes in MPI_COMM_WORLD. The function should use a tree-structured broadcast. The first time the function is called, each process should cache information on the structure of the broadcast with MPI_COMM_WORLD. For example, if there are 8 processes, process 0 should store the information that it will first send the data to process 4, then process 2, and finally process 1. Process 2 should store the information that it will be idle during the first stage of the broadcast, during the second it will receive from 0, and during the third it will send to 3. This information can be stored in an array with one element for each stage. Each element can consist of the operation to be carried out at the stage (send, receive, idle) and the rank of a process if the operation is send or receive. Use the callback functions MPI_DUP_FN and MPI_NULL_DELETE_FN.

2. If you have an implementation of MPI that runs on a network of workstations and the workstations are not all using the same disk for their home directories, use the file I/O functions to write an rcp function. It should take as input the name of a file and two process ranks. The first process has access to the file. The second process should create a copy of the file on its local disk under the same name.

3. Modify your broadcast function so that it uses callback functions that you've defined. The copy function should allocate enough memory to

store the attribute content and copy the attribute content from the old communicator to the new. The delete function should free the memory referenced by the attribute.

4. Write functions for the I/O of arrays that use a block distribution.

5. Write functions for the I/O of arrays that use a block-cyclic distribution. If p is the number of processes, b is the blocksize, and n is the array order, assume that pb evenly divides n.

CHAPTER 9

Debugging Your Program

IN THIS CHAPTER we'll take a look at a somewhat controversial subject: debugging. Why controversial? Well, there are certain individuals who assert that we should design mathematically correct programs and, as a consequence, we should never need to do any debugging. On the other hand, most programmers find that they spend huge amounts of time debugging. So rather than taking the moral high ground (and thereby saving ourselves the trouble of writing this chapter), we will concede that programmers make mistakes and spend some time talking about how to find those mistakes. However, let's stress that the time spent debugging can be minimized by carefully designing and developing the program.

We'll begin with a short review of debugging serial programs. Then we'll continue with a discussion of some additional problems encountered in debugging parallel programs. The bulk of the chapter will be devoted to testing and debugging a small parallel program.

9.1 Quick Review of Serial Debugging

If you do much programming, you probably consider yourself to be an expert on the subject of debugging, but just in case, let's take a few minutes to discuss some of the main issues and techniques in debugging serial programs.

The typical debugging process is cyclical: the program is run. When a bug is encountered, we have a number of options. We'll discuss three that are most frequently used:

1. Examine the source code.

2. Add debugging output statements to the program.

3. Use a symbolic debugger.

After identifying and correcting the bug, we repeat the process. Let's look at each of the methods we listed for locating bugs.

9.1.1 Examine the Source Code

The first approach is most useful if we have a fairly small program and the nature of the errors we're encountering is suggestive of where the problem is located. As an example, let's try to debug the following program:

```
/* bug.c
 * Program that tries to read a list of floats and sort
 *    them in increasing order.
 * Warning!  This program is definitely incorrect!
 *
 * Input:
 *    size of list (int)
 *    list of floats
 *
 * Output:
 *    Sorted list
 *
 * Algorithm:
 *    1. Get list size
 *    2. Get first input float.
 *    3. For each new element
 *        (a) read it in
 *        (b) use linear search to determine where it
 *            should be inserted
 *        (c) insert it by shifting greater elements down
 *            one
 *    4. Print list
 */
#include <stdio.h>

/* Maximum list size */
#define MAX 100

/* Function for printing contents of list */
void Print_x(char* title, float x[], int size);

main() {
     int    num_vals;   /* Input list size                 */
     float x[MAX];      /* Storage for the sorted list     */
     float temp;        /* Most recently read input value  */
     int    i, j, k;    /* Subscripts.  i:  counts input   */
                        /* values, j:  position to insert  */
                        /* new value.                      */
```

```
    printf("How many input values?\n");
    scanf("%d",num_vals);

    printf("Now enter each value.\n");
    /* Get first value */
    scanf("%f", &(x[0]));

    for (i = 1; i < num_vals; i++) {
        scanf("%f", &temp);

        /* Determine where to insert */
        j = i - 1;
        while ((temp < x[j]) && (j > 0))
            j--;

        /* Insert */
        for (k = i; k > j; k++)
            x[k] = x[k-1];
        x[j] = temp;
    }

    Print_x("Contents of x", x, num_vals);
} /* Print_x */

void Print_x(char* title, float x[], int size) {
    int i;

    printf("%s\n", title);
    for (i = 0; i < size; i++)
        printf("%f ", x[i]);
    printf("\n");
} /* Print_x */
```

If we compile the program,

```
% cc -o bug bug.c
```

and we attempt to run it, we get the prompt

```
% bug
How many input values?
```

Then, when we enter a value, we get the dreaded

```
Segmentation fault
```

If you've done much C programming, this is highly suggestive: a segmentation fault just after entering an input value suggests that we made classic error number 1:

```
scanf("%d",num_vals);
```

We forgot to pass a *pointer* to num_vals.

It should be noted that some systems aren't nearly so obliging in identifying errors. For example, one system happily reads in the num_vals and the first two input floats and crashes later on with the message

```
Bus error
```

This evil system evidently decided that the int passed to scanf was OK, and the program failed to crash until it hit the inner for loop. Unfortunately, this would make it *much* more difficult to diagnose. So, we can't blithely assume that programs will crash when they ought to.

This brings up an important point:

It can be virtually impossible to predict the behavior of an erroneous program.

Many students devote tremendous amounts of energy to trying to decide how their program "ought" to have behaved with a given collection of errors. Don't waste your time. Life is too short.

9.1.2 Add Debugging Output

As you may have already noticed, we haven't quite fixed up our program. Let's see what happens when we try again.

```
% cc -o bug bug.c
% bug
How many input values?
3
Now enter each value.
1 2 3
Segmentation fault
```

The dreaded "Segmentation fault" again! Let's attack this error by adding some diagnostic output. Basically, we would like to get a snapshot of the state of the program at various points during execution. One of the easiest ways to do this is to print out the values of the variables at various strategic points. Let's add a new function that takes care of this for us.

```
void Snapshot(char* title, int num_vals, float x[],
    int i, int j,  int k, float temp) {

    printf("*********************\n");
    printf("%s\n", title);
    printf("num_vals = %d, i = %d, temp = %f\n",
        num_vals, i, temp);
```

```
                        printf("j = %d, k = %d\n", j, k);
                        Print_x("x = ", x, i);
                        printf("*********************\n\n");
                        fflush(stdout);
            }
```

The use of fflush as the last statement in the function guarantees that everything is printed. On most systems I/O is buffered, so the output won't actually be printed until the output buffer is full. If our program crashes, data in the output buffer may be lost. However, the use of fflush will force the system to flush the buffer even if it isn't full, and we're assured that we'll see all our output.

Of course, in a large program, it won't be possible to print the values of all the variables, but the principle is the same: you simply print the values of the variables that are of interest.

Now we'll call Snapshot in "strategic" places. Obvious candidates (especially in view of our recent experience) are after the calls to scanf. For variables that are uninitialized we'll simply use "0" as the corresponding argument to Snapshot. The output (together with our input) is now

```
How many input values?
3
*********************
After getting num_vals
num_vals = 3, i = 0, temp = 0.000000
j = 0, k = 0
x =


*********************


Now enter each value.
1 2 3
*********************
After getting first val
num_vals = 3, i = 1, temp = 0.000000
j = 0, k = 0
x =
1.000000
*********************


*********************
After getting next val
num_vals = 3, i = 1, temp = 2.000000
j = 0, k = 0
x =
1.000000
*********************


Segmentation fault
```

Not much help, although we now know that the program is crashing some-
where inside the main `for` loop on its first pass. Let's get rid of these calls to
`Snapshot` and add some calls to the body of the loop: one after the `while`
loop and one after the inner `for` loop.

```
How many input values?
3
Now enter each value.
1 2 3
*********************
After computing j
num_vals = 3, i = 1, temp = 2.000000
j = 0, k = 0
x =
1.000000
*********************

Segmentation fault
```

OK. We never got to the second call to `Snapshot`—the one after the inner `for`
loop. So the immediate problem must be there. Taking a look, we see

```
/* Insert */
for (k = i; k > j; k++)
    x[k] = x[k-1];
```

Well, we should have caught this a while ago: k is being *incremented.* It should
be decremented!

9.1.3 Use a Debugger

In theory, the easiest way to locate bugs is with the use of a symbolic
debugger. A **symbolic debugger**, or, more often, a **debugger,** is a program
that acts as an intermediary between the programmer, the system, and the
program. The description of the capabilities of the GNU debugger (`gdb`) in the
`gdb` man page are instructive:

> `gdb` can do four main kinds of things (plus other things in support of
> these) to help you catch bugs in the act:
> - Start your program, specifying anything that might affect its behavior.
> - Make your program stop on specified conditions.
> - Examine what has happened, when your program has stopped.
> - Change things in your program, so you can experiment with correcting
>   the effects of one bug and go on to learn about another.

Although this excerpt describes the capabilities of `gdb`, it could be applied
equally well to most debuggers.

The big problem is that debuggers tend to be difficult to use. Although their principal function is to help the programmer, the commands tend to have somewhat obscure syntax, and, if we fail to type exactly the correct thing, they may either print a cryptic error message or, even worse, completely ignore our message. In spite of this, they can be extremely useful—especially if they have a well-designed graphical user interface.

Perhaps the most widely used debugger is dbx—most UNIX systems provide some version of it. So let's use it to find the remaining bugs in our program.

In order to use dbx (and most debuggers) we need the compiler to generate a full symbol table: a mapping between the internal representation of the program objects and our source representation. For example, if the variable x begins in memory location 804,780,616, then we need to include in our table the correspondence x $\longleftrightarrow$ 804, 780, 616. With this information, when we request the value of, say, x[0], the debugger can translate that into something like "the value stored at address 804,780,616." On most systems, the full symbol table is generated with the -g option to the compiler. For example,

```
% cc -g -o bug bug.c
```

It should be noted that compiler optimizations can seriously confuse a debugger. So you shouldn't use optimization flags (e.g., -O) when you're debugging and you probably shouldn't use the -g option on "production" codes.

Having compiled the program with the -g option, we can now run it under the control of the debugger.

```
% dbx bug
dbx Version 3.1
Type 'help' for help.
reading symbolic information ...
(dbx)
```

The exact details of the information printed during startup vary from system to system. Eventually, however, we'll get the (dbx) prompt. Now we can run our program by typing run followed by any command line arguments we might use to start our program directly from the shell prompt.

```
(dbx) run
How many input values?
3
Now enter each value.
1 2 3
Contents of x
2.000000 3.000000 1.000000

execution completed (exit code 1)
(dbx)
```

Except for a few comments generated by the debugger, the program runs just the way it runs when we start it from the system prompt. Notice that when our program wants to read input from the keyboard, we can type the input just as we would when we run our program directly from the shell.

OK. Not surprisingly, there are still bugs in our program. But we don't really have any information about where they are. We need to get dbx to give us some information on what the program is doing during execution. In order to do this, we can stop the program during execution and look at what has happened, and in order to do this, we can add some **breakpoints.** That is, we can stop the program at "interesting points" during execution and check things out. Since the elements of the list are incorrectly sorted, it would seem that one interesting point is after the computation of j—the position to insert the new value. How do we find out where to put the breakpoint? We can get dbx to list segments of the source code with the list command:

```
(dbx) list 35,45
    35          for (i = 1; i < num_vals; i++) {
    36              scanf("%f", &temp);
    37
    38              /* Determine where to insert */
    39              j = i - 1;
    40              while ((temp < x[j]) && (j > 0))
    41                  j--;
    42
    43              /* Insert */
    44              for (k = i; k > j; k--)
    45                  x[k] = x[k-1];
```

Its syntax is

```
list <firstline>, <lastline>
```

and it prints the source code starting at line firstline and ending at line lastline. As it can be rather tedious to search through the source program using list, it's usually much more convenient to open a window containing the source code, or use something like C-shell job control to switch back and forth between the source listing and dbx.

We can only insert breakpoints at the beginning of functions or on lines where an executable statement begins. So if we try putting a breakpoint at line 41, 42, or 43, dbx will simply ignore it. Our breakpoint should be at line 44. We can add it by typing

```
(dbx) stop at 44
[2] stop at 44
```

The numeral printed before the echoing of our command is a reference number—dbx has identified this breakpoint with the numeral 2. So if, for example, we want to remove the breakpoint later on, we can reference it with the number 2. We don't have to remember this: we can get a list of active breakpoints with the status command.

```
(dbx) status
[2] stop at 44
```

Incidentally, we also don't need to memorize all of the commands in dbx. Each implementation has a help command. Its details vary from system to system, but you can always get started with just

```
(dbx) help
```

Getting back to our program, we have completed one execution, and we've inserted a breakpoint after the computation of j. Let's run the program and see what happens.

```
(dbx) run
How many input values?
3
Now enter each value.
1 2 3
[2] stopped in main at line 44
    44              for (k = i; k > j; k--)
```

Now let's see what's going on.

```
(dbx) print i
1
(dbx) print x[0]
1.0
(dbx) print temp
2.0
(dbx) print j
0
```

Aha! The program is going to try to insert 2.0 in the wrong place. So whatever else is wrong with our program, it's clear that it's not computing j correctly.

Now we have basically two options: we can continue to run the program under the control of the debugger—trying to analyze under what conditions it fails—or we can go back to the drawing board. For this program, I think we should go back to the drawing board . . . . Whatever, *you* decide, you should correct the program as a matter of conscience. But for the moment, we're done with dbx. So let's

```
(dbx) quit
```

9.2 More on Serial Debugging

Of course, we've barely scratched the surface of debugging. There are a number of other approaches that can be quite useful. It would be very helpful to have a catalog of debugging techniques, common programming errors, and tentative diagnoses of common failures. Fortunately, there are a number of books that address these issues. See the references at the end of the chapter.

9.3 Parallel Debugging

If you've been writing the programs at the ends of the chapters, you've probably already discovered that debugging a parallel program is a good deal more challenging than debugging a serial program. This isn't surprising: we would expect that communication among the processes would increase complexity. Unfortunately, and not surprisingly, the state of the art in parallel debugging is not as far advanced as it is in serial debugging: it remains an active research topic. As we'll discuss below, the development of parallel debuggers remains an active area for research and, as we've already seen, generating output from a parallel program can be extremely difficult.

9.4 Nondeterminism

In addition to all these problems, parallel programs can exhibit **nondeterministic** behavior—the exact sequence of computations and communications performed on each of the processes may vary from execution to execution. As a simple example, consider the following program fragment. Its purpose is to perform a global reduction, where the reduction operation is 2×2 matrix multiplication.

```
/* mat_mult.c
 * Multiply a sequence of 2x2 matrices--1 factor from
 *     each process.  Erroneous.
 *
 * Input: none
 *
 * Output: product of a sequence of 2x2 matrices
 *
 * Algorithm
 *     1. Generate local matrix
 *     2. Send local matrix to process 0
 *     3  if (my_rank == 0)
 *     3a.    for each process, receive matrix and
 *                multiply by product
 *     3b.    print product
```

```
            *
            * Notes:
            *    1. The matrices are stored as linear arrays.  The
            *       correspondence is row major: Matrix[i][j] <->
            *       Array[2*i + j]
            *    2. Local matrices have the form
            *           [my_rank    my_rank+1]
            *           [my_rank+2  my_rank  ]
            */
           #include <stdio.h>
           #include "mpi.h"

           #define MATRIX_ORDER 2
           #define ARRAY_ORDER 4

           void Initialize(float my_matrix[], int my_rank);
           void Mult(float product[], float factor[]);
           void Print_matrix(char* title, float matrix[]);

           main(int argc, char* argv[]) {
               float       my_matrix[ARRAY_ORDER];
               float       temp[ARRAY_ORDER];
               float       product[ARRAY_ORDER] = {1, 0, 0, 1};
                               /* product is the identity matrix */
               int         p;
               int         my_rank;
               MPI_Status  status;
               int         i;

               MPI_Init(&argc, &argv);
               MPI_Comm_size(MPI_COMM_WORLD, &p);
               MPI_Comm_rank(MPI_COMM_WORLD, &my_rank);

               Initialize(my_matrix, my_rank);

               MPI_Send(my_matrix, ARRAY_ORDER, MPI_FLOAT, 0, 0,
                   MPI_COMM_WORLD);

               if (my_rank == 0) {
                   for (i = 0; i < p; i++) {
                       MPI_Recv(temp, ARRAY_ORDER, MPI_FLOAT,
                           MPI_ANY_SOURCE, 0, MPI_COMM_WORLD, &status);
                       Mult(product, temp);
                   }
                   Print_matrix("The product is", product);
               }

               MPI_Finalize();
           } /* main */
```

The first time we run the program with three processes, the output is

```
The product is
10.000000 11.000000
20.000000 14.000000
```

However, when we run the program later, the output is

```
The product is
10.000000 10.000000
22.000000 14.000000
```

What's going on? The local matrices are

$$\text{Process 0:} \quad A_0 = \begin{pmatrix} 0 & 1 \\ 2 & 0 \end{pmatrix}$$

$$\text{Process 1:} \quad A_1 = \begin{pmatrix} 1 & 2 \\ 3 & 1 \end{pmatrix}$$

$$\text{Process 2:} \quad A_2 = \begin{pmatrix} 2 & 3 \\ 4 & 2 \end{pmatrix}$$

So one might guess that the product should be

$$A_0 A_1 A_2 = \begin{pmatrix} 10 & 11 \\ 20 & 14 \end{pmatrix}.$$

How did it come up with

$$\begin{pmatrix} 10 & 10 \\ 22 & 14 \end{pmatrix}?$$

You may have guessed that the key is that matrix multiplication is not commutative, and the program is multiplying the matrices in different orders. In fact,

$$A_0 A_2 A_1 = \begin{pmatrix} 10 & 10 \\ 22 & 14 \end{pmatrix},$$

and this is exactly what's happening. The problem is that our calls to MPI_ Recv have source argument MPI_ANY_SOURCE. So the first time we ran the program, process 0 received the matrices in the order A_0, A_1, A_2; during the second run, the matrices were received in the order A_0, A_2, A_1. This situation is sometimes called a **race**: the processes are in a race to get their matrices sent off to process 0. This time the problem is easy to solve—just replace the source argument to MPI_Recv, MPI_ANY_SOURCE, with the loop index i.

Unless we intentionally introduce randomness into a serial program, it will execute exactly the same statements every time we run it on a fixed data set. So how does this nondeterminism occur in parallel programs? There are several possible reasons for this: they generally have to do with "inequalities" among the physical processors and communication links and the order and rate at which processes are started. For example, recall that in distributed-memory systems, there may be no global clock. So the processors may run at different rates. In our example, if, say, process 1 is loaded onto a relatively fast processor during the first execution, and a relatively slow processor during the second, while the situation is reversed for process 2, we shouldn't be surprised that the order in which they complete their setups is reversed, and, as a consequence, the order in which their matrices arrive at process 0 is reversed. On a network of workstations or any parallel system that allows multitasking on the processors, this effect will be exacerbated by the unpredictable fluctuations in the system and network loads.

In our example, nondeterminism is a bug. However, there are many cases where it is a feature. As an example, suppose we try to search a large tree (e.g., a game tree) using a simple "client-server" program. Process 0 is the server: it keeps a store of subtrees that need to be searched. The other processes are the clients: they request subtrees from process 0, which they, in turn, search. As subtrees are searched, new subtrees will be generated, and "surplus" subtrees can be sent back to process 0. When a client completes a search of a subtree, it can request a new subtree from process 0. It is not difficult to see that the subtrees searched by, say, process 1 may vary from execution to execution, even if the main tree is the same and the number of processes is the same. In this case, there is no reason to regard this as a bug: the output of the program (if it's properly coded) should be equally correct regardless of the actual sequence of subtrees examined by a given process.

9.5 An Example

In order to get a better idea of the problems and methods of debugging parallel programs, let's take a look at an extended example. The program is supposed to find the time that it takes to forward messages of different sizes around a ring of processes. For each message size, it will repeatedly forward a message around a ring and compute the average, maximum, and minimum times for the circuit.

The heart of the program is forwarding the message once around the ring: each process receives the message from its predecessor in the ring and then sends it on to its successor. Although, in general, the sequence defined by process ranks in MPI_COMM_WORLD won't correspond to a ring of underlying physical processors, we'll not worry about this in order to simplify the code. It should be easy to use MPI's topology functions to reorder the processes so that they form a one-dimensional ring.

In order to take the actual timings, we use the MPI function

```
double MPI_Wtime()
```

This function returns the "wall clock" time in seconds since some time in the past.

9.5.1   The Program?

Simplicity itself. So here is the *not entirely bug-free* source code.

```
/* comm_time.c
 * Time communication around a ring of processes.
 *     Guaranteed to have bugs.
 *
 * Input: None (see notes).
 *
 * Output:  Average, minimum, and maximum time for messages
 *     of varying sizes to be forwarded around a ring of
 *     processes.
 *
 * Algorithm:
 *     1.  Allocate and initialize storage for messages
 *         and communication times
 *     2.  Compute ranks of neighbors in ring.
 *     3.  For each message size
 *     3a.     For each test
 *     3b.         Start clock
 *     3c.         Send message around loop
 *     3d.         Add elapsed time to running sum
 *     3e.         Update max/min elapsed time
 *     4.  Print times.
 *
 * Functions:
 *     Initialize:  Allocate and initialize arrays
 *     Print_results:  Send results to IO_process
 *         and print.
 *
 * Notes:
 *     1. Due to difficulties some MPI implementations
 *        have with input, the number of tests, the max
 *        message size, the min message size, and the size
 *        increment are hardwired.
 *     2. We assume that the size increment evenly divides
 *        the difference max_size - min_size
 */
#include <stdio.h>
#include "mpi.h"
#include "cio.h"

void Initialize(int max_size, int min_size, int size_incr,
    int my_rank, float** x_ptr, double** times_ptr,
    double** max_times_ptr, double** min_times_ptr,
    int* order_ptr);
```

```
void Print_results(MPI_Comm io_comm, int my_rank,
    int min_size, int max_size, int size_incr,
    int time_array_order, int test_count,
    double* times, double* max_times, double* min_times);

main(int argc, char* argv[]) {
    int         test_count = 1000;  /* Number of tests */
    int         max_size = 10000;   /* Max msg. length */
    int         min_size = 0;       /* Min msg. length */
    int         size_incr = 1000;   /* Increment for   */
                                    /*    msg. sizes   */
    float*      x;                  /* Message buffer  */
    double*     times;              /* Elapsed times   */
    double*     max_times;          /* Max times       */
    double*     min_times;          /* Min times       */
    int         time_array_order;   /* Size of timing  */
                                    /*    arrays.      */
    double      start;              /* Start time      */
    double      elapsed;            /* Elapsed time    */
    int         i, test, size;      /* Loop variables  */
    int         p, my_rank, source, dest;
    MPI_Comm    io_comm;
    MPI_Status  status;

    MPI_Init(&argc, &argv);
    MPI_Comm_size(MPI_COMM_WORLD, &p);
    MPI_Comm_rank(MPI_COMM_WORLD, &my_rank);
    MPI_Comm_dup(MPI_COMM_WORLD, &io_comm);
    Cache_io_rank(MPI_COMM_WORLD, io_comm);

    Initialize(max_size, min_size, size_incr, my_rank,
        &x, &times, &max_times, &min_times,
        &time_array_order);

    source = (my_rank - 1) % p;
    dest = (my_rank + 1) % p;

    /* For each message size, find average circuit time */
    /*      Loop var size = message size                */
    /*      Loop var i = index into arrays for timings   */
    for (size = min_size, i = 0; size <= max_size;
            size = size + size_incr, i++) {
        times[i] = 0.0;
        max_times[i] = 0.0;
        min_times[i] = 1000000.0;
        for (test = 0; test < test_count; test++) {
            start = MPI_Wtime();
            MPI_Recv(x, size, MPI_FLOAT, source, 0,
                MPI_COMM_WORLD, &status);
            MPI_Send(x, size, MPI_FLOAT, dest, 0,
                MPI_COMM_WORLD);
```

```
                elapsed = MPI_Wtime() - start;
                times[i] = times[i] + elapsed;
                if (elapsed > max_times[i])
                    max_times[i] = elapsed;
                if (elapsed < min_times[i])
                    min_times[i] = elapsed;
            }
        } /* for size . . . */

        Print_results(io_comm, my_rank, min_size, max_size,
            size_incr, time_array_order, test_count, times,
            max_times, min_times);

        MPI_Finalize();
    } /* main */


    /*********************************************************/
    void Initialize(int max_size, int min_size, int size_incr,
        int my_rank, float** x_ptr, double** times_ptr,
        double** max_times_ptr, double** min_times_ptr,
        int* order_ptr) {
        int i;

        *x_ptr = (float *) malloc(max_size*sizeof(float));

        *order_ptr = (max_size - min_size)/size_incr;
        *times_ptr =
            (double *) malloc((*order_ptr)*sizeof(double));
        *max_times_ptr =
            (double *) malloc((*order_ptr)*sizeof(double));
        *min_times_ptr =
            (double *) malloc((*order_ptr)*sizeof(double));

        /* Initialize buffer--why this? */
        for (i = 0; i < max_size; i++)
            (*x_ptr)[i] = (float) my_rank;
    } /* Initialize */



    /*********************************************************/
    /* Send results from process 0 in MPI_COMM_WORLD to     */
    /* I/O process in io_comm, which prints the results.     */
    void Print_results(MPI_Comm io_comm, int my_rank,
        int min_size, int max_size, int size_incr,
        int time_array_order, int test_count, double* times,
        double* max_times, double* min_times) {
        int        i;
        int        size;
        MPI_Status status;
```

```
int         io_process;
int         io_rank;

Get_io_rank(io_comm, &io_process);
MPI_Comm_rank(io_comm, &io_rank);

if (my_rank == 0) {
    MPI_Send(times, time_array_order, MPI_DOUBLE,
        io_rank, 0, io_comm);
    MPI_Send(max_times, time_array_order, MPI_DOUBLE,
        io_process, 0, io_comm);
    MPI_Send(min_times, time_array_order, MPI_DOUBLE,
        io_process, 0, io_comm);
}
if (io_rank == io_process) {
    MPI_Recv(times, time_array_order, MPI_DOUBLE,
        MPI_ANY_SOURCE, 0, io_comm, &status);
    MPI_Recv(max_times, time_array_order, MPI_DOUBLE,
        MPI_ANY_SOURCE, 0, io_comm, &status);
    MPI_Recv(min_times, time_array_order, MPI_DOUBLE,
        MPI_ANY_SOURCE, 0, io_comm, &status);

    printf("Message size (floats):  ");
    for (size = min_size;
        size <= max_size; size += size_incr)
        printf("%10d ", size);
    printf("\n");
    printf("Avg circuit time (ms):  ");
    for (i = 0; i < time_array_order; i++)
        printf("%10f ",1000.0*times[i]/test_count);
    printf("\n");
    printf("Max circuit time (ms):  ");
    for (i = 0; i < time_array_order; i++)
        printf("%10f ",1000.0*max_times[i]);
    printf("\n");
    printf("Min circuit time (ms):  ");
    for (i = 0; i < time_array_order; i++)
        printf("%10f ",1000.0*min_times[i]);
    printf("\n\n");
    fflush(stdout);
}
} /* Print_results */
```

Notice that we hardwired the parameters that specify the message sizes and the number of messages. This was done in order to avoid some of the problems associated with I/O on some implementations of MPI.

Also notice that this program is definitely broken. What? You didn't notice? Well, OK. Let's try to debug it.

9.5.2 Debugging The Program

Perhaps the first thing we should be aware of is that the behavior of a buggy program depends strongly on the system on which it's run. As a consequence, when you run the program on your system, the errors that appear may be different from those that occurred when we ran the program. We'll look at several different systems: an nCUBE 2 running the `mpich` implementation of MPI, a network of workstations running `mpich`, and a network of workstations running the LAM implementation of MPI.

In general, it's a good idea to make initial tests relatively small. If the program is broken, but it doesn't crash, it could run for a long time before we even realize there's a problem, and we'll have wasted a lot of time and compute power. With the given "input" data,

```
int          test_count = 1000;  /* Number of tests  */
int          max_size = 10000;   /* Max msg. length  */
int          min_size = 0;       /* Min msg. length  */
int          size_incr = 1000;   /* Increment for    */
                                 /*     msg. sizes   */
```

our program *should* generate 11,000 full circuits before it completes. Let's change this to something minimal.

```
int          test_count = 2;     /* Number of tests  */
int          max_size = 1000;    /* Max msg. length  */
int          min_size = 1000;    /* Min msg. length  */
int          size_incr = 1000;   /* Increment for    */
                                 /*     msg. sizes   */
```

This should only run through two circuits. Of course, this won't test different sizes. So before we're through testing, we will need to run the program with `min_size < max_size`.

Let's compile it and see what happens with just one process .... (What does the program do with just one process? What is a one-process "circuit"?) On the nCUBE and on a network running LAM, it just hangs. On a network running `mpich`, it prints

```
p0_361: Bailing out
```

and quits. (The "p0" indicates process 0, and the "361" is the process id assigned to the UNIX process started by the program.) So there can't be any doubt that the program is broken.

9.5.3 A Brief Discussion of Parallel Debuggers

The failures didn't give us much information about what's wrong. A seemingly simple solution to the problem of finding out where the program is hanging (or crashing) would be to run it under the control of a debugger. (To check where a program is hanging, we can just send an interrupt when the program hangs, and then do a backtrace with the command where.) Unfortunately, the development of debuggers for parallel systems remains an active research subject, and, as a consequence, there isn't much standardization and it's difficult to provide general guidance in their use.

In this case, however, since we are running under a single process, it shouldn't be too difficult to get things going. The first job is to figure out what command the *system* uses to start your job. For example, suppose you're using the LAM implementation on a network of workstations. Then you probably started your job with something like

```
% mpirun -v n0 comm0
```

Here, comm0 is the name of the executable created by the compiler. The obvious thing to do is to start up dbx:

```
% dbx comm0
dbx version 3.19 Nov  3 1994 19:59:46
Executable /usr/people/peter/mpi.test/comm0
(dbx)
```

and then try starting your program

```
(dbx) mpirun -v n0 comm0

"mpirun" is not a valid command name.

Apparent syntax error in examine command. expected / ? ,
(dbx)
```

The problem is that dbx doesn't know about mpirun. So we need to figure out what mpirun does to start the process, then we can try executing this inside dbx. To do this, we can start the program using mpirun and use the ps command to see what is actually being run.

```
% mpirun -np 1 comm0
14554 comm0 running on n0 (o)
% ps -ef
              ⋮
peter 14554 14523  0 14:40:58 ?         0:00 comm0
              ⋮
%
```

We started the program as usual. The command ps -ef generated a list of all processes on the system. The details of this command will be different on other systems—check with your local expert. We've deleted the processes we're not interested in. The important point is that mpirun simply executes the command comm0

So we can just type

(dbx) run

to start our program in dbx. Be careful here: different systems will be substantially different in the details of how this is done; as usual, check with your
local expert.

Let's see what happens when we start the program under the control of
dbx.

```
% dbx comm0
dbx version 3.19 Nov  3 1994 19:59:46
Executable /usr/people/peter/mpi.lam/comm0
(dbx) run
Process 14576 (comm0) started
^C
Interrupt
Process 14576 (comm0) stopped on signal SIGINT:
Interrupt (handler cipc_catastrophe)
[_recvfrom:12 +0x8,0xfad5b44]
Source (of recvfrom.s) not available for Process 14576
(dbx) where
>  0 _recvfrom(0x6, 0x7fffabec, 0x28, 0x0)
["recvfrom.s":12, 0xfad5b44]
    1 _cio_recvfrom(0x6, 0x7fffabec, 0x28, 0x0)
["../../../otb/t/kreq/clientio2.udp.c":391, 0x41897c]
    2 _cio_kreqback(0x6, 0x7fffabec, 0x28, 0x0)
["../../../otb/t/kreq/clientio.udp.c":244, 0x414e7c]
    3 _cipc_ksr(0x7fffac14, 0x7fffabec, 0x28, 0x0)
["../../../otb/t/kreq/couter.c":301, 0x41b0fc]
    4 ksr(0x7fffac9c, 0x7fffabec, 0x28, 0x0)
["../../../../share/kreq/ksr.c":63, 0x41b870]
    5 dsfr(0x6, 0x7fffabec, 0x7fffacf4, 0x0)
["../../../../share/nreq/dsfr.c":67, 0x418f24]
    6 bfrecvsql(0x7fffadc4, 0x7fffabec, 0x28, 0x0)
["../../../../share/nreq/bfrecvsql.c":112, 0x41604c]
    7 dorecv(0x7fffadc4, 0x7fffae1c, 0x28, 0x0)
["../../../share/mpi/lamrecv.c":252, 0x40c950]
    8 __lam_recv_(0x10004cf0, 0x3e8, 0x10002788, 0x0)
["../../../share/mpi/lamrecv.c":160, 0x40c684]
    9 MPI_Recv(0x10004cf0, 0x3e8, 0x10002788, 0x0)
["../../../share/mpi/recv.c":48, 0x406c84]
    10 main(argc = 1, argv = 0x7fffaf24)
["/usr/people/peter/mpi.lam/comm_time0.c":103, 0x404844]
    11 __start() ["crt1text.s":133, 0x40459c]
(dbx)
```

We started the program as planned; when it hung, we interrupted it with Ctrl-C. Then we checked to see where it was by typing where. Most of the output is from functions that are part of the LAM implementation. It doesn't get to our code until the line numbered 10. Evidently the code hung at line 103 in main in the call to MPI_Recv. This is highly suggestive of what the problem is, but before proceeding with our debugging, let's talk a little more about parallel debuggers.

As we have noted in several places, the details of how to start a parallel program under the control of a debugger will vary considerably from system to system. For example, on the same network running the mpich implementation, we would need to create a procgroup file and start the program inside the debugger with

```
(dbx) run -p4pg <procgroup file name>
```

To make matters worse, on some systems it is difficult, or impossible, to start the program from inside the debugger. Under these circumstances, the most common approach is to start the program, get its process number, and then start the debugger, "attaching" it to the running process. A final solution to starting the debugger is to invoke it when the program crashes. This may be done automatically by the system or it may be done by hand after a core dump. In either case, it should be possible to figure out where the program crashed by executing where. Once again, check with your local expert for details on whether these options are available and, if so, how to use them on your system.

Unfortunately, it may be difficult to get all this sorted out, and even if we do, our troubles may be just beginning. On a network of workstations, if we're running multiple processes on distinct hosts, we'll probably want to start a debugger on each host in a separate window. When we do this, we need to worry about such things as how setting a breakpoint or source stepping one command at a time on one host will affect the processes on the other hosts. The situation with parallel machines is somewhat better, but as we noted earlier, there is little standardization. As a consequence, we'll leave it to you, the ever-interested reader, to explore (in your vast amount of leisure time) the debuggers on your system.

9.5.4 The Old Standby: printf/fflush

Rather than developing a solution using debuggers that probably won't work on your system, let's use the old standby for debugging: printf/fflush.

Before going on, we should note that adding I/O statements to a parallel program comes with no guarantees. Indeed, it may cause more problems than it solves. As we'll see, adding I/O statements to a program can introduce new bugs and hide existing bugs. It isn't scalable: it frequently generates unmanageably large amounts of output; if we're using many processes, I/O statements can dramatically reduce performance. Finally, some systems may have serious problems if too many processes are simultaneously trying to print. In spite of all these drawbacks, it is frequently the only method available. So let's proceed—with caution.

We would like the program to keep a record of what it does so that when it hangs or crashes we'll have a pretty clear idea of where things are going wrong. So let's begin by printing out where we are at a few critical points in the program's execution. Let's print out our location and the values of a few variables before the calls to `Initialize`, `MPI_Recv`, and `MPI_Send`. Since some of us may not be able to use `printf/fflush` statements, let's use `Cprintf` statements on all the processes from the minimal I/O library we developed in Chapter 8. We'll put the following calls in the indicated locations in `main`:

```
Cprintf(io_comm,"","Before Initialize, p = %d,
    my_rank = %d", p, my_rank);
         ⋮
Cprintf(io_comm,"","Before MPI_Recv, source = %d,
    my_rank = %d", source, my_rank);
         ⋮
Cprintf(io_comm,"","Before MPI_Send, dest = %d,
    my_rank = %d", dest, my_rank);
```

Now our output looks like this:

```
Process 0 > Before Initialize, p = 1, my_rank = 0

Process 0 > Before MPI_Recv, source = 0, my_rank = 0
```

and, as before, the program hangs or crashes.

9.5.5 The Classical Bugs in Parallel Programs

The fact that the program hangs in a call to `MPI_Recv` is highly suggestive. Since `MPI_Recv` blocks until it finds data that matches its requirements, it seems likely that the program is hanging for one (or both) of the following reasons:

1. **Trying to receive data before sending in an exchange, or trying to receive data when there has been no send.** The problem here is that since `MPI_Recv` blocks, it will wait forever if there is no data to receive. For example, if process *A* and process *B* are trying to exchange data, then the sends must be carried out before the receives. Consider the code

```
if (my_rank == A) {
    MPI_Recv(&x, count1, datatype1, B, tag1, comm,
        &status);
    MPI_Send(&y, count2, datatype2, B, tag2, comm);
} else { /* my_rank == B */
    MPI_Recv(&y, count2, datatype2, A, tag2, comm,
        &status);
    MPI_Send(&x, count1, datatype1, A, tag1, comm);
}
```

It will almost certainly hang: both *A* and *B* may wait forever to receive messages that will never be sent. Note that this problem applies to situations more general than simple exchanges between two processes—e.g., each process in a ring tries to receive a message from its neighbor.

We've encountered this problem in Chapter 5. It is a very simple example of what is commonly called **deadlock.** In general, a deadlocked program is one in which each process is waiting for something that is supposed to occur on some other process. Since all the processes are waiting, the program just hangs.

2. **Incorrect parameters to send/receive.** How the program fails will depend on the system and which parameters are incorrect. For example, in the code

```
if (my_rank == A)
    MPI_Send(&x, count, datatype, B, 1, comm);
else /* my_rank == B */
    MPI_Recv(&x, count, datatype, A, 2, comm,
        &status);
```

process *B* will probably hang, and *A* will continue. However, in the code

```
if (my_rank == A)
    MPI_Send(&x, count, datatype, B, 0, comm);
else /* my_rank == B.  Should receive from A */
    MPI_Recv(&x, count, datatype, C, 0, comm,
        &status);
```

or the code

```
if (my_rank == A) /* Should send to B */
    MPI_Send(&x, count, datatype, C, 0, comm);
else /* my_rank == B */
    MPI_Recv(&x, count, datatype, A, 0, comm,
        &status);
```

the program may hang or crash.

These are the two classical errors in message-passing programs.

It's probably pretty clear which one is causing us problems: process 0 is trying to receive a message that has never been sent. Indeed, it's pretty clear that the program will hang even if there are more processes: they'll all just sit and wait, since the first message is never sent.

9.5.6   First Fix

In order to fix this, we need to get the message started on process 0. So we should rewrite the code so that process 0 is the unique process that first sends the data. Let's try replacing the nested pair of `for` loops with the following code:

```
for (size = min_size, i = 0; size <= max_size;
          size = size + size_incr, i++) {
    if (my_rank == 0) {
        times[i] =0.0;
        max_times[i] = 0.0;
        min_times[i] = 1000000.0;
        for (test = 0; test < test_count; test++) {
            start = MPI_Wtime();
            MPI_Send(x, size, MPI_FLOAT, dest, 0,
                MPI_COMM_WORLD);
            MPI_Recv(x, size, MPI_FLOAT, source, 0,
                MPI_COMM_WORLD, &status);
            elapsed = MPI_Wtime() - start;
            times[i] = times[i] + elapsed;
            if (elapsed > max_times[i])
                max_times[i] = elapsed;
            if (elapsed < min_times[i])
                min_times[i] = elapsed;
        }
    } else { /* my_rank != 0 */
        for (test = 0; test < test_count; test++) {
            MPI_Recv(x, size, MPI_FLOAT, source, 0,
                MPI_COMM_WORLD, &status);
            MPI_Send(x, size, MPI_FLOAT, dest, 0,
                MPI_COMM_WORLD);
        }
    }
} /* for size . . . */
```

We have just rewritten the code so that process 0 starts the circuit by sending and ends the circuit by receiving. The behavior of the other processes is unchanged (except that they no longer take timing data).

Taking the pessimistic (or realistic) view that the program is probably not completely bug free, let's continue to monitor its progress with `Cprintf` statements. Note, however, that it's no longer clear where we should place the

Cprintf statements, since processes are doing essentially different things. We could try matching the Cprintf associated with the send on 0 with Cprintfs associated with receives on the other processes, and vice versa, but this may cause some problems (see below). A less confusing, albeit not so informative, solution is to just put a single Cprintf before the if--then--else branch.

For the time being, let's take the easy way out and just put the following statement before the if:

```
Cprintf(io_comm,"",
    "Before if, my_rank = %d, source = %d, dest = %d",
    my_rank, source, dest);
```

When we run the program with a single process, the behavior is different on different systems. Two systems (nCUBE running mpich, network of workstations running LAM) produce

```
Process 0 > Before Initialize, p = 1, my_rank = 0

Process 0 > Before if, my_rank = 0, source = 0, dest = 0
Message size (floats):          1000
Avg circuit time (ms):
Max circuit time (ms):
Min circuit time (ms):
```

Let's look at the network running mpich later.

9.5.7 Many Parallel Programming Bugs Are Really Serial Programming Bugs

Clearly something is wrong in Print_results. Why is the message size correctly printed, but none of the times? Recall how Print_results works:

1. The process with rank 0 in MPI_COMM_WORLD sends its timing data to the I/O process. (Since we're only using one process, these are, of course, the same process.)

2. The I/O process receives the data and prints it.

It uses four for loops to generate the output. The first loops over the message sizes, while the other three loop over the order of the arrays storing the timing data. Explicitly, the first for is

```
for (size = min_size; size <= max_size;
    size += size_incr)
```

and the others are

```
for (i = 0; i < time_array_order; i++)
```

So we should check to see what value is being stored in `time_array_order`. Since we're only interested in its value on the I/O process, we can just use `printf/fflush` statements instead of `Cprintf`. Let's check its value just before the first `for` that prints out timing data:

```
printf("io_process = %d, time_array_order = %d\n",
    io_process, time_array_order);
fflush(stdout);
```

Now the output is

```
Process 0 > Before Initialize, p = 1, my_rank = 0

Process 0 > Before if, my_rank = 0, source = 0, dest = 0
Message size (floats):          1000
io_process = 0, time_array_order = 0
Avg circuit time (ms):
Max circuit time (ms):
Min circuit time (ms):
```

As we suspected, `time_array_order` is 0. It should be 1—we're checking circuit times for a single message size (1000 floats). There are several possibilities here:

1. Our argument list in the call to `Print_results` may not correspond properly to the function's parameter list.
2. We may have inadvertently modified `time_array_order` at some point in the program.
3. The argument list in the call to `Initialize` may not correspond properly to the function's parameter list.
4. We computed its value incorrectly in `Initialize`.

Notice that none of these possibilities has anything to do with the message passing in our program. The variable `time_array_order` is completely local on each process: it is initialized locally, and it is never sent to another process. In other words, it appears that this error has nothing to do with parallel computing. Rather, it seems that we have just made an error in C programming. This brings up one of the most important points to keep in mind when you're debugging a parallel program:

> *Many (if not most) parallel program bugs have nothing to do with the fact that the program is a parallel program. Many (if not most) parallel program bugs are caused by the same mistakes that cause serial program bugs.*

Enough moralizing (at least for the time being). Let's search through our source code and see if we can find the error .... Sure enough! We've incorrectly calculated `time_array_order` in the first place. Take a look at the initialization in `Initialize`:

```
*order_ptr = (max_size - min_size)/size_incr;
```

Here `order_ptr` is the formal parameter that corresponds to the argument `&time_array_order` in the call to `Initialize`, and since `max_size` and `min_size` have both been initialized to 1000,

$$(\texttt{max\_size} - \texttt{min\_size})/\texttt{size\_incr} = 0.$$

We want `time_array_order` to be 1! So our basic formula is wrong. A little thought and a few example calculations will convince you that the correct formula should be

```
*order_ptr = (max_size - min_size)/size_incr + 1;
```

9.5.8 Different Systems, Different Errors

Before continuing with our debugging, let's take a look at what happens on another system (a network of workstations running `mpich`). When we run the program on this system with the incorrect value for `time_array_order`, the output is

```
Process 0 > Before Initialize, p = 1, my_rank = 0

Process 0 > Before if, my_rank = 0, source = 0, dest = 0
p0_468:  p4_error: interrupt SIGSEGV: 11
```

That is, the program crashed with a segmentation violation. This suggests that we have either failed to allocate storage correctly, or that a subscript has been calculated incorrectly. So this error also points to a possible problem with `time_array_order`: it suggests that we may not have allocated the correct amount of space for the arrays we're using to store the timings. Indeed, this is what happens: when we try to write values to the timing arrays (which have length 0), a segmentation violation results and the system aborts the program.

You may well ask why the program didn't crash when we ran it on the other systems. This brings up a point we've noted before:

> *Different systems respond in different ways if a program contains a bug. In particular, it's entirely possible that a program that has been "fully debugged" on one system will crash on another. The exact behavior of erroneous programs is impossible to predict.*

9.5.9   Moving to Multiple Processes

Let's move on. After fixing the computation of `time_array_order`, the output of the program run with one process is

```
Process 0 > Before Initialize, p = 1, my_rank = 0

Process 0 > Before if, my_rank = 0, source = 0, dest = 0
Message size (floats):            1000
io_process = 0, time_array_order = 1
Avg circuit time (ms):    1.493990
Max circuit time (ms):    1.518011
Min circuit time (ms):    1.469970
```

Of course, the reported times are different on different systems, but the basic structure of the output is the same.

OK! We've got the program to pass our first test. The next step is to try to get it to run with different size messages. Let's change `min_size` to 0. Now it should send two messages containing 0 floats and two messages containing 1000 floats. (What is actually sent in the messages containing 0 floats?) The output is

```
Process 0 > Before Initialize, p = 1, my_rank = 0

Process 0 > Before if, my_rank = 0, source = 0, dest = 0

Process 0 > Before if, my_rank = 0, source = 0, dest = 0
Message size (floats):          0        1000
io_process = 0, time_array_order = 2
Avg circuit time (ms):    0.533491    1.492471
Max circuit time (ms):    0.533998    1.514971
Min circuit time (ms):    0.532985    1.469970
```

and it seems that we've got a program that works with one process.

So we're finally ready to run the program with more than one process. Before doing so, however, let's remove that `printf` statement from `Print_results` that's messing up our output. With this removed, our output with two processes is

```
Process 0 > Before Initialize, p = 2, my_rank = 0
Process 1 > Before Initialize, p = 2, my_rank = 1

Process 0 > Before if, my_rank = 0, source = -1, dest = 1
Process 1 > Before if, my_rank = 1, source = 0, dest = 0

Process 0 > Before if, my_rank = 0, source = -1, dest = 1
Process 1 > Before if, my_rank = 1, source = 0, dest = 0
Message size (floats):          0        1000
```

```
Avg circuit time (ms):    0.384986   0.599504
Max circuit time (ms):    0.500977   0.606954
Min circuit time (ms):    0.268996   0.592053
```

At first glance, it looks OK. However, closer examination reveals an oddity: process 0 is reporting that the source for its receives is process -1! Of course, there's no process -1, and we've miscalculated the source. Recall that the source is calculated using the formula:

```
source = (my_rank - 1) % p
```

This is fine as long as my_rank is greater than 0. However, when my_rank equals 0, the formula produces a negative value.[1] This can be changed easily enough: guarantee that the dividend is positive by adding in p. That is, a formula that will always produce a nonnegative source is

```
source = (my_rank + p - 1) % p
```

Adding in p doesn't change the congruence class, but it does guarantee that the "representative" of the congruence class is positive.

The real question is, Why didn't the program crash with source -1? We accidentally stumbled across a value that matches one of MPI's special possibilities for a source in MPI_Recv. That is, if we examined the include files for MPI, we might find

```
#define MPI_ANY_SOURCE -1
```

or perhaps

```
#define MPI_PROC_NULL -1
```

If the first definition is used, then the program will actually do what it's supposed to do: process 0 will receive data from any process that attempts to send to it. Since process 1 is the only process that's trying to send to it, the program does exactly what it's supposed to do. However, if the second definition is used, then MPI_Recv simply returns as soon as possible without changing the contents of the receive buffer and the timing results for our program are meaningless. (For a discussion of the meaning and use of MPI_PROC_NULL, see section 13.4.)

This brings up an extremely important point:

During testing and debugging, you must make certain that communications are behaving as they should. In some cases, this can be

---

1   The ANSI standard for C is not explicit about this: it only insists that the absolute value of the remainder be less than the absolute value of the divisor.

determined simply by examining the output of the program. In other cases, however, this may involve printing out the arguments passed to and returned from communication functions.

9.5.10 Confusion about I/O

Since the output of the program doesn't tell us whether the communications functions are behaving as we intended, we should examine the contents of the arguments. As we noted earlier, this can cause problems if we use Cprintf: the program could actually hang if we're not careful. If each process can print, then there's no difficulty. But let's look at what happens to the less fortunate. Suppose we want to examine the arguments being passed into MPI_Send and the arguments being returned from MPI_Recv. Then we might insert Cprintfs as indicated.

```
if (my_rank == 0) {
    ⋮
    for (test = 0; test < test_count; test++) {
        start = MPI_Wtime();
/* 1 */ Cprintf(io_comm,"","Before send, x[0] = . . .);
        /* dest = 1 */
        MPI_Send(x, size, MPI_FLOAT, dest, . . .);
        /* source should be p - 1 */
        MPI_Recv(x, size, MPI_FLOAT, source, . . .);
/* 2 */ Cprintf(io_comm,"","After recv, x[0] = . . .);
    ⋮
    } /* for test */
} else { /* my_rank != 0 */
    for (test = 0; test < test_count; test++) {
        MPI_Recv(x, size, MPI_FLOAT, source, . . .);
/* 1 */ Cprintf(io_comm,"","After recv, x[0] = . . .);
/* 2 */ Cprintf(io_comm,"","Before send, x[0] = . . .);
        MPI_Send(x, size, MPI_FLOAT, dest, . . .);
    } /* for test */
}
```

When we run this program with two processes, the output is

```
Process 0 > Before Initialize, p = 2, my_rank = 0
Process 1 > Before Initialize, p = 2, my_rank = 1

Process 0 > Before if, my_rank = 0, source = 1, dest = 1
Process 1 > Before if, my_rank = 1, source = 0, dest = 0

Process 0 > Before send, x[0] = 0.0, size = 0, dest = 1
```

The program hangs! What's happened? Recollect that `Cprintf` prints a message from *every* process in `io_comm`, and the underlying group of `io_comm` is the same as the underlying group of `MPI_COMM_WORLD`. So the `Cprintf`s that are marked with a "1" will be paired, and the `Cprintf`s marked by a "2" will be paired. Thus, since process 0 in `io_comm` is the same as process 0 in `MPI_COMM_WORLD`, it will block in `Cprintf` until it receives data from *every* process in `io_comm`. So it will never get to `MPI_Send`, since it will never receive a message from process 1 inside the call to `Cprintf`. Is this confusing, or what?

We have another form of deadlock: Process 0 is waiting inside `Cprintf` for a message from process 1, but process 1 is waiting in `MPI_Recv` called from `main` for a message from process 0, and process 0 can't get to `MPI_Send` because it's hung in `Cprintf`.

The moral here is that since `Cprintf` is a collective operation, we must be careful about interlacing calls to it with other communication operations, and we should keep in mind:

> *The addition of debugging output can change the behavior of our program.*

One solution in this case is just to make sure that all processes call `Cprintf` before and after each send and each receive. Another is to have each process call `Cprintf` before any sends or receives are started and after all sends and receives (in a single circuit) are completed. We'll opt for the second alternative. Now our code should look something like this:

```
      if (my_rank == 0) {
         ⋮
         for (test = 0; test < test_count; test++) {
            start = MPI_Wtime();
/* 1 */     Cprintf(io_comm,"","Before send, x[0] = . . .);
            /* dest = 1 */
            MPI_Send(x, size, MPI_FLOAT, dest, . . .);
            /* source should be p - 1 */
            MPI_Recv(x, size, MPI_FLOAT, source, . . .);
/* 2 */     Cprintf(io_comm,"","After recv, x[0] = . . .);

            ⋮

         } /* for test */
      } else { /* my_rank != 0 */
         for (test = 0; test < test_count; test++) {
/* 1 */     Cprintf(io_comm,"","Before recv, x[0] = . . .);
            MPI_Recv(x, size, MPI_FLOAT, source, . . .);
            MPI_Send(x, size, MPI_FLOAT, dest, . . .);
/* 2 */     Cprintf(io_comm,"","After send, x[0] = . . .);
         } /* for test */
      }
```

The output is OK. However, as it is fairly long, we'll omit it. Incidentally, it's easy to get flooded by the output of a parallel program. So we should be careful to consider how much output our program will generate before we run it.

If you prefer not to use Cprintf, and you can't use printf, you may want to consider having each process open its own output file. This can be confusing: it may be difficult to get a comprehensive view of what is happening on all the processes at a given instant, but it does avoid the complexities associated with the use of collective operations. See Chapter 8 for a brief discussion of the mechanics of this.

Finally, it should be noted that in addition to the problems associated with collective output operations, the addition of any output statements may change a race condition, and hence change the details of an error.

9.5.11 Finishing Up

In order to complete the debugging, we still need to test the program with

1. large values of test_count
2. a large range of sizes
3. different numbers of processes

In order to do this and not be swamped by output, we can first test the program with different numbers of processes, but use small values for test_count and only a few sizes. Then we can finish up by removing most of the output statements and testing the program on large values of test_count and many different sizes of messages.

When we run the program with different numbers of processes but with small values of test_count and only a few sizes, it seems to be OK. Once again, we'll omit the output of these runs, since it is fairly extensive.

The "production" output of the program running with two processes on an nCUBE 2 and using only three different message sizes was

```
Message size (floats):          0        500       1000
Avg circuit time (ms):   0.355654   2.665530   4.961305
Max circuit time (ms):   0.364006   2.679050   4.966021
Min circuit time (ms):   0.346959   2.651989   4.944980
```

The test_count was 1000.

We're done! That wasn't so painful ... was it?

9.6 Error Handling in MPI

Our last topic is an option built into MPI that can be used to help analyze program bugs.

An **error handler** is basically a function to which control is transferred
when an error condition is detected by a program. Every implementation of
MPI is required to make two error handlers available to the user. The default
error handler, `MPI_ERRORS_ARE_FATAL`, causes programs to abort when errors are detected. The other standard error handler is `MPI_ERRORS_RETURN`.
When an error is detected, this handler returns an error code to the function
that called the MPI function. Implementations are free to define additional
error handlers. For example, the `mpich` implementation has defined the error handlers `MPE_Errors_call_dbx_in_xterm` and `MPE_Signals_call_`
`debugger`. The first will open a window and start `dbx` when an error occurs.
The second will start a debugger if it catches a signal (e.g., `SIGSEGV`).

Error handlers are associated with communicators. In order to associate
a new error handler with a communicator, one can simply call the function
`MPI_Errhandler_set`:

```
int MPI_Errhandler_set(
        MPI_Comm       comm         /* in */,
        MPI_Errhandler errhandler   /* in */)
```

This has the effect of associating the error handler `errhandler` with the communicator `comm` on the calling process. After calling this function, when an
error is detected in an MPI function that is using the communicator `comm`, the
MPI function will use the error handler `errhandler`.

For example, if we want to examine the error codes generated by MPI
functions instead of aborting, we can associate `MPI_ERRORS_RETURN` with
`MPI_COMM_WORLD` by making the following call on all processes:

```
int error_code;
error_code = MPI_Errhandler_set(MPI_COMM_WORLD,
            MPI_ERRORS_RETURN);
```

Now we can examine errors occurring within MPI functions by testing the error
code after calling an MPI function. For example,

```
char error_message[MPI_MAX_ERROR_STRING];
int message_length;

error_code = MPI_Bcast(&x, 1, MPI_INT, 0, comm);
if (error_code != MPI_SUCCESS) {
    MPI_Error_string(error_code, error_message,
        &message_length);
    fprintf(stderr, "Error in call to MPI_Bcast = %s\n",
        error_message);
    fprintf(stderr, "Exiting from function XXX\n");
    MPI_Abort(MPI_COMM_WORLD, -1);
}
```

If, for example, we fail to properly initialize `comm`, then after the call to `MPI_`
`Bcast` each process will print something like

```
Error in call to MPI_Bcast = Invalid communicator
Exiting from function XXX
```

and the program will abort.

MPI_SUCCESS and MPI_MAX_ERROR_STRING are predefined constants in MPI. In order to be consistent with C usage, MPI_SUCCESS is always 0. MPI_MAX_ERROR_STRING is defined by the implementation. The function MPI_Error_String returns the error message (and the length of the error message) associated with the value in error_code. Both the code and the message are implementation dependent. The second parameter of MPI_Abort is an error code that is returned to the program that started the MPI program (e.g., the shell). It is a good idea to abort after a call that returns an error code: MPI makes no guarantees that it will recover correctly. So it's up to us to clean things up before we try to proceed.

Of course, this code won't work if you can't print from every process. See Chapter 8 for a partial solution.

Error handlers are inherited by newly created communicators. Thus, if the preceding call to MPI_Errhandler_set were placed immediately after the call to MPI_Init, and there were no subsequent calls to MPI_Errhandler_set, then all of the MPI functions would return error codes. Note that since error handlers are associated with communicators, it's entirely possible to have multiple different error handlers simultaneously active in a program. Also note that since the association of error handlers is local, it's possible to have different handlers associated to the same communicator on different processes.

MPI does provide facilities for users to write their own error handlers. See the references for pointers to discussions of this.

Finally, we note that we can use MPI's profiling interface to have our programs generate traces. We'll discuss the profiling interface in section 12.6.1.

9.7 Summary

The most important observation in this chapter has to do with design and development: a carefully designed and developed program should require minimal debugging. This point cannot be overstressed. If, however, our program does contain errors, we discussed some methods for debugging. Typically, the debugging process for both serial and parallel programs is cyclic: The program is run; when an error is detected, one of several methods is used for identifying the cause of the error. After the error is corrected, the process is repeated until no further errors are found. Not surprisingly, debugging parallel programs tends to be much more complex than debugging serial programs. In addition to the complexity added by communication, parallel programs can exhibit nondeterminism because of race conditions in which processes effectively compete against each other to complete tasks. Nondeterminism may not be a bug: it is perfectly natural for some programs to be designed so that faster processes complete more work than slower processes.

The cyclic process on serial programs typically progresses from simple data sets to more complex data sets. That is, after bugs have been eliminated from the program when it is run on the simplest possible input, progressively more complex data is used to exercise all aspects of the program. With parallel programs, this cyclic process should be repeated with varying numbers of processes: first the program is fully debugged with just one process; then the program is debugged with two processes; etc.

We discussed the three most commonly used methods for identifying bugs:

1. Examine the source code.
2. Add debugging output to the source code.
3. Use a symbolic debugger.

All three methods are applicable to both serial and parallel programs. Simply examining the source code is most useful when the program is fairly small and the errors suggest the nature of the problem.

The use of debugging output is the mainstay of both serial and parallel debugging: it is typically used to provide snapshots of the state of the program at various points during execution. When we're debugging parallel programs, the introduction of output statements can change the behavior of the program. Collective output operations (such as Cprintf) can cause deadlock if they are interlaced with other communication operations. Any output statements may change race conditions, and hence the apparent nature of bugs. If all processes don't have access to stdout or stderr, then you may want to consider writing the output of each process to a separate file rather than using a collective output function.

Debuggers can be used to start a program, stop execution of a program at various points, examine the state of a program during execution, and make changes to a program. The development of parallel debuggers remains an active area of research, and, as a consequence, there is little standardization. Currently, the only universally available debuggers are just serial debuggers attached to the various processes of a parallel execution. Starting a debugger for a parallel program is highly system dependent. It may be necessary to start the program and then attach a debugger to the processes started by the program. If the debugger is just a serial debugger, it can be very difficult to monitor and control the execution of a program running multiple processes.

Much of the chapter was devoted to warnings of pitfalls, examples of common bugs, and sage advice:

- Be aware that the manifestation of a bug can change from system to system. Indeed, an apparently bug-free program may crash ignominiously when it is run on a new system.
- The classical bugs in message-passing programs are

—A receive that has no matching send will usually cause the receiving process to hang. If all processes are trying to receive and there is no send, the program will deadlock. A deadlock occurs when each process is waiting on another process.

—A receive or a send with an incorrect argument will usually cause a process to hang or crash.

- Don't be misled into thinking that all your bugs are the result of the fact that the program is parallel. Many, if not most, parallel program bugs are really just serial program bugs.

- Be very careful to check the arguments being passed in and out of communication functions: it can be very dangerous to make assumptions about what is sent or received in a communication.

- It's easy when debugging parallel programs to get flooded by output. Be careful to take into consideration that all your output will typically be multiplied by the number of processes.

We didn't learn a lot of new MPI functions. All the new MPI functions that we studied had to do with MPI's error handling facilities. An error handler is basically a function that is called when an error condition arises. In MPI, error handlers are local to a process and associated with communicators. All implementations of MPI have two error handlers: MPI_ERRORS_ARE_FATAL, the default error handler, and MPI_ERRORS_RETURN, which can be used to get MPI functions to return error codes if they detect errors. In order to associate an error handler with a communicator, we can use the local function

```
int MPI_Errhandler_set(
        MPI_Comm        comm        /* in */,
        MPI_Errhandler  errhandler  /* in */)
```

In order to find out what an error code means, we can obtain a string by calling

```
int MPI_Error_string(
        int     error_code     /* in  */,
        char*   error_message  /* out */,
        int*    message_length /* out */)
```

Except for the predefined constant MPI_SUCCESS, which is always 0, error codes are implementation dependent. The amount of storage needed for an error string is also implementation dependent. However, it will always be less than MPI_MAX_ERROR_STRING. When we use an error handler that does not automatically abort a program, we must be very careful about continuing execution. It is usually a good idea to just print a message and then abort the program whenever MPI detects an error in one of its functions. Recollect that we can abort a program with the function MPI_Abort.

9.8 References

The quotation from the gdb man page can be found in [36]. For an excellent source of information on debugging and testing serial programs, see [35].

See [21], [29], and [34] for discussions of user-defined error handlers.

Both mpich and LAM provide more powerful debugging facilities than we've outlined here. Consult the mpich user's guide [20] or the LAM MPI primer [30] for further information.

9.9 Exercises

1. Fully debug the serial insertion sort program.

2. Modify comm_time.c so that it uses a communicator with a one-dimensional ring topology for its message passing.

3. Although we didn't worry about it in our example, the calls to MPI_Wtime may add a significant overhead to the elapsed time. Modify comm_time.c so that this overhead is subtracted from elapsed time. How does this affect the results of your timings?

9.10 Programming Assignments

1. Write a function that will print out a matrix that uses a block-checkerboard distribution. Assume that the process grid is square and that $\sqrt{p}$ evenly divides n. The output should present a unified picture of the matrix; it shouldn't simply list the blocks from each process.

2. Write a matrix-vector multiplication program that uses a block-checkerboard distribution of the matrix and a block distribution of the vectors along the *processes* on the diagonal. Assume that the processes form a square virtual grid. Use the output function you wrote in programming assignment 1.

3. Take a look at the programming assignments in the previous chapters. Now's a good time to go back and try to write the ones that looked too formidable before.

CHAPTER 10

Design and Coding of Parallel Programs

Now that we have mastered the basics of parallel programming in MPI, it's time to consider the problem of program design and coding.

There are essentially two approaches to designing parallel programs:

1. **The data-parallel approach.** In this approach we partition the data among the processes, and each process executes more or less the same set of commands on its data.

2. **The control-parallel approach.** In this approach we partition the tasks we wish to carry out among the processes, and each process executes commands that are essentially different from some or all of the other processes.

It should be noted that most parallel programs involve both approaches. However, data-parallel programming is more common and it is generally much easier to do. Perhaps most importantly, data-parallel programs tend to **scale** well: loosely, this means that they can be used to solve larger and larger problems with more and more processes.

All of the programs in this text use a mix of both methods, but data parallelism tends to predominate, and, as a consequence, we'll devote most of our attention to the design of data-parallel programs.

10.1 Data-Parallel Programs

We have already seen an example of a data-parallel program: the trapezoidal rule program. In it, the input data is the interval $[a, b]$, which is partitioned equally among the processes, and each process estimates the integral over its subinterval. If we ignore the I/O and estimate the entire integral by using MPI_Allreduce rather than MPI_Reduce, we see that the program is perfectly data parallel: each process executes exactly the same statements on its data.

So how do we design a data-parallel program? Generally, we start by examining serial solutions to the problem. Then we try partitioning the data in various ways among the processes. If the solution can be obtained by simply running the serial algorithm on each subset of the data, we have the simplest possible candidate for a data-parallel solution. This is exactly what happened with the trapezoidal rule. In general, of course, this won't happen—we'll have to write some code for communicating among the processes.

Also note that ideally the program should be designed to run with arbitrarily many input values and arbitrarily many processes. However, in practice, we usually make some simplifying assumptions. For example, in our dot product function, we made the simplifying assumption that n, the order of the vectors, was evenly divisible by p, the number of processes. If the simplifying assumptions are too restrictive, the program should be designed so that it is fairly straightforward to modify it later. In the dot product example, we might replace the parameter n_bar ($= n/p$) by the number of components assigned to the process.

10.2 Jacobi's Method

As a simple example, let's write a program for solving a system of linear equations using Jacobi's method. So suppose $A\mathbf{x} = \mathbf{b}$ is a system of linear equations where $A = (a_{ij})$ is a nonsingular $n \times n$ matrix, $\mathbf{x} = (x_0, x_1, \ldots, x_{n-1})^T$, and $\mathbf{b} = (b_0, b_1, \ldots, b_{n-1})^T$. Recollect that Jacobi's method is an iterative method; that is, after making an initial guess, $\mathbf{x}^0$, to a solution, the method generates a sequence of approximations $\mathbf{x}^k$, $k = 1, 2, 3, \ldots$, to the solution $\bar{\mathbf{x}}$. The ith component, $x_i^{(k+1)}$ of the $(k+1)$st iterate, $\mathbf{x}^{k+1}$, is computed using the ith row of the system:

$$a_{i0}x_0 + a_{i1}x_1 + \cdots + a_{ii}x_i + \cdots + a_{i,n-1}x_{n-1} = b_i.$$

If we solve this equation for x_i and substitute $x_i^{(k+1)}$ for x_i and $x_j^{(k)}$ for $x_j, j \neq i$, we obtain the iteration formula

$$x_i^{(k+1)} = \frac{1}{a_{ii}}\left(b_i - \sum_{j \neq i} a_{ij}x_j^{(k)}\right).$$

In general, this iteration may not converge. However, if the system is **strictly diagonally dominant**, it will. That is, if for $i = 0, 1, \ldots, n-1$, we have

$$|a_{ii}| > \sum_{j \neq i} |a_{ij}|,$$

then Jacobi's method will converge.

In order to terminate the iteration, we can compute the size of the difference between successive estimates,

$$\|\mathbf{x}^{k+1} - \mathbf{x}^k\|,$$

and when this becomes less than some predefined tolerance, the iteration terminates. Since the iteration may not converge, we should also keep track of the number of iterations, and terminate if there is no convergence after some maximum number of iterations.

Given these considerations, we can write a serial version of Jacobi's method.

```
/* Return 1 if iteration converged, 0 otherwise */
/* MATRIX_T is just a 2-dimensional array       */
int Jacobi(
        MATRIX_T  A          /* in  */,
        float     x[]        /* out */,
        float     b[]        /* in  */,
        int       n          /* in  */,
        float     tol        /* in  */,
        int       max_iter   /* in  */) {
    int   i, j;
    int   iter_num;
    float x_old[MAX_DIM];

    float Distance(float x[], float y[], int n);

    /* Initialize x */
    for (i = 0; i < n; i++)
        x[i] = b[i];

    iter_num = 0;
    do {
        iter_num++;

        for (i = 0; i < n; i++)
            x_old[i] = x[i];

        for (i = 0; i < n; i++){
            x[i] = b[i];
            for (j = 0; j < i; j++)
                x[i] = x[i] - A[i][j]*x_old[j];
```

```
            for (j = i+1; j < n; j++)
                x[i] = x[i] - A[i][j]*x_old[j];
            x[i] = x[i]/A[i][i];
        }
    } while ((iter_num < max_iter) &&
            (Distance(x,x_old,n) >= tol));

    if (Distance(x,x_old,n) < tol)
        return 1;
    else
        return 0;
} /* Jacobi */

float Distance(float x[], float y[], int n) {
    int   i;
    float sum = 0.0;

    for (i = 0; i < n; i++) {
        sum = sum + (x[i] - y[i])*(x[i] - y[i]);
    }
    return sqrt(sum);
} /* Distance */
```

10.3   Parallel Jacobi's Method

If there are p processes, and we make the assumption that $n \geq p$, a natural approach to parallelizing Jacobi is to have each process calculate the entries in a subvector of the solution vector **x**. In order to do this, we begin by considering how to distribute the data among the processes. In other words, how should A, n, b, tol, max_iter, x, and x_old be distributed? As a rule of thumb, we can give each process a copy of all the scalar variables—since the amount of memory used by scalars is generally negligible. In our case, these are n, tol, and max_iter. So after process 0 reads these values, it should broadcast them to all the processes.

There are two obvious possibilities for the vectors x, b, and x_old. They can be partitioned into subvectors of more or less the same size and each process can be assigned a distinct subvector, or each process can be assigned an entire copy of the vector. In order to decide, let's look at our initial idea for parallelizing. The heart of the algorithm is

```
Process q:  Calculate the entries in x that are
    assigned to q.
```

In order to do this we need to calculate

```
Process q:
    for each subscript i assigned to q {
```

Table 10.1   Block partitioning of **x**

Process	Components
0	$x_0, x_1, \ldots, x_{\bar{n}-1}$
1	$x_{\bar{n}}, x_{\bar{n}+1}, \ldots, x_{2\bar{n}-1}$
$\vdots$	$\vdots$
q	$x_{q\bar{n}}, x_{q\bar{n}+1}, \ldots, x_{(q+1)\bar{n}-1}$
$\vdots$	$\vdots$
$p-1$	$x_{(p-1)\bar{n}}, x_{(p-1)\bar{n}+1}, \ldots, x_{n-1}$

```
    x[i] = b[i];
    for (j = 0; j < i; j++)
        x[i] =   x[i] - A[i][j]*x_old[j];
    for (j = i+1; j < n; j++)
        x[i] =   x[i] - A[i][j]*x_old[j];
    x[i] = x[i]/A[i][i];
}
```

So in order to carry out the basic calculations, each process needs a *complete* copy of x_old, but only its own entries in x and b.

This calculation also suggests a partitioning of A: each process is assigned the rows of A corresponding to its entries in x and b.

Note that there is considerable ambiguity in the notation x[i]. In the first place, x is to be distributed among the processes. So the variable we called x in the preceding pseudocode is not the same as the variable x in our serial implementation of Jacobi's method. For example, the first x will, in general, reference a smaller block of memory than the second. There is further ambiguity in the use of the subscript i. The implication in the pseudocode is that i is a *global* subscript. That is, the variable i in the pseudocode is the same as the variable i in the serial implementation. This is also not, in general, the case, since array subscripts in C must begin at 0. It is easy enough to remedy the first problem: simply append the string "_local" to arrays that have been distributed. The second problem, however, is not so easily remedied, and it is up to us, the programmers, to make sure that we keep track of the meaning of subscripts.

The only remaining issue is which entries of x (and hence entries of b and rows of A) should be assigned to each process. If there are p processes, in order to balance the computational load, we would like to assign approximately n/p entries to each process. So in order to simplify the assignment, let's assume that p evenly divides n. With this assumption, there are two obvious approaches to partitioning x: a block partitioning and a cyclic partitioning. We've already encountered both. Recall that if $\bar{n} = n/p$, the block partitioning is defined as in Table 10.1. In the cyclic partitioning, each process is assigned the components whose subscripts are equivalent to its rank mod q. That is,

Table 10.2	Cyclic partitioning of **x**

Process	Components
0	$x_0, x_p, x_{2p}, \ldots, x_{(\bar{n}-1)p}$
1	$x_1, x_{p+1}, x_{2p+1}, \ldots, x_{(\bar{n}-1)p+1}$
$\vdots$	$\vdots$
q	$x_q, x_{p+q}, x_{2p+q}, \ldots, x_{(\bar{n}-1)p+q}$
$\vdots$	$\vdots$
p-1	$x_{p-1}, x_{2p-1}, x_{3p-1}, \ldots, x_{n-1}$

assign x_i to process q if $q \equiv i \bmod q$. Thus, if we use the cyclic partitioning, we'll make the assignments shown in Table 10.2.

Is there any reason to prefer one partitioning scheme to the other? For example, if you think about the parallel dot product, you can see that the cyclic partition would work just as well as the block. Indeed, the function we wrote in Chapter 5 can be used without any modification with a cyclic partition of the vectors. Is the same thing true for the parallel Jacobi? Let's look more closely at the solution.

```
Process q:
    Assign entries of b_local to x_local;

    iter_num = 0;
    do {
        iter_num++;
        Copy entries of x_local from each process
            to x_old;

        Calculate entries of x_local;

    } while ((iter_num < max_iter) &&
            (Distance(x_global, x_old, n) >= tol));
```

The only parts of the algorithm that we haven't already looked at are

```
Copy entries of x_local from each process
    to x_old
```

and the calculation of Distance. Since the distance between two vectors **x** and **y** is just

$$\sqrt{(\mathbf{x} - \mathbf{y}) \cdot (\mathbf{x} - \mathbf{y})}$$

(i.e., a dot product), there's no advantage to using one partitioning scheme over the other in the calculation of Distance.

In order to carry out the calculation

```
Copy entries of x_local from each process
    to x_old
```

we want to execute something like the following:

```
Copy x_local to temp;
for (root = 0; root < p; root++) {
    MPI_Bcast(temp, n_bar, MPI_FLOAT, root,
        MPI_COMM_WORLD);
    Copy temp into appropriate locations in x_old;
}
```

If we have used a block partitioning of *x*, this has the same overall effect as a single call to the MPI collective communication function, MPI_Allgather:

```
MPI_Allgather(x_local, n_bar, MPI_FLOAT, x_old,
    n_bar, MPI_FLOAT, MPI_COMM_WORLD)
```

That is, each process's array x_local is sent to every other process, and the received arrays are copied in process rank order into x_old. Clearly we would prefer to use this single command, since it can be optimized for the particular system we're using. In order to use it with the block mapping, we can simply call it with the arguments indicated above, since the subvectors are simply concatenated in process rank order. However, in order to use it with the cyclic mapping, we must "interleave" the entries received from the different processes, and, in order to do this, we must build a derived datatype. Thus, it is somewhat simpler to use the block mapping, and since we have no other reason to prefer one mapping to the other, let's use the block mapping.

Now we're ready to write a parallel Jacobi routine.

```
#define Swap(x,y) {float* temp; temp = x; \
                   x = y; y = temp;}

/* Return 1 if iteration converged, 0 otherwise */
/* MATRIX_T is a 2-dimensional array            */
int Parallel_jacobi(
        MATRIX_T  A_local     /* in  */,
        float     x_local[]   /* out */,
        float     b_local[]   /* in  */,
        int       n           /* in  */,
        float     tol         /* in  */,
        int       max_iter    /* in  */,
        int       p           /* in  */,
        int       my_rank     /* in  */) {
    int    i_local, i_global, j;
    int    n_bar;
    int    iter_num;
    float  x_temp1[MAX_DIM];
```

```
        float    x_temp2[MAX_DIM];
        float*   x_old;
        float*   x_new;

        float Distance(float x[], float y[], int n);

        n_bar = n/p;

        /* Initialize x */
        MPI_Allgather(b_local, n_bar, MPI_FLOAT, x_temp1,
            n_bar, MPI_FLOAT, MPI_COMM_WORLD);
        x_new = x_temp1;
        x_old = x_temp2;

        iter_num = 0;
        do {
            iter_num++;

            /* Interchange x_old and x_new */
            Swap(x_old, x_new);
            for (i_local = 0; i_local < n_bar; i_local++){
                i_global = i_local + my_rank*n_bar;
                x_local[i_local] = b_local[i_local];
                for (j = 0; j < i_global; j++)
                    x_local[i_local] = x_local[i_local] -
                        A_local[i_local][j]*x_old[j];
                for (j = i_global+1; j < n; j++)
                    x_local[i_local] = x_local[i_local] -
                        A_local[i_local][j]*x_old[j];
                x_local[i_local] = x_local[i_local]/
                        A_local[i_local][i_global];
            }

            MPI_Allgather(x_local, n_bar, MPI_FLOAT, x_new,
                n_bar, MPI_FLOAT, MPI_COMM_WORLD);
        } while ((iter_num < max_iter) &&
                (Distance(x_new,x_old,n) >= tol));

        if (Distance(x_new,x_old,n) < tol)
            return 1;
        else
            return 0;
}  /* Jacobi */


float Distance(float x[], float y[], int n) {
    int i;
    float sum = 0.0;
```

```
    for (i = 0; i < n; i++) {
        sum = sum + (x[i] - y[i])*(x[i] - y[i]);
    }
    return sqrt(sum);
} /* Distance */
```

Note that we used storage for an extra temporary vector—x_new. We did this so that each pass through the main loop involved only one communcation—the call to MPI_Allgather. If we wanted to avoid using additional storage, we could have gathered into x_old at the beginning of the loop, and used a call to MPI_Allreduce in Distance. That is, the main loop would look like

```
do {
    MPI_Allgather(x_local, . . . , x_old, . . .);
    Calculate new entries in x_local;
} while ((iter_num < max_iter) &&
        (Distance(x_local,x_old,n) >= tol));
```

and the Distance function would first compute the dot product

```
for (i_local = 0; i_local < n_bar; i++) {
    i_global = i_local + my_rank*n_bar;
    sum += (x[i] - y[i_global])*(x[i] - y[i_global]);
}
```

and then call

```
MPI_Allreduce(&sum, . . . );
```

10.4 Coding Parallel Programs

The mechanics of actually coding a parallel program are much the same as they are for coding a serial program. Before any code is written, we decide on the basic outline of the program and identify the main data structures.

When we actually begin to code, we can either proceed "top down" or "bottom up." Generally, a mix of the two approaches is useful: most of the code can be developed top-down. However, as soon as data structures are (provisionally) determined, it is essential that we write I/O routines and basic access functions (or macros) for the structures.

Thus you typically begin by defining the data structures with "dummy" type definitions—e.g., typedef int MAIN_TYPE. Write functions and/or macros for accessing the data in the structures. By doing this, you only need to modify localized pieces of code when you decide that you need to change your data structures. Write real, working code for the main program, defining subprograms with stubs—e.g., void Sub_program(int param1, int param2){}. When the main program is done, begin defining the subprograms. The definition of the actual data structures should be deferred for as long as possible. The basic rule of thumb is, If it looks hard, procrastinate. If a piece of code seems complicated, defer writing it by assigning it to a subprogram.

As subprograms are completed, the code should be tested. As with serial programs, this involves two phases. First test the subprogram in a **driver**—a complete program whose sole function is to call the subprogram. If it's at all possible, make your driver a serial program. Even if the function being tested involves communication, the driver program can be initially run on a single process.

After testing the subprogram in the driver, test it in the evolving program. For this it will be necessary to add informative output statements to the program skeleton so that you can verify that control is flowing as planned. As we noted in Chapter 8, this can be a problem on some systems. So you may want to use the functions we wrote for output.

Since typical parallel programs are designed to run with varying numbers of processes, at each stage you should test your code on varying numbers of processes. Typically, if your program won't run with just one process, it has no hope of success with two. Of course, even if it runs correctly with one, it may fail with two, etc.

Since I/O tends to be one of the most troublesome aspects of parallel programming, it may be useful to first code a program with hardwired input. That is, rather than write a complete input function, it may be easier to simply assign values to the variables inside the program. For example, if we wish to read in a distributed array of floats, we might first write the following function.

```
void Read_array(float x_local[], int local_order) {
    int i;

    /* Defer writing the code to actually read in the
     * data. */
    for (i = 0; i < local_order; i++)
        x_local[i] = (float) i;
} /* Read_array */
```

Alternatively, you can use the self-initializing code discussed in Chapter 8.

10.5 An Example: Sorting

As an example of parallel program development, let's write a program that sorts a list of keys (e.g., numbers or words) into process-increasing order. That is, the keys on process q are sorted into increasing order, and all the keys on q are greater than all the keys on $q - 1$ and less than all the keys on $q + 1$. If you prefer, you can imagine that we have a linear array distributed in block fashion across the processes, and we want to sort the elements of the array in increasing order.

Perhaps surprisingly, general sorting on parallel processors is a difficult problem and remains an active area of research. So in order to simplify the problem, we'll assume that we know the distribution of the entire set of keys. That is, we know the probability that a randomly selected key falls into a given range of keys. Knowing the distribution, we can determine which process should be assigned which keys. For example, suppose we have integer keys distributed among four processes, and we know that the keys are *uniformly* distributed in the range 1–100. Then process 0 should receive keys in the range 1–25, process 1 should receive keys in the range 26–50, etc.

With this assumption, it's easy to devise an algorithm:

```
Get local keys.
Use distribution to determine which
    process should get each key.
Send keys to appropriate processes.  Receive
    keys from processes.
Sort local keys.
Print results.
```

We still haven't specified the type, the distribution, and the source of the keys. So let's suppose that the keys are nonnegative integers and that they're uniformly distributed. Since, as usual, I/O is a problem, we'll just generate the keys on the processes, and the input to the program will just be the total number of keys. In order to generate the keys, we can use the C function `rand`. The actual range of values generated by `rand` varies from system to system. However, most allow at least the range 0–32,767, so let's use this as the range of our keys.

10.5.1 Main Program

We know we'll be needing storage for the keys on each process, so let's make a dummy type definition.

```
typedef int LOCAL_LIST_T;
```

In the interests of making the program easier to modify, we can also define a type for the keys:

```
typedef int KEY_T;
```

After adding an input function, we can just convert our basic algorithm into a sequence of function calls.

```
/* First Level Program */
#include <stdio.h>
#include <string.h>
#include "mpi.h"
#include "cio.h"
#include "sort.h"

int       p;
int       my_rank;
MPI_Comm  io_comm;

main(int argc, char* argv[]) {
    LOCAL_LIST_T  local_keys;
    int           list_size;
    int           error;

    MPI_Init(&argc, &argv);
    MPI_Comm_size(MPI_COMM_WORLD, &p);
    MPI_Comm_rank(MPI_COMM_WORLD, &my_rank);
    MPI_Comm_dup(MPI_COMM_WORLD, &io_comm);
    Cache_io_rank(MPI_COMM_WORLD, io_comm);

    list_size = Get_list_size();

    /* Return negative if Allocate failed */
    error = Allocate_list(list_size, &local_keys);

    Get_local_keys(&local_keys);
    Print_list(&local_keys);
    Redistribute_keys(&local_keys);
    Local_sort(&local_keys);
    Print_list(&local_keys);

    MPI_Finalize();
} /* main */

int Get_list_size(void) {
    Cprintf(io_comm, "", "%s", "In Get_list_size");
    return 0;
} /* Get_list_size */

/* Return value negative indicates failure */
int Allocate_list(int list_size,
    LOCAL_LIST_T* local_keys) {

    Cprintf(io_comm, "", "%s", "In Allocate_key_list");
    return 0;
} /* Allocate_list */
```

```
void Get_local_keys(LOCAL_LIST_T* local_keys) {
    Cprintf(io_comm, "", "%s", "In Get_local_keys");
} /* Get_local_keys */

void Redistribute_keys(LOCAL_LIST_T* local_keys) {
    Cprintf(io_comm, "", "%s", "In Redistribute_keys");
} /* Redistribute_keys */

void Local_sort(LOCAL_LIST_T* local_keys) {
    Cprintf(io_comm, "", "%s", "In Local_sort");
} /* Local_sort */

void Print_list(LOCAL_LIST_T* local_keys) {
    Cprintf(io_comm, "", "%s", "In Print_list");
} /* Print_list */
```

Notice that we're using a header file sort.h. This is especially convenient when the various definitions haven't been finalized—it gives us a fixed single location for changing typedefs and function prototypes as they evolve. (Unfortunately, we still need to change the actual function calls.)

```
/* sort.h */
#ifndef SORT_H
#define SORT_H

#define KEY_MIN 0
#define KEY_MAX 32767
#define KEY_MOD 32768

typedef int KEY_T;
typedef int LOCAL_LIST_T;

#define List_size(list) (0)
#define List_allocated_size(list) (0)

int Get_list_size(void);
int Allocate_list(int list_size,
    LOCAL_LIST_T* local_keys);
void Get_local_keys(LOCAL_LIST_T* local_keys);
void Redistribute_keys(LOCAL_LIST_T* local_keys);
void Local_sort(LOCAL_LIST_T* local_keys) ;
void Print_list(LOCAL_LIST_T* local_keys) ;
#endif
```

Also notice that we always pass local_keys by reference—in spite of the fact that not every function will modify it. The reason for this is that we expect this data structure to be large, and we don't want to waste time and space copying it when we call a function. Further, we expect the list data structure to contain information on the number of keys stored and the space allocated, so we've written two dummy macros for accessing this information.

Since the program is so simple, the only real purpose in testing at this point is to look for typos. If we do compile it and run it with one process, the output is

```
Process 0 > In Get_list_size

Process 0 > In Allocate_key_list

Process 0 > In Get_local_keys

Process 0 > In Print_list

Process 0 > In Redistribute_keys

Process 0 > In Local_sort

Process 0 > In Print_list
```

If we run it with two processes, the output is

```
Process 0 > In Get_list_size
Process 1 > In Get_list_size

Process 0 > In Allocate_key_list
Process 1 > In Allocate_key_list

Process 0 > In Get_local_keys
Process 1 > In Get_local_keys

Process 0 > In Print_list
Process 1 > In Print_list

Process 0 > In Redistribute_keys
Process 1 > In Redistribute_keys

Process 0 > In Local_sort
Process 1 > In Local_sort

Process 0 > In Print_list
Process 1 > In Print_list
```

10.5.2 The "Input" Functions

OK. Now it's just a matter of filling in the subprograms.

Since input can be a major problem, we'll first write our program with hardwired input. During the initial testing, we're probably going to want to look at the actual contents of the list, so we don't want to be printing thousands of keys. So let's assume that we'll have five keys per process when we begin. That is, Get_list_size should return 5*p*.

```
int Get_list_size(void) {
    Cprintf(io_comm, "", "%s", "In Get_list_size");
    return 5*p;
} /* Get_list_size */
```

We can't actually allocate the list yet, since we haven't decided on the actual structure, but we do want members of the structure to record the number of keys and the space allocated. So we can provisionally define a struct with three members, one of which is a dummy:

```
/* Goes in sort.h */
typedef struct {
    int allocated_size;
    int local_list_size;
    int keys;  /* dummy member */
} LOCAL_LIST_T;

/* Assume list is a pointer to a struct of type
 * LOCAL_LIST_T */
#define List_size(list) ((list)->local_list_size)
#define List_allocated_size(list) ((list)->allocated_size)
```

With these definitions, we can update Allocate_list.

```
 /* Returns negative value if malloc fails.  */
int Allocate_list(
        int           list_size /* in  */,
        LOCAL_LIST_T* local_keys /* out */) {

    List_allocated_size(local_keys) = list_size/p;
    List_size(local_keys) = list_size/p;
    return 0;
} /* Allocate_list */
```

In order to get the keys, we can use the C functions srand and rand. The first function seeds the random number generator. We can use it to make sure that each process gets a different set of keys by seeding each process's random number generator with its rank. The second function, rand, actually generates the keys. Of course, we need to create storage for the list of keys. But this would imply that we know the data structure LOCAL_LIST_T. So we'll avoid this issue by putting the key list accesses into functions, which, for the time being, will be stubs.

```
/* Use random number generator to generate keys */
void Get_local_keys(LOCAL_LIST_T* local_keys) {
    int i;

    /* Seed the generator */
    srand(my_rank);

    for (i = 0; i < List_size(local_keys);  i++)
        Insert_key(rand() % KEY_MOD, i, local_keys);
} /* Get_local_keys */
```

Notice that we are assuming that list_size is evenly divisible by the number of processes.

The stub for Insert_key:

```
void Insert_key(KEY_T key, int i,
    LOCAL_LIST_T* local_keys) {
} /* Insert_key */
```

We omit the call to Cprintf because Insert_key will be called five times by each process and we don't want to be overwhelmed by the output.

10.5.3 All-to-all Scatter/Gather

The heart of the redistribution of the keys is each process's sending of its original local keys to the appropriate process. This is an example of an **all-to-all scatter/gather,** also called a **total exchange.** This is a collective communication operation in which each process sends a distinct collection of data to every other process. Recall that a scatter is a collective communication in which a fixed root process sends a distinct collection of data to every other process, and a gather is a collective communication in which a root process receives data from every other process. Thus an all-to-all scatter/gather, or total exchange, can be viewed as a series of scatters—each process carries out a scatter—or as a series of gathers—each process carries out a gather. As you can probably guess, MPI provides a function for all-to-all scatter/gathers.

There are two forms of total exchange in MPI: MPI_Alltoall and MPI_Alltoallv. The first form is used when we wish to send the same *amount* of data to every process. At first glance it might appear that we have no use for this, since, in general, each process will send a different amount of data to every other process. However, in order to use the second form, we need to know how much data is to be received by each process, and a simple way to communicate this information is to use the first form of MPI_Alltoall.

The syntax of MPI_Alltoall is

```
int MPI_Alltoall(
        void*            send_buffer  /* in  */,
```

```
            int          send_count    /* in  */,
            MPI_Datatype send_type     /* in  */,
            void*        recv_buffer   /* out */,
            int          recv_count    /* in  */,
            MPI_Datatype recv_type     /* in  */,
            MPI_Comm     comm          /* in  */)
```

This is a collective operation, so every process in the communicator comm must call the function. Its effect on process q is to send send_count elements of type send_type to every process (including itself). The first block of send_ count elements goes to process 0, the second block to process 1, etc. Process q will also receive recv_count elements of type recv_type from every process. The elements from process 0 are received into the beginning of recv_buffer. The elements from process 1 are received immediately following those from 0, etc.

The syntax of MPI_Alltoallv is similar:

```
int MPI_Alltoallv(
            void*        send_buffer             /* in  */,
            int          send_counts[]           /* in  */,
            int          send_displacements[]    /* in  */,
            MPI_Datatype send_type               /* in  */,
            void*        recv_buffer             /* out */,
            int          recv_counts[]           /* in  */,
            int          recv_displacements[]    /* in  */,
            MPI_Datatype recv_type               /* in  */,
            MPI_Comm     comm                    /* in  */)
```

Its effect is also similar. The difference is that each process can send (receive) a different amount of data to (from) every process. So send_count and recv_ count have been replaced by arrays of counts and arrays of displacements. The displacements are measured in elements of type send_type (recv_type) from the beginning of send_buffer (recv_buffer). Notice that the various arrays, send_counts, send_displacements, recv_counts, and recv_ displacements all have p entries, where p is the number of processes in comm.

10.5.4 Redistributing the Keys

In view of our newly acquired knowledge of MPI collective communications, we can construct a fairly simple solution to redistribution:

1. Determine what and how much data is to be sent to each process.
2. Carry out a total exchange on the amount of data to be sent/received by each process.
3. Compute the total amount of space needed for the data to be received and allocate storage.

4. Find the displacements of the data to be received.

5. Carry out a total exchange on the actual keys.

6. Free old storage.

An easy way to carry out the first step is to sort the local keys, then simply traverse the list of local keys, determining where the keys going to processor q end and those going to processor $q + 1$ begin. We'll need two lists: one to keep track of where the keys being sent to each process begin and one to keep track of how many keys go to each process. Since this information will be used directly by MPI_Alltoallv, in the form of arrays, we'll allocate arrays for this information.

Note also that MPI_Alltoallv uses arrays for the lists of keys that will be distributed. So if we want to avoid recopying the data in the key lists, it should be stored in arrays also. So let's tentatively define

```
typedef struct {
    int allocated_size;
    int local_list_size;
    KEY_T* keys;
} LOCAL_LIST_T;
```

With these definitions we can write the function Redistribute_keys.

```
void Redistribute_keys(
        LOCAL_LIST_T* local_keys  /* in/out */) {
    int new_list_size, i;
    int* send_counts;
    int* send_displacements;
    int* recv_counts;
    int* recv_displacements;
    KEY_T* new_keys;

    /* Allocate space for the counts and displacements */
    send_counts = (int*) malloc(p*sizeof(int));
    send_displacements = (int*) malloc(p*sizeof(int));
    recv_counts = (int*) malloc(p*sizeof(int));
    recv_displacements = (int*) malloc(p*sizeof(int));

    Local_sort(local_keys);
    Find_alltoall_send_params(local_keys,
        send_counts, send_displacements);

    /* Distribute the counts */
    MPI_Alltoall(send_counts, 1, MPI_INT, recv_counts,
        1, MPI_INT, MPI_COMM_WORLD);

    /* Allocate space for new list */
```

```
        new_list_size = recv_counts[0];
        for (i = 1; i < p; i++)
            new_list_size += recv_counts[i];
        new_keys = (KEY_T*)
            malloc(new_list_size*sizeof(KEY_T));

        Find_recv_displacements(recv_counts, recv_displacements);

        /* Exchange the keys */
        MPI_Alltoallv(List(local_keys), send_counts,
            send_displacements, key_mpi_t, new_keys,
            recv_counts, recv_displacements, key_mpi_t,
            MPI_COMM_WORLD);

        /* Replace old list with new list */
        List_free(local_keys);
        List_allocated_size(local_keys) = new_list_size;
        List_size(local_keys) = new_list_size;
        List(local_keys) = new_keys;

        free(send_counts);
        free(send_displacements);
        free(recv_counts);
        free(recv_displacements);

    } /* Redistribute_keys */
```

The most important thing to notice is that in the process of redistributing the keys, we create an entirely new list of keys—recall that MPI does not allow us to use the same list of keys as both the input argument (first argument) and as the output argument (fifth argument).

Notice also that we access the elements of *local_keys using macros. This makes the program much easier to modify if we decide to change the representation of any of the data. With the definition of LOCAL_LIST_T that we made previously, the following macros should be added to sort.h.

```
#define List_size(list) ((list)->local_list_size)
#define List_allocated_size(list) ((list)->allocated_size)
#define List(list) ((list)->keys)
#define List_free(list) {free List(list);}
```

Also notice that in the call to MPI_Alltoallv we use key_mpi_t. This is a derived datatype—as opposed to the C datatype KEY_T. In general, we would need to write a function defining this type, but since our keys are just ints, we can simply add the definition

```
#define key_mpi_t MPI_INT
```

to sort.h.

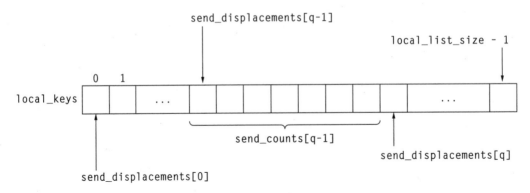

Figure 10.1   Displacements for MPI_Alltoallv

10.5.5 Pause to Clean Up

We leave the writing of the stubs for Find_alltoall_send_params and Find_recv_displacements to you. You should also finish up the incomplete code for Allocate_list and write the functions Local_sort, Insert_key, and Print_list. The Local_sort function can be simply a call to the standard C function qsort, or you can write your own sorting function. It is not very convenient to use the Cprintf function as the basis of Print_List. The difficulty is that Cprintf essentially prints one line of output per process, and if the local lists are long, it can get very tedious filling in the parameters to Cprintf. So you should probably use Cprintf as a model, but instead of sending a short, formatted list, send the list of keys. Be sure to address the problem of variable length lists. We strongly encourage you to update and test your complete code at this point.

10.5.6 Find_alltoall_send_params

In the function Find_alltoall_send_params we need to compute the values of the entries in the arrays send_counts and send_displacements. Since the entries in List(local_keys) have been sorted, we simply traverse this list until we encounter a value too large for the current process. The value in send_counts[q] is incremented as each key is examined. Since send_displacements[q] is the index of the first key to be sent to process q, its value can be computed as

$$\text{send\_displacements[q]} = \text{send\_displacements[q-1]} + \text{send\_counts[q-1]}.$$

See Figure 10.1. In view of the value $q-1$, the calculation for process 0 must be done separately. In order to calculate the cutoff—i.e., the first value that goes to the next higher ranked process—we use our assumption that the keys are uniformly distributed in the range KEY_MIN–KEY_MAX (0–32,767). Hence the cutoff for process q is just

$$\texttt{cutoff} = (q + 1) * (\texttt{KEY\_MAX} + 1)/p$$

We'll put this in a function to allow for the possibility that a future modification of the program may use a different key type or a different distribution. A word of warning here: if your computer uses 16-bit integers and the type of the variable cutoff is int, then the preceding calculation will overflow, since KEY_MAX + 1 = 2^{15}. So you may need to make cutoff a float and cast the values in these calculations to float.

In view of these considerations, we can write the function.

```
void Find_alltoall_send_params(
            LOCAL_LIST_T* local_keys          /* in  */,
            int*          send_counts         /* out */,
            int*          send_displacements  /* out */) {
    KEY_T cutoff;
    int i, j;

    /* Take care of process 0 */
    j = 0;
    send_displacements[0] = 0;
    send_counts[0] = 0;
    cutoff = Find_cutoff(0);
    /* Key_compare > 0 if cutoff > key */
    while ((j < List_size(local_keys)) &&
            (Key_compare(&cutoff,&List_key(local_keys,j))
                > 0)) {
        send_counts[0]++;
        j++;
    }

    /* Now deal with the remaining processes */
    for (i = 1; i < p; i++) {
        send_displacements[i] =
            send_displacements[i-1] + send_counts[i-1];
        send_counts[i] = 0;
        cutoff = Find_cutoff(i);
        /* Key_compare > 0 if cutoff > key */
        while ((j < List_size(local_keys)) &&
                (Key_compare(&cutoff,&List_key(local_keys,j))
                    > 0)) {
            send_counts[i]++;
            j++;
        }
    }
} /* Find_alltoall_send_params */
```

Notice that we have used an additional macro—List_key—and another function—Key_compare. List_key simply finds the *j*th key in the list. Key_compare returns positive if the first key is greater than the second, zero if they're equal, and negative if the first is less than the second. If you used the standard C function qsort, you had to write just such a function. We'll leave the writing of these to you.

A *serial* driver for Find_alltoall_send_params should allocate and initialize local_keys, sort the keys, print them, and print send_counts and send_displacements. We can use our routines, Allocate_list and Get_local_keys, to allocate and initialize. We can use the Local_sort function for sorting.

```c
#include <stdio.h>
#include "sort.h"

int p;
int my_rank;

main() {
    LOCAL_LIST_T local_keys;
    int size;
    int* send_counts;
    int* send_displacements;
    int i, q;

    /* Ctrl-C to exit */
    while (1) {
        printf("Enter p, my_rank, and list size\n");
        scanf("%d %d %d", &p, &my_rank, &size);

        send_counts = (int*) malloc(p*sizeof(int));
        send_displacements =
            (int*) malloc(p*sizeof(int));

        /* Use p*size, since functions assume first
         * argument = global list size */
        Allocate_list(p*size, &local_keys);
        Get_local_keys(&local_keys);

        Local_sort(&local_keys);
        Find_alltoall_send_params(&local_keys,
            send_counts, send_displacements);

        printf("keys = ");
        for (i = 0; i < size; i++)
            printf("%d ",List_key(&local_keys,i));
        printf("\n");
```

```
                    printf("counts = ");
                    for (q = 0; q < p; q++)
                        printf("%d ", send_counts[q]);
                    printf("\n");

                    printf("displacements = ");
                    for (q = 0; q < p; q++)
                        printf("%d ", send_displacements[q]);
                    printf("\n\n");

                    free(List(&local_keys));
                    free(send_counts);
                    free(send_displacements);
                }
            }
```

A run of the driver program produced the following output:

```
Enter p, my_rank, and list size
1 0 10
keys = 824 2495 8741 9255 10552 12096 16011 17326 20464 26067
counts = 10
displacements = 0

Enter p, my_rank, and list size
2 0 10
keys = 824 2495 8741 9255 10552 12096 16011 17326 20464 26067
counts = 7 3
displacements = 0 7

Enter p, my_rank, and list size
2 1 10
keys = 263 6436 9850 10838 10997 15681 19269 20264 21361 22597
counts = 6 4
displacements = 0 6

Enter p, my_rank, and list size
4 0 10
keys = 824 2495 8741 9255 10552 12096 16011 17326 20464 26067
counts = 2 5 2 1
displacements = 0 2 7 9
```

10.5.7 Finishing Up

Now there are essentially two functions left to write: Find_recv_displacements and Get_list_size. If you've understood Find_alltoall_send_params, you won't have any trouble writing Find_recv_displacements. However, Get_list_size brings up the thorny issue of access to stdin. If your system provides no access to stdin, you're either stuck with the version we've just written, you can use command line arguments, or you can use a file for input. See Chapter 8 for details. If you do have access to `stdin`, you should be able to simply call the function `Cscanf` (see Chapter 8) as follows:

```
int size;

Cscanf(io_comm,"How big is the list?","%d", &size);
return size;
```

10.6 Summary

In this chapter we briefly looked at the design and coding of parallel programs. Parallel programs are often classified as *data-parallel* or *control-parallel* programs. As the name implies, data-parallel programs obtain parallelism by dividing the data among the processes, and each process executes more or less the same instructions on its subset of the data. Control-parallel programs divide the tasks we wish to carry out among the processes. So in a control-parallel program, the instructions executed by one process may be completely different from those executed by another. Most parallel programs use both approaches. However, since it is usually easier to write a data-parallel program that will perform well on many processes, the data-parallel parts of most programs tend to predominate. Roughly speaking, a program is said to be *scalable* if, by increasing the amount of data, we can continue to obtain good performance as the program uses more and more processes. Thus, data-parallel programs tend to scale better than control-parallel programs.

We illustrated the design of a data-parallel program by writing a function that solved a linear system using Jacobi's method. We started by studying the serial solution. We saw that we could easily parallelize the serial program by giving each process a copy of the scalar parameters (e.g., n and convergence tolerance) and by partitioning the arrays (coefficient matrix, right-hand side, and solution vector) among the processes. The steps in our parallel solution were almost identical to the steps in the serial solution. The two exceptions were that there was a communication phase in the parallel solution, and we slightly modified the organization of the solution so that we could reduce the amount of communication.

We illustrated the coding of a parallel program by writing a program that sorted a distributed list: when the program completed, the keys assigned to each process were sorted in increasing order, and if $A < B$, the keys assigned to process A were all less than or equal to the keys assigned to process B. Our approach to coding was modelled on standard approaches to coding serial programs. We used both top-down and bottom-up design and coding. Initially we proceeded top-down: we defined the main program and used stubs for the subprograms. However, as soon as we had proceeded far enough in our design that we had partially defined a data structure, we changed to bottom-up coding: we defined output functions for the structure so that we could examine its contents during debugging, and we defined member access functions or macros so that if the design changed, we would only need to change the access functions.

Since input can be a major problem on parallel systems, we avoided the problem of dealing with input functions until the program was nearly complete.

The only new MPI functions we learned about were `MPI_Alltoall` and `MPI_Alltoallv`.

```
int MPI_Alltoall(
        void*         send_buffer   /* in  */,
        int           send_count    /* in  */,
        MPI_Datatype  send_type     /* in  */,
        void*         recv_buffer   /* out */,
        int           recv_count    /* in  */,
        MPI_Datatype  recv_type     /* in  */,
        MPI_Comm      comm          /* in  */)

int MPI_Alltoallv(
        void*         send_buffer                 /* in  */,
        int           send_counts[]               /* in  */,
        int           send_displacements[]        /* in  */,
        MPI_Datatype  send_type                   /* in  */,
        void*         recv_buffer                 /* out */,
        int           recv_counts[]               /* in  */,
        int           recv_displacements[]        /* in  */,
        MPI_Datatype  recv_type                   /* in  */,
        MPI_Comm      comm                        /* in  */)
```

Both functions scatter the contents of each process's `send_buffer` among the processes in `comm`. In the first, each process sends the same amount of data to every other process, while with the second, the amount of data sent to process B from A is specified by `send_counts[A]`, `send_displacements[A]`, and `send_type`.

10.7 References

We've just suggested a few of the issues in parallel software engineering. For a much more comprehensive treatment, see [17].

10.8 Exercises

1. Rewrite the parallel Jacobi function so that it no longer assumes that n is evenly divisible by p. What changes will have to be made in the calling program?

2. The C functions `drand48` and `srand48` can be used to generate random `doubles`. If you were using these functions to generate `doubles` or `floats` that were distributed across a set of processes, how would you try to insure that the numbers generated on distinct processes were independent?

10.9 Programming Assignments

1. Write a calling program for the parallel Jacobi function. Use your random number generator from exercise 2 to generate most of the entries in the matrix. What will you do for the diagonal entries?

2. If your system provides I/O access to process 0, write input and output functions to be used in the sorting program. Process 0 will read in the input list and distribute it by blocks to the processes. When the computation is complete, process 0 will gather the blocks of the list from the processes and print the sorted list.

3. Use `MPI_Alltoall` to write a matrix transpose function. Suppose the $n \times n$ matrix A is distributed by block rows among the processes and p divides n. After the operation is complete, A^T should also be distributed by block rows. Should your program overwrite A with A^T or use additional storage? What modifications need to be made to your program if you use a cyclic row distribution? What modifications need to be made if n isn't evenly divisible by p?

4. A two-dimensional binary cellular automaton consists of a two-dimensional rectangular grid together with an initial assignment of zeroes and ones to the vertices, or cells, of the grid and a "next-state" function for updating the values at the vertices. The updating function is applied simultaneously to all the cells. Typically, the value of the next-state function at an individual cell will depend on the current value at the grid point and the four neighbors immediately above, below, to the right, and to the left of the cell. However, it is also quite common for the next-state function to depend on the four diagonally adjacent neighbors as well—upper-left neighbor, upper-right neighbor, lower-left neighbor, and lower-right neighbor.

   John Conway's game of Life is a well-known example. In it, cells with ones are "alive," while cells with zeroes are dead. Updating corresponds to finding the "next generation," and the new value of a cell depends on all eight immediately adjacent neighbors. The rules are the following:

   a. Living cells with one or zero neighbors will die from loneliness.
   b. Living cells with two or three neighbors will survive into the next generation.
   c. Living cells with four or more neighbors will die from overcrowding.
   d. Empty cells with exactly three neighbors will come to life.

Write a parallel program that simulates a two-dimensional binary cellular automaton. Use Conway's Life as an example to clarify your thinking, but allow for the possibility that the update rule can be changed.

The program should take as input the order of the automaton (number of rows and number of columns), the maximum number of generations, and an initial configuration. After each new generation is computed, the program should print it out.

How should the cells of the automaton be partitioned among the processes? Should you use a block-row partitioning? A cyclic row partitioning? A block-checkerboard partitioning? How should this be decided?

CHAPTER 11

Performance

OF COURSE, WE WANT TO WRITE PARALLEL PROGRAMS so that we can solve bigger problems in less time. If our serial programs were fast enough to solve all the problems we were interested in, and if they could store all our data, parallel programming would just be an intellectual exercise. So in our discussion of writing parallel programs in Chapter 10, we omitted a critical part of the design process: performance estimation. Before going to the trouble to write a nontrivial program, we should attempt to determine whether its performance will satisfy our needs. In this chapter we'll discuss methods for estimating parallel program performance.

Note that we do not use the more conventional asymptotic methods for analyzing program performance. Although these methods are very useful, especially in the analysis of serial program performance, we have found that they don't provide sufficient detail in the analysis of parallel programs. Rather, we have found that an empirical approach is the most useful. We should also note that, although we will focus on speed, there are many aspects to the evaluation of a parallel program. In particular, you should always keep in mind the cost of developing a parallel program. Many parallel programs are designed in order to obtain the maximum possible performance and, as a consequence, take years to develop. Clearly, you should always ask how much more it will cost to develop a faster, more complex program than a slower, simpler program.

We'll begin by discussing serial program performance.

11.1 Serial Program Performance

We view program performance analysis as an ongoing, integral part of program development. Thus, there are varying degrees of precision implicit in the expression "performance analysis." Before any code has been written, we can only provide performance estimates that involve arbitrary symbolic constants obtained by estimating the number of statements executed. As the development proceeds, we can replace the symbolic constants with numerical constants that are valid for a particular system and compiler. Thus, in our a priori analysis we will specify runtime by counting statements; as details of the performance emerge, we may specify runtime in milliseconds or microseconds.

When discussing the runtime of a program, we would like to be able to say something like, "The running time of this program is $T(n)$ units if the input has size n." Of course the actual time a program takes to solve a problem—the time from the beginning of execution to the completion of execution—will depend on factors other than the input size. For example, it will depend on

1. the hardware being used
2. the programming language and compiler
3. details of the input other than its size

In order to avoid dealing with the first factor, we will, as we already mentioned, count "statements executed" in our initial analyses. This, brings up the second factor: if we're counting statements executed, are these assembler statements? If so, what type of assembler, RISC or CISC? Or are the statements high-level language statements, and if so, which high-level language? Also, is counting statements reasonable, since, in general, different statements will require different execution times?

Finally, it's easy to come up with examples of programs that behave very differently with different inputs, even if the inputs have the same size. For example, an insertion sort that sorts integers into increasing order and that uses linear search will run much faster if the input is 1, 2, ... , n than if the input is n, $n - 1$, ... , 2, 1. We can avoid this problem by discussing worst-case runtime or possibly average-case runtime; in general, when we discuss runtime, we will mean worst-case runtime.

However, when we're counting statements, we can't entirely avoid the first two problems without introducing some imprecision into our measurements. Most authors deal with this imprecision by using **asymptotic analysis.** In asymptotic analysis, we specify bounds on the performance of a program. As an example, people often say that the sorting algorithm commonly known as "bubble sort" is an n^2 algorithm. What is meant by this is that if you apply the bubble sort algorithm to a list consisting of n items, the number of statements executed will be less than some constant multiple of n^2, provided that n is sufficiently large. If you're not accustomed to seeing this type of analysis, this statement may sound very vague. However, for estimating serial program performance, it has proved to be very useful.

Since it is not as useful for parallel program performance, we won't pursue this avenue. Rather, we will count statements executed and include all "constant" multiples explicitly in our formulas—at least until we've determined that they're not necessary. Let's illustrate the ideas by looking at a simple example.

11.2 An Example: The Serial Trapezoidal Rule

Let's estimate the runtime of the serial trapezoidal rule. (If you are skipping around in your reading, take a look at Chapter 4.) Recollect that the serial program reads in the left and right endpoints (a and b), the number of trapezoids (n), and then computes a running sum: it computes the area of the ith trapezoidal and adds it into the sum of the areas of the previous $i - 1$ trapezoids. When this is completed, it prints the result. For ease of reference, the heart of the program is

```
h = (b-a)/n;
integral = (f(a) + f(b))/2.0;
x = a;
for (i = 1; i <= n-1; i++) {
    x = x + h;
    integral = integral + f(x);
}
integral = integral*h;
```

The number of statements executed before and after the for loop doesn't depend on the input size, n. Say there are c_1 of these statements. If we assume that evaluation of $f(x)$ requires a constant number of statements, then the number of statements executed in each pass through the for loop is also a constant: call it c_2. So the total number of statements executed is

$$T(n) = c_1 + c_2(n - 1).$$

That is, $T(n)$ is a linear polynomial in n; after regrouping and renaming the constants, we have

$$T(n) = k_1 n + k_2.$$

For this simple program, it is not unreasonable to assume that the execution time of the various statements isn't too different. Furthermore, we would expect the total number of statements executed inside the for loop to be much greater than the number of statements executed outside the loop. That is, $k_1 n \gg k_2$. Hence, T(n) can be approximated by

$$T(n) \approx k_1 n.$$

So we would predict that if we increase n by a factor of r, $T(n)$ should increase by the same factor. That is, if $T(n) = t$, then we would predict that the runtime for input size rn, $T(rn)$, would be about rt.

OK. How do our predictions compare to actual performance? We'll discuss the problem of taking program timings later. For now, it suffices to say that if our system isn't running any other processes, we can simply check the system clock at the beginning and the end of the code segments, and take the difference to get the elapsed time.

The actual execution times on a single processor of an nCUBE 2 correspond very well with our estimates. (Here $f(x) = e^{-x^2}, a = -2$, and $b = 2$.)

n	512	1024	1536	2048
Time in ms	11.4	22.8	34.2	45.6

Observe, for example, that if we double n, we double the total execution time. Observe also that we can actually estimate the constant k_1 to be 11.4/512 milliseconds/trapezoidal, which is about 22.3 microseconds/trapezoid. We'll make use of this later, when we try to analyze the performance of the parallel trapezoidal rule.

11.3 What about the I/O?

A couple of things should be bothering you about our analysis. We omitted the scanf and printf statements. Why? They're certainly an important and expensive part of the computation. There are two reasons for leaving them out. The first has to do with how the program might be used in a practical application. In an application, the trapezoidal rule program would probably not be of interest in its own right. It would be part of a larger problem that happens to need to do some integration. So the input values, a, b, and n, would be supplied by the program—not by the user. Similarly, the result of the integration would, in all likelihood, not be of interest—it would be used by the rest of the program to complete its "bigger" calculation.

The second reason has to do with the fundamental difference between I/O statements and statements that simply use the computer's CPU and RAM: I/O statements are *much* slower—typically several orders of magnitude. For example, in a 33 MHz 486 PC running Linux and the gcc compiler, a multiplication takes about a microsecond, while a printf of a single float takes about 300 microseconds. On a single processor of an nCUBE 2, a multiplication takes about 2.5 microseconds, and a printf takes about 500 microseconds.[1] Furthermore these are relatively slow processors. On faster systems, the ratios may be worse, since the arithmetic times will decrease, but the I/O times may remain about the same. In any case, it definitely does not make sense to count I/O statements with statements that only involve the CPU and RAM. Thus, when we are analyzing programs that include I/O statements, our initial

---

1   These times are for unbuffered output. If the output is buffered, average times can be reduced by about 50%.

analyses will include two terms: one for the calculation and one for I/O:

$$T(n) = T_{calc}(n) + T_{i/o}(n).$$

In our serial trapezoidal rule, we would estimate $T_{i/o} = k$ for some constant k, since we will always read three values and print a single float. (Since we're interested in performance, we'll omit such niceties as self-documenting I/O.) We can estimate k by taking the preceding timings and subtracting them from the time it takes to run the program with the I/O.

The runtimes with the two I/O statements on an nCUBE 2 are

n	512	1024	1536	2048
Time in ms	12.6	24.0	35.4	46.8

So the two I/O statements add about 1.2 milliseconds to the overall runtime, and our new performance estimate is

$$T(n) = 22.3n + 1200.$$

11.4 Parallel Program Performance Analysis

One clear difference between serial and parallel program performance estimation is that the runtime of a parallel program should depend on two variables: input size and number of processes. Thus, instead of using $T(n)$ to denote performance, we'll use a function of two variables, $T(n, p)$. It is the time that has elapsed from the moment when the first process to start actually begins execution of the program to the moment when the last process to complete execution executes its last statement. In many of our programs, $T(n, p)$ will simply be the number of statements executed by process 0 (or whichever process is responsible for I/O), since typically execution will begin with process 0 gathering and distributing input data, and it will end with process 0 printing results.

Note that this definition implies that if multiple processes are running on a single physical processor, the runtime will in all likelihood be substantially greater than if processes are running on separate physical processors. In general, we won't worry about this issue—we'll assume that each process is running on a separate physical processor.

Generally, when parallel program performance is discussed, the subject of how the parallel program compares to the serial program arises. The most commonly used measures are speedup and efficiency. Loosely, **speedup** is the ratio of the runtime of a serial solution to a problem to the parallel runtime. That is, if $T_\sigma(n)$ denotes the runtime of the serial solution and $T_\pi(n, p)$ denotes the runtime of the parallel solution with p processes,[2] then the speedup of the

---

2   We use the subscripts σ and π so that they can't be confused with S (the speedup) and p (the number of processes).

parallel program is

$$S(n,p) = \frac{T_\sigma(n)}{T_\pi(n,p)}.$$

There is some ambiguity in this definition. For example, is the serial program just the parallel program running with one process, or is it the fastest known serial program that solves the problem? Is the serial program to run on the fastest possible serial machine, or is it to run on a single processor of the parallel system? Most authors define the speedup to be the ratio of the runtime of the fastest known serial program on one processor of the parallel system to that of the parallel program running on p processors of the parallel system.

For a fixed value of p, it will usually be the case that $0 < S(n,p) \leq p$. If $S(n,p) = p$, a program is said to have **linear speedup.** This is, of course, a rare occurrence since most parallel solutions will add some overhead because of communication among the processes. Unfortunately, a far more common occurrence is **slowdown.** That is, the parallel program running on more than one process is actually slower than the serial program. This unfortunate occurrence usually results from an excessive amount of overhead, and this overhead is usually due to communication among the processes.

An alternative to speedup is **efficiency.** Efficiency is a measure of process utilitization in a parallel program, relative to the serial program. It is defined as

$$E(n,p) = \frac{S(n,p)}{p} = \frac{T_\sigma(n)}{pT_\pi(n,p)}$$

Since $0 < S(n,p) \leq p$, $0 < E(n,p) \leq 1$. If $E(n,p) = 1$, the program is exhibiting linear speedup, while if $E(n,p) < 1/p$, the program is exhibiting slowdown.

11.5 The Cost of Communication

In several places in the text we've already noted that communication, like I/O, is significantly more expensive than local calculation. Thus, in order to make reasonable estimates of parallel program performance, we should count the cost of communication separately from the cost of calculation and I/O. That is,

$$T(n,p) = T_{calc}(n,p) + T_{i/o}(n,p) + T_{comm}(n,p).$$

In view of this, we need to get a better understanding of what happens when two processes communicate. So suppose we are running a parallel program and process q is sending a message to process r. When process q executes the statement

```
MPI_Send(message, count, datatype, r, tag, comm)
```

and process r executes the statement

```
MPI_Recv(message, count, datatype, q, tag, comm,
    &status)
```

the details of what happens at the hardware level will vary. Different systems use different communication protocols, and a single system will execute two different sets of machine-level commands depending on whether the processes reside on the same or distinct physical processors.

We are mainly interested in the case where the processes reside on distinct processors, and for this case we can make some general observations about what happens on most systems. In this situation, the execution of the send/receive pair can be divided into two phases: a start-up phase and a communication phase. Once again, details of what the system does during these phases will vary. Typically, however, during the start-up phase the message may be copied into a system-controlled message buffering area, and the envelope data, consisting of the source rank (q), the destination rank (r), the tag, the communicator, and possibly other information, may be appended to the message. During the communication phase, the actual data is transmitted between the physical processors. There may be another phase, analogous to the start-up phase, on the receiving process, during which the message may be copied from a system-controlled buffering area into user-controlled memory.

The costs of these phases will vary from system to system, so we'll use symbolic constants to denote the costs. We'll use t_s to denote the runtime of the start-up phase, including any time spent on the receiving process copying the message into user-controlled memory, and t_c will denote the time it takes to transmit a single unit of data from one processor to another. The unit of data can be either a byte, a word, or some larger unit of data. If it isn't clear from the context, we'll specify which. Using this notation, the cost of sending a single message containing k units of data will be

$$t_s + kt_c.$$

The time t_s is sometimes called message **latency,** and the reciprocal of t_c is sometimes called the **bandwidth.**

It is surprisingly difficult to obtain reliable estimates of t_s and t_c. For a particular system, the best thing to do is to actually write programs that send messages and take timings. However, we can make some broad generalizations. On most systems, t_c is within one order of magnitude of the cost of an arithmetic operation, t_a, and t_s is from one to three orders of magnitude greater than t_c. For example, on the nCUBE 2, t_c is about 2.5 microseconds/float, and t_s is about 170 microseconds. Table 11.1 contains data on several systems.[3]

Such values should not be taken too seriously for a variety of reasons:

---

3   Most of the data in this table is taken from [12]. The t_a figures are times for a double precision addition and a multiplication on the 1000 × 1000 Linpack benchmark. The t_c figures were computed for a message size of 1 megabyte.

Table 11.1 Estimates of t_s, t_c, and t_a on several systems (all times are in microseconds; SM denotes use of shared-memory functions; t_c is time per double)

Machine	Operating System	t_a	t_s	t_c
Cray T3D (PVM)	MAX 1.2.0.2	0.011	21	0.30
Cray T3D (SM)	MAX 1.2.0.2	0.011	3	0.063
Intel Paragon	OSF 1.0.4	0.030	29	0.052
Intel iPSC/860	NX 3.3.2	0.030	65	2.7
Intel iPSC/2	NX 3.3.2	–	370	2.9
IBM SP-1	MPL	0.0096	270	1.1
IBM SP-2	MPI	0.0042	35	0.23
Meiko CS2 (SM)	Solaris 2.3	0.010	11	0.20
Meiko CS2	Solaris 2.3	0.010	83	0.19
nCUBE 2	Vertex 3.2	0.50	170	4.7
TMC CM-5	CMMD 2.0	–	95	0.89
Ethernet	TCP/IP	–	500	8.9

1. The communication figures tend to become dated very quickly, since computer manufacturers are always tweaking their hardware and software in order to improve the figures.

2. On many systems, MPI is layered on top of proprietary message-passing software, and, as a consequence, figures for MPI may not be as good as those reported in the table.

3. Floating point performance tends to depend highly on the application, and figures for a given application may vary widely from those in the table.

11.6 An Example: The Parallel Trapezoidal Rule

As an example of the use of these ideas, let's estimate the runtime of the parallel trapezoidal rule. We'll also try to estimate its speedup.

Once again, for ease of reference, we include the part of our parallel program that corresponds to the serial program we analyzed earlier. (As before, we'll omit the I/O.)

```
h = (b-a)/n;     /* h is the same for all processes */
local_n = n/p;   /* So is the number of trapezoids */

/* Length of each process's interval of
 * integration = local_n*h.  So my interval
 * starts at: */
local_a = a + my_rank*local_n*h;
local_b = local_a + local_n*h;

/* Call the serial trapezoidal function */
integral = Trap(local_a, local_b, local_n, h);
```

```
/* Add up the integrals calculated by each process */
MPI_Reduce(&integral, &total, 1, MPI_FLOAT,
    MPI_SUM, 0, MPI_COMM_WORLD);
```

Except for the function calls, `Trap` and `MPI_Reduce`, all of the statements take constant time and hence add a constant, c_1, to the total runtime. The `Trap` function just executes the preceding serial trapezoidal rule code on each process's interval of integration. Since each process sums the areas of n/p trapezoids, this part of the code has runtime $c_2(n/p - 1) + c_3$. If the parallel implementation of `MPI_Reduce` uses the tree-structured communication pattern we discussed in Chapter 5, then it will have runtime

$$c_4 \log_2(p)(t_s + t_c + t_a) + c_5,$$

for some constants c_4 and c_5. Here, t_a is the cost of an arithmetic operation (the sum computed after each communication phase). So the total runtime for the parallel program is

$$T(n, p) = k_1 \frac{n}{p} + k_2 \log_2(p) + k_3,$$

for some constants k_1, k_2, and k_3.

From our previous discussion, we expect k_3 to be negligible, and we've already estimated $k_1 = 22.3$ microseconds/trapezoid on an nCUBE 2. Furthermore, from our previous estimates of t_a, t_s, and t_c, we can estimate that

$$k_2 \approx 170 + 2.5 + 1.5 \approx 175 \, \mu sec.$$

Thus, our overall first estimate of $T(n, p)$ on an nCUBE 2 is

$$T(n, p) = 22.3 \frac{n}{p} + 175 \log_2(p),$$

and our predicted speedup is

$$S(n, p) = \frac{22.3n}{22.3n/p + 175 \log_2(p)}.$$

How does our prediction compare to the actual performance? Table 11.2 contains the predicted speedups and the actual speedups on an nCUBE 2 running a somewhat optimized version of the `mpich` implementation of MPI. (The limits of integration are $a = -2$ and $b = 2$. The function being integrated is e^{-x^2}.) Figure 11.1 illustrates some of these numbers graphically. As you can see, our speedup estimates are quite good if p is small. However, as p increases, our estimates deteriorate—especially if p is large and n is small. When p is small and n is large, the term $22.3n/p$ will dominate the overall runtime; when p is large and n small, its relative contribution to the parallel runtime will shrink. This suggests that our estimate of the time spent in calculating the

Table 11.2   Predicted and actual speedups of trapezoidal rule

| | Number of trapezoids | | | | | | | |
| | 512 | | 1024 | | 1536 | | 2048 | |
Processes	Pred.	Act.	Pred.	Act.	Pred.	Act.	Pred.	Act.
2	1.9	2.0	2.0	2.0	2.0	2.0	2.0	2.0
4	3.6	3.6	3.8	3.8	3.8	3.9	3.9	3.9
8	5.8	5.7	6.8	6.7	7.1	7.1	7.3	7.4
16	8.1	7.6	10.7	10.4	12.1	11.8	12.8	12.7
32	9.3	8.1	14.4	13.4	17.6	16.3	19.8	19.0

local integrals is fairly accurate, but we have underestimated the cost of the call to MPI_Reduce.

If we try fitting the formula

$$k_1 \frac{n}{p} + k_2 \log_2(p) + k_3$$

to the actual runtimes, we find that $k_1 = 22.2, k_2 = 190$, and $k_3 = 0$. Thus, our a posteriori analysis seems to be correct. That is, we have underestimated the runtime of the global sum function. In fact, if we take timings of the global sum, we find that there is an additional 15 μsec overhead that we didn't consider in our earlier estimate. This additional overhead is probably due to the cost of the function call and the cost of calculating the addresses (source and destination) for the message passing.

11.7 Taking Timings

If you have exclusive access to the processors on which you will be running your program, it's fairly easy to time your program: synchronize the processes at the beginning of the code you wish to time, start a clock on each process, synchronize the processes at the end of the code you wish to time, stop the clock, and compute the elapsed time. If, as in the trapezoidal rule program, the runtime of one process (process 0 in this case) dominates the runtime—i.e., starts first and finishes last—the synchronization steps can be omitted.

In order to synchronize the processes, you can call MPI_Barrier:

```
int MPI_Barrier(
        MPI_Comm  comm  /* in */)
```

This function causes each process in comm to block until every process in comm has called it.

In order to actually take the timings, there are a number of possibilities. MPI provides a timer:

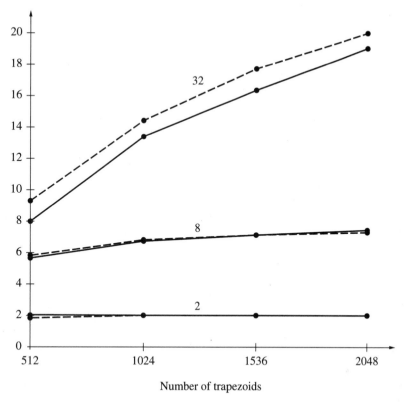

Number of trapezoids

Figure 11.1   Plot of predicted (dashed curves) and actual (solid curves) speedups of trapezoidal rule for p = 2, 8, 32

```
double MPI_Wtime(void)
```

It returns a double precision value that represents the number of seconds that
have elapsed since some point in the past. Its precision can be found by calling
MPI_Wtick:

```
double MPI_Wtick(void)
```

For example if MPI_Wtime is incremented every microsecond, then MPI_Wtick
will return 10^{-6}.

Thus, an MPI program can determine elapsed time as follows:

```
double start, finish;

MPI_Barrier(comm);
start = MPI_Wtime();
    ⋮
/* Code being timed */
```

```
                  ⋮
MPI_Barrier(comm);
finish = MPI_Wtime();
if (my_rank == 0)
    printf("Elapsed time = %e seconds\n",
        finish - start);
```

If the code you're timing is very short, you can estimate the cost of MPI_Barrier and MPI_Wtime by writing a program that estimates their cost and subtract this cost from the elapsed time.

It should be stressed that MPI_Wtime returns *wall-clock* time. That is, it makes no allowance for such things as system time. So if a process is interrupted by the system, the time it spends idle will be added into the elapsed time.

11.8 Summary

To summarize, in order to estimate the performance of a parallel program, we should carry out the following steps:

1. Develop a formula for the runtime of the serial program that contains symbolic constants.

2. Estimate the size of the symbolic constants in the formula for the serial runtime. Some of these can be estimated from your knowledge of the algorithm and your knowledge of the performance characteristics of your system. In our example, we were able to determine that in our linear formula, the constant term was close to zero. In order to determine the slope, however, we had to actually take timings.

3. Develop a formula for the runtime of the parallel program that contains symbolic constants.

4. Estimate the value of the symbolic constants on the basis of the performance characteristics of your system and the results of the serial program analysis.

5. Estimate the speedup.

In order to actually take the timings, you can use the function MPI_Barrier to synchronize the processes and MPI_Wtime to measure elapsed time. Their syntax is

```
int MPI_Barrier(
        MPI_Comm  comm  /* in */)

double MPI_Wtime(void)
```

11.9 References

Foster [17] provides an excellent discussion of the performance analysis of parallel programs.

Most of our machine-specific performance figures are based on the work of Dongarra and Dunigan. See [12] for a more complete discussion of these figures.

Kumar et al. [26] derive a number of asymptotic parallel program performance estimates.

Bailey [4] has a nice discussion of tricks that have been used to obscure poor performance of parallel programs.

11.10 Exercises

You may want to write programming assignment 1 before working on the exercises.

1. There are some anomalous examples where $S(n, p) > p$. Such programs are said to exhibit **superlinear** speedup. Can you think of a program that might show superlinear speedup?

2. Estimate the runtime of the trapezoidal rule program that used a simple loop of receives on process 0. Compare your predicted speedups with the actual speedups.

3. a. Estimate the runtime of a simple serial matrix multiplication program (see section 7.1). Write a serial matrix multiplication program and compare your prediction to the actual times.
   b. Estimate the performance of the basic parallel matrix multiplication algorithm that partitions the matrix by block rows. Compare your prediction of the performance with the actual performance.
   c. Estimate the performance of Fox's algorithm. (See [26] if you need some help with the formulas.) Compare your prediction of the performance with the actual performance.
   d. Use least squares to determine the size of the constants that will make your predicted runtimes best fit the parallel runtimes.

4. In order to estimate the runtime of Jacobi's method, we need to include a constant representing the number of iterations. Estimate the cost of a single iteration of the serial and parallel Jacobi's method programs. Compare your estimates to the actual performance.

5. Recall programming assignment 4 from Chapter 10, involving a cellular automaton. In it you were asked to try to determine which distribution of the grid was preferred. In light of your recently acquired knowledge of the cost of communication and computation, which distribution of the grid do you think will minimize the runtime?

11.11 Programming Assignments

1. Write a short program that estimates t_s and t_c for your system. This can be done by repeatedly sending fixed-size messages from one process to another. When the receiving process receives its message, it should reply to the sending process. This process should then be repeated with messages of different sizes. You can use least squares to fit a line to the resulting (message size, time) pairs. The intercept will approximate t_s and the slope t_c.

2. Modify your solution to programming assignment 1 so that it uses different derived datatypes (contiguous, vector, indexed, and struct) to communicate various amounts of data. Compare the costs of sending the different derived datatypes.

3. Modify your solution to programming assignment 1 so that the data is first packed on the sending process and then unpacked on the receiving process. Compare the costs to the costs you determined in the preceding two exercises.

4. Study the performance of the cellular automaton program (programming assignment 4 from Chapter 10) using different distributions of the grid. Don't include the printing of the grid in your timings. How does the actual performance compare to the performance you predicted in exercise 5?

CHAPTER 12

More on Performance

IN THIS CHAPTER WE CONTINUE our discussion of performance. We'll begin with a discussion of Amdahl's law, which seems to imply that there is little hope that large-scale parallel systems will be able to achieve large speedups. During the period 1967–1988, Amdahl's law was the bête noire of researchers in parallel computing. In 1988, however, three researchers at Sandia National Labs reported speedups of more than 1000 on a 1024-processor nCUBE. This resulted in a serious reexamination of Amdahl's law. One of the principal outcomes of this reexamination was the idea of **scalability**. Essentially, a parallel program is scalable if it is possible to maintain a given efficiency as the number of processes is increased by simultaneously increasing the problem size.

After our discussion of these somewhat theoretical issues, we turn to some more practical issues. We discuss some potential problems with estimating parallel program performance, and we discuss MPI's profiling interface. We close with a brief discussion of a software tool that has been developed to analyze the performance of parallel programs.

12.1 Amdahl's Law

Suppose that a certain program requires time T_σ to solve an instance of a problem using a single process. By an "instance" of a problem, we mean the problem together with a specific set of input data—e.g., integrating e^{-x^2} over the interval $[0, 1]$ using the trapezoidal rule with 512 trapezoids. Suppose also that this program contains a fraction, r, of statements $(0 \leq r \leq 1)$ that are "perfectly parallelizable." That is, regardless of how large p is, this fraction of the program has linear speedup and hence runtime rT_σ/p when it is parallelized and run with p processes. However, suppose that the remaining fraction, $1 - r$, of the program is inherently serial. That is, regardless of how large p is, the runtime of this fraction is $(1 - r)T_\sigma$ when it is parallelized with p processes. An example of what might be inherently serial code is an input segment, where a single value is needed by all the processes. We'll defer, for the moment, a discussion of how reasonable these assumptions are.

Under these assumptions, the speedup of the parallellized program with p processes is

$$S(p) = \frac{T_\sigma}{(1 - r)T_\sigma + rT_\sigma/p}$$

$$= \frac{1}{(1 - r) + r/p}.$$

If we differentiate S with respect to p, we get

$$\frac{dS}{dp} = \frac{r}{[(1 - r)p + r]^2} \geq 0.$$

So $S(p)$ is an increasing function of p, and as $p \to \infty$, we see that

$$S(p) \to \frac{1}{1 - r}.$$

So $S(p)$ is bounded above by $(1 - r)^{-1}$. For example, if $r = 0.5$, the maximum possible speedup is 2. If $r = 0.75$, the maximum possible speedup is 4, and if $r = 0.99$, the maximum possible speedup is 100. In particular, if $r = 0.99$, even if we use 10,000 processes, we can't get a speedup of better than 100, which would correspond to an efficiency of 0.01!

Is Amdahl's law correct? If so, it would seem to imply that it's hopeless for us to try to use massive parallelism (i.e., hundreds or thousands of processes). The mathematics is clearly correct. Hence, insofar as we can trust its hypotheses, it is correct. So is it reasonable then, to accept its hypotheses? Certainly given an instance of a problem and a program for solving the problem, it seems reasonable to assume that a certain fraction of statements in the program cannot be parallelized. Indeed, it seems excessively optimistic to assume that the remainder of the statements are "perfectly" parallelizable.

However, what may not be reasonable is the use of arbitrarily many processes to solve a given instance of the problem. In other words, the parameter n, the problem size, is conspicuously absent from all these equations. As an extreme example, it seems clear that if we try to use more than 500 processes to solve a problem instance that only requires 500 calculations, we'll be wasting our resources. Rather, we should use more processes to solve larger instances of a problem, and perhaps if we take a larger instance of a problem, the serial fraction will get smaller. This was one of the key ideas in the development of the first programs that obtained speedups of more than 1000. For example, in our trapezoidal program, there are essentially two serial statements: reading the input values and printing the solution. So as n, the number of trapezoids, gets larger, the serial fraction of the program will approach zero.

12.2 Work and Overhead

The observation that in many programs, as the problem size increases, the inherently serial fraction decreases, suggests a general view of parallel programming that allows us to make more optimistic predictions than Amdahl's law. An inherently serial segment of a program can be parallelized in essentially one of two ways: one process can execute the statements in the segment while the others remain idle, or all the processes can execute the statements—that is, the statements in the segment are replicated by each process. Both of these approaches are sources of parallel **overhead**: they increase the total amount of work performed by the parallel program over the amount performed by the serial program.

Let's make this idea precise. The amount of **work** done by a serial program is simply the runtime:

$$W_\sigma(n) = T_\sigma(n).$$

The amount of work done by a parallel program is the sum of the amounts of work done by each process:

$$W_\pi(n, p) = \sum_{q=0}^{p-1} W_q(n, p),$$

where $W_q(n, p)$ is the amount of work done by the program executed by process q. Now observe that (unlike in the real world) *work includes idle time.* If we're timing a serial program and it remains idle for some reason (e.g., it's waiting for input), then this idle time is included in the total runtime or the work. Thus, each $W_q(n, p)$ should include the time that process q is idle. But this vastly simplifies our calculations, for it implies that for each q, $W_q(n, p) = T_\pi(n, p)$. That is, $W_q(n, p)$ is simply the parallel runtime because process q is either doing useful work or idle for the duration of the execution of the parallel program. So our formula for $W_\pi(n, p)$ is simply

$$W_\pi(n, p) = pT_\pi(n, p).$$

Thus, an alternative definition of efficiency is

$$E(n, p) = \frac{T_\sigma(n)}{pT_\pi(n, p)} = \frac{W_\sigma(n)}{W_\pi(n, p)}.$$

So in this setting, linear speedup, or $E(n, p) = 1$, is equivalent to the statement "The amount of work done by the parallel program is the same as the amount of work done by the serial program."

We can formalize our definition of overhead: since it is the amount of work done by the parallel program that is not done by the serial program, it's simply

$$T_O(n, p) = W_\pi(n, p) - W_\sigma(n) = pT_\pi(n, p) - T_\sigma(n).$$

Alternatively, we could define **per-process overhead** as the difference between the parallel runtime and the ideal parallel runtime that would be obtained with linear speedup:

$$T'_O(n,p) = T_\pi(n,p) - T_\sigma(n)/p.$$

In this setting we can think of our definition of overhead as "total overhead":

$$T_O(n,p) = pT'_O(n,p).$$

As an example, let's find $T_O(n,p)$ for the trapezoidal rule program. In our analysis of its runtime, we found that

$$T_\sigma(n) = k_1 n,$$

and

$$T_\pi(n,p) = k_1 n/p + k_2 \log_2(p).$$

Hence, the work done by the parallel program is

$$W_\pi(n,p) = k_1 n + k_2 p \log_2(p)$$

and the overhead function for the parallel trapezoidal rule program is

$$T_O(n,p) = k_2 p \log_2(p).$$

In other words, the total work done by the parallel program will differ from the total work done by the serial program by $k_2 p \log_2(p)$. This is true regardless of the value of n. So if n is large relative to p, we would expect that the amount of work done by the parallel program would be very close to the amount of work done by the serial program.

12.3 Sources of Overhead

Although we haven't formalized this observation, previous comments imply that there are three main sources of overhead:

1. communication
2. idle time
3. extra computation

It's clear that interprocess communication is not an issue in a serial program. Hence, any interprocess communication will contribute to T_O. Idle time may or may not contribute to overhead. Unfortunately, it generally does: one or more processes will remain idle while they wait for information from another process. For example, in the trapezoidal rule program, processes 1, 2, ..., $p-1$ must remain idle while process 0 reads in the input data. Finally, there are numerous opportunities for a parallel program to do extra computation. Some of the most obvious are performing calculations not required by the serial program and replicated calculations. An example of the former is the calculation in the trapezoidal rule program of each process's subinterval of integration. Clearly this calculation isn't required in the serial program. An example of the latter occurs when each process calculates the number of trapezoids used in estimating the integral over its subinterval. Since the program assumes that p divides n, this value is the same on all the processes. (Note that this is also an example of a calculation not required by the serial program.)

The formula for the overhead in the parallel trapezoidal program is simply $p \times$ (the time to execute MPI_Reduce). That is, if we ignore I/O, the vast majority of the overhead comes from the call to MPI_Reduce. The bulk of the time for this function comes from communication. However, there is also idle time and extra computation: recall that using the tree-structured communication, each process other than the root (in our case, process 0) is eventually idled before the computation is complete. Also, each process must do some calculations at each stage in order to determine which process it communicates with.

12.4 Scalability

Amdahl's law says that there is a definite upper bound on the speedup that can be attained in a parallel program. In terms of efficiency, it asserts that if r is the fraction of the program that can be parallelized, then

$$E = \frac{T_\sigma}{p(1-r)T_\sigma + rT_\sigma}$$
$$= \frac{1}{p(1-r) + r}.$$

So an equivalent formulation of Amdahl's law would conclude that the efficiency achievable by a parallel program on a given problem instance will approach zero as the number of processes is increased.

Let's look at this assertion in terms of overhead. Since

$$T_O(n,p) = pT_\pi(n,p) - T_\sigma(n),$$

efficiency can be written as

$$E(n,p) = \frac{T_\sigma(n)}{pT_\pi(n,p)}$$
$$= \frac{T_\sigma(n)}{T_O(n,p) + T_\sigma(n)}$$
$$= \frac{1}{T_O(n,p)/T_\sigma(n) + 1}.$$

Thus, we might reply to Amdahl that the behavior of the efficiency as p is increased is completely determined by the overhead function, $T_O(n, p)$. In the trapezoidal rule program, since

$$T_O = k_2 p \log_2(p),$$

the efficiency attained on a given problem instance will approach zero as the number of processes is increased. This, is completely expected: both our theoretical estimates and our actual timings show that for a given value of n, the efficiency decreases as p is increased. However, this formula also shows that for fixed p, as n is increased, we can obtain efficiencies as close to one as we like. What happens if we increase both n and p simultaneously? If we substitute our formulas for T_σ and T_O into the new formula for E, we get

$$E(n, p) = \frac{1}{k_2 p \log_2(p)/k_1 n + 1}.$$

Thus, if we increase n and p at the same rate, our efficiency will decrease since $p \log_2(p)$ will grow slightly faster than $n = p$. However, if n is increased as fast as $p \log_2(p)$, then we can maintain a constant efficiency.

For example, if we examine the speedups in Table 11.2, we see that if $p = 4$ and $n = 512$, the efficiency is $E = 3.6/4 = 0.90$. If we wish to maintain this efficiency with $p = 8$ processes, we shouldn't double n. Rather, we should choose n so that the value of

$$\frac{k_2 p \log_2(p)}{k_1 n}$$

is constant. Substituting our values for n and p, we see that

$$\frac{k_2 4 \log_2(4)}{k_1 512} = \frac{k_2 8 \log_2(8)}{k_1 n},$$

and hence the new value of n should be 1536. Examining the table of speedups again, we see that if $p = 8$ and $n = 1536$, then the efficiency is $E = 7.1/8 = 0.89$. More generally, we see that if n is increased at the same rate as $p \log(p)$, then we can maintain any desired level of efficiency.

This last observation is the key to scalability: a parallel program is **scalable** if, as the number of processes (p) is increased, we can find a rate of increase for the problem size (n) so that efficiency remains constant. Of course, this definition suggests that there are varying degrees of scalability. If we can solve our efficiency formula for n in terms of p, we can obtain an explicit formula for the rate at which n must grow. For example, the efficiency formula for the trapezoidal rule program is

$$E(n, p) = \frac{k_1 n}{k_2 p \log_2(p) + k_1 n}.$$

Solving for n gives

$$n = \frac{E}{1 - E} \frac{k_2}{k_1} p \log_2(p).$$

That is, in order to maintain a constant efficiency E, n should grow at the same rate as $p \log_2(p)$ (which we just observed).

A couple of caveats are in order. First, in general it may be very difficult to solve for n in terms of p. For example, if $T_\sigma(n)$ has degree 5 in n, there is no general approach that will allow us to solve for n in terms of E and p. Second, and more important, don't lose sight of practical considerations when manipulating formulas. For example, suppose we have written a parallel program that achieves linear speedup. Then

$$T_O(n, p) = pT_\pi(n, p) - T_\sigma(n) = pT_\sigma(n)/p - T_\sigma(n) = 0.$$

So in theory, $E = 1$, regardless of n and p. However, in a real-world problem this formula will fail very quickly.

For example, suppose we have to add two distributed vectors that are to remain distributed after addition. Then each process simply adds its local components. If n, the order of the vectors, is evenly divisible by p, and each process is assigned n/p components of each vector, then the program achieves linear speedup. The key here is that n is evenly divisible by p. In particular, if $p > n$, then some processors will remain idle and the overhead will no longer be 0. In other words, in order to maintain an efficiency of 1, for arbitrary p, n must grow as p.

12.5 Potential Problems in Estimating Performance

Now that we've developed a theoretical underpinning for performance estimation, let's return to a discussion of practical performance estimation and discuss some problems that we might encounter. In Chapter 11 we have already discussed several difficulties. The most important of these was getting reliable estimates of t_a, t_s, and t_c. Another problem we encountered was underestimating the cost of a collective communication function. Both of these problems have to do with an empirical analysis of a *component* of the program, and as such are relatively easy to solve. For example, as soon as we suspect that our estimate of the runtime of MPI_Reduce is inaccurate, we can write a short timing analysis program and determine whether this is, in fact, a problem. However, there are other problems that are not so easily remedied. In this section we'll discuss some of the more common problems.

12.5.1 Networks of Workstations and Resource Contention

Unfortunately, timings on networks of workstations are almost always suspect. If we write a parallel program for a network of workstations, the ideal environment should allow the user exclusive access to processors, peripherals, and network during execution. That is, only the absolute minimum set of system processes and no other user processes should run on each workstation, and there should be no network traffic other than that generated by our program. Of course, this ideal environment is virtually impossible to achieve. Even if we manage to find a time when no one else is logged on to any of the machines, it's still entirely possible, for example, that a mail message might be received by one of the machines during the execution of our program. However, unless we have a program that runs for a long time, such interruptions will be relatively rare, and if our program does run for a long time, we should expect such random interruptions and, as a consequence, we should be cautious about rejecting predicted timing analyses that differ from actual runtimes.

So the first rule of thumb here is to try to run our programs when there are as few users and as little network traffic as possible. Unfortunately, this tends to be at unpleasant times like 3 AM, but, heck, we're programmers, and programmers like to stay up all night. Right? The second rule of thumb is that if our program takes a long time to run and/or we are using a network with relatively heavy traffic, we should expect to get timings that are at variance with our predicted timings. In most settings (e.g., ethernet-connected workstations), this variance is more often due to network traffic than reduced access to processors. In other words, it's more likely that the network is saturated than that the processors are heavily loaded, but this will depend on your particular installation.

In order to compare predicted times with actual times, it's not unreasonable to run the program repeatedly and see if the runtimes are clustering around a fixed value. Usually this will be the case. If it is, this cluster time is probably more reliable than an average of all runtimes.

Networks of workstations provide an extreme example of a problem that can be encountered on virtually any parallel system: resource contention. For example, if a program generates large amounts of data that are stored on a single disk, the processes may be forced to access the disk sequentially—even on a dedicated parallel system. The situation could be even worse if a parallel system provided virtual memory but very limited I/O capabilities.

12.5.2 Load Balancing and Idle Time

We've mentioned idle time as a source of overhead in a parallel program. The most common cause of idle time is load imbalance: one or more processes must carry out more computation than one or more other processes. There can be other causes. A common source occurs when one process must wait for some system resource to become available before it can proceed with its computations. For example, in a network of workstations, if the network is saturated, a process may be forced to wait to send a message. In any case, when we're carrying out performance analyses, we can identify two basic sources of idle time: predictable or regular, and unpredictable or irregular.

By *predictable* or *regular* idle time, we mean idle time that will occur every time the program is run with more than one process—regardless of the input data. For example, when we use a tree-structured broadcast to communicate a value from one process to the other processes, if there is a point of synchronization before a broadcast, most of the processes will necessarily be idle while they wait for the data to propagate through the broadcast tree.

By *unpredictable* or *irregular* idle time, we mean idle time that does not occur every time the program is run. For example, a program that searches a binary tree might partition the problem by assigning disjoint subtrees to different processes. If the number of nodes in the different subtrees varies, then one or more of the processes may be idle. However, this is clearly data dependent. For example, if the tree is generated as the program is run, there may be no way of knowing before the program is run whether one subtree will contain fewer nodes than another. Another source has been previously alluded to: system limitations. If your program doesn't have exclusive access to the system resources when it's run, then one or more processes may be idled while some system resources are used by another program.

The reason for this distinction is clear: we can anticipate regular idle time in our performance analysis, and, as a consequence, it should not be a source of inaccurate performance prediction. The second type of idle time is more problematic. We've already discussed various options if we don't have exclusive access to the system. If, on the other hand, the source of the imbalance is in the data or algorithm, we need to determine how serious the resulting load imbalances will be.

As an example, consider the search tree problem. If we can make reasonable a priori estimates of the structure of the trees, we can determine how serious the load imbalances will be. If we determine that, in the vast majority of cases, each nonleaf node will have the same number of children, and all the leaves will be in about the same level, then simply assigning a distinct subtree to each process will cause little difficulty with load imbalance and idle time. If, on the other hand, we determine that the structure of the trees is highly variable, we should probably look for another partitioning algorithm.

None of this should be taken to imply that we believe that any idle time is desirable. We are simply observing that, in some cases, we can include predicted idle time in our performance analysis, while in other cases it may be very difficult to do so, and, as a consequence, our analyses will be unreliable.

12.5.3 Overlapping Communication and Computation

If each compute node of your system contains a communication coprocessor, or if you use nonblocking communications (see Chapter 13), it's possible that communications and computation can be overlapped. This can cause difficulties in performance prediction because it may be extremely difficult to make any a priori estimate of the extent to which these are overlapped. For example, we can estimate t_s and t_c by running the following code and using least squares to fit a line to the data:

```
/* two process ping-pong */
if (my_rank == 0) {
```

```
        for (test = 0, size = min_size;
                size <= max_size; size = size + incr, test++) {
            for (pass = 0; pass < MAX; pass++) {
                MPI_Barrier(comm);
                start = MPI_Wtime();
                MPI_Send(x, size, MPI_FLOAT, 1, 0, comm);
                MPI_Recv(x, size, MPI_FLOAT, 1, 0, comm,
                    &status);
                finish = MPI_Wtime();
                raw_time = finish - start - wtime_overhead;
                printf("%d %f\n", size, raw_time);
            }
        }
    } else { /* my_rank == 1 */
        for (test = 0, size = min_size; size <= max_size;
                size = size + incr, test++) {
            for (pass = 0; pass < MAX; pass++) {
                MPI_Barrier(comm);
                MPI_Recv(x, size, MPI_FLOAT, 0, 0, comm,
                    &status);
                MPI_Send(x, size, MPI_FLOAT, 0, 0, comm);
            }
        }
    }
}
```

However, consider the following segment of code:

```
MPI_Barrier(comm);
if (my_rank == src)
    MPI_Send(x, m, MPI_FLOAT, dest, tag, comm);
else if (my_rank == dest)
    MPI_Recv(x, m, MPI_FLOAT, src, tag, comm,
        &status);
for (i = 0; i < k; i++)
    y[i] = w[i] + z[i];
```

We would predict that the runtime for the code following the call to MPI_ Barrier would be

$$t_s + mt_c + kt_a.$$

However, if we have communication coprocessors (and smart compilers), the send/receive pair may be run simultaneously with the for loop, and the actual runtime might be

$$\max\{t_s + mt_c, kt_a\}.$$

In this simple situation, it's not difficult to predict the actual runtime. However, if we repeatedly encounter these situations or fail to synchronize the processes before they occur, the cumulative effects may make it extremely difficult to accurately predict runtime. In such cases, it is necessary to rely almost completely on empirical data.

12.5.4 Collective Communication

The problem of overlapping communication and computation can further complicate the prediction of the runtime of collective communication. However, even greater difficulties can arise if you don't know what algorithm(s) a given collective communication is using. For example, some implementations of MPI simply use a linear `for` loop and `MPI_Send/Recv` to implement a broadcast:

```
if (my_rank == root) {
    for (proc = 0; proc < p; proc++)
        MPI_Send(x, size, datatype, proc, tag, comm);
}
MPI_Recv(x, size, datatype, root, tag, comm, &status);
```

while, as we've already seen, other implementations use a tree structure. This problem isn't very difficult to diagnose. However, an implementation may use several different algorithms depending on, for example, the size of the message. There may also be lower-level optimizations that can be exploited by coding in assembler. So, once again, it may be necessary to simply rely on empirical data for runtime prediction.

12.6 Performance Evaluation Tools

You may already be familiar with some performance evaluation tools that are commonly available for serial programs. Many UNIX systems provide the tool `prof` (an abbreviation for *profile*). This program is used to provide information on how much time is being spent in various parts of the program during execution—such information is called an **execution profile.** Typically `prof` is used by compiling a program with the `-p` flag. Then each time the program is run, a **log file** called `mon.out` is created. The log file contains information on how much time is spent in various parts of the program, and this data can be examined by calling the function `prof`.

The exact contents of `mon.out` and the data displayed by `prof` will vary from system to system. Typically they will have one of two forms: counts of the number of times various parts of the program have been executed or, more often, percentages of execution time spent in various parts of the program. (This latter form of the data is, properly speaking, an execution profile.) In order to generate the counts, one typically links the program with special libraries. These libraries contain copies of all the functions in the libraries you normally link your program with, except that the functions in the special libraries contain counters that record the number of times each function is called. In order to generate the times, the program is interrupted at fixed intervals by the operating system and data is collected on which function (or statement) is being executed. This data can then be used to get a rough picture of how much time is being spent in various parts of the programs.

Typically both forms of profiling are available to users of MPI. For example, if you are running a program on a network of workstations, you can simply compile your MPI program with the -p option, and your system will generate a mon.out file on each machine. (Note that this may cause problems if the directory containing your executable is NFS-mounted on multiple machines in your network.)

Unfortunately, simply generating a serial profile of each executable frequently doesn't provide us with enough information to make detailed analyses of where the time is being spent in our programs. For example, the profiling data may tell you that 50% of process 0's execution time was spent in calls to MPI_Recv, but this won't tell you whether the time was spent equally in all calls to MPI_Recv or whether one call took most of the time, and, if the latter is the case, it won't tell you which call it was and which process called the matching MPI_Send. Even worse, the profiling may show that, say, 80% of the runtime was spent in function A, while 20% was spent in B, but A was perfectly parallel, while B was executed sequentially by the processes. In this situation, we're liable to ignore B and spend all our time trying to improve A.

So we need a unified profile of the behavior of a parallel program. There are several difficulties with providing such a profile. In the first place, many distributed-memory systems don't have a single, "universal" clock, and the clocks on the various processors are not synchronized. So it is very difficult to tell how events on one process correspond to events on another. Further, even if we could synchronize the clocks, there's no guarantee that each of the clocks runs at the same rate. Finally, in trying to overcome these difficulties, we may find that we've seriously affected the overall performance of the program, and that it may be difficult to distinguish performance problems that are a result of our code and performance problems that are a result of the profiling code. It should be mentioned that this last problem may be encountered in profiling serial programs. However, on most modern systems, its effect is either very small or nonexistent, while on parallel systems, the effect may be very large. For example, the profiling software may create a single log file recording events. Since the events themselves will, in general, be distributed, the recording of the information may involve communication so that the data can be stored in a single location.

As a consequence of these problems, the development of performance evaluation tools for parallel programs remains an active area of research, and there are a number of tools currently under development. Since a comprehensive discussion of these tools is beyond the scope of this text, we'll limit ourselves to a discussion of MPI's profiling interface and one tool that is commonly available with MPI implementations.

12.6.1 MPI's Profiling Interface

We mentioned earlier that in order to use some serial profiling tools, it's necessary to link in special libraries before your program is executed (or at execution time for dynamically linked libraries). In order to understand the reason for this, suppose, for example, that you wish to determine how many times a function is called during execution of your program. If you wrote the function, you could define a static global counter and make the first executable statement of the function increment this variable. Before the program completes, you could simply print the value of the variable.

If you haven't written the function, however, this basic strategy could be very painful, or even impossible, to use. Since you haven't written the function, the global counter must be incremented outside the function. Thus, each time you call the function, you'll have to add a statement to your source code incrementing the counter. Furthermore, this may actually be impossible: if calls to the function are contained in other system-defined functions, you won't be able to count these calls. A solution to this problem is use a system-defined function with its own built-in counter. Of course, you don't want to waste CPU cycles on incrementing counters or taking timings during a production run. So a simple solution to the problem is to have two distinct libraries of functions: a profiling library in which each function has a built-in counter or timer, and a production library in which each function is optimized and, as a consequence, doesn't contain counters or timers.

This idea is at the heart of MPI's profiling interface. The MPI standard requires that each implementation allow each MPI function to be called by its usual name, and the usual name preceded by a capital "P". For example, a process can send the float stored in x to process 0 with either

```
MPI_Send(&x, 1, MPI_FLOAT, 0, 0, MPI_COMM_WORLD)
```

or

```
PMPI_Send(&x, 1, MPI_FLOAT, 0, 0, MPI_COMM_WORLD)
```

How does this help? Each user can write his or her own profiling implementation—even if he or she doesn't have access to the MPI source code.

For example, suppose we want to find out how much time is being spent by our program in calls to MPI_Send—including the calls made by the MPI functions themselves. We can write our own MPI_Send function:

```
static double send_time = 0.0;

int MPI_Send(void* buffer, int count, MPI_Datatype datatype,
        int dest, int tag, MPI_Comm comm) {
    double start_time;
    double finish_time;
    int return_val;
```

```
        start_time = MPI_Wtime();
        return_val = PMPI_Send(buffer, count, datatype,
                            dest, tag, comm);
        finish_time = MPI_Wtime();
        send_time = send_time + finish_time - start_time;
        return return_val;
}
```

Now when we link our program, we first link with the file containing this code. Then we link with the MPI libraries. So when MPI_Send is called, our own version will be executed. It, in turn, will call the real MPI_Send using the call to PMPI_Send.

12.6.2   Upshot

Upshot is a parallel program performance analysis tool that comes bundled with the public domain mpich implementation of MPI. See the references at the end of the chapter and Appendix B for information on obtaining a copy. It should be stressed that Upshot is not a part of MPI. We discuss it here because it has many features in common with other parallel performance analysis tools, and it is readily available for use with MPI.

Upshot provides some of the information that is not easily determined if we use data generated by serial tools such as prof or simply add counters and/or timers using MPI's profiling interface. It attempts to provide a unified view of the profiling data generated by each process by modifying the time stamps of events on different processes so that all the processes start and end at the same time. It also provides a convenient form for visualizing the profiling data in a **Gantt chart**. A Gantt chart is simply a series of timelines—one per process–running side by side. The timeline corresponding to process q shows the state of process q at each instant of time by color-coded bars. For examples of Gantt charts, see Figures 12.1 and 12.2.

There are basically two methods of using Upshot. In the simpler approach, we can link our source code with appropriate libraries and obtain information on the time spent by our program in each MPI function. If we desire information on more general segments or states of our program, we can get it to provide custom profiling data by adding appropriate function calls to our source code.

Let's look at each approach. Using the parallel trapezoidal rule program as an example, in order to use the first approach, we just link our program with the profiling library that comes with the code. When we run the program, it generates a log file containing information on the time spent in the various MPI communication functions. After execution is completed, we simply run Upshot on the log file. If the parallel trapezoidal rule is run on four processors of an nCUBE with 2048 trapezoids, the Gantt chart generated from the log file

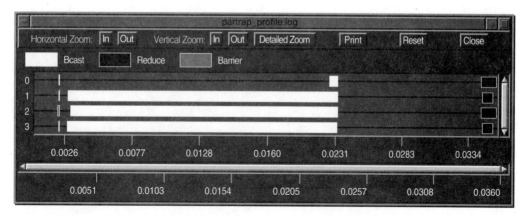

Figure 12.1   Upshot output using automatic profile generation

looks something like Figure 12.1. Note that bars are generated only for MPI communication function calls; other parts of the program are indicated by a horizontal line. Also note the huge amount of time spent by processes 1–3 in the call to `MPI_Bcast`. Most of this clearly represents idle time. When `Get_data` is called, all the processes build the derived type before the broadcast, but process 0 must also read in the limits of integration and the number of trapezoids, which evidently takes a long time. While process 0 is reading in this data, the remaining processes block in the call to `MPI_Bcast`, waiting for process 0 to finish reading in the data and initiate the broadcast.

Alternatively, we can define various parts of the code that we wish to study. For example, we might want information on the following parts of the trapezoidal rule program:

1. Construction of derived datatype
2. Broadcast
3. Local calculations for trapezoidal rule
4. Reduce

In order to get this information, we need to define the states we're interested in. This involves three additional function calls for each state. The first describes the state, and the remaining two mark its beginning and end. In our example, we could describe the states by adding the following code before the call to `Get_data`:

```
if (my_rank == 0) {
    MPE_Describe_state(1, 2, "Derived", "gray");
    MPE_Describe_state(3, 4, "Broadcast", "black");
    MPE_Describe_state(5, 6, "Trapezoid", "white");
    MPE_Describe_state(7, 8, "Reduce", "gray");
}
```

These calls specify a pair of integers, a name, and a color for each state. The integers are used to mark the beginning and the end of code corresponding to the state. The name and the color are used in the display generated by Upshot.

In order to identify the states, we place calls to MPE_Log_event at the beginning and end of each code segment corresponding to one of our states. For example, in order to mark the code segments for building the derived datatype and the broadcast, the body of Get_data would be modified as follows:

```
if (my_rank == 0){
    scanf("%f %f %d", a_ptr, b_ptr, n_ptr);
}

MPE_Log_event(1,0,"start Derived");
Build_derived_type(a_ptr, b_ptr, n_ptr, &mesg_mpi_t);
MPE_Log_event(2,0,"end Derived");

MPE_Log_event(3,0,"start Bcast");
MPI_Bcast(a_ptr, 1, mesg_mpi_t, 0,
    MPI_COMM_WORLD);
MPE_Log_event(4,0,"end Bcast");
```

So we mark the start of the state with the first integer we defined in MPE_Describe_state, and we mark the end of the state with the second. We won't make use of the remaining arguments: it suffices to know that the second is an int and the third is a string.

In order to start and finish logging, we need to include calls to MPE_Init_log and MPE_Finish_log. MPE_Init_log takes no arguments, and it should be called at some point between the call to MPI_Init and the calls to MPE_Describe_state. MPE_Finish_log takes a single argument (a string), the name of the log file. For example, we might use

```
MPE_Finish_log("customprof.log")
```

This would create a log file called customprof.log.

Finally, it should be stressed that none of these MPE functions is part of MPI. Consequently, it's necessary to add the preprocessor directive

```
#include "mpe.h"
```

It's also necessary to link your program with the mpe libraries. Ask your local expert for details.

With our trapezoidal rule function modified as we've described, Upshot would create the Gantt chart in Figure 12.2.

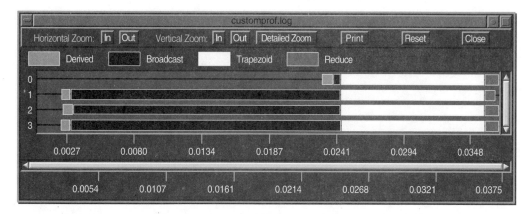

Figure 12.2 Upshot output using custom profile generation

12.7 Summary

Amdahl's law asserts that if a fraction s of a program that solves an instance of a problem is inherently serial, then $1/s$ is an upper bound on the speedup that can be achieved by any parallel program—regardless of the number of processes. An inherently serial part of a program is one that cannot be parallelized. For example, if a program needs to read in a value, this will probably be an inherently serial part of the program.

Amdahl's law seems to imply that many problems are not amenable to solution on a parallel system. For example, if 25% of a program is inherently serial, then the maximum possible speedup is $1/(1/4) = 4$. So even if we use 100 processes, we can't do better than a speedup of 4, which would be an efficiency of 0.04.

We saw that Amdahl's law can be unnecessarily pessimistic. Indeed, it is true that, for a fixed problem instance, increasing the number of processes will decrease efficiency. That is, if we fix n (the problem size) and increase p (the number of processes), then it is more than likely that efficiency will diminish. However, if we increase our computational power (p), we will, in all likelihood, also increase the size of the problem we want to solve. As an extreme example, it wouldn't make much sense to use 1000 processes to run the trapezoidal rule with only 500 trapezoids.

This critical observation leads to the idea of *scalability*. A program is *scalable* if we can maintain constant efficiency by increasing the problem size at the same time that we increase the number of processes.

In order to understand scalability, we defined two additional concepts: *work* and *overhead*. The work done by a serial program is just its runtime. The work done by a parallel program is the sum of the work done by each of its processes. Thus, the work done by a parallel program is simply $W_\pi(n,p) = pT_\pi(n,p)$. The overhead incurred by a parallel program is the difference between the work done by the parallel program and the corresponding serial program:

$$T_O(n, p) = W_\pi(n, p) - W_\sigma(n) = pT_\pi(n, p) - T_\sigma(n).$$

Thus, the efficiency of a parallel program can be written

$$E(n, p) = \frac{T_\sigma(n)}{pT_\pi(n, p)}$$

$$= \frac{1}{T_O(n, p)/T_\sigma(n) + 1}.$$

If, as p is increased, we can increase n so that the fraction T_O/T_σ remains constant, then we can maintain a constant efficiency.

There are three main sources of overhead in parallel programs:

1. interprocess communication

2. process idle time

3. additional computation (computation carried out by the parallel program that is not carried out by the serial program)

There are many situations in which it may be very difficult to make accurate a priori estimates of parallel program performance. Some of the most common problems occur in the following situations:

1. Resource contention. In any parallel system, we can run into problems of resource contention: processes attempting to simultaneously use the same system facility (e.g., a disk). This problem is especially troublesome in networks of workstations, where we almost never have exclusive access to system resources, and, as a consequence, our programs are subject to unpredictable delays.

2. Load imbalance. In some situations, it is possible to predict idle time. For example, if a value is read by, say, process 0 and distributed to the other processes, we can predict that the processes other than 0 will be idle for the duration of the input operation. However, there are many situations where we can't predict idle time with any reliability. For example, if our program distributes a tree by assigning subtrees to different processes, and the tree is unbalanced, the computational load may be unevenly distributed among the processes.

3. Overlapping communication with computation. Our simple formula for communication, $t_s + mt_c$, may not accurately predict the cost of communication if it's possible that communication and computation can be overlapped. This can happen if each node of the parallel system has a separate communication coprocessor, or if we use nonblocking communications.

4. Collective communication. Our system may use complicated, proprietary algorithms for collective communication. An unfortunate consequence of this is that we may be unable to predict the runtime of collective operations.

In order to help users analyze program performance, MPI provides a profiling interface. Essentially, this allows users to create their own profiling library for any MPI functions that they wish to study. The key to this is that any implementation of MPI must allow a program to call each MPI function, MPI_Xxx, by both MPI_Xxx and PMPI_Xxx. Thus, by defining your own version of MPI_Xxx that calls PMPI_Xxx, you can study such matters as length of time spent in MPI_Xxx.

We closed the chapter with a brief discussion of Upshot, a program that can be used to study the behavior of parallel programs. Although Upshot is not a part of MPI, it is commonly available with MPI implementations. It can be used to generate Gantt charts of parallel programs. It can be used either with or without modification to the source program.

12.8 References

Amdahl's law was originally formulated by Gene Amdahl [2]. The development of programs that achieved efficiencies near 1 on a 1024-processor system was reported in [23]. The resulting reconsideration of Amdahl's law was published in [22].

Our discussion of overhead and scalability is largely based on Kumar et al. [26]. They also provide a very complete discussion of other measures of parallel program performance.

See the MPI Standard [28, 29], Gropp et al. [21], and Snir et al. [34] for discussions of MPI's profiling interface.

The *User's Guide for* mpich [20] discusses the features of Upshot. Upshot can be downloaded from Argonne National Lab at ftp:// info.mcs.anl.gov. Foster [17] provides an extensive discussion of profiling parallel programs.

12.9 Exercises

1. Determine T_O for the solution to the trapezoidal rule that uses a simple loop of receives on process 0. Compare the scalability of this implementation with the implementation that uses a tree-based reduce.

2. Determine T_O for the basic parallel matrix multiplication algorithm (see section 7.1) and Fox's algorithm (section 7.2). Can you devise simple formulas describing the scalability of these algorithms? If not, how might we go about studying their scalability?

12.10   Programming Assignments

1. Write a program that generates timing statistics on your collective communication functions. Compare your data with predicted runtimes. Do your collective communication functions use the algorithms you thought they used?

2. Use MPI's profiling interface and a profiling tool such as Upshot (if you have access to one) in order to study the performance of the basic parallel matrix multiplication algorithm (section 7.1). Does the profile indicate that there is a significant amount of idle time on any process? Do the results of your profiling suggest possible improvements in the algorithm?

3. Repeat assignment 2 for Fox's algorithm (section 7.2).

4. Repeat assignment 2 for Jacobi's method (section 10.3).

5. Repeat assignment 2 for our parallel sorting program (section 10.5).

CHAPTER 13

Advanced Point-to-Point Communication

UP UNTIL NOW THE ONLY POINT-TO-POINT communication functions we've used are the blocking operations MPI_Send and MPI_Recv. In this chapter, we'll explore the much richer set of point-to-point functions provided by MPI. We'll begin by developing a couple of simple implementations of an allgather function using MPI_Send and MPI_Recv. With this under our belts, we'll spend the remainder of the chapter discussing how we might modify our functions to make them more reliable and faster.

The first new communication functions we'll discuss are MPI_Sendrecv and MPI_Sendrecv_replace, which provide a simple means of organizing paired communications to avoid deadlock. We'll continue with a discussion of the basic nonblocking functions, MPI_Isend and MPI_Irecv. As we'll see, these nonblocking functions provide a means of overlapping communication and computation, and hence a means of improving performance. We'll go on to a discussion of persistent communication requests, which provide the possibility of even greater overlap between communication and computation. We'll close with a discussion of communication modes: up to now, we've left a number of decisions about how communication is managed to the system. For example, we've let the system manage buffering of messages. Using different communication modes, we can explicitly tell the system whether we want messages buffered and, if so, where they should be buffered.

13.1 An Example: Coding Allgather

MPI provides a collective communication operation that allows us to take data that is distributed across a collection of processes and gather the distributed data onto each process. The name of the MPI function that does this is MPI_Allgather. As an example, let's implement our own allgather functions, first using MPI_Send and MPI_Recv, then using more advanced point-to-point communications.

There are *many* possible implementations of allgather in terms of point-to-point operations. If our processes were physically configured as a full binary tree, a natural solution would be to write a tree-structured gather to the root process, and then follow that by a tree-structured broadcast from the root. The cost of the startups for this would be $2(\lceil \log_2(p) \rceil - 1)t_s$.

If our processors were physically configured as a ring, a **ring pass** would be a natural solution. The idea is that each process sends its data to the process immediately adjacent in, say, the counterclockwise direction. Then this operation can be repeated, but instead of using the original data, each process sends the data it received during the previous stage. Figure 13.1 shows a four-processor ring pass. Since it takes exactly $p-1$ stages for each processor to receive all the data, the cost of the startups is $(p - 1)t_s$.

An alternative that is natural for hypercubes involves a sequence of pair-wise exchanges among the processes. At each stage, the processes are split into two groups of equal sizes, each process in the first group is paired with a process in the second, and the paired processes exchange *all* of their data. See Figure 13.2 for an example with four processes. If there are $p = 2^d$ processes, then at each stage each process will double the amount of data it contains. Hence there will be $d = \log_2(p)$ stages and $\log_2(p)$ startups.

Let's write a ring pass allgather and a hypercube allgather.

13.1.1 Function Parameters

We'll assume that the data to be gathered from each process consists of a block of floats, and each process is storing the same number of floats. Thus the input parameters should be an array of floats containing the data to be gathered from the local process, the size of the array (which will be the same on each process), and a communicator whose members are the processes that will participate in the allgather. The output will consist of a single parameter: an array containing the floats that have been gathered from each process. Thus, the output array will have order pb, where p is the size of the communicator and b is the order of the input array. As with the MPI collective functions, we will assume that the input and output arrays are distinct. This will mean that in each function we will need to copy the contents of the input array into the appropriate location in the output array.

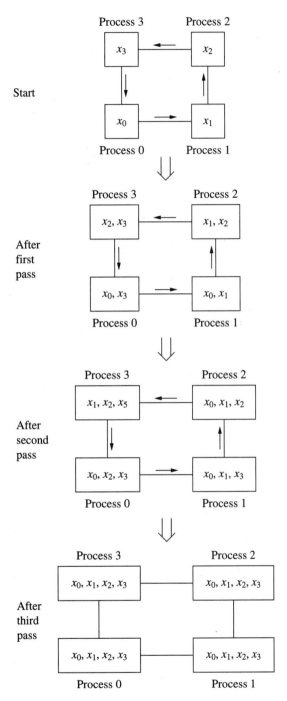

Figure 13.1   A four-processor ring pass

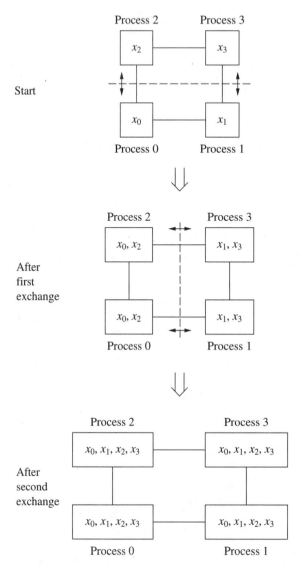

Figure 13.2   Four-process pairwise exchange

13.1.2   Ring Pass Allgather

The heart of the code is a loop: during each pass through the loop we send the most recently received block of data to the successor processor and receive a new block of data from the predecessor processor. Thus, we will execute the body of the loop $p - 1$ times; before we execute the loop, we need to compute the ranks of the predecessor and successor processes, as well as copying the data from the input array into the output array.

In the body of the loop we will need to compute offsets into the array that tell us where the data to be sent begin and where the data to be received should begin. This involves some modular arithmetic: we work backward through the array one block at a time; after we've hit the beginning of the array, we move to the end of the array. The block we're receiving will always be one block before the block we're sending. Since we start with our own block, the block we send on pass i, $i = 0, 1, \ldots, p - 1$, will be

$$(\texttt{my\_rank} - i) \bmod p.$$

Since the C programming language does not guarantee that the result of a % b is positive, we should add in p to the dividend. That is, the block that we should send on the ith pass can be computed in C as

```
(my_rank - i + p) % p
```

In order to convert this to the offset in floats instead of blocks, we can multiply by the blocksize

```
((my_rank - i + p) % p)*blocksize
```

The block that we're receiving will be the block immediately preceding the one we're sending. So to get the offset in floats for the receive, we simply subtract one from the dividend:

```
((my_rank - i + p - 1) % p)*blocksize
```

Then we execute our send and receive.

```
void Allgather_ring(
         float      x[]        /* in  */,
         int        blocksize  /* in  */,
         float      y[]        /* out */,
         MPI_Comm   ring_comm  /* in  */) {

    int        i, p, my_rank;
    int        successor, predecessor;
    int        send_offset, recv_offset;
    MPI_Status status;

    MPI_Comm_size(ring_comm, &p);
    MPI_Comm_rank(ring_comm, &my_rank);

    /* Copy x into correct location in y */
    for (i = 0; i < blocksize; i++)
        y[i + my_rank*blocksize] = x[i];

    successor = (my_rank + 1) % p;
```

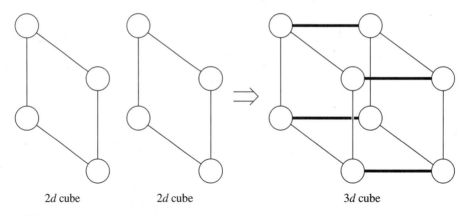

2*d* cube   2*d* cube   3*d* cube

Figure 13.3   Forming a three-dimensional hypercube from two two-dimensional hypercubes

```
predecessor = (my_rank - 1 + p) % p;

for (i = 0; i < p - 1; i++) {
    send_offset = ((my_rank - i + p) % p)*blocksize;
    recv_offset =
        ((my_rank - i - 1 + p) % p)*blocksize;
    MPI_Send(y + send_offset, blocksize, MPI_FLOAT,
        successor, 0, ring_comm);
    MPI_Recv(y + recv_offset, blocksize, MPI_FLOAT,
        predecessor, 0, ring_comm, &status);
}
} /* Allgather_ring */
```

Note that we execute all the sends first and then all the receives. This assumes that the system can buffer the messages: indeed, the code could fail if there is inadequate system buffering. We'll return to this point later.

13.2 Hypercubes

For the hypercube allgather, we'll assume that p is a power of two, so that we don't have to worry about how to deal with processes that aren't paired up. As with most hypercube algorithms, it's usually easiest to understand how the algorithm works by looking at the binary representation of the process ranks.

Recall that hypercubes are defined inductively: a hypercube of dimension 0 consists of a single process, and a hypercube of dimension $d + 1$ can be constructed from two hypercubes of dimension d by joining corresponding processes in the d-dimensional hypercubes with communication wires. See Figure 13.3.

This "doubling" process leads to a natural scheme for assigning binary addresses to the processes: each process in a d-dimensional hypercube has a

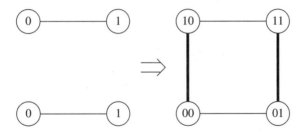

Figure 13.4   Addresses in a two-dimensional hypercube built from two one-dimensional hypercubes

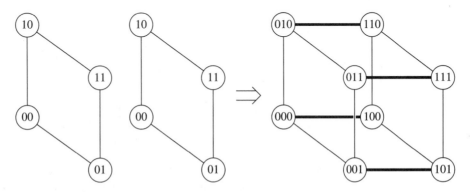

Figure 13.5   Addresses in a three-dimensional hypercube built from two two-dimensional hypercubes

unique d-bit address. (What happens in a zero-dimensional hypercube?) In a one-dimensional hypercube, one process has rank 0 and the other has rank 1. Now if we form a two-dimensional hypercube from two one-dimensional hypercubes, we'll join the two processes with rank 0 with a wire and we'll join the two processes with rank 1 with a wire. In order to get unique addresses, we'll use 2-bit addresses in our new hypercube: the low-order bits will be the same as they were in the original one-dimensional hypercubes, but the high-order bit will be 0 in one of the original one-dimensional hypercubes and 1 in the other one-dimensional hypercube. See Figure 13.4.

In order to assign addresses in a three-dimensional hypercube, we use the same idea that we used to assign addresses in the two-dimensional hypercube: after we join the two two-dimensional hypercubes, the two low-order bits of the address are the same as they were in the original hypercubes, but the high-order bit is 0 for all the processes in one of the original two-dimensional hypercubes and the high-order bit is 1 for all the processes in the other. See Figure 13.5.

The idea generalizes to arbitrary dimensions, and it results in an addressing scheme that has the following property:

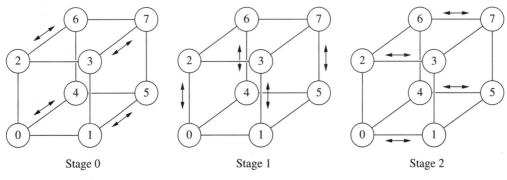

| Stage 0 | Stage 1 | Stage 2 |

Figure 13.6   Process pairing during the stages

Two processes in a hypercube are adjacent if and only if their binary addresses differ in exactly one bit.

Now we can formulate our pairing scheme in allgather more precisely. Suppose the hypercube has dimension d. During the first stage, we'll assign all the processes that have 0 as their most significant bit to one group, and all the processes that have 1 as their most significant bit to the other group. Each process in the first group will be paired with the process in the second group whose binary address differs only in the most significant bit. Then each communication will occur between adjacent processes, and no two pairs of communicating processes will attempt to use the same communication wire. During the next stage, we'll use the same idea, except that now we'll use the second most significant bit. That is, the first group will now consist of all processes with 0 as their second most significant bit, and the second group will consist of all processes with 1 as their second most significant bit. We'll pair processes whose binary addresses are identical in all but the second most significant bit. Continuing this process: next we use the third most significant bit, then the fourth, etc., until we've formed the groups and pairs on the least significant bit.

An example always helps. Suppose that the blocksize is 1, and we have a three-dimensional cube. Then the stages are illustrated in Figures 13.6–13.9.

13.2.1   Additional Issues in the Hypercube Exchange

At each stage, each process will need to compute the rank of the process with which it will exchange data. But observe that this won't be enough: the amount of data to be transmitted and its layout change with each stage. In our example, during the first stage, each process simply sends and receives a single float. During the second stage, each process sends and receives two floats that are spaced four floats apart, and during the third stage, each process sends and receives four floats that are spaced two floats apart. In general, we will need

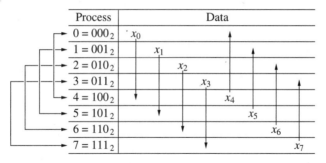

Figure 13.7 Exchanges during stage 0

Process	Data			
$0 = 000_2$	x_0		x_4	
$1 = 001_2$	x_1		x_5	
$2 = 010_2$	x_2		x_6	
$3 = 011_2$	x_3		x_7	
$4 = 100_2$	x_0		x_4	
$5 = 101_2$	x_1		x_5	
$6 = 110_2$	x_2		x_6	
$7 = 111_2$	x_3		x_7	

Figure 13.8 Exchanges during stage 1

Process	Data			
$0 = 000_2$	x_0	x_2	x_4	x_6
$1 = 001_2$	x_1	x_3	x_5	x_7
$2 = 010_2$	x_0	x_2	x_4	x_6
$3 = 011_2$	x_1	x_3	x_5	x_7
$4 = 100_2$	x_0	x_2	x_4	x_6
$5 = 101_2$	x_1	x_3	x_5	x_7
$6 = 110_2$	x_0	x_2	x_4	x_6
$7 = 111_2$	x_1	x_3	x_5	x_7

Figure 13.9 Exchanges during stage 2

to use blocks of floats instead of simple floats, but the problem is essentially the same.

There are a number of approaches to dealing with this. We list a few possibilities:

1. We can build a new derived datatype before each exchange.
2. We can pack the data before each exchange and unpack it afterward.

3. We can send/receive the data into contiguous memory locations at every stage and sort the data when we're done.

4. We can work under the assumption that the function will be called many times with the same blocksize and prebuild all the derived types we'll need.

The fourth approach is clearly less general than the preceding three. Is there a clear reason for choosing among the first three? Probably, but it will depend on your system and the problem size. For example, if your system has a very efficient implementation of derived types, then the first alternative will probably be faster than the second, especially if the number of processes and the blocksize are very large: the use of pack and unpack will involve a lot of copying from one buffer to another. The third alternative, although inelegant, could be very fast relative to the other methods, especially on a large number of processes with a small blocksize: the sort would be a very fast operation, and there would be almost no overhead associated with the exchanges other than that required for the actual message passing. However, if the blocksize is large, we'll once again run into the problem of lots of recopying of the data. In the absence of a clear choice, we'll opt for the solution we consider the most natural and elegant: derived types.

13.2.2 Details of the Hypercube Algorithm

As we mentioned earlier, it is usually easiest to understand the details of algorithms for hypercubes if we look at process ranks as binary integers rather than decimal integers. Recall that during the initial stage, two processes communicate if their addresses differ only in the most significant bit. For example, process 2, binary 010_2, exchanges with process 6, binary 110_2. So how do processes 2 and 6 determine the ranks of their partners? More generally, how do we determine the process that differs in rank from my_rank in the most significant bit? Conceptually, we just look at the most significant bit in my_rank; if it's a 0, we change it to a 1; if it's a 1, we change it to a 0. However, it's probably not immediately obvious how we program a computer to do this; at least, it's probably not obvious if you aren't accustomed to using C's bitwise operators. If you are, you'll recognize this as a clear case for a "bitwise exclusive or."

So recall the definition of "exclusive or":

A	B	A eor B
0	0	0
0	1	1
1	0	1
1	1	0

Observe that if we "exclusive or" a bit (0 or 1) with a 1, the resulting bit will be inverted ($0 \rightarrow 1$, $1 \rightarrow 0$), while if we "exclusive or" a bit with a 0, the resulting bit will be the same as the original bit. So if we can compute an integer whose binary representation consists of a 1 in the most significant bit and 0 everywhere else, we can "bitwise exclusive or" this integer with my_rank to compute the rank of our partner during stage 0. If there are $p = 2^d$ processes, then the most significant bit is the dth bit, and $d = \log_2(p)$ can be computed by counting the number of times we need to right-shift the binary representation of p until the result is 1. For example, $8 = 1000_2 = 2^3$, and if we right-shift 1000_2 three times, the result will be 1. Thus, we can write a simple $\log_2$ function to get the number of bits:

```
int log_base2(int p) {
/* Just counts number of bits to right of most significant
 * bit.  So for p not a power of 2, it returns the floor
 * of log_2(p).
 */
    int return_val = 0;
    unsigned q;

    q = (unsigned) p;
    while(q != 1) {
        q = q >> 1;
        return_val++;
    }
    return return_val;
}   /* log_base2 */
```

Since some implementations of C fill leading bits with a sign bit instead of a 0 when an int is right-shifted, we copied p into a variable having type unsigned before shifting; C does guarantee that leading bits of an unsigned will be filled with 0s.

Now we can use the result of this operation to compute our eor_bit and the rank of our partner.

```
    unsigned eor_bit;
    int d;
    int partner;

    d = log_base2(p);
    eor_bit = 1 << (d-1); /* fills low-order bits with 0s */
    partner = my_rank ^ eor_bit; /* ^ = bitwise eor in C */
```

Of course, we also need to calculate our partner at subsequent stages, but recall that during the next stage, our partner's rank differs from ours in the second most significant bit. Thus, if we right-shift our eor_bit by 1 bit, we can compute the rank of the partner during the next stage. In general, there will be d exchanges or d stages, and the basic outline of the hypercube exchange will be something like this:

```
/* eor_bit should be unsigned so that
 * right shift will fill leftmost bits with 0
 */
d = log_base2(p);
eor_bit = 1 << (d-1);

for (stage = 0; stage < d; stage++) {
    partner = my_rank ^ eor_bit;
    Build derived data type;
    Exchange data;
    eor_bit = eor_bit >> 1;
}
```

The derived datatypes we use in the exchanges will, in general, consist of equally spaced blocks of floats. MPI_Type_vector is specifically designed for this purpose. Recall the syntax:

```
int MPI_Type_vector(
    int         number_of_blocks  /* in  */,
    int         blocksize         /* in  */,
    int         stride            /* in  */,
    MPI_Datatype old_type         /* in  */,
    MPI_Datatype* new_type        /* out */)
```

The stride is just the number of elements between the start of successive blocks. For example, suppose we have an array x containing 16 floats, and we want to send x_0, x_1, x_8, and x_9 to another process. Then we can use a type built with MPI_Type_vector. The number_of_blocks is 2, the blocksize is 2, the stride is 8, and the old_type is MPI_FLOAT.

For our allgather function, the blocksize is in the parameter list. If we take a look at Figures 13.7–13.9, we'll see that each process sends one block during stage 0, two blocks during stage 1, and four blocks during stage 2. In general, then, we start with one block and double number_of_blocks at each stage. If we again look at Figures 13.7–13.9, it's not immediately clear what the stride should be during stage 0, since we're only sending a single block. However, during stage 1, the stride is four, and during stage 2, the stride is two. Since there is only one block exchanged during stage 0, we can make the stride anything we want. So in order to be consistent with the remaining stages, we can make the stride eight at stage 0. Note that in general, these strides should be multiplied by the blocksize. To summarize, during stage stage, we can build the derived datatype with

```
number_of_blocks = 1 << stage;        /* 2^stage    */
stride = (1 << (d-stage))*blocksize; /* 2^(d-stage) */

MPI_Type_vector(number_of_blocks, blocksize,
    stride, MPI_FLOAT, &hole_type)
```

Table 13.1 Offsets in eight-processor pairwise exchange (Pt. = partner, S/O = send offset, R/O = receive offset)

	Stage								
	0			1			2		
Process	Pt.	S/O	R/O	Pt.	S/O	R/O	Pt.	S/O	R/O
0 = 000	100	000	100	010	000	010	001	000	001
1 = 001	101	001	101	011	001	011	000	001	000
2 = 010	110	010	110	000	010	000	011	000	001
3 = 011	111	011	111	001	011	001	010	001	000
4 = 100	000	100	000	110	000	010	101	000	001
5 = 101	001	101	001	111	001	011	100	001	000
6 = 110	010	110	010	100	010	000	111	000	001
7 = 111	011	111	011	101	011	001	110	001	000

The only remaining issue is the offsets to be used in the sends and receives. Once again, using binary representations of the offsets and process ranks makes it easier to understand the pattern. In Table 13.1, we've summarized the offsets from our eight-process example. Let's take a look at the send offsets. Rules such as "My send offset during the current stage is the minimum of my send offset and my receive offset during the last stage" don't seem as elegant as the underlying binary pattern: start with send offset my_rank; during the next stage change the most significant bit to a zero; during the next stage change the next most significant bit to a zero; etc. It looks once again like a bitwise operation: leave all the bits of the previous send offset, except one, intact. For this single bit, leave it alone if it's a 0, and change it to a 0 if it's a 1. You may have already guessed that the appropriate operator is "bitwise and." Recall the table defining "bitwise and".

A	B	A and B
0	0	0
0	1	0
1	0	0
1	1	1

If we "and" a bit with a 1, the resulting bit is the same as the original bit, while if we "and" a bit with a 0, the resulting bit is 0, regardless of what the original bit was. So we would like our bitmask to consist initially of all 1s, and then we can right-shift it after each stage. To do this, we can compute $p = 2^d = 100\ldots00_2$, and subtract 1, $100\ldots00_2 - 1_2 = 011\ldots11_2$. In C, this is

```
unsigned and_bits;
int d;
int send_offset;
```

```
d = log_base2(p);
and_bits = (1 << d) - 1; /* or just p - 1 */
```

Now the send offset can be computed at each stage as follows:

```
for (stage = 0; stage < d; stage++) {
    send_offset = (my_rank & and_bits)*blocksize;
        ⋮
    and_bits = and_bits >> 1;
} /* for stage */
```

Notice that we need to multiply the general send offset by blocksize.

Now it's easy to figure out what the receive offset should be! Our partner is using the same formula to calculate the send offset that we're using, except that she's using her rank. Thus

```
recv_offset = (partner & and_bits)*blocksize
```

To summarize, here's the code:

```
void Allgather_cube(
        float    x[]       /* in  */,
        int      blocksize /* in  */,
        float    y[]       /* out */,
        MPI_Comm comm      /* in  */) {

    int          i, d, p, my_rank;
    unsigned     eor_bit;
    unsigned     and_bits;
    int          stage, partner;
    MPI_Datatype hole_type;
    int          send_offset, recv_offset;
    MPI_Status   status;

    int log_base2(int p);

    MPI_Comm_size(comm, &p);
    MPI_Comm_rank(comm, &my_rank);

    /* Copy x into correct location in y */
    for (i = 0; i < blocksize; i++)
        y[i + my_rank*blocksize] = x[i];

    /* Set up */
    d = log_base2(p);
    eor_bit = 1 << (d-1);
    and_bits = (1 << d) - 1;
```

```
for (stage = 0; stage < d; stage++) {
    partner = my_rank ^ eor_bit;
    send_offset = (my_rank & and_bits)*blocksize;
    recv_offset = (partner & and_bits)*blocksize;

    MPI_Type_vector(1 << stage, blocksize,
        (1 << (d-stage))*blocksize, MPI_FLOAT,
        &hole_type);
    MPI_Type_commit(&hole_type);

    MPI_Send(y + send_offset, 1, hole_type,
        partner, 0, comm);
    MPI_Recv(y + recv_offset, 1, hole_type,
        partner, 0, comm, &status);

    MPI_Type_free(&hole_type);  /* Free type so we  */
            /* can build new type during next pass */
    eor_bit = eor_bit >> 1;
    and_bits = and_bits >> 1;
    }
} /* Allgather_cube */
```

A couple of caveats are in order. The program assumes that there will be some system buffering, since it executes all sends first. Also, this code may fail with a blocksize of 0: `hole_type` may be an invalid datatype.

13.3 Send-receive

We've remarked after completing both `Allgather_ring` and `Allgather_cube` that the functions could fail if there is no system buffering. We briefly discussed this issue in Chapter 5: in MPI parlance our functions are *unsafe*. A couple of natural questions might occur: why are they unsafe, and, if they are, what can we do to make them safe?

First, why are the functions unsafe? Consider the case that we have two processes. Then there will be a single exchange of data between process 0 and process 1. If we synchronize the processes before the exchanges we'll have approximately the following sequence of events:

Time	Process 0	Process 1
1	MPI_Send to 1	MPI_Send to 0
2	MPI_Recv from 1	MPI_Recv from 0

However, if there's no buffering, the MPI_Sends will never return: when a blocking function is called, the function won't return until it's safe for the program to modify the arguments to the function, and if there's no buffering, the buffer passed to MPI_Send can't be modified until the data has been copied over to the other processor—i.e., until MPI_Recv is called. So process 0 will wait in MPI_Send until process 1 calls MPI_Recv, and process 1 will wait in MPI_Send until process 0 calls MPI_Recv. We've encountered this situation several times before: it's called *deadlock.*

Of course, the harder question is how to make them safe. We have basically two options: we can figure out how to make them safe by reorganizing the sends and receives, or we can let MPI make them safe.

In order to make them safe by reorganizing the sends and receives, we need to decide who will send first and who will receive first. A standard solution is to have the processors with even ranks send first, and the processors with odd ranks receive first. So the sequence of events in our function would now be

Time	Process 0	Process 1
1	MPI_Send to 1	MPI_Recv from 0
2	MPI_Recv from 1	MPI_Send to 0

Note that this solution works even if we have an odd number of processes. For example, if we used alternating sends and receives in our ring pass with three processes, the approximate sequence of events might be as follows:

Time	Process 0	Process 1	Process 2
1	MPI_Send to 1	MPI_Recv from 0	Start MPI_Send to 0
2	MPI_Recv from 2	Start MPI_Send to 2	Finish MPI_Send
3	Done	Finish MPI_Send	MPI_Recv from 1

So there may be a delay in the completion of one communication, but the program will complete successfully.

A simpler solution is to let MPI take care of the problem. In fact, we encountered this solution in our implementation of Fox's algorithm (Chapter 7). The function MPI_Sendrecv, as its name implies, performs both a send and a receive, and it organizes them so that even in systems with no buffering the calling program won't deadlock—at least not in the way that the MPI_Send/MPI_Recv implementation deadlocks! The syntax of MPI_Sendrecv is

```
int MPI_Sendrecv(
        void*        send_buf      /* in  */,
        int          send_count    /* in  */,
        MPI_Datatype send_type     /* in  */,
        int          destination   /* in  */,
        int          send_tag      /* in  */,
        void*        recv_buf      /* out */,
        int          recv_count    /* in  */,
        MPI_Datatype recv_type     /* in  */,
        int          source        /* in  */,
```

```
int         recv_tag    /* in  */,
MPI_Comm    comm        /* in  */,
MPI_Status* status      /* out */ )
```

Notice that the parameter list is basically just a concatenation of the parameter lists for MPI_Send and MPI_Recv. The only difference is that the communicator parameter is not repeated. The destination and the source parameters can be the same. The "send" in an MPI_Sendrecv can be matched by an ordinary MPI_Recv, and the "receive" can be matched by an ordinary MPI_Send. The basic difference between a call to this function and MPI_Send followed by MPI_Recv (or vice versa) is that MPI can try to arrange that no deadlock occurs since it knows that the sends and receives will be paired. We leave it as an exercise to modify Allgather_ring and Allgather_cube so that they use the MPI_Sendrecv.

Recollect that MPI doesn't allow a single variable to be passed to two distinct parameters if one of them is an output parameter. Thus, we can't call MPI_Sendrecv with send_buf = recv_buf. Since it is very common in practice for paired send/receives to use the same buffer, MPI provides a variant that does allow us to use a single buffer:

```
int MPI_Sendrecv_replace(
        void*        buffer      /* in/out */,
        int          count       /* in     */,
        MPI_Datatype datatype    /* in     */,
        int          destination /* in     */,
        int          send_tag    /* in     */,
        int          recv_tag    /* in     */,
        MPI_Comm     comm        /* in     */,
        MPI_Status*  status      /* out    */)
```

Note that this implies the existence of some system buffering.

13.4 Null Processes

A typical use of MPI_Sendrecv and MPI_Sendrecv_replace is to shift data in a process ring: this is exactly what we do in Allgather_ring. How would we manage this if, instead of a process ring, we had a linear array of processes? The obvious answer is we would have to test for boundary processes:

```
if (my_rank == 0)
    MPI_Send(send_buf, count, . . . );
else if (my_rank == p-1)
    MPI_Recv(recv_buf, count, . . . );
else
    MPI_Sendrecv(send_buf, count, . . . );
```

An elegant alternative is provided by MPI in the dummy process MPI_PROC_NULL. If a process executes a send with destination MPI_PROC_NULL, the send simply returns as soon as possible, with no change to its arguments. If a process executes a receive with source MPI_PROC_NULL, the receive returns without modifying the receive buffer. The return value of status.MPI_Source is MPI_PROC_NULL, and the return value of status.MPI_Tag is the MPI constant MPI_ANY_TAG. If we call

```
MPI_Get_count(&status, datatype, &count),
```

the value returned in count will be 0.

In our example, if we set source = MPI_PROC_NULL on process 0 and destination = MPI_PROC_NULL on process $p - 1$, then each process can call MPI_Sendrecv.

Another example of the use of MPI_PROC_NULL is provided by Allgather_cube. It can be modified so that p can be any positive integer, not just a power of two. If we test the value of partner before the communication and find that its value is greater than $p - 1$, we can assign it the value MPI_PROC_NULL. We'll discuss the details of this modification in a programming assignment.

13.5 Nonblocking Communication

Since MPI_Send, MPI_Recv, and MPI_Sendrecv are blocking operations, they will not return until the arguments to the functions can be safely modified by subsequent statements in the program. For MPI_Send, this means that the message envelope has been created and the message has been sent or that the contents of the message have been copied into a system buffer. For MPI_Recv, it means that the message has been received into the buffer specified by the buffer argument. For MPI_Sendrecv, it implies that the outgoing message has been sent or buffered, and the incoming message has been received.

All of these semantics may imply that the resources available to the sending or receiving process are not being fully utilized. For example, if the MPI process controls two physical processors, a processor for computation and a processor for communication, then the send operation should be able to proceed concurrently with some computation, as long as the computation doesn't modify any of the arguments to the send operation. Also if, during execution of a receive operation, a process finds that the data to be received is not yet available, then the process should be able to continue with useful computation as long as it doesn't interfere with the arguments to the receive.

Nonblocking communication is explicitly designed to meet these needs. A call to a nonblocking send or receive simply starts, or **posts**, the communication operation. It is then up to the user program to explicitly complete the communication at some later point in the program. Thus, any nonblocking op-

eration requires a minimum of two function calls: a call to start the operation
and a call to complete the operation.

The basic functions in MPI for starting nonblocking communications are
MPI_Isend and MPI_Irecv. The "I" stands for "immediate," i.e., they return
(more or less) immediately. Their syntax is very similar to the syntax of MPI_
Send and MPI_Recv:

```
int MPI_Isend(
      void*        buffer       /* in  */,
      int          count        /* in  */,
      MPI_Datatype datatype     /* in  */,
      int          destination  /* in  */,
      int          tag          /* in  */,
      MPI_Comm     comm         /* in  */,
      MPI_Request* request      /* out */)
```

and

```
int MPI_Irecv(
      void*        buffer       /* in  */,
      int          count        /* in  */,
      MPI_Datatype datatype     /* in  */,
      int          source       /* in  */,
      int          tag          /* in  */,
      MPI_Comm     comm         /* in  */,
      MPI_Request* request      /* out */)
```

The parameters that they have in common with MPI_Send and MPI_Recv
have the same meaning. However, the semantics are different. Both calls
only *start* the operation. For MPI_Isend this means that the system has been
informed that it can start copying data out of the send buffer (either to a system
buffer or to the destination). For MPI_Irecv, it means that the system has
been informed that it can start copying data into the buffer. Neither send nor
receive buffers should be modified until the operations are explicitly completed
or cancelled.

The request parameter is a *handle* associated to an *opaque object*. Recollect that this means, effectively, that the object referenced by request is
system defined, and that it cannot be directly accessed by the user. Its purpose is to identify the operation started by the nonblocking call. So it will
contain information on such things as the source or destination, the tag, the
communicator, and the buffer. When the nonblocking operation is completed,
the request initialized by the call to MPI_Isend or MPI_Irecv is used to
identify the operation to be completed.

There are a variety of functions that MPI uses to complete nonblocking
operations. The simplest of these is MPI_Wait. It can be used to complete any
nonblocking operation.

```
int MPI_Wait(
    MPI_Request* request   /* in/out */,
    MPI_Status*  status    /* out    */ )
```

The `request` parameter corresponds to the `request` parameter returned by
`MPI_Isend` or `MPI_Irecv`. `MPI_Wait` blocks until the operation identified
by `request` completes: if it was a send, either the message has been sent
or buffered by the system; if it was a receive, the message has been copied
into the receive buffer. When `MPI_Wait` returns, `request` is set to `MPI_`
`REQUEST_NULL`. This means that there is no pending operation associated to
`request`. If the call to `MPI_Wait` is used to complete an operation started by
`MPI_Irecv`, the information returned in the `status` parameter is the same as
the information returned in `status` by a call to `MPI_Recv`.

Finally, it should be noted that it is perfectly legal to match blocking
operations with nonblocking operations. For example, a message sent with
`MPI_Isend` can be received by a call to `MPI_Recv`.

13.5.1 Ring Allgather with Nonblocking Communication

Let's illustrate the use of nonblocking communication with our allgather
functions.

When we use nonblocking communication, we want to do as much *local*
computation as possible between the start of the nonblocking operation and
the call to `MPI_Wait`. Thus, when we convert code that uses blocking communications to the use of nonblocking communications, we usually reorganize
the statements so that we can defer the completion calls. The basic loop in the
blocking version of `Allgather_ring` looks like this:

```
for (i = 0; i < p - 1; i++) {
    send_offset = ((my_rank - i + p) % p)*blocksize;
    recv_offset = ((my_rank - i - 1 + p) % p)*blocksize;
    MPI_Send(y + send_offset, blocksize, MPI_FLOAT,
        successor, 0, ring_comm);
    MPI_Recv(y + recv_offset, blocksize, MPI_FLOAT,
        predecessor, 0, ring_comm, &status);
}
```

In order to somewhat overlap communication and computation, we can compute the offsets for the next pass through the loop before completing the communications. This will necessitate our initializing the offsets before we enter
the loop:

```
MPI_Request send_request;
MPI_Request recv_request;
        :
send_offset = my_rank*blocksize;
```

Table 13.2 Runtimes of Allgather_ring (times are in milliseconds; blocksize = 1; both systems running mpich)

Processes	Paragon		SP2	
	Blocking	Nonblocking	Blocking	Nonblocking
2	0.14	0.10	0.11	0.080
8	1.0	0.94	0.85	0.54
32	4.9	4.2	3.9	2.5

```
recv_offset = ((my_rank - 1 + p) % p)*blocksize;
for (i = 0; i < p - 1; i++) {
    MPI_Isend(y + send_offset, blocksize, MPI_FLOAT,
        successor, 0, ring_comm, &send_request);
    MPI_Irecv(y + recv_offset, blocksize, MPI_FLOAT,
        predecessor, 0, ring_comm, &recv_request );

    send_offset = ((my_rank - i - 1 + p) % p)*blocksize;
    recv_offset = ((my_rank - i - 2 + p) % p)*blocksize;

    MPI_Wait(&send_request, &status);
    MPI_Wait(&recv_request, &status);
}
```

Table 13.2 shows the runtimes of both the blocking and nonblocking versions of Allgather_ring on a Paragon and an SP2. If we take into consideration the relatively small amount of computation between the calls to MPI_Isend and MPI_Irecv and the calls to MPI_Wait, the performance improvements, especially on the SP2, are quite good.

13.5.2 Hypercube Allgather with Nonblocking Communication

Recollect that during each pass through the main loop of Allgather_cube, we build a new derived datatype. Since this is a fairly expensive operation, it would seem that we might obtain a significant increase in performance if we can overlap the building of the datatype with the communications. So recall the blocking code:

```
for (stage = 0; stage < d; stage++) {
    partner = my_rank ^ eor_bit;
    send_offset = (my_rank & and_bits)*blocksize;
    recv_offset = (partner & and_bits)*blocksize;

    MPI_Type_vector(1 << stage, blocksize,
        (1 << (d-stage))*blocksize, MPI_FLOAT,
        &hole_type);
    MPI_Type_commit(&hole_type);
```

```
        MPI_Send(y + send_offset, 1, hole_type,
            partner, 0, comm);
        MPI_Recv(y + recv_offset, 1, hole_type,
            partner, 0, comm, &status);

        MPI_Type_free(&hole_type);  /* Free type so we  */
                /* can build new type during next pass */
        eor_bit = eor_bit >> 1;
        and_bits = and_bits >> 1;
    }
```

It seems that we can indeed make the overlap, but note that once again, we will have to perform some extra initialization.

```
    partner = my_rank ^ eor_bit;
    send_offset = (my_rank & and_bits)*blocksize;
    recv_offset = (partner & and_bits)*blocksize;
    MPI_Type_contiguous(blocksize, MPI_FLOAT, &hole_type);
    MPI_Type_commit(&hole_type);

    for (stage = 0; stage < d; stage++) {
        MPI_Isend(y + send_offset, 1, hole_type,
            partner, 0, comm, &send_request);
        MPI_Irecv(y + recv_offset, 1, hole_type,
            partner, 0, comm, &recv_request);

        if (stage < d-1) {
            eor_bit >>= 1;
            and_bits >>= 1;
            partner = my_rank ^ eor_bit;
            send_offset = (my_rank & and_bits)*blocksize;
            recv_offset = (partner & and_bits)*blocksize;
            MPI_Type_free(&hole_type);
            MPI_Type_vector(1 << (stage+1), blocksize,
                (1 << (d-stage-1))*blocksize, MPI_FLOAT,
                &hole_type);
            MPI_Type_commit(&hole_type);
        }

        MPI_Wait(&send_request, &status);
        MPI_Wait(&recv_request, &status);
    }  /* for */
```

Note that since the first derived datatype consists of a single block, we can build it during the initialization phase using MPI_Type_contiguous instead of MPI_Type_vector.

Table 13.3 shows the runtimes of both the blocking and nonblocking versions of Allgather_cube on a Paragon and an SP2. Once again the perfor-

Table 13.3 Runtimes of `Allgather_cube` (times are in milliseconds; blocksize = 16,384; both systems running `mpich`)

	Paragon		SP2	
Processes	*Blocking*	*Nonblocking*	*Blocking*	*Nonblocking*
2	11	11	12	12
8	58	51	49	45
32	270	250	220	190

mance improvements are good, although not as substantial as they were for `Allgather_ring`.

13.6 Persistent Communication Requests

It is not uncommon for message-passing programs to repeatedly call communication functions inside a loop with exactly the same arguments. For example, consider the calls to `MPI_Isend` and `MPI_Irecv` in our ring allgather:

```
MPI_Isend(y + send_offset, blocksize, MPI_FLOAT,
    successor, 0, ring_comm, &send_request);
MPI_Irecv(y + recv_offset, blocksize, MPI_FLOAT,
    predecessor, 0, ring_comm, &recv_request );
```

Observe that during each pass, the only argument that changes in each call is the buffer argument: `send_offset` and `recv_offset` are recomputed during each pass, but the other arguments are identical. If we pack the contents of `y + send_offset` into a buffer and send the buffer, and then receive into another buffer and unpack its contents into `y + recv_offset`, then all our calls to `MPI_Isend` will use exactly the same arguments and all our calls to `MPI_Irecv` will use exactly the same arguments.

Clearly, the repeated calls to, say, `MPI_Isend` are performing redundant work. For example, the envelope of all the messages will contain exactly the same information. Thus, we might get some further improvement in performance if we could get MPI to do this redundant work just once, and, as you probably anticipated, we can. The mechanism is called a **persistent communication request.** The idea is that we do all the work (building envelopes, etc.) associated with the message passing just once; i.e., we build the appropriate request just once. Then we can reuse the request for all the appropriate communications, rather than continually rebuilding them.

Here's how this is done if we pack/unpack the data in our ring allgather:

```
#define MAX_BYTES MAX*sizeof(float)

float send_buf[MAX];
```

```
float recv_buf[MAX];
int position;
        ⋮
MPI_Send_init(send_buf, blocksize*sizeof(float),
    MPI_PACKED, successor, 0, ring_comm,
    &send_request);
MPI_Recv_init(recv_buf, blocksize*sizeof(float),
    MPI_PACKED, predecessor, 0, ring_comm,
    &recv_request );

send_offset = my_rank*blocksize;
for (i = 0; i < p - 1; i++) {
    position = 0;
    MPI_Pack(y+send_offset, blocksize, MPI_FLOAT,
        send_buf, MAX_BYTES, &position, ring_comm);
    MPI_Start(&send_request);
    MPI_Start(&recv_request);
    recv_offset = send_offset =
        ((my_rank - i - 1 + p) % p)*blocksize;
    position = 0;
    MPI_Wait(&send_request, &status);
    MPI_Wait(&recv_request, &status);
    MPI_Unpack(recv_buf, MAX_BYTES, &position,
        y+recv_offset, blocksize, MPI_FLOAT, ring_comm);
}
MPI_Request_free(&send_request);
MPI_Request_free(&recv_request);
```

The calls to MPI_Pack and MPI_Unpack make this code appear radically different from the earlier nonblocking version. However, if you put these calls aside, it becomes apparent that there are three main differences. The first is the calls to MPI_Send_init and MPI_Recv_init before the loop: these "allocate" the persistent requests. Then, in order to actually start the communications, there are two calls to MPI_Start. Finally, since the requests are "persistent," it is up to us to free them. We do this with the calls to MPI_Request_free. We'll discuss each of these new functions in turn.

The parameter lists for the calls to MPI_Send_init and MPI_Recv_init are identical to those for MPI_Isend and MPI_Irecv:

```
int MPI_Send_init(
    void*        buffer       /* in  */,
    int          count        /* in  */,
    MPI_Datatype datatype     /* in  */,
    int          destination  /* in  */,
    int          tag          /* in  */,
    MPI_Comm     comm         /* in  */,
    MPI_Request* request      /* out */)
```

and

```
int MPI_Recv_init(
    void*        buffer       /* in  */,
    int          count        /* in  */,
    MPI_Datatype datatype     /* in  */,
    int          source       /* in  */,
    int          tag          /* in  */,
    MPI_Comm     comm         /* in  */,
    MPI_Request* request      /* out */)
```

However, their effect is simply to set up persistent requests for a send and a receive, respectively.

The calls to MPI_Start actually start the communication. The syntax is simply

```
int MPI_Start(
    MPI_Request* request /* in/out */ )
```

Thus, the pair of calls

```
MPI_Send_init( . . . , &persistent_send_request);
MPI_Start(&persistent_send_request);
```

has much the same effect as the single call

```
MPI_Isend( . . . , &send_request);
```

Similarly the pair of calls

```
MPI_Recv_init(. . . , &persistent_recv_request);
MPI_Start(&persistent_recv_request);
```

has much the same effect as the single call

```
MPI_Irecv( . . . , &recv_request);
```

The key difference lies in the way MPI_Wait deals with the requests. In the case of the persistent requests, MPI_Wait does not set the requests to MPI_REQUEST_NULL after completion. In the parlance of MPI, the persistent requests become **inactive.** This means simply that there is no pending operation associated to the request (e.g., a send or receive), and the requests can be reactivated by calls to MPI_Start. In order to deallocate a request, we call

```
MPI_Request_free(&request)
```

This has the effect of setting request to MPI_REQUEST_NULL.

It should be noted that sends or receives started with MPI_Start can be matched by any other type of receive or send, respectively.

Table 13.4   Runtimes of `Allgather_ring` (times are in milliseconds; blocksize = 1; B = blocking, NB = nonblocking, P = persistent; both systems running `mpich`)

Processes	Paragon			SP2		
	B	NB	P	B	NB	P
2	0.14	0.10	0.21	0.11	0.08	0.09
8	1.0	0.94	1.1	0.85	0.54	0.53
32	4.9	4.2	4.4	3.9	2.5	2.6

Table 13.4 shows the runtimes of all three versions of `Allgather_ring` on a Paragon and an SP2. Generally the times for the version that uses persistent requests are comparable to the times for the version that uses basic nonblocking communication. The cost of the calls to `MPI_Pack` and `MPI_Unpack` offsets the savings obtained by not recreating the requests. Indeed in some cases (Paragon, p = 2, 8), the cost of these calls makes the version that uses persistent requests slower than the version that uses blocking communication.

13.7 Communication Modes

At several points during our discussions, in both this and other chapters, we've encountered the idea of *safety* in MPI. Recollect that a program is safe if it will produce correct results *even if the system provides no buffering.* Most programmers of message-passing systems expect the system to provide some buffering, and, as a consequence, they routinely write unsafe programs. Consider, for example, our initial implementations of `Allgather_ring` and `Allgather_cube`.

If we are writing a program that must absolutely be portable to any system, we can guarantee the safety of our program in two ways:

1. We can reorganize our communications so that the program will not deadlock if sends cannot complete until a matching receive is posted. We discussed an example of this in section 13.3.

2. A possibly less painful solution is to organize our own buffering.

In either case, we are, effectively, changing the **communication mode** of our program.

There are four communication modes in MPI: **standard, buffered, synchronous,** and **ready.** They correspond to four different types of send operations. There is only a standard mode for receive operations. In standard mode, it is up to the system to decide whether messages should be buffered. A typical implementation might buffer only relatively small messages. Up until now all of our sends, whether blocking, nonblocking, or persistent, have used the standard mode.

13.7.1 Synchronous Mode

In synchronous mode a send won't complete until a matching receive has been posted and the matching receive has begun reception of the data. MPI provides three synchronous mode send operations:

```
int MPI_Ssend(
    void*        buffer       /* in */,
    int          count        /* in */,
    MPI_Datatype datatype     /* in */,
    int          destination  /* in */,
    int          tag          /* in */,
    MPI_Comm     comm         /* in */ );

int MPI_Issend(
    void*        buffer       /* in  */,
    int          count        /* in  */,
    MPI_Datatype datatype     /* in  */,
    int          destination  /* in  */,
    int          tag          /* in  */,
    MPI_Comm     comm         /* in  */,
    MPI_Request* request      /* out */ );

int MPI_Ssend_init(
    void*        buffer       /* in  */,
    int          count        /* in  */,
    MPI_Datatype datatype     /* in  */,
    int          destination  /* in  */,
    int          tag          /* in  */,
    MPI_Comm     comm         /* in  */,
    MPI_Request* request      /* out */ );
```

Their effect is much the same as the corresponding standard mode sends. However, MPI_Ssend and the waits corresponding to MPI_Issend and MPI_Ssend_init will not complete until the corresponding receives have started. Thus, synchronous mode sends require no system buffering, and we can assure that our program is safe if it runs correctly using only synchronous mode sends.

Observe that if we replace the standard sends in, say, Allgather_ring with synchronous sends, then the function will hang, since none of the sends will complete until the corresponding receive has started. Thus, if we wish to use synchronous sends, we need to do something like this:

```
if ((my_rank % 2) == 0){ /* Even ranks send first */
    MPI_Ssend(y + send_offset, blocksize, MPI_FLOAT,
        successor, 0, ring_comm);
    MPI_Recv(y + recv_offset, blocksize, MPI_FLOAT,
        predecessor, 0, ring_comm, &status);
```

```
} else {   /* Odd ranks receive first */
   MPI_Recv(y + recv_offset, blocksize, MPI_FLOAT,
      predecessor, 0, ring_comm, &status);
   MPI_Ssend(y + send_offset, blocksize, MPI_FLOAT,
      successor, 0, ring_comm);
}
```

13.7.2 Ready Mode

On some systems it's possible to improve the performance of a message transmission if the system knows, before a send has been initiated, that the corresponding receive has already been posted. For such systems, MPI provides the ready mode. The parameter lists of the ready sends are identical to the parameter lists for the corresponding standard sends:

```
int MPI_Rsend(
    void*        buffer      /* in */,
    int          count       /* in */,
    MPI_Datatype datatype    /* in */,
    int          destination /* in */,
    int          tag         /* in */,
    MPI_Comm     comm        /* in */ );

int MPI_Irsend(
    void*        buffer      /* in  */,
    int          count       /* in  */,
    MPI_Datatype datatype    /* in  */,
    int          destination /* in  */,
    int          tag         /* in  */,
    MPI_Comm     comm        /* in  */,
    MPI_Request* request     /* out */ );

int MPI_Rsend_init(
    void*        buffer      /* in  */,
    int          count       /* in  */,
    MPI_Datatype datatype    /* in  */,
    int          destination /* in  */,
    int          tag         /* in  */,
    MPI_Comm     comm        /* in  */,
    MPI_Request* request     /* out */ );
```

The only difference between the semantics of the various ready sends and the corresponding standard sends is that the ready sends are erroneous if the matching receive hasn't been posted, and the behavior of an erroneous program is unspecified. Also note that it should be possible to replace all ready sends in a program with standard sends without affecting the output, although the program with the standard sends may be slower.

If we don't have too many processes, we could rewrite our allgathers by posting all the receives with MPI_Irecv and then executing the sends with one of the ready sends. For example, we might do something like this in Allgather_ring:

```
MPI_Request  request[p-1];

for (i = 0; i < p - 1; i++) {
    recv_offset =
        ((my_rank - i - 1 + p) % p)*blocksize;
    MPI_Irecv(y + recv_offset, blocksize, MPI_FLOAT,
        predecessor, i, ring_comm, &(request[i]));
}

MPI_Barrier(ring_comm);

for (i = 0; i < p - 1; i++) {
    send_offset = ((my_rank - i + p) % p)*blocksize;
    MPI_Rsend(y + send_offset, blocksize, MPI_FLOAT,
        successor, i, ring_comm);
    MPI_Wait(&(request[i]), &status);
}
```

Note that the call to MPI_Barrier is necessary since otherwise some process might enter the loop of sends before a receive had been posted.

13.7.3 Buffered Mode

The final mode, and the only one that has additional associated functions, is buffered mode. In buffered mode, a send operation is **local**. In other words, its completion does not depend on the existence of a matching receive. The other send modes are **nonlocal**; i.e., their completion may depend on the existence of a matching receive posted by another process. If a send is started in buffered mode and the matching receive hasn't been posted, the process *must* buffer the data. Of course, it's possible to exceed the available buffer space, in which case the program is erroneous.

The buffered mode sends have the same parameter lists as the other sends.

```
int MPI_Bsend(
    void*        buffer      /* in */,
    int          count       /* in */,
    MPI_Datatype datatype    /* in */,
    int          destination /* in */,
    int          tag         /* in */,
    MPI_Comm     comm        /* in */ );

int MPI_Ibsend(
    void*        buffer      /* in  */,
```

```
        int          count      /* in  */,
        MPI_Datatype datatype   /* in  */,
        int          destination /* in  */,
        int          tag        /* in  */,
        MPI_Comm     comm       /* in  */,
        MPI_Request* request    /* out */ );

    int MPI_Bsend_init(
        void*        buffer     /* in  */,
        int          count      /* in  */,
        MPI_Datatype datatype   /* in  */,
        int          destination /* in  */,
        int          tag        /* in  */,
        MPI_Comm     comm       /* in  */,
        MPI_Request* request    /* out */ );
```

The semantics are much the same as the corresponding standard sends. However, as we just noted, the system *must* buffer the data and return if the matching receive hasn't already been posted.

The missing ingredient in buffered mode is the buffer. In order to use buffered mode, it's up to the user, not the system, to allocate the buffer. This can be done with MPI_Buffer_attach:

```
    int MPI_Buffer_attach(
            void* buffer       /* in */,
            int   buffer_size  /* in */)
```

This is used by the system to buffer messages sent in buffered mode only, and there can only be one buffer attached at any time.

Thus, if we wanted to guarantee the safety of our program, we could try to estimate the maximum amount of data that would be buffered at any given time, attach a buffer of this size, and carry out all our sends in buffered mode.

Finally, if we know that we no longer need a buffer, it can be released from control by MPI with

```
    int MPI_Buffer_detach(
            void* buffer_address /* out */,
            int*  size_ptr       /* out */ )
```

This function removes the previously attached buffer from control by the system. If there are pending buffered sends, it will block until they have completed. Thus, when it completes, the user program can reuse or free the buffer. Note that it returns a pointer to the previously attached buffer and a pointer to its size. (Recollect that void indicates a pointer to an arbitrary type, including a pointer to a pointer.)

Thus, we could guarantee the safety of, say, Allgather_ring by just preceding the loop of sends and receives with a call to MPI_Buffer_attach, and following the loop with a call to MPI_Buffer_free:

```
        char buffer[MAX_BUF];
        int  buffer_size = MAX_BUF;
            :
        MPI_Buffer_attach(buffer, buffer_size);

        for (i = 0; i < p - 1; i++) {
            send_offset = ((my_rank - i + p) % p)*blocksize;
            recv_offset =
                ((my_rank - i - 1 + p) % p)*blocksize;
            MPI_Bsend(y + send_offset, blocksize, MPI_FLOAT,
                successor, 0, ring_comm);
            MPI_Recv(y + recv_offset, blocksize, MPI_FLOAT,
                predecessor, 0, ring_comm, &status);
        }

        MPI_Buffer_detach(&buffer, &buffer_size);
```

Be aware that this may not work if some other part of the program has already attached a buffer. Thus, we should only use buffered mode sends if we know whether other parts of the program are using them.

13.8 The Last Word on Point-to-Point Communication

As you've probably already observed, MPI provides a very rich set of point-to-point communication functions, and there are more than a few that we haven't examined in this chapter. We will explore more point-to-point functions in the exercises. However, for the sake of completeness, we'll list a couple of the categories of functions we have not yet covered.

Most of the remaining functions have to do with completing nonblocking operations. There are variants of MPI_Wait that have arrays of requests as parameters. These variants can be used to wait on any one of the requests, a subset of the requests, or all of the requests.

There is also a function, MPI_Test, that can be used simply to check whether an operation has completed. If the operation hasn't completed, the program can carry out further local computation, while if it has, MPI_Test will behave in the same manner as MPI_Wait. There are also variants of MPI_Test that can be used to check for the completion of multiple operations.

13.9 Summary

We've covered quite a lot of material in this chapter. We studied (in gruesome detail) two algorithms for allgather and in the process learned quite a bit about programming a hypercube and using bit operations in C.

After coding the two algorithms, we discussed MPI_Sendrecv and MPI_Sendrecv_replace:

```
int MPI_Sendrecv(
        void*        send_buf      /* in  */,
        int          send_count    /* in  */,
        MPI_Datatype send_type     /* in  */,
        int          destination   /* in  */,
        int          send_tag      /* in  */,
        void*        recv_buf      /* out */,
        int          recv_count    /* in  */,
        MPI_Datatype recv_type     /* in  */,
        int          source        /* in  */,
        int          recv_tag      /* in  */,
        MPI_Comm     comm          /* in  */,
        MPI_Status*  status        /* out */ )

int MPI_Sendrecv_replace(
        void*        buffer        /* in/out */,
        int          count         /* in     */,
        MPI_Datatype datatype      /* in     */,
        int          destination   /* in     */,
        int          send_tag      /* in     */,
        int          recv_tag      /* in     */,
        MPI_Comm     comm          /* in     */,
        MPI_Status*  status        /* out    */)
```

As their names suggest, these functions perform both a send and a receive. They also take care of any buffering of messages that may be necessary. They are especially convenient if processes are exchanging data or if there is a shift of data (e.g., 0 sends to 1, 1 sends to 2, 2 sends to 3, etc.). The second version can be used if we want to use the same storage for both the data sent and the data received.

In many cases, it's convenient to be able to send or receive data from a nonexistent process. For example, in the shift of the data in the previous paragraph, it might be useful to have process 0 receive from a nonexistent process, and process $p - 1$ send to a nonexistent process. MPI provides MPI_PROC_NULL for this purpose. Sends to and receives from MPI_PROC_NULL simply return without changing the arguments.

Perhaps the most important idea in the chapter is *nonblocking communication*. Nonblocking communication functions provide us with an explicit means for overlapping communication and computation. By using nonblocking communication we may be able to hide some of the cost of communication and obtain significantly improved performance. The basic functions for nonblocking communication are

```
int MPI_Isend(
        void*        buffer        /* in */,
        int          count         /* in */,
        MPI_Datatype datatype      /* in */,
        int          destination   /* in */,
```

```
                    int         tag        /* in  */,
                    MPI_Comm    comm       /* in  */,
                    MPI_Request* request   /* out */)

            int MPI_Irecv(
                    void*       buffer     /* in  */,
                    int         count      /* in  */,
                    MPI_Datatype datatype  /* in  */,
                    int         source     /* in  */,
                    int         tag        /* in  */,
                    MPI_Comm    comm       /* in  */,
                    MPI_Request* request   /* out */)

            int MPI_Wait(
                    MPI_Request* request   /* in/out */,
                    MPI_Status*  status    /* out    */ )
```

MPI_Isend and MPI_Irecv initiate a send and a receive, respectively. When MPI_Isend returns, however, the send may not have completed. So the contents of buffer should not be modified. Similarly, when MPI_Irecv returns, the data may not have been received and buffer should not be used to store other data. In order to complete either operation, we can call MPI_Wait with the request argument returned by the call to MPI_Isend or MPI_Irecv. When MPI_Wait returns, the send or receive will have completed. So in order to exploit the full power of nonblocking communication, we should try to structure our code so that we do useful work between a call to MPI_Isend or MPI_Irecv and the corresponding call to MPI_Wait.

If we are repeatedly calling MPI_Isend with exactly the same arguments, we will be repeatedly carrying out many of the same operations on the same data. For example, since the arguments are the same each time, the message envelope will be the same each time, but each time we call MPI_Isend the contents of the envelope will be recomputed. MPI provides a way for us to avoid some of this repeated effort with *persistent communication requests*. We use one function, MPI_Send_init, to do all the work necessary for setting up the communication only once. A call to this function will create a *persistent* or reusable request. Each time we're ready to initiate a send (with the same arguments), we call a second function, MPI_Start, which is passed the persistent request. When we're ready to complete the send, we can call MPI_Wait as usual. The same ideas can be used for receives. The syntax of the functions is

```
        int MPI_Send_init(
                void*       buffer      /* in  */,
                int         count       /* in  */,
                MPI_Datatype datatype   /* in  */,
                int         destination /* in  */,
                int         tag         /* in  */,
                MPI_Comm    comm        /* in  */,
                MPI_Request* request    /* out */)
```

```
int MPI_Recv_init(
    void*        buffer      /* in  */,
    int          count       /* in  */,
    MPI_Datatype datatype    /* in  */,
    int          source      /* in  */,
    int          tag         /* in  */,
    MPI_Comm     comm        /* in  */,
    MPI_Request* request     /* out */)

int MPI_Start(
        MPI_Request* request /* in  */)
```

We also discussed MPI's different communication modes: standard, synchronous, ready, and buffered. All receives in MPI use standard mode; only sends can use different modes. Up to this point we've been using standard mode; in standard mode it is up to the system to decide whether a message should be buffered. In synchronous mode, a send won't complete until the matching receive has begun receiving the data, so no buffering is needed. Some systems can optimize the performance of a send if it is known that the corresponding receive has been posted before the send is initiated; in ready mode, a send is erroneous unless the corresponding receive has already been posted. We can use buffered mode to guarantee the safety of our communications. If a matching receive hasn't already been posted and the send uses buffered mode, the system must buffer the data being sent in a user-supplied buffer.

For each of the different modes, there is a blocking send, a nonblocking send, and a persistent send. They are distinguished by the addition of the letter "S" for synchronous, "R" for ready, and "B" for buffered. Thus, MPI defines

```
MPI_Ssend,       MPI_Rsend,       MPI_Bsend,
MPI_Issend,      MPI_Irsend,      MPI_Ibsend,
MPI_Ssend_init,  MPI_Rsend_init, MPI_Bsend_init.
```

Their parameter lists are the same as the parameter lists for the corresponding standard mode sends.

In order to use the buffered mode sends the user must set aside a buffer. This can be done by calling

```
int MPI_Buffer_attach(
        void* buffer      /* in */,
        int   buffer_size /* in */)
```

The buffer size is in bytes. A buffer can be freed with

```
int MPI_Buffer_detach(
        void* buffer_address /* out */,
        int*  size_ptr       /* out */ )
```

At any time during the execution of a program there may be only one buffer attached on a process.

We closed the chapter with a brief mention of some other point-to-point communication functions. These fell into two categories: variants of `MPI_Wait`, which can be used to complete multiple nonblocking operations, and `MPI_Test`, which can be used to test for the completion of a nonblocking operation.

13.10 References

Additional information on point-to-point communication can be found in the MPI Standard [28, 29], Gropp et al. [21], and Snir et al. [34].

Kumar et al. [26] have extensive discussions of algorithms for allgather and other collective communication functions.

13.11 Exercises

1. Complete the coding of `Allgather_ring` using synchronous sends and receives. Compare its performance to the performance of the function using blocking sends and receives.

2. Complete the coding of `Allgather_ring` using ready sends. Compare its performance to the performance of the function using blocking sends and receives.

3. `MPI_Test` can be used to check whether a nonblocking operation has completed. Its syntax is

```
int MPI_Test(
        MPI_Request*  request  /* in/out */,
        int*          flag     /* out    */,
        MPI_Status*   status   /* out    */)
```

It checks for completion of the communication operation associated with `request`. If the operation has completed, it returns a nonzero value in `flag`. Otherwise it returns 0 in `flag`. If the operation associated with the request is a receive and the operation completed, information on the receive will be returned in `status`. If the operation completed and the request was not started by a persistent operation, it will be set to `MPI_REQUEST_NULL`. If the operation completed and the request was started by a persistent operation, it will be made inactive.

Modify `Allgather_ring` so that it starts all of its receives using nonblocking receives (be careful to use different tags!) and then checks its list of requests using `MPI_Test`. When it finds a request that has been completed, it should send the received data on to the next process. Can this function deadlock?

4. `MPI_Waitany` can be used to wait for one of a list of operations. Its syntax is

```
int MPI_Waitany(
        int          count        /* in      */,
        MPI_Request  requests[]    /* in/out */,
        int*         index         /* out     */,
        MPI_Status*  status        /* out     */)
```

`MPI_Waitany` blocks until the operation associated with one of the elements of `requests` has completed. The `requests` array consists of `count` elements. When the operation completes, it returns the subscript of the completed operation in `*index`. The element of `requests` is either set to `MPI_REQUEST_NULL` or made inactive. If the operation was a receive, status information is returned in `status`.

Modify the solution to exercise 3 so that it uses `MPI_Waitany`. How does its performance compare to the other ring allgathers?

13.12 Programming Assignments

1. Modify `Allgather_cube` so that it can deal with p not a power of two. The main idea is to test the value of `partner`: if it's greater than p, set it to `MPI_PROC_NULL`. However there are a number of other issues that need to be addressed. The `log_base2` function needs to be changed so that it returns $\lceil p \rceil$ rather than $\lfloor p \rfloor$. A more complex problem arises from the ordering of the exchanges. For example, if $p = 8$, process 5 is first paired with process 1, then process 7, and finally process 4. If $p = 6$ and we try to use the same sequence of pairings, the data stored on processes 2 and 3 will never get to process 5. (Work an example!) The problem here is that we're moving from high order to low order; i.e., `eor_bit` is being *right-shifted*. If we reverse this process, we won't run into this problem. Of course, this will mean that we need to change the sequence of offsets as well.

2. Write a ring-based all-to-all function. What type of nonblocking communications should you use?

3. Write a hypercube exchange all-to-all function. What type of nonblocking communications will you use?

4. Modify your cellular automaton program (see programming assignment 4 from Chapter 10) so that it uses nonblocking sends and receives. Should your code be reorganized so that you can obtain a better overlap between communication and computation? Is there any advantage to using persistent sends and receives in your program? You may want to suppress printing of the output to study the program's performance.

CHAPTER 14

Parallel Algorithms

IN MANY INSTANCES THE BEST ALGORITHM for a parallel computer is not a parallelized serial algorithm. Rather it is an entirely new algorithm specifically designed for parallel computers. In this chapter we'll discuss a couple of parallel algorithms. Our purpose is not to provide an overview of the field; such an effort would require at least as much space as the rest of the book. Rather, we want to illustrate some of the issues in parallel algorithm design and give some indication of the breadth of the field.

14.1 Designing a Parallel Algorithm

Parallel algorithms can be roughly divided into two basic categories: those that are obtained by a direct parallelization of a standard serial algorithm, and those that either have no serial counterpart or have been obtained in an indirect way from a serial algorithm. The parallel trapezoidal rule program and the parallel Jacobi's method program are examples of direct parallelization, while the hypercube allgather function has no serial counterpart, and Fox's algorithm might be viewed as having been obtained in an indirect way from the standard serial matrix multiplication program. When we're designing parallel algorithms, we need to keep both approaches in mind. In most cases the design and development cost of programs that use the direct route will be substantially less. However, as a number of our examples illustrate, if we follow the indirect route, the improvement in performance can be substantial.

Our first example illustrates the indirect route. We design and code an algorithm for sorting that is based on a little known and not very efficient serial sorting algorithm. The reason we choose this indirect route is that the direct route doesn't produce a very good parallel algorithm. In our second example,

315

we take the direct route. We design an algorithm for tree searching that is a natural extension of serial depth-first search. The development illustrates the immense care needed to successfully parallelize a fairly simple and standard serial algorithm.

In our discussions we'll focus on coding and correctness. We leave it to you to decide whether the algorithms meet the criteria we've outlined in Chapters 11–12, i.e., performance, scalability, load balance, etc.

14.2 Sorting

In Chapter 10 we wrote a simple program for parallel sorting. It made the possibly unrealistic assumption that we knew the distribution of the keys to be sorted before we actually sorted them. In this section we'll discuss a parallel algorithm for sorting that doesn't make this assumption. We'll assume that there are n keys to be sorted, and, when the algorithm begins, each process is assigned n/p keys. When the algorithm completes, each process should contain a sorted subset of n/p keys, and if the rank of process q is less than the rank of process r, then each key on process q should be less than or equal to every key on process r.

Quicksort, the "standard" serial algorithm for sorting, might, at first glance, seem to be a good choice for the basis of a parallel algorithm for sorting. Recall that quicksort is a divide-and-conquer algorithm: It chooses a pivot from the list of keys, and splits the list into two sublists: the first sublist consists of keys less than or equal to the pivot, the second consists of keys greater than the pivot. It then calls itself recursively on the two sublists. The obvious parallelization would choose a global pivot and broadcast it to all the processes. It would then assign the first sublist to the processes with rank less than or equal to $p/2$, and the second sublist to the processes with rank greater than $p/2$. However, unless we have some a priori information on the distribution of the keys, there is no guarantee that the first sublist contains the same number of elements as the second, and the algorithm can quickly lead to serious imbalances. So we'll look at a parallel algorithm that is not based on serial quicksort.

14.3 Serial Bitonic Sort

The bitonic sorting algorithm is based on the idea of a sorting network. For further information on this approach, see the references at the end of the chapter. We'll simply view it as a (somewhat unusual) serial algorithm.

Recollect that a **monotonic** sequence is one that either increases or decreases, but not both. The word "bitonic" was coined to describe sequences that increase and then decrease. More formally, a sequence of keys $(a_0, a_1, \ldots, a_{n-1})$ is **bitonic** if

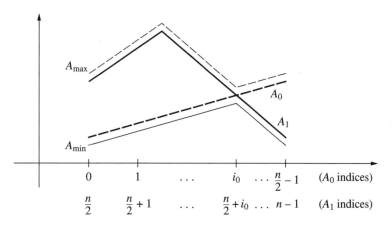

Figure 14.1   A bitonic split

1. there exists an index $m, 0 \leq m \leq n - 1$, such that

$$a_0 \leq a_1 \leq \cdots \leq a_m \geq a_{m+1} \geq \cdots \geq a_{n-1},$$

   or

2. there exists a cyclic shift σ of $(0, 1, \ldots, n - 1)$ such that the sequence $(a_{\sigma(0)}, a_{\sigma(1)}, \ldots, a_{\sigma(n-1)})$ satisfies condition 1. A cyclic shift sends each index i to $(i + s)$ mod n, for some integer s.

Thus, the sequence $(1, 5, 6, 9, 8, 7, 3, 0)$ is bitonic, as is the sequence $(6, 9, 8, 7, 3, 0, 1, 5)$, since it can be obtained from the first by a cyclic shift.

Now observe that if the sequence $A = (a_0, a_1, \ldots, a_{n-1})$ is bitonic, then we can form two bitonic sequences from A as follows. Define

$$A_{\min} = (\min\{a_0, a_{n/2}\}, \min\{a_1, a_{n/2+1}\} \ldots, \min\{a_{n/2-1}, a_{n-1}\}),$$

and

$$A_{\max} = (\max\{a_0, a_{n/2}\}, \max\{a_1, a_{n/2+1}\} \ldots, \max\{a_{n/2-1}, a_{n-1}\}).$$

$A_{\min}$ and $A_{\max}$ are bitonic sequences. Furthermore, each element of $A_{\min}$ is less than every element of $A_{\max}$. It's easy to see that this is the case if we represent the two subsequences $A_0 = (a_0, a_1, \ldots, a_{n/2-1})$ and $A_1 = (a_{n/2}, \ldots, a_{n-1})$ of A in a graph. See Figure 14.1. The figure makes it clear that there is an index $i_0, 0 \leq i_0 \leq n/2 - 1$, with the property that up to index i_0 all the elements of $A_{\min}$ are the corresponding elements of A_0, and after i_0, all the elements of $A_{\min}$ are the corresponding elements of A_1. This process of creating two bitonic sequences from a single bitonic sequence is called a **bitonic split.**

Because every element in $A_{\min}$ is less than every element in $A_{\max}$, and both sequences are bitonic, we can recursively split $A_{\min}$ and $A_{\max}$ until we

Table 14.1 Bitonic sort of a bitonic sequence

Step	Elements							
Start	1	5	6	9	8	7	3	0
1	1	5	3	0	8	7	6	9
2	1	0	3	5	6	7	8	9
3	0	1	3	5	6	7	8	9

obtain sequences of length 1. When this has happened, we will have obtained a sorted sequence.

As an example, consider the sequence $(1, 5, 6, 9, 8, 7, 3, 0)$. Table 14.1 illustrates the process of successively splitting to ultimately obtain a sorted sequence.

Of course, we still need to arrange that we have a bitonic sequence to start off with. Let's start small: observe that any sequence containing two elements is bitonic—in fact, any sequence containing two elements is monotonic. Now suppose for the moment that we have an unsorted list of four elements, $A = (a_0, a_1, a_2, a_3)$. In order for A to be bitonic, it's not enough for both two element sequences, (a_0, a_1) and (a_2, a_3) to be monotonic. We need for, say, the first to be increasing and the second to be decreasing. Of course this is easy enough to arrange: just compare the two elements in each two element sequence and make the appropriate switch.

How does this generalize? If we have an eight-element sequence, $A = (a_0, a_1, \ldots, a_7)$, we can use the preceding method to convert it into two bitonic sequences. That is, we can assume that (a_0, a_1, a_2, a_3) and (a_4, a_5, a_6, a_7) are bitonic. Indeed we can assume that $a_0 \le a_1$, $a_2 \ge a_3$, $a_4 \le a_5$, and $a_6 \ge a_7$. But how can we arrange that the sequence A itself is bitonic? Recall that the iterated bitonic split converts a bitonic sequence into a sorted sequence. Thus, we can arrange that (a_0, a_1, a_2, a_3) is increasing. Can we also arrange that (a_4, a_5, a_6, a_7) is decreasing? It's easy; we just "reverse" our bitonic splits. That is, we put the minima in the second half and the maxima in the first half.

An example will help. Suppose we have the sequence

$$(5, 3, 6, 2, 1, 9, 0, 8).$$

We can convert it into two bitonic sequences easily enough: $(3, 5, 6, 2)$ and $(1, 9, 8, 0)$. Now we can convert the sequence $(3, 5, 6, 2)$ into an increasing sequence using bitonic splits:

Step	Elements			
Start	3	5	6	2
1	3	2	6	5
2	2	3	5	6

Similarly, we can convert $(1, 9, 8, 0)$ into a decreasing sequence:

Step	Elements			
Start	1	9	8	0
1	8	9	1	0
2	9	8	1	0

Now we can perform a sequence of bitonic splits on $(2, 3, 5, 6, 9, 8, 1, 0)$ to obtain a sorted list.

If we assume that n is a power of two, it's easy to code a serial bitonic sort. The following code contains some excerpts:

```
            ⋮
/* Successive subsequences will switch between
 * increasing and decreasing bitonic splits.
 */
#define INCR 0
#define DECR 1
#define Reverse(ordering) ((ordering) == INCR ? DECR : INCR)

main() {
            ⋮

    for (list_length = 2; list_length <= n;
            list_length = list_length*2)
        for (start_index = 0, ordering = INCR;
                start_index < n;
                start_index = start_index + list_length,
                ordering = Reverse(ordering))
            if (ordering == INCR)
                Bitonic_sort_incr(list_length,
                    A + start_index);
            else
                Bitonic_sort_decr(list_length,
                    A + start_index);
            ⋮
void Bitonic_sort_incr(
        int       length /* in     */,
        KEY_T     B[]    /* in/out */) {
    int i;
    int half_way;

    /* This is the bitonic split */
    half_way = length/2;
    for (i = 0; i < half_way; i++)
        if (B[i] > B[half_way + i])
            Swap(B[i],B[half_way+i]);
```

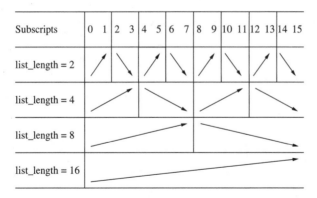

| Subscripts | 0 | 1 | 2 | 3 | 4 | 5 | 6 | 7 | 8 | 9 | 10 | 11 | 12 | 13 | 14 | 15 |

Figure 14.2   Orientation of subsequences during stages of bitonic sort

```
    if (length > 2) {
        Bitonic_sort_incr(length/2, B);
        Bitonic_sort_incr(length/2, B + half_way);
    }
} /* Bitonic_sort_incr */
```

The nested for loops in the main program arrange first that successive two-element subsequences are monotone (increasing or decreasing), then successive four-element subsequences are monotone, etc. For a 16-element sequence, the effect of the algorithm can be visualized as illustrated in Figure 14.2. An up arrow indicates an increasing subsequence, a down arrow a decreasing subsequence.

The only differences between Bitonic_sort_incr and Bitonic_sort_decr will be that the conditional

```
    if (B[i] > B[half_way + i])
```

should be replaced by

```
    if (B[i] < B[half_way + i])
```

and Bitonic_sort_decr should recursively call itself.

14.4 Parallel Bitonic Sort

As with the serial bitonic sort, we'll assume that the number of keys n is a power of two. We'll also assume that the number of processes p is a power of two, and that the underlying architecture of our system is a hypercube. (We'll relax the first restriction later on.) So we'll assume that the process ranking in MPI_COMM_WORLD is the natural hypercube ranking we discussed in Chapter 13. At each stage of the algorithm, each process will have a sublist of the global list containing n/p keys.

Let's first consider the case $p = 4$. We can begin by using a fast local sorting algorithm (e.g., quicksort) to convert the local keys on each process into an increasing or decreasing sequence. The ordering will be determined by the parity of the process rank: even-numbered processes will sort into increasing order, odd-numbered processes will sort into decreasing order. Then, each pair of processes, $(0, 1)$ and $(2, 3)$, jointly owns a bitonic sequence, and, if they perform the appropriate bitonic splits, each pair will own a monotonic sequence, and the global sequence will be bitonic. That is, the 4-tuple of processes, $(0, 1, 2, 3)$, jointly owns a bitonic sequence.

Observe that we can now carry out a bitonic split on the entire distributed sequence by carrying out a bitonic split on the sequence shared by processes 0 and 2 and by carrying out a bitonic split on the sequence shared by processes 1 and 3.

An example will clarify this. Suppose that the following sequences have been assigned to processes 0, 1, 2, and 3:

Process 0:	9, 12, 16, 23
Process 1:	26, 39, 42, 61
Process 2:	43, 17, 14, 13
Process 3:	12, 7, 6, 5

If we perform an (increasing) bitonic split on the sequence

$$(9, 12, 16, 23, 26, 39, 42, 61, 43, 17, 14, 13, 12, 7, 6, 5),$$

and divide the keys among the processes, we'll get the following assignment:

Process 0:	9, 12, 14, 13
Process 1:	12, 7, 6, 5
Process 2:	43, 17, 16, 23
Process 3:	26, 39, 42, 61

However, if we perform a bitonic split on the subsequence shared by processes 0 and 2,

$$(9, 12, 16, 23, 43, 17, 14, 13),$$

and assign the lower half of the result to process 0 and the upper half to process 2, processes 0 and 2 will get the same keys. Similarly, if we perform a bitonic split on the sequence shared by processes 1 and 3, $(12, 7, 6, 5, 26, 39, 42, 61)$, and assign the lower half to process 1 and the upper half to process 3, processes 0 and 3 will also get the same keys. That is, a bitonic split on the entire sequence has the same effect as two separate, independent bitonic splits: one on the subsequence shared by processes 0 and 2, and the other on the subsequence shared by processes 1 and 3. Further, in a hypercube, the paired processes are adjacent.

To finish up and obtain a sorted sequence on the four processes, we can perform a bitonic split on the sequence shared by processes 0 and 1 and a bitonic split on the sequence shared by processes 2 and 3.

The difference between the four-processor case and the p-processor case, $p = 2^d$, should be pretty clear. We obtain successively larger bitonic sequences by applying the process-pair bitonic splits to larger collections of processes. For example, suppose a bitonic sequence is distributed across eight processes. Then process pairs $(0, 4)$, $(1, 5)$, $(2, 6)$, and $(3, 7)$ will perform the initial bitonic splits. The next set of bitonic splits will pair processes $(0, 2)$, $(1, 3)$, $(4, 6)$, and $(5, 7)$. The final splits will pair processes $(0, 1)$, $(2, 3)$, $(4, 5)$, and $(6, 7)$.

A final observation. Suppose processes A and B, $A < B$, share a bitonic sequence, with A's keys increasing and B's keys decreasing. We can obtain a monotonic sequence if, instead of performing a bitonic split, we sort the keys on B in increasing order, merge the keys from the two processes, and assign the smaller keys to A and the larger keys to B. In other words, we can replace our bitonic splits with "merge splits." This is a cheaper operation, since it always maintains a sorted list. If there are n/p keys per process, we only have to sort these n/p keys once. If we used bitonic splits, we would sort them every time we sorted across a set of processes. Note also that if we use merge splits, we can relax the restriction that the number of keys is a power of two.

Let's make all of this precise by writing some of the code for carrying it out. The heart of the algorithm, the bitonic split, is replaced by a merge split.

```
#include "mpi.h"

KEY_T temp_list[MAX]; /* buffer for keys received */
                      /* in Merge_split          */
                      /* KEY_T is a C type        */


/* Merges the contents of the two lists. */
/* Returns the smaller keys in list1     */
void Merge_list_low(
        int    list_size  /* in     */,
        KEY_T  list1[]     /* in/out */,
        KEY_T  list2[]     /* in     */);

/* Returns the larger keys in list 1.    */
void Merge_list_high(
        int    list_size  /* in     */,
        KEY_T  list1[]     /* in/out */,
        KEY_T  list2[]     /* in     */);

void Merge_split(
        int       list_size    /* in     */,
        KEY_T     local_list[] /* in/out */,
        int       which_keys   /* in     */,
        int       partner      /* in     */,
        MPI_Comm  comm         /* in     */ ) {
```

```
        MPI_Status status;

        /* key_mpi_t is an MPI (derived) type */
        MPI_Sendrecv(local_list, list_size, key_mpi_t,
                     partner, 0, temp_list, list_size,
                     key_mpi_t, partner, 0, comm, &status);
        if (which_keys == HIGH)
            Merge_list_high(list_size, local_list,
                            temp_list);
        else
            Merge_list_low(list_size, local_list,
                           temp_list);
    } /* Merge_split */
```

Since we are effectively parallelizing the inner loop of the serial main program, the main program will now have a single for loop:

```
main(int argc, char* argv[]) {
        :
    Local_sort(list_size, local_list);

    /* and_bit is a bitmask that, when "anded" with  */
    /* my_rank, tells us whether we're working on an  */
    /* increasing or decreasing list                  */
    for (proc_set_size = 2, and_bit = 2;
         proc_set_size <= p;
         proc_set_size = proc_set_size*2,
         and_bit = and_bit << 1)
        if ((my_rank & and_bit) == 0)
            Par_bitonic_sort_incr(list_size,
                    local_list, proc_set_size, comm);
        else
            Par_bitonic_sort_decr(list_size,
                    local_list, proc_set_size, comm);
        :
```

As with most hypercube algorithms, the processes that have been grouped for a bitonic sort are paired by "exclusive or'ing" the process rank with a bitmask consisting of a single bit successively right-shifted. (See section 13.2 for a detailed discussion.)

```
void Par_bitonic_sort_incr(
        int       list_size      /* in     */,
        KEY_T     local_list[]   /* in/out */,
        int       proc_set_size  /* in     */,
        MPI_Comm  comm           /* in     */ ) {
        :
```

```
    /* type of eor_bit should be unsigned: otherwise
     * right shift may fill most significant bits with
     * sign bit */
    proc_set_dim = log_base2(proc_set_size);
    eor_bit = 1 << (proc_set_dim - 1);
    for (stage = 0; stage < proc_set_dim; stage++) {
        partner = my_rank ^ eor_bit;
        if (my_rank < partner)
            Merge_split(list_size, local_list, LOW,
                partner, comm);
        else
            Merge_split(list_size, local_list, HIGH,
                partner, comm);
        eor_bit = eor_bit >> 1;
    }
} /* Par_bitonic_sort_incr */
```

We have effectively replaced the recursive calls in `Bitonic_sort_incr` by an iterative loop. The only difference between `Par_bitonic_sort_incr` and `Par_bitonic_sort_decr` is that the test

```
    if (my_rank < partner)
```

should be replaced with

```
    if (my_rank > partner)
```

We'll leave to the exercises discussions of the performance of parallel bitonic sort and parallel quicksort.

14.5 Tree Searches and Combinatorial Optimization

Many optimization problems can be solved by searching a tree. As an example, consider the famous travelling salesman problem: a salesman has a list of cities he must visit and a set of costs associated to travelling between each city (e.g., airfare, car rental). His problem is to visit each city exactly once and return to the starting city, ordering the cities so that the cost of his trip is minimized.

The problem can be formalized by defining a weighted, directed graph. Each vertex of the graph corresponds to a city, and the weight of each edge is the cost of travelling from the city corresponding to the tail of the edge to the city corresponding to its head. Thus, the problem can be viewed as finding a listing of the vertices or cities so that the first vertex is the same as the last, and every other vertex appears exactly once in the list. Any such listing is called a **tour**. We want to find a tour with the property that the sum of the weights on the edges joining consecutive vertices is minimized.

The problem can be solved in several ways by using a tree search. In one approach the root of the tree corresponds to all possible tours. Children are generated by choosing an edge: the left subtree corresponds to all tours that traverse the chosen edge, and the right subtree corresponds to all tours that don't traverse the edge.

Another combinatorial optimization problem that has applications to parallel computing is graph partitioning. Many problems in scientific computing can be abstracted as (possibly weighted) graphs: solving differential equations using finite elements, modelling electronic circuits, etc. If we are solving one of these problems on a parallel system, we may wish to partition the graph among the processes. Typically the vertices of the graphs correspond to computations, and the edges correspond to communications. Thus, we would like to partition the graph so that the sums of the weights of the vertices assigned to the processes are equalized (i.e., the computational load is balanced), and the weights of the edges cut by the partitioning is minimized. A simple-minded solution to the problem of partitioning a graph into two subsets is to build a binary tree with the root corresponding to all solutions. Children are generated by choosing an unassigned vertex: the left subtree corresponds to all solutions that assign that vertex to the first subset in the partition; the right subtree corresponds to all solutions that assign that vertex to the second.

Most combinatorial optimization problems of interest are NP-hard or NP-complete, which means, for all practical purposes, that there is no general algorithm that is better in every instance than the brute force algorithm, which examines every possible solution and chooses the optimal solution. Furthermore, if we try to express the size of the set of all possible solutions in terms of the size of the input (e.g., the number of cities in the travelling salesman problem), it will usually contain an exponential term. For such problems, parallel computing won't improve matters unless we happen to have a parallel system with a processor set that also grows exponentially with the problem size. However, there are many important special cases that can be solved in less than exponential time, and for practical applications, we are often willing to settle for a "good" solution rather than an optimal one.

14.6 Serial Tree Search

There are a number of approaches to searching the trees generated during the solution of a combinatorial optimization problem. One of the simplest and most commonly used is **depth-first search.** In depth-first search, we begin at the root; after a node in the tree is "expanded" (i.e., its children are generated), one of the children is chosen for expansion. This process continues until we reach a node that is either a solution or cannot possibly lead to a solution, at which point we backtrack to the first ancestor with children that are still unexpanded. When we find a solution, we can compare it to the best known solution and either save it or discard it. A simple example using the travelling salesman problem is illustrated in Figures 14.3 and 14.4.

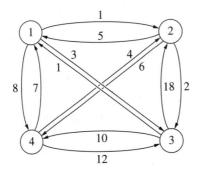

Figure 14.3   Four-vertex travelling salesman problem

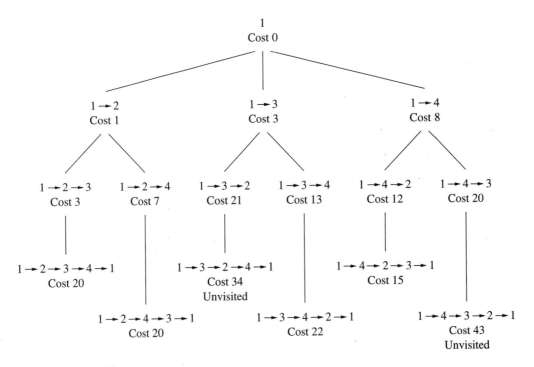

Figure 14.4   Search tree for four-vertex travelling salesman problem

There are two standard implementations of serial depth-first search. The first uses recursion:

```
/* Recursive depth-first search          */
/* Assume the parameter node is "feasible" -- */
/*     i.e., it can lead to a solution    */
void Dfs_recursive(
        NODE_T node  /* in */) {
```

```
int    i;
int    num_children;
NODE_T child_list[MAX_CHILDREN];

Expand(node, child_list, &num_children);

for (i = 0; i < num_children; i++)
    if (Solution(child_list[i])) {
        if (Evaluate(child_list[i])
            < best_solution)
            /* A solution has no children */
            best_solution =
                Evaluate(child_list[i]);
    } else if (Feasible(child_list[i])) {
        Dfs_recursive(child_list[i]);
    }
} /* Dfs_recursive */
```

Note that the function Expand may order the children so that more promising nodes are expanded first. Also note that in its simplest form, depth-first search will not be able to determine whether a node that doesn't correspond to a solution is feasible, and the test

```
if (Feasible(child_list[i]))
```

will be omitted.

The second standard implementation eliminates recursion by pushing un-expanded nodes onto a stack.

```
/* Iterative depth-first search using a stack */
void Dfs_stack(
        NODE_T root  /* in */) {
    NODE_T   node;
    STACK_T  stack;

    /* Allocate empty stack */
    Initialize(&stack);

    /* Expand root; push children onto stack */
    Expand(root, stack);

    while (!Empty(stack)) {
        node = Pop(stack);
        if (Solution(node)) {
            if (Evaluate(node) < best_solution)
                best_solution = Evaluate(node);
        } else if (Feasible(node)) {
            Expand(node, stack);
        }
    }
}
```

```
        Free(stack);
} /* Dfs_stack */
```

A possible problem with depth-first search becomes evident in the iterative solution: can it happen that there are no acceptable solutions? If so, what
does the program do? Clearly the answer to the first question should be yes.
For example, we might want all solutions to an optimization problem that are
better than some value, and there might not be any. In such a case, we should
have initialized best_solution to be the cut-off value, and the program can
simply check whether the result in best_solution is better than this initialization. We'll return to this problem when we look at parallel depth-first
search.

For alternatives to depth-first search, see the references at the end of the
chapter.

14.7 Parallel Tree Search

The obvious, perhaps too obvious, parallelization of depth-first search is simply to distribute disjoint subtrees among the processes. For example, if the tree
is a binary tree, and there are four processes, we can have process 0 expand
the root and its two children, and distribute the four grandchildren among the
processes: one grandchild to each process. Indeed this approach works very
well if we know that the tree is *balanced*. In this case "balanced" means that
each of the subtrees rooted at the grandchildren contains approximately the
same number of nodes. Of course, this won't necessarily be the case, and we
may run into serious problems with load imbalance. Indeed, some solutions
to optimization problems that use tree search intentionally generate a highly
unbalanced tree.

In order to avoid this problem, parallel implementations of depth-first
search usually rely on a *dynamic* load-balancing scheme. There are several
methods for dynamic load balancing. On a shared-memory machine, we can
simply put the stack in shared memory, and processes can push nodes onto
and pop nodes from the stack. On a distributed-memory machine, a single
process could be responsible for managing the stack, and the other processes
could access the stack through message passing. However, even on a shared-
memory machine, this can lead to serious problems with processes competing
for access to the stack. Thus, it may be better to distribute the stack among
the processes. If a process exhausts its stack, it can send requests to other
processes for work.

The basic outline for a parallel tree search based on serial depth-first search
might be something like this:

```
/* root == NULL if rank != 0 */
void Par_tree_search(
        NODE_T      root      /* in */,
        MPI_Comm    comm      /* in */ ) {
```

```
            STACK_T  local_stack;
            NODE_T*  node_list;
            NODE_T   node;
            int      p;
            int      my_rank;

            MPI_Comm_size(comm, &p);
            MPI_Comm_rank(comm, &my_rank);

            /* Generate initial set of nodes, 1 per process */
            if (my_rank == 0) {
                Generate(root, &node_list, p);
            }

            Scatter(node_list, &node, comm);
            Initialize(node, &local_stack);

            do {
                /* Search for a while */
                Par_dfs(local_stack, comm);

                /* Service requests for work. */
                Service_requests(local_stack, comm);

                /* If local_stack isn't empty, return.        */
                /* If local_stack is empty, send              */
                /* requests until either we get work, or we   */
                /* receive a message terminating program.     */
            } while(Work_remains(local_stack, comm));

            Update_solution(comm);
            Free(local_stack);
            Print_solution(comm);
    } /* Par_tree_search */
```

Thus, process 0 receives the root of the tree from the calling function and generates a list of p nodes—possibly using depth-first search. It then scatters the nodes among the processes, and each process does a local depth-first search. The local depth-first search continues until either the process exhausts its subtree, or it expands some predefined maximum number of nodes. In either case, it returns and services any requests it has received for work: if local_stack doesn't contain enough work, it will send a rejection; otherwise it will split its stack and send part to the requesting process. After returning from the call to Service_requests, it either continues with more searching or, if its stack is empty, it requests further work. Eventually, it will either receive work from another process, in which case it will continue, or it will receive a termination message. After termination, each process will update its value for the solution, process 0 will print the result, and `Par_tree_search` will return.

Let's look at each of the functions `Par_dfs`, `Service_requests`, and `Work_remains`.

14.7.1 Par_dfs

`Par_dfs` is basically the same as `Dfs_stack`. There are two main differences: The first is that `Par_dfs` doesn't necessarily run until the local stack is empty: it will return after it has expanded `MAX_WORK` nodes regardless of the state of the local stack. The reason for this is that the calling function `Par_tree_search` needs to periodically service requests for work from other processes. The parameter `MAX_WORK` must be chosen so that it balances two conflicting requirements. On the one hand, we want each process to do as much local work as possible—i.e., the amount of communication should be minimized. This suggests that `MAX_WORK` should be chosen to be as large as possible. On the other hand, we don't want processes sitting idle, and if a process is assigned a small subtree and `MAX_WORK` is large, it may wait a long time before it receives any new work from another process.

The second main difference with `Dfs_stack` is the fact that in `Par_dfs` the "quality" of a solution may depend on the work done by other processes. For example, in the solution of the travelling salesman problem, we only want the *best* tour. When we are executing `Par_dfs` and we generate a new solution, we can evaluate it strictly on the basis of whether it is better than all local solutions so far, or we can compare it to the best solution on all processes so far. Similarly, if we can evaluate partial solutions (e.g., a partial tour in the travelling salesman problem), we will not want to complete all partial solutions. Those that cannot possibly be better than the current best solution or upper bound on the best possible solution (given the current state of our knowledge) should not be completed. Once again, this decision can be made on the basis of local or global information. In either case, we have a trade-off: We can improve the quality of our estimates if we use global information; however, the use of global information involves communication and, as a consequence, is expensive. In our code we have chosen to make the decisions on the basis of global information. Consequently, the function `Feasible` takes a communicator argument as well as a node argument, and we define a new function, `Best_solution`, which checks for new solutions from other processes.

```
void Par_dfs(
         STACK_T    local_stack  /* in/out */,
         MPI_Comm   comm         /* in      */) {
    int     count;
    NODE_T  node;
    float   temp_solution;
```

```
/* Search local subtree for a while */
count = 0;
while (!Empty(local_stack) && (count < MAX_WORK)) {
    node = Pop(local_stack);
    if (Solution(node)) {
        temp_solution = Evaluate(node);
        if (temp_solution < Best_solution(comm)) {
            Local_solution_update(temp_solution, node);
            Bcast_solution(comm);
        }
    } else if (Feasible(node, comm)) {
        Expand(node, local_stack);
    }
    count++;
} /* while */
} /* Par_dfs */
```

Note that the stack is no longer local to the depth-first search routines: other functions (e.g., those that service requests) will also need to access the stack. Also note that we will need to use at least two communication functions: a function that checks the message queue for new best solutions (to be called by Best_solution and Feasible) and a broadcast function.

Checking the message queue can be implemented with the MPI function

```
int MPI_Iprobe(
    int         source /* in  */,
    int         tag    /* in  */,
    MPI_Comm    comm   /* in  */,
    int*        flag   /* out */,
    MPI_Status* status /* out */ )
```

This function searches for an incoming message that matches source, tag, and comm. If it finds a message that matches, it returns flag = TRUE, and status will contain the same information that would be contained in the status argument returned by a call to MPI_Recv. In particular, it will contain information on the number of elements in the message. Thus, MPI_Iprobe can be used when we want to receive a message of unknown size. The source and tag arguments can be wildcards; i.e., we can call MPI_Iprobe with

```
source = MPI_ANY_SOURCE;
tag    = MPI_ANY_TAG;
```

If there are multiple messages that can match the call, information is returned on the message that would be received by a call to MPI_Recv at that point. Thus, in order to correctly implement checking the message queue, it will be necessary to loop until all messages that contain new best solutions have been received. Note that MPI_Iprobe doesn't actually receive the message: you still need to call MPI_Recv.

Since `MPI_Bcast` requires the participation of all the processes in `comm`, and the only process that "knows" about the new solution is the one that finds it, `MPI_Bcast` cannot be used in `Par_dfs`. A simple, albeit unscalable, solution is to use a loop of buffered sends. In most cases, the number of new solutions will be quite small and this won't be a serious problem. If it is, it's possible to write a nonblocking broadcast using attributes (see Chapter 8).

14.7.2 Service_requests

The function that services requests needs to read all requests for data and either service them or send a refusal. It might look something this.

```
void Service_requests(
        STACK_T    local_stack /* in/out */,
        MPI_Comm   comm        /* in      */) {
    STACK_T send_stack;
    int     destination;

    while (Work_requests_pending(comm)) {
        destination = Get_dest(comm);
        if (Nodes_available(local_stack)) {
            Split(local_stack, &send_stack);
            Send_work(destination, send_stack, comm);
        } else {
            Send_reject(destination, comm);
        }
    }
} /* Service_requests */
```

The function `Work_requests_pending` uses `MPI_Iprobe` to see if there's a message with a previously defined tag that is used only for requests. If there is such a message, `Get_dest` will return the source of the message.

Both `Nodes_available` and `Split` are highly problem dependent. We'll explore some alternatives in the exercises. For further information, see the references at the end of the chapter.

14.7.3 Work_remains

The function `Work_remains` determines whether there are any remaining nodes to be expanded either locally or globally. If there are, it returns `TRUE` and a nonempty stack. Otherwise it returns `FALSE`.

```
int Work_remains(
        STACK_T    local_stack /* in/out */,
        MPI_Comm   comm        /* in      */ ) {

    int     work_available;
```

```
        int        request_sent = FALSE;
        int        work_request_process;

    if (!Empty(local_stack)) {
        return TRUE;
    } else {
        Out_of_work(comm);
        while (TRUE) {
            Send_all_rejects(comm);
            if (Search_complete(comm)) {
                return FALSE;
            } else if (!request_sent) {
                work_request_process = New_request(comm);
                Send_request(work_request_process, comm);
                request_sent = TRUE;
            } else if (Reply_received(work_request_process,
                        &work_available, local_stack, comm)) {
                if (work_available)
                    return TRUE;
                else
                    request_sent = FALSE;
            }
        }
    } /* while (TRUE) */
    }
} /* Work_remains */
```

The function Out_of_work posts a notice that we've finished all local work. Search_complete tests whether all the processes are done. We'll discuss these in more detail in the next section.

The function Send_all_rejects sends rejection messages to all processes that have requested work. This is necessary to avoid a "busy" deadlock. If we omitted it, two processes that are out of work could send requests to each other. These requests would never be either satisfied or rejected, and the other processes would do all the remaining work.

The function New_Request simply returns the rank of a process to which the work request will be sent. There are many possibilities for this function. One possibility is for it to just generate a random process rank. Another possibility would be for each process to simply increment, modulo p, the rank of the process from which work was last requested, with the initial request being sent to process (my_rank + 1) mod p. A third possibility is for a single process, say process 0, to maintain the rank of the process to which the next request will be sent, and when a process runs out of work, it gets the rank from 0, and 0 increments it. Since the first two approaches make no use of global information, it can happen that many processes simultaneously request work from the same process. In the third approach, process 0 may find itself spending all its time servicing requests for a process address, and each request for work requires four communications (send request for process rank to 0, receive process rank, send work request, receive work) and hence $4t_s$ instead of just $2t_s$.

The function `Send_request` simply sends a message using the request tag to the process `work_request_process`. `Reply_received` uses `MPI_Iprobe` to check whether there has been a reply to our request. If there hasn't, it returns false. Otherwise, if the reply was affirmative, it copies the received data into `local_stack` and sets `work_available` to true. If the reply was negative, it sets `work_available` to false.

Alternatively, `Send_request` can post a nonblocking receive, and `Reply_received` can use `MPI_Test` to check for a reply.

14.7.4 Distributed Termination Detection

This is a popular topic in computer science, and there is an extensive literature on the subject. We'll limit our discussion to a single approach that is especially well suited to parallel tree search. See the references at the end of the chapter for further discussion.

The idea behind this algorithm is that when the program begins, process 0 has a certain quantity of some indestructible resource: call it energy. Process 0 can transfer some of the energy to other processes, and they can, in turn, transfer some to yet other processes, but, of course, energy is conserved. So no matter how the energy is distributed among the processes, the total energy will always be the same as it was when the program started. The rules governing the energy are as follows:

1. When the program begins, process 0 has all the energy: its total energy is 1.

2. Energy is only transferred in three circumstances:
   a. during the initial distribution of the tree
   b. when a process fills a request for work
   c. when a process runs out of work

3. During the initial distribution phase, the energy is divided into p parts. So after the initial distribution, each process has energy $1/p$.

4. When a process fills a request for work, it keeps half its energy and transfers half to the process that requested the work.

5. When a process runs out of work, it transfers whatever energy it has left to process 0.

Now observe that energy is conserved: we never actually dispose of energy. Also observe that when every process (except possibly 0) has run out of work, each process will have 0 energy, and process 0 will have energy 1. Thus, whenever process 0 completes its work and finds it has energy 1, it should broadcast a termination message to all the processes.

Of course, there will be problems with keeping track of the energy if we try to use floating point arithmetic and keep halving the energy. However, we can avoid this by representing fractions as pairs of integers: $a/b = (a, b)$. Then dividing by p converts (a, b) to (a, pb) and adding $(a, b) + (c, d) = (ad + bc, bd)$. The only work here is reducing to lowest terms. However, the only possible divisors of the denominator are 2 and divisors of p.

Also note that even if process 0 is receiving lots of energy returns, it only needs to tally them when it runs out of work. So this shouldn't seriously interfere with process 0's performance. Alternatively, we can form a spanning tree, rooted at process 0. Then rather than returning energy to process 0, each process can return energy to its parent in the spanning tree.

14.8 Summary

In this chapter we took a very brief look at the field of parallel algorithms. We saw that parallel algorithms can be roughly divided into two categories: those that are more or less direct parallelizations of standard serial algorithms and those that aren't.

We took in-depth looks at the design and coding of two parallel algorithms: parallel bitonic sort and parallel tree search. The first algorithm used the indirect approach to the development of parallel algorithms, since the standard serial algorithm for sorting, quicksort, doesn't seem to parallelize very well.

The second algorithm, parallel tree search, was a natural generalization of serial depth-first search. However, in order to obtain load balance, we had to be very careful about the details of our implementation.

In our discussion of parallel tree search we touched briefly on a well-known problem in parallel and distributed computing: distributed termination detection. The problem is to determine when a collection of processes working asynchronously (as in the parallel tree search) are finished computing. The solution we looked at assigns a fixed quantity of an indestructible resource to process 0 at the start of execution. Each time work is sent from one process to another process, the process sending the work also sends half of its resource. When a process runs out of work, it sends its resource back to process 0. When process 0 has recovered all of the original resource, the program should terminate.

We only learned one new MPI function, MPI_Iprobe. It can be used to check to see whether a message from a specified source, a message with a given tag, or a message in a certain communicator is available. Its syntax is

```
int MPI_Iprobe(
    int          source /* in  */,
    int          tag    /* in  */,
    MPI_Comm     comm   /* in  */,
    int*         flag   /* out */,
    MPI_Status*  status /* out */ )
```

If `flag` is nonzero, then a message matching the criteria specified by `source`, `tag`, and `comm` has arrived. The `source` and `tag` arguments can be wildcards, but there is no wildcard for communicators. The `status` will return a reference to the status that would be returned if `MPI_Recv` were called with the same `source`, `tag`, and `comm` arguments. Note that since the `status` specifies the amount of storage needed for the message, we can guarantee that the buffer in a subsequent call to `MPI_Recv` will be large enough to receive the entire message.

14.9 References

The literature on parallel algorithms is quite extensive. Two excellent starting points are Fox et al. [18] and Kumar et al. [26]. Both books provide discussions of parallel sorting algorithms. Fox et al. provide empirical performance data on several sorting algorithms, including bitonic sort and quicksort. The efficiency of parallel quicksort actually begins to decrease on large datasets. Kumar et al. also discuss how bitonic sort can be mapped to a mesh.

Much of our discussion of parallel tree search is based on Kumar et al. They also discuss alternatives to depth-first search, and they provide performance analyses and empirical data on the performance of various implementations of parallel depth-first search.

There is also an extensive literature on serial algorithms. Perhaps the best known reference is Knuth's classic, *The Art of Computer Programming* [25]. The third volume discusses searching and sorting.

Reingold et al. [32] have an extensive discussion of approaches to the travelling salesman problem.

14.10 Exercises

1. If we wish to predict the performance of any *comparison-based* sorting algorithm— serial or parallel—we run into difficulties with the constants in our formulas. Unlike the algorithms we've considered thus far, it is not possible to say something like "The runtime of a serial bubble sort is $T(n) = kn^2$." The reason is that the exact time of a bubble sort (and other comparison-based algorithms) depends in large measure on the number of swaps, and for fixed n, this can vary considerably. A reasonable approach to this difficulty is to empirically determine an average value for k by timing the program on a large number of datasets.

   Use this approach to derive a formula for the average runtimes of serial bitonic sort on your system.

2. Use the method outlined in exercise 1 to derive a formula for the average runtime for the local sorting algorithm you're using in your implementation of parallel bitonic sort. Use this formula to develop a formula for the

runtime of parallel bitonic sort. How do your predicted runtimes compare to the actual runtimes?

3. Modify the parallel bitonic sort program so that it can handle lists whose length isn't divisible by p. There are several ways this can be done. For example, we might pad the list with "huge" keys—keys larger than any actual key—or we might modify Merge_split so it uses two list sizes: the size of the local list and the size of the partner's list. Which method do you think will result in better performance? Which method is easier to implement?

14.11 Programming Assignments

1. Reingold et al. [32] provide an extensive discussion of the *branch and bound* solution to the travelling salesman problem (TSP).

   a. Write a serial program that uses branch and bound to solve the travelling salesman problem. Input to the program will consist of n, the number of cities, and an adjacency matrix for the graph representing intercity costs. Output should be an optimal tour.

   b. Complete the coding of the parallel tree search program so that it uses branch and bound to solve the travelling salesman problem. Add MAX_WORK to the input data. For the Nodes_available function, return TRUE if there are at least two nodes in local_stack. For the Split function, send every other node in the local_stack. If a process runs out of work, it should simply generate a random process rank, and send a request for work to this process. How do different values of MAX_WORK affect the performance of the program?

   c. Compare the performance of the serial program to the parallel program. Does the program seem to be scalable?

   d. Kumar et al. [26] suggest that the Nodes_available function should depend on a cut-off depth. (The depth of a node in a tree is its distance from the root.) The idea is that if a node is very deep in the tree, it won't have many descendants, and hence it won't provide much additional work to a process that's run out of data. Modify your tree-search program so that it takes a cut-off depth as an additional input parameter. The Nodes_available function should return TRUE only if there are nodes in local_stack above the cut-off depth. If there are, the Split function should send every other node above the cut-off depth. Can you significantly improve the performance of the program by choosing a good cut-off depth?

2. Both Fox et al. [18] and Kumar et al. [26] discuss parallel shellsort. Implement a parallel shellsort algorithm. Compare its performance to parallel bitonic sort. Is one algorithm consistently better than the other?

CHAPTER 15

Parallel Libraries

IF WE'RE TRYING TO DEVELOP AN APPLICATION, we would probably prefer not to take the time to design, code, and debug parallel algorithms. We would prefer to take some preexisting code and simply plug it into our program. Indeed, one of the principal reasons for the development of MPI was that it would make it possible for software developers to write portable parallel libraries. So we will discuss how we can use parallel libraries to solve a couple of simple problems. The libraries we'll discuss are ScaLAPACK and PETSc. Both are large, complex libraries. ScaLAPACK can be used for solving problems in linear algebra, especially problems involving dense matrices. PETSc can be used to solve a variety of problems in scientific computing. It is one of the first libraries to use MPI.

15.1 Using Libraries: Pro and Con

What's wrong with parallel computing? Go to the mall and ask the man in the street. Nine times out of 10, he'll say, "No software." As we have repeatedly seen, writing even a small parallel program can be an extremely difficult undertaking. As a consequence, most of the people who use parallel computing are specialists in parallel hardware or software: certainly not your average scientist or engineer.

There is a solution to the software problem, though. It's the development of libraries of parallel software. If we wanted to, say, solve a system of differential equations and we could simply write a program that involved setting up the equations, calling a solver, and printing the solution, we wouldn't hesitate to do so. Indeed, if we want to solve a system on a serial computer, this is just what we do: thousands of scientists and engineers do this on an almost daily basis. If they could do the same, and solve problems that are hundreds or even thousands of times larger than what they are now capable of solving, many wouldn't hesitate to use parallel computing.

So go out and spread the gospel! Libraries of Parallel Software for the Masses!

Ahem. On a more serious note, one of the strongest points of MPI is its support for parallel libraries. The use of communicators allows us to isolate the communication universe of one part of a program from that of another. In some sense communicators do for communication what functions do for computation: they provide a means of logically separating a collection of inter-related communications from other communications, just as functions allow us to logically separate a set of interrelated computations from other computations. The analogy can be taken further: functions allow us to define a hierarchy of logical views of computations, and communicators allow us to define a hierarchy of logical views of communications. In particular, communicators allow us to separate the communications required by the functions in a library from other communications, just as the functions themselves allow us to separate the library's computations from those of the rest of the program.

However, if writing a small parallel program is a big undertaking, writing even a modest parallel library is a project of colossal proportions. In such a situation, programmers, especially the programmers in research environments who write most parallel software, tend to skimp on the development and documentation of the application/library interface. The reason is quite simple: their job is to write fast software, not easy-to-use software. Unfortunately, in using larger libraries, understanding the library interface can be the biggest hurdle the application programmer faces.

Most library writers attempt to address these problems by providing a comprehensive user's guide. However, the difficulties facing a user can be greatly reduced if the following documentation is also provided:

1. Quick-start documentation: a concise introduction to a few of the library's features. A simple way to do this is to provide a well-documented, small application program illustrating the use of some of the library's functions.

2. An explanation of all nonstandard terminology. Since most terms used by computing professionals are not standard, this probably means: "Explain your terms."

Our example libraries, ScaLAPACK and PETSc, are both excellent examples of well-designed and well-documented libraries. Indeed, they could be taken as models for other library developers.

15.2 Using More than One Language

Currently most of ScaLAPACK is written in Fortran. So before we try to use it, we need to briefly discuss some of the issues involved in writing programs that call Fortran subprograms from C. Many of the issues are system dependent, so we can't provide a prescription that will work on all systems. However, we can indicate what the problems are likely to be and suggest possible means for solving them.

There are two main areas of system-specific problems we're likely to encounter:

- Many compilers change the names of Fortran subprograms. So if we're trying to call the Fortran subprogram moo from a C program, and we simply type

  ```
  moo(x);
  ```

  in our C program, the linker is very likely to report that there is an undefined symbol. The reason is probably that the compiler has modified the subprogram name. The most common changes are appending an underscore (moo becomes moo_) or converting to capitals (moo becomes MOO). You can find out what your system does by writing a short Fortran subprogram and translating it into assembly. It should be clear from the assembly listing what's happened to the name.

- When we compile a C program with cc, it won't be automatically linked with the Fortran libraries. We can either try to find the Fortran libraries and explicitly link them, or we can write a Fortran main program whose sole purpose is to call the C main program. Although the latter course appears to be the path of least resistance, we may run into problems if our program uses command line arguments since standard Fortran 77 doesn't provide access to them.

The following problems will be encountered on any system, since they have to do with the specifications of C and Fortran 77:

- In Fortran all parameters are passed by address, while in C all parameters are passed by value. A further source of confusion is the fact that arrays in C are pointers, so they can be passed to Fortran subprograms without changes. The simplest solution to this problem is to make sure that each time we call a Fortran subprogram, each scalar argument is passed as a pointer. A more robust solution is to write **wrappers** for the Fortran subprograms. A wrapper is just a function whose sole purpose is to call another function. If we use wrappers, we can pass the parameters naturally, and let the wrapper subprogram worry about making sure that the correct information is passed to the Fortran subprogram. We'll illustrate this in our ScaLAPACK example.

- Two-dimensional arrays in Fortran are stored in *column-major* order, while in C they're stored in *row-major* order. For example, the matrix

$$\begin{pmatrix} 1 & 2 & 3 \\ 4 & 5 & 6 \end{pmatrix}$$

would be stored in sequential memory locations as

$$(1, 4, 2, 5, 3, 6)$$

in Fortran, while in C it would be stored as

$$(1, 2, 3, 4, 5, 6).$$

The simplest solution to this problem is to just use one-dimensional arrays and store the elements by hand in column-major order.

These suggestions may not solve all the problems you encounter in trying to call Fortran subprograms from C, but they should give you a good start. Your system's compiler documentation may also provide some pointers.

15.3 ScaLAPACK

ScaLAPACK is a large library of functions for solving problems in linear algebra on distributed-memory systems. Among other things it provides subprograms for linear system solution and solution of the symmetric eigenvalue problem. It is based on the library LAPACK, which was written for conventional and shared-memory systems. LAPACK stands for "Linear Algebra Package," and ScaLAPACK stands for "Scalable LAPACK." LAPACK obtains both portability and high performance by relying on another library, the BLAS, or "Basic Linear Algebra Subprogram" library. The BLAS performs common operations such as dot product, matrix-vector multiply, and matrix-matrix multiply. Most computer manufacturers have a BLAS library that has been specially written to obtain maximum performance from their systems. However, even though most BLAS implementations are system specific, the interface to the BLAS is completely standard. The LAPACK library exploits this by using the BLAS as much as possible. Both LAPACK and the BLAS were originally written in Fortran, although they have been rewritten in C.

Unfortunately, the problem of porting LAPACK and the BLAS to distributed-memory systems is an extremely difficult one. For example, suppose we wish to multiply a distributed matrix by a distributed vector. In order to do this, we must be able to determine whether the distributions are compatible, and, if not, we should probably be able to automatically redistribute one of the operands so that we can carry out the operation. Thus, we must associate with each distributed matrix or vector information on how it is distributed. Since Fortran 77 does not permit the use of mixed datatypes, this information must be added to all function-calling sequences. Furthermore, this information must be accessible to the user so that she can modify the distributions as she sees fit. In other words, any distributed linear algebra package must provide both a different interface to existing routines for conventional and shared-memory systems, and additional functionalities not available in the library for other types of systems. Thus, ScaLAPACK is necessarily very different from LAPACK.

a_{00}	a_{01}	a_{02}	a_{03}	a_{04}	a_{05}	a_{06}
a_{10}	a_{11}	a_{12}	a_{13}	a_{14}	a_{15}	a_{16}
a_{20}	a_{21}	a_{22}	a_{23}	a_{24}	a_{25}	a_{26}
a_{30}	a_{31}	a_{32}	a_{33}	a_{34}	a_{35}	a_{36}
a_{40}	a_{41}	a_{42}	a_{43}	a_{44}	a_{45}	a_{46}
a_{50}	a_{51}	a_{52}	a_{53}	a_{54}	a_{55}	a_{56}
a_{60}	a_{61}	a_{62}	a_{63}	a_{64}	a_{65}	a_{66}

Figure 15.1   Partitioning of a 7×7 matrix into 3×2 blocks

None of this should be taken to imply that LAPACK and the BLAS were simply tossed and that ScaLAPACK was written from scratch. To the contrary, both of the earlier libraries are used extensively for *local* operations. However, it was necessary to write completely new libraries for carrying out distributed operations.

By analogy with LAPACK, ScaLAPACK is based on underlying libraries that can be highly optimized for a particular system, but still provide a uniform interface to both ScaLAPACK and the user. Because of the increased complexity of ScaLAPACK, its developers partitioned the underlying functions into several different classes and wrote a separate library for each class. The separate libraries that we shall be concerned with are the PBLAS (Parallel BLAS) and the BLACS (Basic Linear Algebra Communication Subprograms). The routines in the PBLAS provide a highly optimized set of operations analogous to the BLAS for distributed matrices and vectors. As you can probably guess, the parts of the PBLAS that are concerned with operating on local matrices and vectors make extensive use of the BLAS. The communication that is necessary in both the PBLAS and ScaLAPACK is concentrated in the BLACS, and there is an implementation of the BLACS that uses MPI for its communication.

In order to map matrices and vectors to processes, the libraries (BLACS, PBLAS, and ScaLAPACK) rely on the complementary concepts of process grid and block-cyclic mapping. Rather than forcing the user to decide how best to map the matrices and vectors to physical processors, the libraries create a virtual rectangular grid of processes—much like a topology in MPI. Each matrix or vector is decomposed into rectangular blocks, and the matrix blocks are mapped cyclically to the virtual processes in each of the process dimensions. For example, suppose we have a 7×7 matrix decomposed into 3×2 blocks as indicated in Figure 15.1. If, in addition, we have a virtual 2×2 grid of processes, then a typical mapping of the entries to the processes might look something like the mapping shown in Figure 15.2.

Each virtual process grid forms a communication universe. Thus, a BLACS process grid is very similar to an MPI communicator with a topology. However, the terminology used in the BLACS may be somewhat confusing to an MPI user: a virtual grid is also called a **context.** (We'll avoid using this term and always call them grids.) The underlying description of the grid is invisible to the user, and each grid is accessed by a handle, which is just an integer.

Process 0				Process 1		
a_{00}	a_{01}	a_{04}	a_{05}	a_{02}	a_{03}	a_{06}
a_{10}	a_{11}	a_{14}	a_{15}	a_{12}	a_{13}	a_{16}
a_{20}	a_{21}	a_{24}	a_{25}	a_{22}	a_{23}	a_{26}
a_{60}	a_{61}	a_{64}	a_{65}	a_{62}	a_{63}	a_{66}
Process 2				Process 3		
a_{30}	a_{31}	a_{34}	a_{35}	a_{32}	a_{33}	a_{36}
a_{40}	a_{41}	a_{44}	a_{45}	a_{42}	a_{43}	a_{46}
a_{50}	a_{51}	a_{54}	a_{55}	a_{52}	a_{53}	a_{56}

Figure 15.2   Mapping of a 7×7 matrix onto a 2×2 grid

In order to completely describe a distributed matrix, the libraries make use of a data structure called a **descriptor.** Since the routines in the libraries are callable from Fortran, descriptors are arrays of integers rather than structs. Each descriptor consists of the following information:

1. The global dimensions of the matrix—the number of rows and columns.

2. The dimensions of the matrix blocks.

3. The process row and column of the first entry of the matrix. The libraries allow for the possibility that the matrix begins in a process different from the process with row and column rank 0.

4. The handle of the BLACS grid.

5. The leading dimension of the local storage for the matrix. If we were storing the local entries of the matrices in statically allocated two-dimensional Fortran arrays, this would allow the libraries to skip over empty storage in the event that we allocated more space than was actually needed. However, since we'll be simulating two-dimensional storage with a one-dimensional array (as discussed above), we'll just use the number of local matrix rows for this value.

Since the libraries view vectors as matrices with one row or one column, the same information can be used to describe vectors. However, in most situations, a vector will not be significant on the entire process grid; only the values stored on a single process row or column will be accessed by the routines. Whether the vector is stored in a process row or a process column is determined by another integer variable, the increment. Currently, there are two possible values for the increment: 1 or the row block size of the vector. In the former case, the vector is a column vector, and in the latter, it is a row vector. This convention originated in the Fortran convention that two-dimensional arrays are stored in column-major order. Thus, if the increment is 1, the next entry in the vector is in the same column, while if the increment is the row block size, the next entry is in the next column. The increment is not part of the descriptor. So in addition to the contents of the vector and the descriptor, routines that operate on vectors will be passed a value for the increment.

15.4 An Example of a ScaLAPACK Program

Now that we have a feel for some of the basic ideas in the BLACS, the PBLAS, and ScaLAPACK, let's write a short program that solves a linear system. In brief, we'll initialize system data structures, generate a coefficient matrix, generate a right-hand side for the system, solve the system, and determine the error in our solution and the amount of time it took to solve the system. We can generate a coefficient matrix by using a random number generator. A simple way to guarantee that we know the exact solution is to form a vector of, say, all ones, and multiply the coefficient matrix by the vector of ones to obtain the right-hand side. Then the exact solution is just the vector of ones, and we can easily compare the computed solution.

Before proceeding to write the program, we need to address the issue of language. All three libraries are written in a mix of C and Fortran. Presently, the PBLAS and ScaLAPACK only present a Fortran interface to the user, although the ScaLAPACK project plans to include a C interface with a release that will be made available in 1996. The BLACS, however, have both a Fortran and C interface, and even if we use the C user interface, its functions will still interface properly with the PBLAS and ScaLAPACK. Thus, we can use the C interfaces to both MPI and the BLACS, and we only need to worry about inter-language communication when we use the PBLAS and ScaLAPACK. When we call a Fortran function, we will use the convention that Fortran subprograms have underscores appended to their names. Be aware that this may not be the case with your system.

The input to the program is

- n: the global order of the system
- nproc_rows: the number of process rows
- nproc_cols: the number of process columns
- row_block_size: the number of rows in a block of the matrix
- col_block_size: the number of columns in a block of the matrix

The output is just the two-norm of the error and time it took to solve the system.

Here's the main program:

```
#include <stdio.h>
#include "mpi.h"
#include "linsolve.h"
    /* Function prototypes, including BLACS prototypes   */

main(int argc, char* argv[]) {
    float*  b_local;     /* Local part of rhs of Ax = b */
    int     b_local_size;
    int     b_descrip[DESCRIPTOR_SIZE];
```

```
             /* For each distributed array, the descrip- */
             /* tor is named <array_name>_descrip        */

float*   exact_local;    /* Local part of exact soln. */
int      exact_local_size;
int      exact_descrip[DESCRIPTOR_SIZE];

float*   A_local;                    /* Local part of A */
int      local_mat_rows;
int      local_mat_cols;
int      A_descrip[DESCRIPTOR_SIZE];
int*     pivot_list;         /* Pivots used by solver */

int      p, my_rank;
int      nproc_rows, nproc_cols;  /* proc. grid dims */
int      m, n;            /* global matrix order, m = n */
int      row_block_size;  /* Solver requires square   */
int      col_block_size;  /*      blocks.             */
int      blacs_grid;        /* handle for process grid */

int      my_process_row, my_process_col;
float    error_2;     /* 2-norm of error in solution */
double   start_time, elapsed_time;

MPI_Init(&argc, &argv);
MPI_Comm_size(MPI_COMM_WORLD, &p);
MPI_Comm_rank(MPI_COMM_WORLD, &my_rank);

Get_input(p, my_rank, &n, &nproc_rows, &nproc_cols,
          &row_block_size, &col_block_size);

/* The matrix is square */
m = n;

/* Build BLACS grid */
/* First get BLACS System Grid */
Cblacs_get(0, 0, &blacs_grid);

/* blacs_grid is in/out.                            */
/* "R": process grid will use row major ordering. */
Cblacs_gridinit(&blacs_grid, "R", nproc_rows,
    nproc_cols);

/* Get my process coordinates in the process grid */
Cblacs_pcoord(blacs_grid, my_rank, &my_process_row,
    &my_process_col);

/* Figure out space needs for the arrays and       */
/* malloc storage.  Get_dimension is a wrapper for */
```

```
/* the ScaLAPACK function numroc, which computes   */
/* the number of rows and columns needed for local */
/* storage.                                         */
local_mat_rows = Get_dimension(m, row_block_size,
                      my_process_row, nproc_rows);
local_mat_cols = Get_dimension(n, col_block_size,
                      my_process_col, nproc_cols);
/* Last parameter = 1, allocate floats */
Allocate(my_rank, "A", &A_local,
    local_mat_rows*local_mat_cols, 1);

b_local_size = Get_dimension(m, row_block_size,
                      my_process_row, nproc_rows);
Allocate(my_rank, "b", &b_local, b_local_size, 1);

exact_local_size = Get_dimension(m, col_block_size,
                      my_process_row, nproc_rows);
Allocate(my_rank, "exact", &exact_local,
    exact_local_size, 1);

/* Now build the matrix descriptors.  Build_descrip */
/* is a wrapper for the ScaLAPACK subroutine         */
/* descinit, which initializes descriptor arrays     */
Build_descrip(my_rank, "A", A_descrip, m, n,
    row_block_size, col_block_size, blacs_grid,
    local_mat_rows);
Build_descrip(my_rank, "B", b_descrip, m, 1,
    row_block_size, 1, blacs_grid, b_local_size);
Build_descrip(my_rank, "Exact", exact_descrip, n, 1,
    col_block_size, 1, blacs_grid, exact_local_size);

/* Initialize A_local and exact_local */
Initialize(p, my_rank, A_local, local_mat_rows,
    local_mat_cols, exact_local, exact_local_size);

/* Set b = A*exact.  Mat_vect_mult is a wrapper for */
/* the PBLAS subroutine, psgemv, which computes      */
/* y = alpha*A*x + beta*y, for scalars alpha and     */
/* beta, matrix A, and vectors x and y.              */
Mat_vect_mult(m, n, A_local, A_descrip, exact_local,
                exact_descrip, b_local, b_descrip);

/* Allocate storage for pivots. Last parameter 0, */
/* allocate ints                                   */
Allocate(my_rank, "pivot_list", &pivot_list,
        local_mat_rows + row_block_size, 0);

/* Done with setup!  Solve the system. */
MPI_Barrier(MPI_COMM_WORLD);
```

```
start_time = MPI_Wtime();

/* Solve is a wrapper for the ScaLAPACK subroutine */
/* psgesv which solves Ax = b, and returns the     */
/* solution in b.                                   */
Solve(my_rank, n, A_local, A_descrip, pivot_list,
        b_local, b_descrip);
elapsed_time = MPI_Wtime() - start_time;

/* Use PBLAS routines psaxpy and psnrm2 to compute */
/* 2-norm of error                                 */
error_2 = Norm_diff(n, b_local, b_descrip,
            exact_local, exact_descrip);

/* Print results */
if (my_rank == 0) {
    printf("2-norm of error = %g\n",error_2);
    printf("Elapsed time for solve = %g msec\n",
        1000.0*elapsed_time);
}


/* Now free up allocated resources and shut down */
/* Call Cblacs_exit.  Argument != 0 says, "User  */
/*      program will shut down MPI."              */
Cblacs_exit(1);
MPI_Finalize();
}   /* main */
```

Since the complete source code is fairly extensive, we include here only a couple of the wrappers. The first is a wrapper for the PBLAS function psgemv. The subroutine psgemv will compute

$$\bar{\mathbf{y}} = \alpha \bar{A}\bar{\mathbf{x}} + \beta\bar{\mathbf{y}},$$

or

$$\bar{\mathbf{y}} = \alpha \bar{A}^T\bar{\mathbf{x}} + \beta\bar{\mathbf{y}},$$

where $\bar{A}$ is a submatrix of A and $\bar{\mathbf{x}}$ and $\bar{\mathbf{y}}$ are subvectors of $\mathbf{x}$ and $\mathbf{y}$, respectively. However, since we only need to compute $\mathbf{y} = A\mathbf{x}$, we only pass A, $\mathbf{x}$, $\mathbf{y}$ and their associated descriptors to the wrapper.

```
void Mat_vect_mult(int m, int n, float* A_local,
        int* A_descrip, float* x_local,
        int* x_descrip, float* y_local, int* y_descrip) {

    char transpose = 'N';
            /* Don't take the transpose of A */
```

```
        float alpha = 1.0;
        float beta = 0.0;

        int first_row_A = 1;
        int first_col_A = 1;
        int first_row_x = 1;
        int first_col_x = 1;
        int first_row_y = 1;
        int first_col_y = 1;
                /* Don't use submatrices or subvectors */
                /* Multiply all of x by all of A        */

        int x_increment = 1;
        int y_increment = 1;
                /* x and y are column vectors. So next */
                /* value is obtained by adding one to  */
                /* current subscript. Remember fortran */
                /* arrays are column major!            */

        extern void psgemv_(char* trans, int* m, int* n,
                float* alpha,
                float* A_local, int* ia, int* ja, int* A_descrip,
                float* x_local, int* ix, int* jx, int* x_descrip,
                    int* incx,
                float* beta,
                float* y_local, int* iy, int* jy, int* y_descrip,
                    int* incy);

        psgemv_(&transpose, &m, &n, &alpha,
            A_local, &first_row_A, &first_col_A, A_descrip,
            x_local, &first_row_x, &first_col_x, x_descrip,
                &x_increment,
            &beta,
            y_local, &first_row_y, &first_col_y, y_descrip,
                &y_increment);
}   /* Mat_vect_mult */
```

The linear system solution is carried out by the ScaLAPACK subroutine psgesv. Our Solve function is a simplified wrapper. If the subroutine successfully solves the system, it returns 0 in error_info. If there's either an erroneous argument or if the system is singular, error_info is nonzero.

```
void Solve(int my_rank, int order,
        float* A_local, int* A_descrip, int* pivot_list,
        float* b_local, int* b_descrip) {
    int rhs_count = 1;
    int first_row_A = 1;
    int first_col_A = 1;
    int first_row_b = 1;
```

```
        int first_col_b = 1;
                /* Use all of A and b */
        int error_info;

        /* Solve the system Ax = b.  Return solution in b */
        /* Blocks of A must be square.                    */
        extern void psgesv_(int* order, int* rhs_count,
                float* A_local, int* first_row_A,
                    int* first_col_A, int* A_descrip,
                int* pivot_list,
                float* b_local, int* first_row_b,
                    int* first_col_b, int* b_descrip,
                int* error_info);

        psgesv_(&order, &rhs_count, A_local, &first_row_A,
                &first_col_A, A_descrip, pivot_list,
                b_local, &first_row_b,
                &first_col_b, b_descrip, &error_info);

    if (error_info != 0) {
        fprintf(stderr,"Process %d > Psgesv failed!\n",
            my_rank);
        fprintf(stderr,"Process %d > Error_info = %d\n",
                my_rank, error_info);
        fprintf(stderr,"Process %d > Quitting\n",my_rank);
        MPI_Abort(MPI_COMM_WORLD, -1);
    }
}   /* Solve */
```

15.5 PETSc

PETSc (Portable Extensible Toolkit for Scientific Computation) is a large library
for use in the solution of partial differential equations and related problems
(such as linear system solution). It can solve both sparse and dense linear
and nonlinear systems of equations; it provides an extensive error traceback
facility; and it provides functions and utilities for basic graphics. (It obtains
part of its functionality from LAPACK and the BLAS.) Although PETSc provides
a Fortran interface, it has been primarily designed for use by C and C++ applications, and it provides a distinctly object-oriented interface: the basic data
structures and associated operations are hidden from the user and are accessed
mainly through the use of generic datatypes and functions. For example, if the
user so desires, she can use exactly the same program interface regardless of
whether she is working with dense or sparse matrices. Although the underlying data structures and functions may be different, the user functions for such
things as initialization and matrix-vector multiplication can be identical.

Another striking feature of PETSc is the provision of many complex nonblocking operations. For example, if A is a distributed matrix, it is permissible for any process to initialize *any* entry in A. Thus, after initialization, PETSc must check whether any redistribution is necessary and, if so, carry out the redistribution. PETSc provides two functions for this: `MatAssemblyBegin` and `MatAssemblyEnd`. In the first function, each process determines how much data it will receive, allocates storage for the data to be received, and posts the necessary nonblocking receives and sends. In the second function, each process waits on the receives, inserts the received values into the correct storage locations, and waits on the sends. Thus, these two functions can—and if there is data to be redistributed, should—be separated by other useful work.

PETSc also provides a huge number of options that can be selected at runtime. For example, it provides a large collection of linear system solvers, all of which use the same application interface. The particular solver can be specified by a command line option at runtime. This is a great convenience during development; rather than recompiling the program so that it will use a different solver, we can simply change a command line argument. It is also extremely useful for the development of general-purpose programs; for example, a single program can be used to solve a variety of different types of problems by simply choosing a different solver.

A large collection of linear system solvers lies at the heart of PETSc. Currently, all of the parallel linear system solvers use iterative methods. Recall (see section 10.2) that an iterative method makes an initial estimate to a solution, and then refines the estimate through a sequence of iterations. Iterative methods are frequently used for solving sparse linear systems. Basically, a sparse system, as opposed to a dense system, has a coefficient matrix with a large number of zero entries. By "large" we mean that there will be a significant gain in the performance of our programs if we use a compressed storage format—a storage format that only records the nonzero entries in the matrix. For example, the most expensive basic operation in many iterative methods is matrix-vector multiplication, and if the matrix is sparse and our code is well designed, it should be much cheaper to multiply a sparse matrix of a given order by a vector than it is to multiply a dense matrix of the same order by the vector.

Most of the solvers in PETSc belong to a family of iterative solvers known as **Krylov subspace methods.** A Krylov subspace is simply a subspace of euclidean space, $\mathbf{R}^n$, spanned by a set of vectors having the form

$$\{\mathbf{p}, A\mathbf{p}, A^2\mathbf{p}, \dots, A^{m-1}\mathbf{p}\}.$$

If A is the coefficient matrix of a linear system and $\mathbf{x}_0$ denotes the initial guess, then a Krylov subspace method chooses the qth iterate from the translated Krylov subspace

$$\mathbf{x}_0 + \mathrm{Span}\{\mathbf{p}, A\mathbf{p}, \dots, A^{q-1}\mathbf{p}\},$$

for some vector $\mathbf{p}$. That is, if $\mathbf{x}_q$ denotes the qth approximation to the solution, then

$$\mathbf{x}_q = \mathbf{x}_0 + \sum_{i=0}^{q-1} \eta_i A^i \mathbf{p},$$

for some scalars $\eta_0, \eta_1, \ldots, \eta_{q-1}$. The various Krylov subspace methods are distinguished by their method for choosing the iterate, $\mathbf{x}_q$, from the translated Krylov subspace. These methods usually terminate by testing the norm or relative norm of the **residual,**

$$\mathbf{r}_q = \mathbf{b} - A\mathbf{x}_q,$$

where $\mathbf{b}$ is the right-hand side of the system; i.e., $A\mathbf{x} = \mathbf{b}$. Observe that this is much easier to compute than the error, which is the difference between the true solution, $A^{-1}\mathbf{b}$, and the estimate. That is, the **error** in the qth iterate is

$$\mathbf{e}_q = A^{-1}\mathbf{b} - \mathbf{x}_q.$$

Krylov subspace methods may converge very slowly or even diverge. As a consequence, most solvers employ a **preconditioner.** Basically a preconditioner is a matrix M with the property that the system

$$M^{-1}A\mathbf{b} = M^{-1}\mathbf{b}$$

is much easier to solve than the original system $A\mathbf{x} = \mathbf{b}$. Choosing M is generally regarded as an art rather than a science, and, as a consequence, PETSc provides a variety of possible preconditioners with which the user can experiment.

For further information on Krylov subspace methods, see the references at the end of the chapter.

15.6 A PETSc Example

Let's write a small program that solves a sparse linear system. It will use a user-specified runtime option to choose a solver and/or a preconditioner. We'll initialize MPI and PETSc, get input data describing the linear system and how we want the coefficient matrix initialized, allocate and initialize matrices and vectors, solve the system, and print results.

We'll generate the coefficient matrix by using a random number generator. Since the matrix is sparse, before generating an entry, we'll generate a (uniformly distributed) random value in $(0, 1)$. If the value is less than a user-specified threshold, we'll generate another random value from $(0, 1)$, scale it so that it lies in $(-1, 1)$, and insert it into the matrix. Since this procedure may generate a singular or near-singular matrix, the diagonal entries of the matrix will be assigned a user-specified value. We'll use the standard C functions srand48 and drand48 to generate the random numbers. The first function is used to seed the generator, while the second is used to generate the actual entries.

In order to illustrate PETSc's simple redistribution facilities, we'll also let the user specify the initial distribution of the matrix. Depending on a user-specified flag, we'll either generate the entire matrix on process 0, or each process can generate its entries in the matrix. We'll use the default internal matrix representation, which partitions the matrix by block rows and stores only the nonzero entries of the matrix. Thus, in order to use the second option, we only need to call a function that returns the minimum and maximum row numbers for the calling process. Note that the first option should only be used for relatively small matrices.

So user input should be

- n: order of the linear system
- diagonal: value of the diagonal entries in the matrix
- prob: probability that an off-diagonal entry is nonzero
- initial_dist: the initial distribution of the coefficient matrix (0 indicates that the entire matrix initially resides on process 0; 1 indicates that it will be distributed among the processes)

After starting the redistribution of the matrix with MatAssemblyBegin, we can allocate storage for the right-hand side vector b, the exact solution exact, and the computed solution x. As with the ScaLAPACK example, we can set exact to be a vector of all ones, and we can generate the right-hand side by multiplying the exact solution by the coefficient matrix. Thus, before generating the entries in b, we need to finish redistribution of the matrix with MatAssemblyEnd.

The solution of the system will use four function calls. The first call will be to SLESCreate. This sets up internal storage, communicators, etc., needed by the solver. The second call will be to SLESSetOperators. This identifies the coefficient matrix and the matrix on which the preconditioner is based. For this example, our preconditioners will be based on the original coefficient matrix. Before actually solving the system, we'll call SLESSetFromOptions. This will examine the command line options and determine what type of solver and preconditioner to use. After this setup phase, we can solve the system by calling SLESSolve.

To complete the program, we'll print information on the solution method, compute the norm of the error, print the results, free up storage, and shutdown PETSc and MPI.

There are only three user-defined functions: Get_input, Initialize, and Allocate. The second uses a PETSc function, MatSetValues, to assign the randomly generated values to the matrix entries.

Before presenting the code, we should note that almost all PETSc functions return an error code. This error code can be processed with some PETSc macros so that tracebacks will be generated in the event the program crashes.

We are omitting this from our code simply to make it more readable. In order
to include it, we would replace a call to the PETSc function XXX

```
XXX(param, list);
```

with

```
ierr = XXX(param, list); CHKERRA(ierr);
```

if the call is in main, or

```
ierr = XXX(param, list); CHKERRQ(ierr);
```

if the function is being called from a subprogram.

Here's the main program:

```
#include <stdio.h>
#include <stdlib.h> /* Needed for drand48 and srand48   */
#include "sles.h"   /* Includes headers needed by PETSc */
#include "mpi.h"
#include "sparse_linsolve.h"
            /* function prototypes, etc. */

/* Required in all PETSc programs: brief description of */
/*      program                                         */
static char help[] = "Solve a random sparse linear system";

int main(int argc, char* argv[]) {
        Vec      x;              /* computed solution       */
        Vec      b;              /* right-hand side         */
        Vec      exact;          /* exact solution          */
        int      p, my_rank;
        int      n;              /* order of system         */
        double   diagonal;       /* diagonal matrix entries */
        double   prob;           /* probability of an off-  */
                                 /* diagonal nonzero        */
        int      initial_dist;   /* =0 matrix initialized   */
                                 /* on process 0. =1 dist-  */
                                 /* tributed initialization */
        Mat      A;              /* coefficient matrix      */
        double   one = 1.0;
        double   minus_one = -1.0;
        SLES     sles;           /* context for solver      */
        int      iterations;     /* number of iterations    */
                                 /* used by solver          */
        double   error;          /* 2-norm of error in sol- */
                                 /* ution                   */

        MPI_Init(&argc, &argv);
```

```
PetscInitialize(&argc,&argv,0,0,help);

MPI_Comm_rank(MPI_COMM_WORLD,&my_rank);
MPI_Comm_size(MPI_COMM_WORLD,&p);

Get_input(my_rank, &n, &diagonal, &prob,
    &initial_dist);

/* PETSc function for creating a matrix */
MatCreate(MPI_COMM_WORLD, n, n, &A);

/* Assign random values to matrix entries.  Uses  */
/* PETSc function MatSetValues to actually assign */
/* randomly generated values to matrix entries     */
Initialize_matrix(my_rank, A, n, diagonal, prob,
                  initial_dist);

MatAssemblyBegin(A, FINAL_ASSEMBLY);

/* Create and set vectors, all PETSc functions */
VecCreate(MPI_COMM_WORLD,n,&x);
VecDuplicate(x, &exact);
VecDuplicate(x, &b);
VecSet(&one, exact);

MatAssemblyEnd(A, FINAL_ASSEMBLY);

MatMult(A, exact, b);

/* Set up solver */
SLESCreate(MPI_COMM_WORLD, &sles);

/* Identify coefficient matrix and preconditioning */
/* matrix                                          */
SLESSetOperators(sles, A, A, 0);

/* Use solver and preconditioner specified */
/* by command line options                 */
SLESSetFromOptions(sles);

/* Now solve the system */
SLESSolve(sles, b, x, &iterations);

/* Take a look at info on the solution */
SLESView(sles, STDOUT_VIEWER_WORLD);

/* Check solution: First compute x - exact */
VecAXPY(&minus_one, exact, x);
/* Now compute two-norm of x - exact */
```

```
        VecNorm(x, NORM_2, &error);

        /* MPIU_printf is a PETSC utility */
        if (error >= 1.0e-12)
            MPIU_printf(MPI_COMM_WORLD,
                "Norm of error %g, Iterations %d\n",
                error, iterations);
        else
            MPIU_printf(MPI_COMM_WORLD,
                "Norm of error < 1.0e-12, Iterations %d\n",
                iterations);

        /* Free work space */
        VecDestroy(x);
        VecDestroy(exact);
        VecDestroy(b);
        MatDestroy(A);
        SLESDestroy(sles);

        PetscFinalize();
        MPI_Finalize();
}   /* main */
```

In order to illustrate how we assign values to the matrix entries, we also
include the function Initialize. It first determines the range of rows to
which the process should assign data and allocates temporary storage for the
entries. Then, for each row of the matrix, it generates the entries and assigns
them to the matrix. Recall that if initial_dist is 0, we generate the entire
matrix on process 0. If it's 1, each process generates its own entries.

```
void Initialize_matrix(int my_rank, Mat A, int n,
                double diagonal, double prob,
                int initial_dist) {
    int*      columns;  /* temporary storage for col */
    double*   temp_row; /* indices and row entries    */
    int       nonzero_count;
    int       my_min_row;
    int       my_max_row;
    int       i, j;

    if (initial_dist == 0) {
        if (my_rank == 0) {
            my_min_row = 0;
            my_max_row = n;
        } else {
            return;
        }
    } else {
        /* Have PETSc determine which rows of matrix  */
```

```
        /*      are assigned to this process           */
        MatGetOwnershipRange(A, &my_min_row, &my_max_row);
    }

    /* Allocate temporary storage, last parameter 0 => */
    /*      allocate ints, last parameter 1 => floats  */
    Allocate(my_rank, "columns", &columns, n, 0);
    Allocate(my_rank, "temp_row", &temp_row, n, 1);

    /* Seed random number generator */
    srand48((long) (my_rank*my_rank));

    /* Generate 1 row and insert into matrix */
    for (i = my_min_row; i < my_max_row; i++) {
        nonzero_count = 0;
        for (j = 0; j < n; j++) {
            if (i == j) {
                temp_row[nonzero_count] = diagonal;
                columns[nonzero_count] = j;
                nonzero_count++;
            } else if (drand48() <= prob) {
                temp_row[nonzero_count] =
                    2.0*drand48()-1.0;
                columns[nonzero_count] = j;
                nonzero_count++;
            }
        }
        /* Insert entries in a single row (row i) into */
        /* the matrix                                  */
        MatSetValues(A, 1, &i, nonzero_count, columns,
                    temp_row, INSERT_VALUES);
    }
    free(columns);
    free(temp_row);
}   /* Initialize_matrix */
```

The number of command line options is quite extensive. Among other options, we can choose the type of the solver, we can set a number of parameters for testing convergence, and we can choose the type of preconditioning. For example, if we are using the mpich implementation of MPI, we can use four processes to solve the system using GMRES with ILU preconditioning by starting the program with the command

```
% mpirun -np 4 a.out -ksp_method GMRES -pc_method ilu
```

See the references at the end of the chapter for pointers to a full description of the command line options.

15.7 Summary

One of the most important features of MPI is that it provides strong support for the development of parallel libraries. This could go a long way to bringing parallel computing into the mainstream of computational science and engineering by making parallel systems relatively easy to use. It is not, however, an unmixed blessing. The development of powerful parallel libraries is an extremely difficult undertaking, and the programmers who do most of the development of parallel software are research oriented. As a consequence, they tend to concentrate more on functionality and performance than they do on developing and documenting the application/library interface. Of course, this can result in code that is extremely difficult to use. There are a couple of things library writers can do to make things easier: provide quick-start documentation that gives a brief introduction to the library, and explain all nonstandard terminology.

Two libraries that provide well-designed and well-documented interfaces are ScaLAPACK and PETSc. ScaLAPACK is based on the well-known LAPACK library for conventional and shared-memory systems. Like LAPACK, its purpose is to provide a portable, efficient library for the solution of problems in dense numerical linear algebra. At this time ScaLAPACK only provides a Fortran 77 interface. Thus, in order to use it, we had to briefly discuss some of the issues involved in calling Fortran functions from C. We noted four main concerns: the modification of Fortran subprogram names by the compiler, linking with the Fortran library, passing parameters to a Fortran function, and the ordering of two-dimensional array elements. Dealing with the first two problems is system dependent. We dealt with the third by writing *wrappers* for the ScaLAPACK functions. A wrapper is just a function whose purpose is to call another function. We dealt with the last problem by only using one-dimensional arrays and ordering the elements according to the Fortran convention.

PETSc can be used to solve both sparse and dense, linear and nonlinear equations. It also provides an error traceback facility and basic I/O and graphics facilities. It has been written primarily for use with C and C++, and it provides an object-oriented interface. Data structures such as matrices and vectors are hidden from the user and accessed only through PETSc functions. Further, data structures and data access are generic. For example, we can use the same type declarations and functions for accessing both sparse and dense matrices, even if the program is using different underlying representations. PETSc also provides a large number of nonblocking operations, and it provides many command line options that can be used for such things as specifying solvers and preconditioners at run time.

We wrote a couple of simple programs. One used ScaLAPACK to solve a dense linear system. The other used PETSc to solve a sparse linear system. In both cases, once the basics of the library had been illustrated, the coding of the solution was completely straightforward.

15.8 References

There is an extensive collection of articles on the development of ScaLAPACK, the PBLAS, and the BLACS. It forms a subset of an even larger set called *LAPACK Working Notes*. Most of the *Working Notes* are available over the World Wide Web at `http://www.netlib.org/lapack/lawns/`. *Working Notes 55* and *95* [6, 7] discuss ScaLAPACK. *Working Note 100* [8] discusses the PBLAS, and *Working Note 94* [13] is a user's guide to the BLACS.

The *LAPACK User's Guide* [3] contains a comprehensive and elementary discussion of LAPACK. The BLAS have all been published in the *ACM Transactions on Mathematical Software* [27, 14, 15].

The *PETSc Users Manual* [33] is available over the World Wide Web at the PETSc home page: `http://www.mcs.anl.gov/petsc/petsc.html/`.

Golub and Ortega [19] provide an elementary introduction to Krylov subspace methods in the context of parallel computing.

15.9 Exercises

1. Use our sparse linear solver program to experiment with the different solvers and preconditioners provided by PETSc. Is there a solver/preconditioner pair that seems to be consistently better than the others, or is the best solver/preconditioner pair dependent on such things as the order, sparsity, and number of processes?

2. Write a serial version of our ScaLAPACK solver that uses LAPACK. Compare the performance of the two solvers.

15.10 Programming Assignments

1. a. Write a serial program that uses the LAPACK function DSYEV to find all the eigenvalues of a random $n \times n$ matrix of doubles.
   b. Write a parallel program that uses the ScaLAPACK function PDSYEVX to find all the eigenvalues of a random $n \times n$ matrix of doubles.

2. Suppose $\mathbf{x} = (x_0, x_1, \ldots, x_{n-1})$, $\mathbf{y} = (y_0, y_1, \ldots, y_{n-1})$, and A is a random nonsingular sparse matrix. Further, if $\mathbf{u}$ is the n-dimensional vector all of whose components are 1, let $\mathbf{b} = A\mathbf{u}$. Use the nonlinear solver in PETSc, SNES, to solve the system

$$A\mathbf{y} = \mathbf{b},$$
$$y_i = x_i^2, \quad i = 0, \ldots, n-1$$

for $\mathbf{x}$.

CHAPTER 16

Wrapping Up

BEFORE YOU MOVE ON TO BIGGER AND BETTER THINGS, we'd like to take a minute to provide a few pointers to additional sources of information on MPI and to discuss the future of MPI.

16.1 Where to Go from Here

Presumably, at this point you've covered most of the material in the book, so you should have a very solid grounding in MPI. If, for some reason, you've only been reading the book, as opposed to reading, coding, and debugging, you'll probably want to start writing some programs. Appendix B contains pointers to implementations of MPI that can be freely obtained over the Internet.

If there are some thorny problems concerning MPI that we haven't solved, you have several options. The first place to go for further information is the MPI Standard [28, 29]. If you find the Standard too dry or difficult, several members of the MPI Forum have produced an annotated edition of the Standard, *MPI: The Complete Reference* [34]. It follows the basic organization of the Standard, but provides considerably more discussion and examples than the Standard.

If you want to continue your study of MPI, *Using MPI* [21] provides an excellent point of departure. It provides well-documented, extended examples that will help to clarify technical details. It illustrates how MPI should be used in large applications, and it provides a guide to porting codes written using various parallel systems.

If you feel that your view of parallel computing is a little too parochial, too "MPI-centric," take a look at *Designing and Building Parallel Programs* [17]. It provides discussions of several other parallel programming languages.

Perhaps, more importantly, it provides a comprehensive approach to parallel software engineering.

Finally, there are numerous additional resources on the Internet. To name a few, there is an MPI FAQ (a list of frequently asked questions about MPI), there are several tutorial introductions to MPI, and there is a Usenet newsgroup devoted to MPI. More detailed pointers are provided in Appendix B.

16.2 The Future of MPI

As we noted in Chapter 1, message passing is sometimes called the "assembly language" of parallel processing. The implication is that it requires an excessive command of detail. To a degree, this is a valid objection, and it might lead you to believe that MPI will soon take its place in the dustbin of failed parallel programming systems. However, this conclusion is almost certainly wrong for several reasons. First, it is the *first* truly portable, universally available standard for programming parallel systems. Furthermore, because of the care exercised in its design, it's possible to develop applications that obtain very high performance on a variety of systems. This will open the way for the development of a parallel software industry. Since the standard is bound to gain acceptance in the short term, its users will become an entrenched interest in the long term, making it almost certain that for the forseeable future virtually all parallel systems will include an MPI implementation.

This should not be construed to imply that in the near future MPI will be a millstone hanging around the neck of parallel software developers. The MPI Forum has anticipated this possibility and, as a consequence, is continuing to develop MPI. *The Return of MPI,* or *The Son of MPI,* or, more often, MPI-2, is a collection of extensions to MPI that should prevent its becoming obsolescent for a long time to come. Among other things, standards for dynamic process management, one-sided communications, extended collective communications, external interfaces, a C + + class library, real-time programming, and interlanguage interoperability are currently under development. These standards address deficiencies in the current standard (e.g., lack of functionality in some of the collective communication operations) and add new and powerful functionalities to MPI (e.g., operations allowing processes to directly access remote memory locations). Furthermore, taking MPI as a model, other groups are working on the development of one of the most important omissions from the original standard: standards for I/O on parallel systems.

MPI has addressed a serious deficiency in parallel programming: the absence of a powerful, portable standard for programming parallel systems. Furthermore, the excellence of its original design, its portability, and its continued development will make it one of the best systems for parallel programming for years to come.

APPENDIX A

Summary of MPI Commands

IN THIS APPENDIX WE BRIEFLY SUMMARIZE the syntax of each MPI function and list MPI constants and type definitions. Within each subsection, functions are listed alphabetically. The order of the constants and type definitions follows the MPI Standard [28]. The MPI Standard [28, 29] is available online in both PostScript and hypertext from `http://www.mcs.anl.gov/mpi`.

Unless otherwise noted, function return values are error codes.

A.1 Point-to-Point Communication Functions

For general discussions of point-to-point communication, see Chapters 3 and 13.

A.1.1 Blocking Sends and Receives

`MPI_Get_count`

Returns in `count` the number of elements received by the operation that initialized the `status` parameter (e.g., `MPI_Recv`). Discussed in section 3.3.4, p. 49.

```
int MPI_Get_count(
        MPI_Status*    status      /* in  */,
        MPI_Datatype   datatype    /* in  */,
        int*           count       /* out */)
```

MPI_Recv

Receives data sent by process source into memory referenced by message. Discussed in section 3.3, especially section 3.3.4, p. 47.

```
int MPI_Recv(
        void*        message     /* out */,
        int          count       /* in  */,
        MPI_Datatype datatype    /* in  */,
        int          source      /* in  */,
        int          tag         /* in  */,
        MPI_Comm     comm        /* in  */,
        MPI_Status*  status      /* out */)
```

MPI_Send

Sends the data referenced by message to the process with rank dest. Discussed in section 3.3, especially section 3.3.4, p. 47.

```
int MPI_Send(
        void*        message     /* in */,
        int          count       /* in */,
        MPI_Datatype datatype    /* in */,
        int          dest        /* in */,
        int          tag         /* in */,
        MPI_Comm     comm        /* in */)
```

A.1.2 Communication Modes

MPI_Bsend

Buffered send. Uses user-allocated buffer (see p. 365). Discussed in section 13.7.3, p. 307.

```
int MPI_Bsend(
        void*        message     /* in */,
        int          count       /* in */,
        MPI_Datatype datatype    /* in */,
        int          dest        /* in */,
        int          tag         /* in */,
        MPI_Comm     comm        /* in */)
```

MPI_Rsend

Ready send. Use ready mode for send: matching receive must be posted before the call to MPI_Rsend. Discussed in section 13.7.2, p. 306.

```
int MPI_Rsend(
        void*             message     /* in */,
```

```
        int         count       /* in */,
        MPI_Datatype datatype   /* in */,
        int         dest        /* in */,
        int         tag         /* in */,
        MPI_Comm    comm        /* in */)
```

MPI_Ssend

Synchronous send. Use synchronous mode for send: function won't return until a matching receive has been posted and data reception has begun. Discussed in section 13.7.1, p. 305.

```
int MPI_Ssend(
        void*       message     /* in */,
        int         count       /* in */,
        MPI_Datatype datatype   /* in */,
        int         dest        /* in */,
        int         tag         /* in */,
        MPI_Comm    comm        /* in */)
```

A.1.3 Buffer Allocation

MPI_Buffer_attach

Informs the system that memory referenced by buffer is to be used for buffering outgoing messages sent in buffered mode. Discussed in section 13.7.3, p. 307.

```
int MPI_Buffer_attach(
        void*  buffer    /* in */,
        int    size      /* in */)
```

MPI_Buffer_detach

Informs system that attached buffer is no longer to be used for buffering messages. Discussed in section 13.7.3, p. 307.

```
int MPI_Buffer_detach(
        void*  buffer_address   /* out */,
        int*   size_ptr         /* out */)
```

A.1.4 Nonblocking Communication

MPI_Ibsend

Start a nonblocking send in buffered mode. Discussed in section 13.7.3, p. 307.

```
int MPI_Ibsend(
        void*           message    /* in */,
```

```
        int             count       /* in  */,
        MPI_Datatype    datatype    /* in  */,
        int             dest        /* in  */,
        int             tag         /* in  */,
        MPI_Comm        comm        /* in  */,
        MPI_Request*    request     /* out */)
```

MPI_Irecv

Starts a nonblocking receive. Discussed in section 13.5, p. 296.

```
int MPI_Irecv(
        void*           message     /* out */,
        int             count       /* in  */,
        MPI_Datatype    datatype    /* in  */,
        int             source      /* in  */,
        int             tag         /* in  */,
        MPI_Comm        comm        /* in  */,
        MPI_Request*    request     /* out */)
```

MPI_Irsend

Start a nonblocking send in ready mode. Discussed in section 13.7.2, p. 306.

```
int MPI_Irsend(
        void*           message     /* in  */,
        int             count       /* in  */,
        MPI_Datatype    datatype    /* in  */,
        int             dest        /* in  */,
        int             tag         /* in  */,
        MPI_Comm        comm        /* in  */,
        MPI_Request*    request     /* out */)
```

MPI_Isend

Start a nonblocking send in standard mode. Discussed in section 13.5, p. 296.

```
int MPI_Isend(
        void*           message     /* in  */,
        int             count       /* in  */,
        MPI_Datatype    datatype    /* in  */,
        int             dest        /* in  */,
        int             tag         /* in  */,
        MPI_Comm        comm        /* in  */,
        MPI_Request*    request     /* out */)
```

MPI_Issend

Start a nonblocking send in synchronous mode. Discussed in section 13.7.1, p. 305.

```
int MPI_Issend(
        void*        message    /* in  */,
        int          count      /* in  */,
        MPI_Datatype datatype   /* in  */,
        int          dest       /* in  */,
        int          tag        /* in  */,
        MPI_Comm     comm       /* in  */,
        MPI_Request* request    /* out */)
```

MPI_Request_free

Mark the memory referenced by request for deallocation, and set request to MPI_REQUEST_NULL. Discussed in section 13.6, p. 301.

```
int MPI_Request_free(
        MPI_Request* request   /* in/out */)
```

MPI_Test

Check for completion of the nonblocking operation associated with request. Discussed in Chapter 13, exercise 3, p. 313.

```
int MPI_Test(
        MPI_Request* request   /* in/out */,
        int*         flag      /* out    */,
        MPI_Status*  status    /* out    */)
```

MPI_Testall

Check whether all the operations associated to elements of the array requests have completed.

```
int MPI_Testall(
        int          array_size   /* in     */,
        MPI_Request  requests[]    /* in/out */,
        int*         flag          /* out    */,
        MPI_Status   statuses[]    /* out    */)
```

MPI_Testany

Check whether at least one of the operations associated to elements of the array requests has completed.

```
int MPI_Testany(
        int          array_size        /* in     */,
        MPI_Request  requests[]         /* in/out */,
        int*         completed_index    /* out    */,
        int*         flag               /* out    */,
        MPI_Status*  status             /* out    */)
```

MPI_Testsome

Return information on all the operations associated with the elements of requests that have completed.

```
int MPI_Testsome(
        int          array_size      /* in     */,
        MPI_Request  requests[]      /* in/out */,
        int*         completed_count /* out    */,
        int          indices[]       /* out    */,
        MPI_Status   statuses[]      /* out    */)
```

MPI_Wait

Return when the operation that initialized request is complete. Discussed in
section 13.5, p. 296.

```
int MPI_Wait(
        MPI_Request*  request  /* in/out */,
        MPI_Status*   status   /* out    */)
```

MPI_Waitall

Wait for all the operations associated to elements of the array requests to
complete.

```
int MPI_Waitall(
        int          array_size /* in     */,
        MPI_Request  requests[] /* in/out */,
        MPI_Status   statuses[] /* out    */)
```

MPI_Waitany

Block until the operation associated with one of the elements of requests has
completed. Discussed in Chapter 13, exercise 4, p. 314.

```
int MPI_Waitany(
        int          array_size      /* in     */,
        MPI_Request  requests[]      /* in/out */,
        int*         completed_index /* out    */,
        MPI_Status*  status          /* out    */)
```

MPI_Waitsome

Wait for the completion of at least one of the operations associated with the
elements of requests.

```
int MPI_Waitsome(
        int          array_size      /* in     */,
        MPI_Request  requests[]      /* in/out */,
```

```
        int*        completed_count  /* out  */,
        int         indices[]        /* out  */,
        MPI_Status  statuses[]       /* out  */)
```

A.1.5 Probe and Cancel

`MPI_Cancel`

Mark the operation associated with request for cancellation.

```
int MPI_Cancel(
        MPI_Request*  request  /* in */)
```

`MPI_Iprobe`

Check whether a message matching the arguments supplied in source, tag, and comm can be received. Discussed in section 14.7.1, p. 330.

```
int MPI_Iprobe(
        int         source  /* in  */,
        int         tag     /* in  */,
        MPI_Comm    comm    /* in  */,
        int*        flag    /* out */,
        MPI_Status* status  /* out */)
```

`MPI_Probe`

Block until a message matching the source, tag, and comm arguments is available.

```
int MPI_Probe(
        int         source  /* in  */,
        int         tag     /* in  */,
        MPI_Comm    comm    /* in  */,
        MPI_Status* status  /* out */)
```

`MPI_Test_cancelled`

Check whether the completed operation associated with status was successfully cancelled.

```
int MPI_Test_cancelled(
        MPI_Status* status  /* in  */,
        int*        flag    /* out */)
```

A.1.6 Persistent Communication Requests

`MPI_Bsend_init`

Create a persistent buffered-mode send request. Discussed in section 13.7.3, p. 307.

```
int MPI_Bsend_init(
        void*         message    /* in  */,
        int           count      /* in  */,
        MPI_Datatype  datatype   /* in  */,
        int           dest       /* in  */,
        int           tag        /* in  */,
        MPI_Comm      comm       /* in  */,
        MPI_Request*  request    /* out */)
```

MPI_Recv_init

Create a persistent request for a receive. Discussed in section 13.6, p. 301.

```
int MPI_Recv_init(
        void*         message    /* out */,
        int           count      /* in  */,
        MPI_Datatype  datatype   /* in  */,
        int           source     /* in  */,
        int           tag        /* in  */,
        MPI_Comm      comm       /* in  */,
        MPI_Request*  request    /* out */)
```

MPI_Rsend_init

Create a persistent ready-mode send request. Discussed in section 13.7.2, p. 306.

```
int MPI_Rsend_init(
        void*         message    /* in  */,
        int           count      /* in  */,
        MPI_Datatype  datatype   /* in  */,
        int           dest       /* in  */,
        int           tag        /* in  */,
        MPI_Comm      comm       /* in  */,
        MPI_Request*  request    /* out */)
```

MPI_Send_init

Create a persistent standard-mode send request. Discussed in section 13.6, p. 301.

```
int MPI_Send_init(
        void*         message    /* in  */,
        int           count      /* in  */,
        MPI_Datatype  datatype   /* in  */,
        int           dest       /* in  */,
        int           tag        /* in  */,
        MPI_Comm      comm       /* in  */,
        MPI_Request*  request    /* out */)
```

```
MPI_Ssend_init
```

Create a persistent synchronous-mode send request. Discussed in section 13.7.1, p. 305.

```
int MPI_Ssend_init(
        void*           message     /* in  */,
        int             count       /* in  */,
        MPI_Datatype    datatype    /* in  */,
        int             dest        /* in  */,
        int             tag         /* in  */,
        MPI_Comm        comm        /* in  */,
        MPI_Request*    request     /* out */)
```

```
MPI_Start
```

Start the nonblocking operation associated with request. Discussed in section 13.6, p. 301.

```
int MPI_Start(
        MPI_Request  *request  /* in/out */)
```

```
MPI_Startall
```

Start the nonblocking operations associated with the elements of the array requests.

```
int MPI_Startall(
        int             array_size  /* in     */,
        MPI_Request     requests[]  /* in/out */)
```

A.1.7 Send-receive

```
MPI_Sendrecv
```

Send the contents of sendbuf to dest and receive from source into recvbuf. Discussed in section 13.3, p. 293.

```
int MPI_Sendrecv(
        void*           sendbuf     /* in  */,
        int             sendcount   /* in  */,
        MPI_Datatype    sendtype    /* in  */,
        int             dest        /* in  */,
        int             sendtag     /* in  */,
        void*           recvbuf     /* out */,
        int             recvcount   /* in  */,
        MPI_Datatype    recvtype    /* in  */,
        int             source      /* in  */,
        int             recvtag     /* in  */,
        MPI_Comm        comm        /* in  */,
        MPI_Status*     status      /* out */)
```

MPI_Sendrecv_replace

Send the contents of buf to dest and then receive from source into buf.
Discussed in section 13.3, p. 293.

```
int MPI_Sendrecv_replace(
        void*          message    /* in/out */,
        int            count      /* in      */,
        MPI_Datatype   datatype   /* in      */,
        int            dest       /* in      */,
        int            sendtag    /* in      */,
        int            source     /* in      */,
        int            recvtag    /* in      */,
        MPI_Comm       comm       /* in      */,
        MPI_Status*    status     /* out     */)
```

A.2 Derived Datatypes and MPI_Pack/Unpack

For general discussions of derived datatypes and MPI_Pack/Unpack, see Chapters 6 and 8.

A.2.1 Derived Datatypes

MPI_Address

Return the byte address of location in *address. Discussed in section 6.2, p. 90.

```
int MPI_Address(
        void*       location   /* in  */,
        MPI_Aint*   address    /* out */)
```

MPI_Get_elements

Return the number of primitive elements that were received.   See also
MPI_Get_count, p. 363.

```
int MPI_Get_elements(
        MPI_Status*    status     /* in  */,
        MPI_Datatype   datatype   /* in  */,
        int*           count      /* out */)
```

MPI_Type_commit

Finalize construction of a derived datatype so that it can be used in communication operations. Discussed in section 6.2, p. 90.

```
int MPI_Type_commit(
        MPI_Datatype*   datatype   /* in/out */)
```

MPI_Type_contiguous

Create a new datatype consisting of the concatenation of count copies of oldtype. Discussed in section 6.3, p. 96.

```
int MPI_Type_contiguous(
        int           count    /* in  */,
        MPI_Datatype  oldtype  /* in  */,
        MPI_Datatype* newtype  /* out */)
```

MPI_Type_extent

Return the extent of datatype. The extent of a type is discussed in section 8.4.5, p. 164.

```
int MPI_Type_extent(
        MPI_Datatype  datatype  /* in  */,
        MPI_Aint*     extent    /* out */)
```

MPI_Type_free

Mark datatype for deallocation. Example in section 13.2.2, p. 288.

```
int MPI_Type_free(
        MPI_Datatype*  datatype  /* in/out */)
```

MPI_Type_hindexed

Build a derived type consisting of copies of oldtype with a variety of block lengths and displacements. Displacements are measured in bytes. See also MPI_Type_indexed, p. 374.

```
int MPI_Type_hindexed(
        int           count             /* in  */,
        int           blocklengths[]     /* in  */,
        MPI_Aint      displacements[]    /* in  */,
        MPI_Datatype  oldtype            /* in  */,
        MPI_Datatype* newtype            /* out */)
```

MPI_Type_hvector

Build a derived type consisting of count copies of blocks of oldtype uniformly displaced stride bytes apart. See also MPI_Type_vector, p. 375.

```
int MPI_Type_hvector(
        int           count        /* in  */,
        int           blocklength  /* in  */,
        MPI_Aint      stride       /* in  */,
        MPI_Datatype  oldtype      /* in  */,
        MPI_Datatype* newtype      /* out */)
```

MPI_Type_indexed

Build a derived type consisting of copies of oldtype with a variety of block lengths and displacements. Displacements are measured by the extent of old-type. Discussed in section 6.3, p. 96.

```
int MPI_Type_indexed(
        int          count              /* in  */,
        int          blocklengths[]      /* in  */,
        int          displacements[]     /* in  */,
        MPI_Datatype oldtype            /* in  */,
        MPI_Datatype* newtype           /* out */)
```

MPI_Type_lb

Find the lower bound of datatype. See also MPI_Type_ub, p. 374.

```
int MPI_Type_lb(
        MPI_Datatype datatype     /* in  */,
        MPI_Aint*    displacement /* out */)
```

MPI_Type_size

Return the size in bytes of the type signature of datatype. Type signatures are discussed in section 6.4, p. 98.

```
int MPI_Type_size(
        MPI_Datatype datatype /* in  */,
        int*         size     /* out */)
```

MPI_Type_struct

Build a general derived type. Discussed in section 6.2, p. 90.

```
int MPI_Type_struct(
        int          count              /* in  */,
        int          blocklengths[]      /* in  */,
        MPI_Aint     displacements[]     /* in  */,
        MPI_Datatype types[]            /* in  */,
        MPI_Datatype* newtype           /* out */)
```

MPI_Type_ub

Find the upper bound of datatype. Upper bounds are discussed in section 8.4.5, p. 164.

```
int MPI_Type_ub(
        MPI_Datatype datatype     /* in  */,
        MPI_Aint*    displacement /* out */)
```

MPI_Type_vector

Build a derived type consisting of `count` copies of blocks of `oldtype` uniformly displaced `stride` units apart, where one unit is the extent of `oldtype`. Discussed in section 6.3, p. 96.

```
int MPI_Type_vector(
        int             count         /* in  */,
        int             blocklength   /* in  */,
        int             stride        /* in  */,
        MPI_Datatype    oldtype       /* in  */,
        MPI_Datatype*   newtype       /* out */)
```

A.2.2 MPI_Pack and MPI_Unpack

MPI_Pack

Pack the contents of `inbuf` into `pack_buf`. Discussed in section 6.5, p. 100.

```
int MPI_Pack(
        void*           inbuf           /* in      */,
        int             incount         /* in      */,
        MPI_Datatype    datatype        /* in      */,
        void*           pack_buf        /* out     */,
        int             pack_buf_size   /* in      */,
        int*            position        /* in/out  */,
        MPI_Comm        comm            /* in      */)
```

MPI_Pack_size

Return an upper bound on the storage needed to pack a message consisting of `incount` elements of type `datatype`.

```
int MPI_Pack_size(
        int             incount   /* in  */,
        MPI_Datatype    datatype  /* in  */,
        MPI_Comm        comm      /* in  */,
        int*            size      /* out */)
```

MPI_Unpack

Unpack the contents of `pack_buf` into `outbuf`. Discussed in section 6.5, p. 100.

```
int MPI_Unpack(
        void*           pack_buf        /* in      */,
        int             pack_buf_size   /* in      */,
        int*            position        /* in/out  */,
        void*           outbuf          /* out     */,
```

```
      int            outcount    /* in    */,
      MPI_Datatype   datatype    /* in    */,
      MPI_Comm       comm        /* in    */)
```

A.3 Collective Communication Functions

For a general discussion of collective communication functions, see Chapter 5. A variable that is passed as an out or an in/out argument cannot be passed as an argument corresponding to another parameter. For example, the following call is *illegal.*

```
    int x;
    MPI_Allreduce(&x, &x, 1, MPI_INT, MPI_SUM,
        MPI_COMM_WORLD);
```

The second argument is an out argument, and hence it cannot appear elsewhere in the argument list.

A.3.1 Barrier and Broadcast

MPI_Barrier

Block the calling process until all processes in comm have entered the function. Discussed in section 11.7, p. 254.

```
int MPI_Barrier(
      MPI_Comm   comm    /* in */)
```

MPI_Bcast

Send the contents of buffer on the process with rank root to every process (including root) in comm. Discussed in section 5.2, p. 69.

```
int MPI_Bcast(
      void*          buffer      /* in/out */,
      int            count       /* in     */,
      MPI_Datatype   datatype    /* in     */,
      int            root        /* in     */,
      MPI_Comm       comm        /* in     */)
```

A.3.2 Gather and Scatter

MPI_Allgather

Gather the contents of each process's sendbuf into recvbuf on all the processes in comm. Discussed in section 5.8, p. 82.

```
int MPI_Allgather(
        void*         sendbuf      /* in  */,
        int           sendcount    /* in  */,
        MPI_Datatype  sendtype     /* in  */,
        void*         recvbuf      /* out */,
        int           recvcount    /* in  */,
        MPI_Datatype  recvtype     /* in  */,
        MPI_Comm      comm         /* in  */)
```

MPI_Allgatherv

Gather the contents of each process's sendbuf into recvbuf on all the processes in comm. Extends the functionality of MPI_Allgather by allowing different type signatures. See also MPI_Allgather, p. 376.

```
int MPI_Allgatherv(
        void*         sendbuf          /* in  */,
        int           sendcount        /* in  */,
        MPI_Datatype  sendtype         /* in  */,
        void*         recvbuf          /* out */,
        int           recvcounts[]     /* in  */,
        int           displacements[]  /* in  */,
        MPI_Datatype  recvtype         /* in  */,
        MPI_Comm      comm             /* in  */)
```

MPI_Alltoall

Carry out an all-to-all gather/scatter: scatter the contents of each process's sendbuf among the processes in comm. Discussed in section 10.5.3, p. 232.

```
int MPI_Alltoall(
        void*         sendbuf      /* in  */,
        int           sendcount    /* in  */,
        MPI_Datatype  sendtype     /* in  */,
        void*         recvbuf      /* out */,
        int           recvcount    /* in  */,
        MPI_Datatype  recvtype     /* in  */,
        MPI_Comm      comm         /* in  */)
```

MPI_Alltoallv

Carry out an all-to-all gather/scatter: scatter the contents of each process's sendbuf among the processes in comm. Extends the functionality of MPI_Allgather by allowing different type signatures. Discussed in section 10.5.3, p. 232.

```
int MPI_Alltoallv(
        void*         sendbuf          /* in  */,
        int           sendcounts[]     /* in  */,
```

```
        int          send_displacements[]  /* in  */,
        MPI_Datatype sendtype              /* in  */,
        void*        recvbuf               /* out */,
        int          recvcounts[]          /* in  */,
        int          recv_displacements[]  /* in  */,
        MPI_Datatype recvtype              /* in  */,
        MPI_Comm     comm                  /* in  */)
```

MPI_Gather

Collect the contents of each process's sendbuf into recvbuf on the process
with rank root. Discussed in section 5.7, p. 78.

```
int MPI_Gather(
        void*        sendbuf    /* in  */,
        int          sendcount  /* in  */,
        MPI_Datatype sendtype   /* in  */,
        void*        recvbuf    /* out */,
        int          recvcount  /* in  */,
        MPI_Datatype recvtype   /* in  */,
        int          root       /* in  */,
        MPI_Comm     comm       /* in  */)
```

MPI_Gatherv

Collect the contents of each process's sendbuf into recvbuf on the process
with rank root. Extends the functionality of MPI_Gather by allowing different type signatures. See also MPI_Gather, p. 378.

```
int MPI_Gatherv(
        void*        sendbuf         /* in  */,
        int          sendcount       /* in  */,
        MPI_Datatype sendtype        /* in  */,
        void*        recvbuf         /* out */,
        int          recvcounts[]    /* in  */,
        int          displacements[] /* in  */,
        MPI_Datatype recvtype        /* in  */,
        int          root            /* in  */,
        MPI_Comm     comm            /* in  */)
```

MPI_Scatter

Distributes the contents of sendbuf on the process with rank root among the
processes in comm. Discussed in section 5.7, p. 78.

```
int MPI_Scatter(
        void*        sendbuf    /* in  */,
        int          sendcount  /* in  */,
        MPI_Datatype sendtype   /* in  */,
        void*        recvbuf    /* out */,
```

```
              int             recvcount    /* in  */,
              MPI_Datatype    recvtype     /* in  */,
              int             root         /* in  */,
              MPI_Comm        comm         /* in  */)
```

MPI_Scatterv

Distributes the contents of sendbuf on the process with rank root among
the processes in comm. Extends the functionality of MPI_Scatter by allowing
different type signatures. See also MPI_Scatter, p. 378.

```
int MPI_Scatterv(
        void*           sendbuf                 /* in  */,
        int             sendcounts[]            /* in  */,
        int             displacements[]         /* in  */,
        MPI_Datatype    sendtype                /* in  */,
        void*           recvbuf                 /* out */,
        int             recvcount               /* in  */,
        MPI_Datatype    recvtype                /* in  */,
        int             root                    /* in  */,
        MPI_Comm        comm                    /* in  */)
```

A.3.3 Reduction Operations

See section A.8, p. 395, for a list of predefined operations and section A.8,
p. 395, for a list of special datatypes that can be used in reduction operations.

MPI_Allreduce

Combine the contents of each process's operand using the operation operator. Store the result in result on all the processes in comm. Discussed in
section 5.6, p. 76.

```
int MPI_Allreduce(
        void*           operand     /* in  */,
        void*           result      /* out */,
        int             count       /* in  */,
        MPI_Datatype    datatype    /* in  */,
        MPI_Op          operator    /* in  */,
        MPI_Comm        comm        /* in  */)
```

MPI_Op_create

Create an operation that can be used in global reduction operations. Type
definition for MPI_User_function is in section A.8, p. 396.

```
int MPI_Op_create(
        MPI_User_function*    function    /* in  */,
        int                   commute     /* in  */,
        MPI_Op*               operator    /* out */)
```

MPI_Op_free

Free the user-defined operation `operator`.

```
int MPI_Op_free(
        MPI_Op*   operator  /* in/out */)
```

MPI_Reduce

Combine the contents of each process's `operand` using the operation `oper-ator`. Store the result on process with rank `root`. Discussed in section 5.4, p. 73.

```
int MPI_Reduce(
        void*          operand    /* in  */,
        void*          result     /* out */,
        int            count      /* in  */,
        MPI_Datatype   datatype   /* in  */,
        MPI_Op         operator   /* in  */,
        int            root       /* in  */,
        MPI_Comm       comm       /* in  */)
```

MPI_Reduce_scatter

Combine the contents of each process's `operand` using the operation `oper-ator`. Scatter the result across the processes in `comm`. See also `MPI_Reduce`, p. 380, and `MPI_Scatterv`, p. 379.

```
int MPI_Reduce_scatter(
        void*          operand       /* in  */,
        void*          recvbuf       /* out */,
        int            recvcounts[]  /* in  */,
        MPI_Datatype   datatype      /* in  */,
        MPI_Op         operator      /* in  */,
        MPI_Comm       comm          /* in  */)
```

MPI_Scan

Carry out a parallel prefix operation: on each process q in `comm`, store the result of combining the operands on processes with ranks less than or equal to q using the operation `operator`.

```
int MPI_Scan(
        void*          operand    /* in  */,
        void*          result     /* out */,
        int            count      /* in  */,
        MPI_Datatype   datatype   /* in  */,
        MPI_Op         operator   /* in  */,
        MPI_Comm       comm       /* in  */)
```

A.4 Groups, Contexts, and Communicators

For a general discussion of groups, contexts, and communicators, see Chapters 7 and 8.

A.4.1 Group Management

All the group management functions are local operations.

MPI_Comm_group

Return the group underlying the communicator comm. If comm is an inter-communicator, return the local group. Discussed in section 7.4, p. 117.

```
int MPI_Comm_group(
        MPI_Comm    comm    /* in  */,
        MPI_Group*  group   /* out */)
```

MPI_Group_compare

Compare group1 and group2. Values of result are listed in section A.8, p. 395. See also MPI_Comm_compare, p. 383.

```
int MPI_Group_compare(
        MPI_Group   group1  /* in  */,
        MPI_Group   group2  /* in  */,
        int*        result  /* out */)
```

MPI_Group_difference

Form a new group consisting of the processes belonging to group1 that are not also in group2.

```
int MPI_Group_difference(
        MPI_Group   group1    /* in  */,
        MPI_Group   group2    /* in  */,
        MPI_Group*  newgroup  /* out */)
```

MPI_Group_excl

Form a new group by deleting the processes listed in ranks from group.

```
int MPI_Group_excl(
        MPI_Group   group     /* in  */,
        int         n         /* in  */,
        int         ranks[]   /* in  */,
        MPI_Group*  newgroup  /* out */)
```

MPI_Group_free

Free the group group. See also MPI_Comm_free, p. 384.

```
int MPI_Group_free(
        MPI_Group* group  /* in/out */)
```

MPI_Group_incl

Form a new group from the processes belonging to group whose ranks are listed in ranks. Discussed in section 7.4, p. 117.

```
int MPI_Group_incl(
        MPI_Group   group     /* in  */,
        int         n         /* in  */,
        int         ranks[]   /* in  */,
        MPI_Group*  newgroup  /* out */)
```

MPI_Group_intersection

Form a new group consisting of the processes belonging to both group1 and group2, ordered as in group1.

```
int MPI_Group_intersection(
        MPI_Group   group1    /* in  */,
        MPI_Group   group2    /* in  */,
        MPI_Group*  newgroup  /* out */)
```

MPI_Group_range_excl

Form a new group by deleting the ranges of processes specified in ranges. Each element of ranges consists of a first rank, last rank, and stride.

```
int MPI_Group_range_excl(
        MPI_Group   group        /* in  */,
        int         n            /* in  */,
        int         ranges[][3]  /* in  */,
        MPI_Group*  newgroup     /* out */)
```

MPI_Group_range_incl

Form a new group from the ranges of processes specified in ranges. Each element of ranges consists of a first rank, last rank, and stride.

```
int MPI_Group_range_incl(
        MPI_Group   group        /* in  */,
        int         n            /* in  */,
        int         ranges[][3]  /* in  */,
        MPI_Group*  newgroup     /* out */)
```

`MPI_Group_rank`

Return the rank of the calling process in group. See also `MPI_Comm_rank`, p. 384.

```
int MPI_Group_rank(
        MPI_Group  group  /* in  */,
        int*       rank   /* out */)
```

`MPI_Group_size`

Return the number of processes in group. See also `MPI_Comm_size`, p. 384.

```
int MPI_Group_size(
        MPI_Group  group  /* in  */,
        int*       size   /* out */)
```

`MPI_Group_translate_ranks`

Determine the rank in group2 of processes in group1. Discussed in section 8.1.4, p. 144.

```
int MPI_Group_translate_ranks (
        MPI_Group  group1   /* in  */,
        int        n        /* in  */,
        int        ranks1[] /* in  */,
        MPI_Group  group2   /* in  */,
        int        ranks2[] /* out */)
```

`MPI_Group_union`

Form a new group consisting of the processes in group1 followed by those processes in group2 that don't belong to group1.

```
int MPI_Group_union(
        MPI_Group   group1    /* in  */,
        MPI_Group   group2    /* in  */,
        MPI_Group*  newgroup  /* out */)
```

A.4.2 Communicator Management

Operations that create communicators are collective and may require communication among processes.

`MPI_Comm_compare`

Compare the communicators comm1 and comm2. Values of `result` are listed in section A.8, p. 395. Discussed in section 8.1.4, p. 144.

```
int MPI_Comm_compare(
        MPI_Comm   comm1    /* in  */,
        MPI_Comm   comm2    /* in  */,
        int*       result   /* out */)
```

MPI_Comm_create

Create a new communicator from the processes listed in new_group. Collective across the members of comm. Discussed in section 7.4, p. 117.

```
int MPI_Comm_create(
        MPI_Comm   comm        /* in  */,
        MPI_Group  new_group   /* in  */,
        MPI_Comm*  new_comm    /* out */)
```

MPI_Comm_dup

Create a new communicator with the same underlying group as comm but a different context. Collective across the members of comm. Discussed in section 8.1.1, p. 139.

```
int MPI_Comm_dup(
        MPI_Comm   comm       /* in  */,
        MPI_Comm*  new_comm   /* out */)
```

MPI_Comm_free

Free the communicator comm. Collective across comm. Discussed in section 8.1.2, p. 141.

```
int MPI_Comm_free(
        MPI_Comm*  comm   /* in/out */)
```

MPI_Comm_rank

Return the rank of the calling process in the group underlying the communicator comm. If comm is an inter-communicator, return the rank in the local group. Discussed in section 3.3.2, p. 44.

```
int MPI_Comm_rank(
        MPI_Comm   comm   /* in  */,
        int*       rank   /* out */)
```

MPI_Comm_size

Return the number of processes in the group underlying comm. If comm is an inter-communicator, return the size of the local group. Discussed in section 3.3.2, p. 44.

```
int MPI_Comm_size(
        MPI_Comm   comm   /* in  */,
        int*       size   /* out */)
```

```
MPI_Comm_split
```

Partition old_comm into a set of new communicators; processes with the same value in split_key belong to the same communicator. Collective across old_comm. Discussed in section 7.5, p. 120.

```
int MPI_Comm_split(
        MPI_Comm   old_comm    /* in  */,
        int        split_key   /* in  */,
        int        rank_key    /* in  */,
        MPI_Comm*  new_comm    /* out */)
```

A.4.3 Inter-communicators

```
MPI_Comm_remote_group
```

Return the remote group underlying the inter-communicator comm.

```
int MPI_Comm_remote_group(
        MPI_Comm    comm    /* in  */,
        MPI_Group*  group   /* out */)
```

```
MPI_Comm_remote_size
```

Return the size of the remote group of the inter-communicator comm.

```
int MPI_Comm_remote_size(
        MPI_Comm  comm  /* in  */,
        int*      size  /* out */)
```

```
MPI_Comm_test_inter
```

Determine whether comm is an inter-communicator.

```
int MPI_Comm_test_inter(
        MPI_Comm  comm  /* in  */,
        int*      flag  /* out */)
```

```
MPI_Intercomm_create
```

Create an inter-communicator from local_comm and a remote communicator. Collective across local_comm and the remote communicator. Discussed in Chapter 7, programming assignment 2, p. 133.

```
int MPI_Intercomm_create(
        MPI_Comm   local_comm     /* in  */,
        int        local_leader   /* in  */,
        MPI_Comm   peer_comm      /* in  */,
        int        remote_leader  /* in  */,
        int        tag            /* in  */,
        MPI_Comm*  intercomm      /* out */)
```

`MPI_Intercomm_merge`

Form an intra-communicator from the processes in the inter-communicator `intercomm`. The processes of the local group providing zero for `high` will receive the lower ranks. Collective across the two groups.

```
int MPI_Intercomm_merge(
        MPI_Comm   intercomm  /* in  */,
        int        high       /* in  */,
        MPI_Comm*  intracomm  /* out */)
```

A.4.4   Attribute Caching

These are all local operations.

`MPI_Attr_delete`

Delete the previously cached attribute identified by `keyval`. Discussed in section 8.1.2, p. 141.

```
int MPI_Attr_delete(
        MPI_Comm   comm    /* in  */,
        int        keyval  /* in  */)
```

`MPI_Attr_get`

Return a pointer to the previously cached attribute identified by `keyval`. Discussed in section 8.1.1, p. 139.

```
int MPI_Attr_get(
        MPI_Comm   comm           /* in  */,
        int        keyval         /* in  */,
        void*      attribute_ptr  /* out */,
        int*       flag           /* out */)
```

`MPI_Attr_put`

Assign a value to the attribute identified by `keyval`. Discussed in section 8.1.1, p. 139.

```
int MPI_Attr_put(
        MPI_Comm   comm       /* in  */,
        int        keyval     /* in  */,
        void*      attribute  /* in  */)
```

`MPI_Keyval_create`

Generate a new attribute key. Type definitions for `MPI_Copy_function` and `MPI_Delete_function` are in section A.8, p. 396. `MPI_Keyval_Create` is discussed in subsections 8.1.1, p. 139, and 8.1.2, p. 141.

```
int MPI_Keyval_create(
        MPI_Copy_function*    copy_fn     /* in  */,
        MPI_Delete_function*  delete_fn   /* in  */,
        int*                  keyval      /* out */,
        void*                 extra_arg   /* in  */)
```

MPI_Keyval_free

Free the key value keyval.

```
int MPI_Keyval_free(
        int*  keyval  /* in/out */)
```

A.5 Process Topologies

For a general discussion of process topologies, see section 7.6.

A.5.1 General Topology Functions

MPI_Topo_test

Determine whether comm has a topology and its type. Return values for top_type are listed in section A.8, p. 396.

```
int MPI_Topo_test(
        MPI_Comm  comm       /* in  */,
        int*      top_type   /* out */)
```

A.5.2 Cartesian Topology Management

MPI_Cart_coords

Return the coordinates of the process with rank rank in the Cartesian communicator comm. Discussed in section 7.6, p. 121.

```
int MPI_Cart_coords(
        MPI_Comm  comm       /* in  */,
        int       rank       /* in  */,
        int       max_dims   /* in  */,
        int       coords[]   /* out */)
```

MPI_Cart_create

Create a communicator with a Cartesian coordinate structure on the processes. Collective across old_comm. Discussed in section 7.6, p. 121.

```
int MPI_Cart_create(
        MPI_Comm    old_comm    /* in  */,
        int         ndims       /* in  */,
        int         dims[]      /* in  */,
        int         periods[]   /* in  */,
        int         reorder     /* in  */,
        MPI_Comm*   cart_comm   /* out */)
```

MPI_Cartdim_get

Return the number of dimensions in the Cartesian topology cached with comm.

```
int MPI_Cartdim_get(
        MPI_Comm    comm    /* in  */,
        int*        ndims   /* out */)
```

MPI_Cart_get

Retrieve the Cartesian topology previously cached with comm.

```
int MPI_Cart_get(
        MPI_Comm    comm        /* in  */,
        int         max_dims    /* in  */,
        int         dims[]      /* out */,
        int         periods[]   /* out */,
        int         coords[]    /* out */)
```

MPI_Cart_map

Low-level function attempts to compute an optimal placement of the calling process in a Cartesian coordinate system.

```
int MPI_Cart_map(
        MPI_Comm    comm        /* in  */,
        int         ndims       /* in  */,
        int         dims[]      /* in  */,
        int         periods[]   /* in  */,
        int*        newrank     /* out */)
```

MPI_Cart_rank

Return the rank of the process with coordinates coords in the Cartesian topology associated with comm. Discussed in section 7.6, p. 121.

```
int MPI_Cart_rank(
        MPI_Comm    comm        /* in  */,
        int         coords[]    /* in  */,
        int*        rank        /* out */)
```

MPI_Cart_shift

Return ranks of source and destination processes for a subsequent call to MPI_Sendrecv that performs a shift of data in a coordinate direction in the Cartesian communicator comm.

```
int MPI_Cart_shift(
        MPI_Comm  comm          /* in  */,
        int       direction     /* in  */,
        int       displacement  /* in  */,
        int*      rank_source   /* out */,
        int*      rank_dest     /* out */)
```

MPI_Cart_sub

Partition the Cartesian communicator comm. Discussed in section 7.7, p. 124.

```
int MPI_Cart_sub(
        MPI_Comm  comm           /* in  */,
        int       free_coords[]  /* in  */,
        MPI_Comm* newcomm        /* out */)
```

MPI_Dims_create

Choose dimension sizes for a Cartesian coordinate system.

```
int MPI_Dims_create(
        int nnodes  /* in     */,
        int ndims   /* in     */,
        int dims[]  /* in/out */)
```

A.5.3 Graph Topology Management

MPI_Graph_create

Create a communicator with a graph structure on the processes. Collective across the processes in old_comm.

```
int MPI_Graph_create(
        MPI_Comm  old_comm    /* in  */,
        int       nnodes      /* in  */,
        int       index[]     /* in  */,
        int       edges[]     /* in  */,
        int       reorder     /* in  */,
        MPI_Comm* graph_comm  /* out */)
```

MPI_Graphdims_get

Return the number of vertices and the number of edges in the graph topology associated with comm.

```
int MPI_Graphdims_get(
        MPI_Comm  comm      /* in  */,
        int*      nnodes    /* out */,
        int*      edges     /* out */)
```

MPI_Graph_get

Retrieve the graph structure cached with comm by a previous call to
MPI_Graph_create.

```
int MPI_Graph_get(
        MPI_Comm  comm        /* in  */,
        int       max_index   /* in  */,
        int       max_edges   /* in  */,
        int       index[]     /* out */,
        int       edges[]     /* out */)
```

MPI_Graph_map

Low-level function attempts to compute an optimal placement of the calling
process in a graph coordinate system.

```
int MPI_Graph_map(
        MPI_Comm  comm      /* in  */,
        int       nnodes    /* in  */,
        int       index[]   /* in  */,
        int       edges[]   /* in  */,
        int*      newrank   /* out */)
```

MPI_Graph_neighbors

Return the ranks of the neighbors of the process with rank rank in the graph
communicator comm.

```
int MPI_Graph_neighbors(
        MPI_Comm  comm            /* in  */,
        int       rank            /* in  */,
        int       max_neighbors   /* in  */,
        int       neighbors[]     /* out */)
```

MPI_Graph_neighbors_count

Return the number of neighbors of the process with rank rank in the graph
communicator comm.

```
int MPI_Graph_neighbors_count(
        MPI_Comm  comm         /* in  */,
        int       rank         /* in  */,
        int*      nneighbors   /* out */)
```

A.6 Environmental Management

See the appropriate subsection for references to the rest of the book.

A.6.1 Implementation Information

Most implementation information is cached with `MPI_COMM_WORLD`. See section A.8 for a list of the predefined attribute keys. See section 8.1.1, p. 139 for a discussion of attribute caching.

`MPI_Get_processor_name`

Return the name of the processor on which the function was called.

```
int MPI_Get_processor_name(
        char*   name        /* out */,
        int*    resultlen   /* out */)
```

A.6.2 Error Handling

See section 9.6, p. 210 for a general discussion of error handling in MPI. All of the error handler functions are local operations.

`MPI_Errhandler_create`

Register the user-defined function `function` as an error handler. Type definition for `MPI_Handler_function` is in section A.9, p. 396.

```
int MPI_Errhandler_create(
        MPI_Handler_function*   function    /* in  */,
        MPI_Errhandler*         errhandler  /* out */)
```

`MPI_Errhandler_free`

Free the error handler referenced by `errhandler`.

```
int MPI_Errhandler_free(
        MPI_Errhandler *errhandler  /* in/out */)
```

`MPI_Errhandler_get`

Return the error handler currently associated with comm.

```
int MPI_Errhandler_get(
        MPI_Comm          comm        /* in  */,
        MPI_Errhandler*   errhandler  /* out */)
```

MPI_Errhandler_set

Associate the error handler `errhandler` with the communicator `comm`. Discussed in section 9.6, p. 210.

```
int MPI_Errhandler_set(
        MPI_Comm        comm        /* in */,
        MPI_Errhandler  errhandler  /* in */)
```

MPI_Error_class

Return the error class (MPI defined) corresponding to `errorcode` (implementation defined). See section A.8, p. 394 for a list of error classes.

```
int MPI_Error_class(
        int    errorcode   /* in  */,
        int*   errorclass  /* out */)
```

MPI_Error_string

Return the string associated with an error code or error class. Discussed in section 9.6, p. 210.

```
int MPI_Error_string(
        int    errorcode   /* in  */,
        char*  string      /* out */,
        int*   resultlen    /* out */)
```

A.6.3 Timers

The timing functions are discussed in section 11.7, p. 254. These are local functions.

MPI_Wtick

Return the precision of `MPI_Wtime`. Discussed in section 11.7, p. 254.

```
double MPI_Wtick(void)
```

MPI_Wtime

Return a double precision number representing the number of seconds (wall-clock time) that have elapsed since some time in the past. Discussed in section 11.7, p. 254.

```
double MPI_Wtime(void)
```

A.6.4 Startup

These functions are discussed in several different locations in the text. See the function summary for references.

`MPI_Abort`

Shut down all the processes in `comm` and return `error_code` to the invoking environment. Discussed in section 8.1.8, p. 152.

```
int MPI_Abort(
        MPI_Comm  comm         /* in */,
        int       error_code   /* in */)
```

`MPI_Finalize`

Shut down MPI. No MPI function (except `MPI_Initialized`) may be called after this function is called. Discussed in section 3.3.1, p. 44.

```
int MPI_Finalize(void)
```

`MPI_Init`

Start up MPI. Must be called before any other MPI function (except `MPI_Initialized`). Discussed in section 3.3.1, p. 44.

```
int MPI_Init(
        int*      argc_ptr     /* in/out */,
        char**    argv_ptr[]   /* in/out */)
```

`MPI_Initialized`

Check whether `MPI_Init` has been called.

```
int MPI_Initialized(
        int*   flag   /* out */)
```

A.7 Profiling

MPI's profiling interface is discussed in section 12.6.1, p. 271.

`MPI_Pcontrol`

Set the level of profiling. Syntax details are implementation dependent.

```
int MPI_Pcontrol(
        const int level   /* in */,
        ...)
```

A.8 Constants

These defined constants are in the file `mpi.h`.

Error Classes

```
MPI_SUCCESS
MPI_ERR_BUFFER
MPI_ERR_COUNT
MPI_ERR_TYPE
MPI_ERR_TAG
MPI_ERR_COMM
MPI_ERR_RANK
MPI_ERR_REQUEST
MPI_ERR_ROOT
MPI_ERR_GROUP
MPI_ERR_OP
MPI_ERR_TOPOLOGY
MPI_ERR_DIMS
MPI_ERR_ARG
MPI_ERR_UNKNOWN
MPI_ERR_TRUNCATE
MPI_ERR_OTHER
MPI_ERR_INTERN
MPI_PENDING
MPI_ERR_IN_STATUS
MPI_ERR_LASTCODE
```

Assorted Constants

```
MPI_BOTTOM
MPI_PROC_NULL
MPI_ANY_SOURCE
MPI_ANY_TAG
MPI_UNDEFINED
MPI_BSEND_OVERHEAD
MPI_KEYVAL_INVALID
```

Error Handling Specifiers

```
MPI_ERRORS_ARE_FATAL
MPI_ERRORS_RETURN
```

Maximum Sizes for Strings

```
MPI_MAX_PROCESSOR_NAME
MPI_MAX_ERROR_STRING
```

Basic Datatypes

```
MPI_CHAR
MPI_SHORT
MPI_INT
MPI_LONG
MPI_UNSIGNED_CHAR
```

```
            MPI_UNSIGNED_SHORT
            MPI_UNSIGNED
            MPI_UNSIGNED_LONG
            MPI_FLOAT
            MPI_DOUBLE
            MPI_LONG_DOUBLE
            MPI_BYTE
            MPI_PACKED
            MPI_LONG_LONG_INT  /* optional */
```

Datatypes for Reduction Functions

```
            MPI_FLOAT_INT
            MPI_DOUBLE_INT
            MPI_LONG_INT
            MPI_2INT
            MPI_SHORT_INT
            MPI_LONG_DOUBLE_INT
```

Datatypes for Building Derived Types

```
            MPI_UB
            MPI_LB
```

Predefined Communicators

```
            MPI_COMM_WORLD
            MPI_COMM_SELF
```

Results of Communicator and Group Comparisons

```
            MPI_IDENT
            MPI_CONGRUENT
            MPI_SIMILAR
            MPI_UNEQUAL
```

Attribute Keys for Implementation Information

```
            MPI_TAG_UB
            MPI_IO
            MPI_HOST
            MPI_WTIME_IS_GLOBAL
```

Collective Reduction Operations

```
            MPI_MAX
            MPI_MIN
            MPI_SUM
            MPI_PROD
            MPI_MAXLOC
```

```
MPI_MINLOC
MPI_BAND
MPI_BOR
MPI_BXOR
MPI_LAND
MPI_LOR
MPI_LXOR
```

Null Handles

```
MPI_GROUP_NULL
MPI_COMM_NULL
MPI_DATATYPE_NULL
MPI_REQUEST_NULL
MPI_OP_NULL
MPI_ERRHANDLER_NULL
```

Empty Group

```
MPI_GROUP_EMPTY
```

Topologies

```
MPI_GRAPH
MPI_CART
```

A.9   Type Definitions

The following type definitions are in the file mpi.h.

Opaque Types

```
MPI_Aint
MPI_Status
```

Handles to Assorted Structures

```
MPI_Group
MPI_Comm
MPI_Datatype
MPI_Request
MPI_Op
```

Prototypes for User-Defined Functions

```
typedef int MPI_Copy_function(
        MPI_Comm    oldcomm,
        int         keyval,
        void*       extra_arg,
```

```
                    void*       attribute_val_in,
                    void*       attribute_val_out,
                    int*        flag)

          typedef int MPI_Delete_function(
                    MPI_Comm    comm,
                    int         keyval,
                    void*       attribute_val,
                    void*       extra_arg)

          typedef void MPI_Handler_function(
                    MPI_Comm*   comm,
                    int*        error_code,
                                ...)

          typedef void MPI_User_function(
                    void*          invec,
                    void*          inoutvec,
                    int*           len,
                    MPI_Datatype*  datatype)
```

MPI on the Internet

THERE ARE A LARGE NUMBER of MPI resources available on the internet. This appendix is a pointer to just a few of them.

B.1 Implementations of MPI

There are several freely available implementations of MPI.

1. The `mpich` implementation developed at Argonne National Lab and Mississippi State University can be downloaded from

    `ftp://info.mcs.anl.gov/pub/mpi`

    `Upshot` is bundled with this implementation. It is also available as a separate package.

2. The LAM implementation developed at the Ohio Supercomputer Center can be downloaded from

    `http://www.mpi.nd.edu/lam/download`

3. The CHIMP implementation developed at the Edinburgh Parallel Computing Centre can be downloaded from

    `ftp://ftp.epcc.ed.ac.uk/pub/chimp/release`

4. There are two implementations of MPI that run under Windows. `WinMPI` runs under Windows 3.1 and is available at

   `ftp://csftp.unomaha.edu/pub/rewini/WinMPI`

   W32MPI is an implementation for Win32 available at

   `http://dsg.dei.uc.pt/wmpi/intro.html`

B.2 The MPI FAQ

The MPI FAQ (frequently asked questions) list is available at

   `http://www.erc.msstate.edu/mpi/mpi-faq.html`

B.3 MPI Web Pages

There are a number of World Wide Web pages devoted to MPI. The following three sites contain many pointers to other information:

1. The Argonne National Lab web page:

   `http://www-unix.mcs.anl.gov/mpi`

2. The Mississippi State web page:

   `http://www.erc.msstate.edu/mpi`

3. The Oak Ridge National Lab MPI Resource Center:

   `http://www.epm.ornl.gov/~walker/mpi`

B.4 MPI Newsgroup

There is a Usenet newsgroup devoted to MPI:

   `comp.parallel.mpi`

B.5 MPI Forum

The MPI Forum home page is

   `http://www.mpi-forum.org`

B.6   Parallel Programming with MPI

Finally, the book home page is linked to

```
http://www.mkp.com
```

and programs and errata can be downloaded from

```
http://www.cs.usfca.edu/mpi
```

Bibliography

[1] George S. Almasi and Allan Gottlieb. *Highly Parallel Computing*, 2nd ed. Redwood City, CA: Benjamin/Cummings, 1994.

[2] Gene M. Amdahl. Validity of the single processor approach to achieving large scale computing capabilities. In *AFIPS Conference Proceedings*, pp. 483–485, 1967.

[3] Edward Anderson et al. *LAPACK User's Guide, Second Edition*. Philadelphia: Society for Industrial and Applied Mathematics, 1995.

[4] David H. Bailey. Twelve ways to fool the masses when giving performance results on parallel supercomputers. *Supercomputing Review* 4(8):54–55, August 1991. Also available over the World Wide Web at http://www.nas.nasa.gov/NAS/TechReports/RNRreports/dbailey/RNR-91-020/RNR020.html

[5] Thomas Bulfinch. *Mythology*. Edmund Fuller, ed. New York: Dell, 1959.

[6] Jae Young Choi et al. *LAPACK Working Note 55. ScaLAPACK: A Scalable Linear Algebra Library for Distributed Memory Concurrent Computers*. University of Tennessee Technical Report CS-92-181, November 1992. Available over the World Wide Web at http://www.netlib.org/lapack/lawns/lawn55

[7] Jae Young Choi et al. *LAPACK Working Note 95. ScaLAPACK: A Portable Linear Algebra Library for Distributed Memory Computers—*

Design and Performance Issues. University of Tennessee Technical Report, CS-95-283, March 1995. Available over the World Wide Web at `http://www.netlib.org/lapack/lawns/lawn95`

[8] Jae Young Choi et al. *LAPACK Working Note 100. A Proposal for a Set of Parallel Basic Linear Algebra Subprograms*. University of Tennessee Technical Report, CS-95-293, May, 1995. Available over the World Wide Web at `http://www.netlib.org/lapack/lawns/lawn100.ps`

[9] Peter Corbett et al. *MPI-IO: A Parallel File I/O Interface for MPI*, Version 0.4. December 1995. Available over the World Wide Web at `http://lovelace.nas.nasa.gov/MPI-IO`

[10] Juan Miguel del Rosario and Alok N. Choudhary. High performance I/O for massively parallel computers: Problems and prospects. *IEEE Computer* 27(3):59–68, March 1994.

[11] James Demmel. *Lecture Notes for Intro to Parallel Computing*. Spring 1995. Available over the World Wide Web at `http://www.cs.berkeley.edu/~demmel/cs267`

[12] Jack J. Dongarra and Thomas H. Dunigan. *Message-passing Performance of Various Computers*. Report ORNL/TM-13006, Oak Ridge National Laboratory, Oak Ridge, TN. February 1996. Available over the World Wide Web at `http://www.epm.ornl.gov/~dunigan/comm.ps`

[13] Jack J. Dongarra and R. Clint Whaley. *LAPACK Working Note 94. A User's Guide to the BLACS v1.0*. University of Tennessee Technical Report CS-95-281, June 7, 1995. Available over the World Wide Web at `http://www.netlib.org/lapack/lawns/lawn94.ps`

[14] Jack J. Dongarra et al. An extended set of Fortran basic linear algebra subprograms. *ACM Transactions on Mathematical Software* 14:1–17, 1988.

[15] Jack J. Dongarra et al. A set of level 3 basic linear algebra subprograms. *ACM Transactions on Mathematical Software* 16:1–17, 1990.

[16] Michael Flynn. Very high-speed computing systems. *Proceedings of the IEEE* 54:1901–1909, December 1966.

[17] Ian Foster. *Designing and Building Parallel Programs*. Reading, MA: Addison-Wesley, 1995. Available over the World Wide Web at `http://www.mcs.anl.gov/dbpp`

[18] Geoffrey Fox et al. *Solving Problems on Concurrent Processors*. Englewood Cliffs, NJ: Prentice Hall, 1988.

[19] Gene Golub and James M. Ortega. *Scientific Computing: An Introduction with Parallel Computing*. San Diego: Academic Press, 1993.

[20] William Gropp and Ewing Lusk. *Users' Guide for* `mpich`, *a Portable Implementation of MPI*. February 1996. Available by anonymous ftp from `ftp.mcs.anl.gov`

[21] William Gropp, Ewing Lusk, and Anthony Skjellum. *Using MPI: Portable Parallel Programming with the Message-Passing Interface*. Cambridge, MA: MIT Press, 1994.

[22] John L. Gustafson. Reevaluating Amdahl's Law. *Communications of the ACM* 31(5):532–533, 1988.

[23] John L. Gustafson, Gary R. Montry, and Robert E. Benner. Development of parallel methods for a 1024-processor hypercube. *SIAM Journal on Scientific and Statistical Computing* 9(4):609–638, 1988.

[24] Brian W. Kernighan and Dennis M. Ritchie. *The C Programming Language*, 2nd ed. Englewood Cliffs, NJ: Prentice Hall, 1988.

[25] Donald Knuth. *The Art of Computer Programming: Searching and Sorting*. Reading, MA: Addison-Wesley, 1973.

[26] Vipin Kumar et al. *Introduction to Parallel Computing: Design and Analysis of Algorithms*. Redwood City, CA: Benjamin/Cummings, 1994.

[27] Charles L. Lawson et al. Basic linear algebra subprograms for Fortran usage. *ACM Transactions on Mathematical Software* 5:308-323, 1979.

[28] Message Passing Interface Forum. MPI: A message-passing interface standard. *International Journal of Supercomputer Applications* 8(3-4), 1994. Also available by anonymous ftp from `ftp.netlib.org` as Computer Science Dept. Technical Report, CS-94-230, University of Tennessee, Knoxville, TN, May 5, 1994.

[29] Message Passing Interface Forum. *MPI: A Message-Passing Interface Standard*, version 1.1. June 12, 1995. Available by anonymous ftp from `ftp.mcs.anl.gov`

[30] Ohio Supercomputer Center. *MPI Primer/Developing with LAM*. Ohio

State University. December, 1995. Available by anonymous ftp as `ftp://ftp.osc.edu/pub/lam/lam60.doc.ps.Z`

[31] *The Performance Database Server.* Available via the World Wide Web at `http://performance.netlib.org/performance/html/PDStop.html`

[32] Edward M. Reingold, Jurg Nievergelt, and Narsingh Deo. *Combinatorial Algorithms: Theory and Practice.* Englewood Cliffs, NJ: Prentice Hall, 1977.

[33] Barry Smith, William Gropp, and Lois Curfman McInnes. *PETSc 2.0 Users Manual.* Argonne National Laboratory Report ANL-95/11, 1995. Available by anonymous ftp from `ftp.mcs.anl.gov`

[34] Marc Snir, Steve Otto, Steven Huss-Lederman, David Walker, and Jack Dongarra. *MPI: The Complete Reference.* Cambridge, MA: MIT Press, 1996. Available over the World Wide Web at `http://www.netlib.org/utk/papers/mpi-book/mpi-book.html`

[35] David A. Spuler. *C++ and C Debugging, Testing, and Reliability.* Englewood Cliffs, NJ: Prentice Hall, 1994.

[36] Richard M. Stallman and Roland H. Pesch. *Debugging with GDB*, edition 4.12. Cambridge, MA: The Free Software Foundation, 1995.

[37] Thorsten von Eicken, David E. Culler, Seth Copen Goldstein, and Klaus Erik Schauser. Active messages: A mechanism for integrated communication and computation. In *Proceedings of the 19th International Symposium on Computer Architecture.* ACM Press, 1992. Also University of California, Computer Science Department Technical Report CSD-92-675.

Index

Page numbers in boldface type indicate discussions containing code examples.

Active messages, 34
addresses, relative, 91–92
algorithms, 315–337. *See also*
     sorting algorithms; tree
     search algorithms
     designing, 315–316
     direct vs. indirect paral-
       lelization, 315
     distributed termination de-
       tection, 334–335
     Fox's algorithm, 113–115,
       125–128
     hypercube allgather,
       288–292
     Jacobi's method, 218–219
     simple matrix multiplica-
       tion, **111–113**
     sorting, 227, 316–324
     tree searches, 324–335
aliasing arguments, 75
Allgather_cube, 284–293
     bitwise exclusive or,
       288–290
     coding, **292–293**

derived datatypes, 290
hypercube addressing
     scheme, 284–286
with nonblocking commu-
     nication, **299–301**
offsets in sends and re-
     ceives, **291–292**
rank of processes, 286–287
send-receive issues,
     293–295
Allgather_ring, 280–284
coding, **282–284**
four-processor ring pass,
     280, 281
four-process pairwise ex-
     change, 280, 282
function parameters, 280
with nonblocking commu-
     nication, **298–299**
persistent communication
     requests, **301–302**
runtimes, 299, 304
send-receive issues,
     293–295

with synchronous sends,
     305–306
Allocate_list, **228**, 230,
     231, 236
allocating buffers, 308, **309**,
     365
all-to-all scatter/gather,
     232–233
Amdahl's law, 259–260
array I/O, 158–171
     C vs. Fortran, 341–342
     data distribution types,
       159–161
     derived datatypes, 162–164
     example, **170–171**
     extent of derived datatypes,
       164–166
     input code, **166–168**
     input distribution, 162
     model problem, 161–162
     printing the array, **168–169**
asymptotic analysis, 245, 246
asynchronous processing, 15

attribute caching
  attribute key creation,
    140–142
  callback functions, 141–142
  command summary,
    386–387
  identifying I/O process
    rank, **142–144**
  I/O process rank, **144–148**
  MPI_IO attribute, 143–144
  overview, 138–139
  topologies, 121–125
attribute retrieval, **140–141**,
  148–149

Bandwidth, 251
barriers, 28–29, 376
Basic Linear Algebra Com-
  munication Subprograms
  (BLACS), 343–345
Basic Linear Algebra Subprogram (BLAS), 342–343
Best_solution, 330, 331
binary semaphore, 27–28, 29
bitonic sort algorithms
  bitonic sequences, 316–317,
    318
  bitonic splits, 317–319,
    321–322
  parallel coding, **322–324**
  serial coding, **319–320**
Bitonic_sort_incr,
  319–320
bitwise exclusive or, **288–290**
BLACS (Basic Linear Algebra
  Communication Subpro-
  grams), 343–345
BLAS (Basic Linear Algebra
  Subprogram), 342–343
block-cyclic distribution. *See*
  block-cyclic mapping
block-cyclic mapping, 35–36
  and array I/O, 159–160
block-cyclic partitioning. *See*
  block-cyclic mapping
block distribution. *See* block
  mapping

blocking communication,
  31–32, 363–364
block mapping, 35
  and array I/O, 159
  for Jacobi's method,
    221–223
block partitioning. *See* block
  mapping
block-row distribution
  allgather function, 82–83
  gather function, 79–81
  overview, 78–79
  scatter function, 81–82
bottleneck, von Neumann, 12
broadcasts, 69–73
  Get_Data using, **70–71**
  MPI_Bcast syntax, 70, 376
buffered send mode, 30–31,
  307–309, 364
buffering
  allocating buffers, 308, **309**,
    365
  and broadcasts, 71–72
  command summary, 365
  and deadlocks, 72, 294
  and I/O performance, 248
  messages, 30–31
  releasing buffers, 308, **309**
  send-receive issues,
    293–295
bus-based networks, 24
bus-based shared-memory
  MIMD, 16, 18
busses, 12

C++
  and MPI-2, 362
  and PETSc, 350
cache coherence, 18
cache consistency, 18
caching attributes
  attribute key creation,
    140–142
  callback functions, 141–142
  command summary,
    386–387
  identifying I/O process
    rank, **142–144**

I/O process rank, **144–148**
  MPI_IO attribute, 143–144
  overview, 138–139
  topologies, 121–125
caching in von Neumann machines, 12
callback functions, 141–142
cancel commands, 369
Cartesian topology management, **121–128**, 387–389
checkerboard distribution of
  matrices, 113
CHIMP implementation, 399
coding parallel programs,
  225–226
collective communication
  all-to-all scatter/gather,
    232–233
  broadcast, 69–73, 376
  command summary,
    376–380
  definition, 69
  gather, 78–83, 376–378
  and performance, 269
  redistributing keys,
    233–236
  reduction, 73–78
  scatter, 78–82, 377–379
combinatorial optimization,
  324–325
command line arguments
  with PETSc, 351–352, 357
  processes' access to,
    154–155
command summary, 363–397.
  See also MPI functions
  attribute caching, 386–387
  blocking sends and re-
    ceives, 363–364
  buffer allocation, 365
  cancel, 369
  collective communication
    functions, 376–380
  communication modes,
    364–365
  communicator manage-
    ment, 383–385
  constants, 393–396
  derived datatypes, 372–375

environmental manage-
ment, 391–393
group management,
381–383
inter-communicators,
385–386
MPI_Pack and MPI_
Unpack, 375–376
nonblocking communica-
tion, 365–369
persistent communication
requests, 369–371
point-to-point communica-
tion functions, 363–372
probe, 369
process topologies,
387–390
profiling, 393
send-receive, 371–372
type definitions, 396–397
comm_time.c example,
191–210
buggy source code,
192–195
dbx example, 197–199
described, 191
initial tests, 196
using printf/fflush,
182–184, 199–200
communication. See col-
lective communication;
message passing
communication coprocessors,
267–268
communication modes,
304–309
buffered, **307–309**, 364
command summary,
364–365
ready, **306–307**, 364–365
standard, 304
synchronous, **305–306**, 365
communication-phase performance costs, 251
communicators. See also attribute caching; rank of
processes
caching topologies,
121–125

command summary,
383–386
constants, 395
creating multiple, 120–121
definition, 45, 47, 111
groups, **116–120**, 381–383
inter-communicators, 116,
385–386
intra-communicators,
116–120
and libraries, 340
in message envelope, 45,
47
predefined, 395
for rows and columns,
124–125
compiling programs, 42
Fortran subprograms, 341
completing nonblocking operations, 297–298
constants, 44, 393–396
contexts
creating communicators,
119–120
overview, 116–117
control-parallel design, 217
coordinates
finding from rank, 122–123
finding rank from, 122–123
Copy_attr, **144–148**
copying cached attributes,
141–142
count, **89–90**, 103
Cprintf, **150–152**
for debugging, 199–200,
208–210
in sort program, 236
critical section, 27
crossbar switches, 16–18
Cscanf, **149–150**
cut-through routing, 25
cyclic distribution. See cyclic
mapping
cyclic mapping, 35
and array I/O, 159–160
for Jacobi's method,
221–222
cyclic partitioning. See cyclic
mapping

Data distributions. See data
mapping
data locality issues, 34–35
data mapping, 34–36
and array I/O, 159–161,
162, **166–168**
and data locality, 34–35
and data parallelism, 33
for Jacobi's method,
221–223
and load balancing, 35
types of mapping, 35–36
data-parallelism
design issues, 218
overview, 6, 32–33, 217
trapezoidal rule program,
56–60, 218
data partitioning. See data
mapping
datatypes. See also derived
datatypes
command summary,
396–397
constants, 394–395
matching, 98–100
MPI vs. C, 48
sorting program example,
227
type signature, 99
dbx
with parallel programs,
197–199
with serial programs,
185–187
deadlocks
and buffering, 72, 294
debugging, 200–201
deallocating requests, 303
debuggers
parallel, 196–199
serial, 184–187
debugging, 179–215. See also
testing programs
adding debugging out-
put, 182–184, 199–200,
208–210
classical parallel program
bugs, 200–202

debugging (*continued*)
  comm_time.c example,
    191–210
  errors on different systems,
    205
  examining source code,
    180–182
  final testing, 210
  initial tests, 196
  nondeterminism, 188–191
  parallel debuggers, 196–199
  serial bugs in parallel pro-
    grams, 203–205
  serial debuggers, 184–187
  serial debugging, 179–188
  testing multiple processes,
    206–207
definite integrals
  I/O example, **60–62**
  parallel program, **56–60**
  serial program, **55–56**
  trapezoidal rule, 53–55
deleting cached attributes,
  141–142
depth-first search
  overview, 325–326
  parallel search based on,
    328–330
  using recursion, **326–327**
  without recursion, **327–328**
derived datatypes, 90–100.
    See also datatypes
  and array I/O, 162–166
  command summary,
    372–375
  constants, 395
  extent of, **164–166**
  for hypercube allgather, 290
  matching types, 98–100
  overview, 90–92
  using MPI_Scatter,
    162–166
  using MPI_Type_
    contiguous, 97–98
  using MPI_Type_indexed,
    97–98
  using MPI_Type_struct,
    92–95

  using MPI_Type_vector,
    96–97
  when to use, 103–104
descriptors, 344
design, 217–243
  of algorithms, 315–316
  coding parallel programs,
    225–226
  control-parallel, 217
  data-parallel, 6, 32–33, 217,
    218
  Jacobi's method example,
    218–225
  sorting example, 226–240
Dfs_recursive, **326–327**
Dfs_stack, **327–328**
displacements, 91–92
distributed-memory MIMD,
  19–24
  bus-based networks, 24
  dynamic networks, 19,
    20–21
  fully connected networks,
    19–20
  and libraries, 342
  message passing, 29–32
  network types, 19–20
  routing issues, 24–25
  static networks, 19, 21–24
distributed termination detection, 334–335
distribution of data. *See* data
  mapping
dot product. *See also* matrix
  multiplication
  using all reduce, 78
  using reduction, **75–76**
downloading
  MPI implementations,
    399–400
  programs and errata, 401
drivers for testing subprograms, 226
dynamic load balancing, 328
dynamic networks, 19, 20–21
dynamic process creation,
  26–29

Efficiency
  and Amdahl's law,
    259–260, 263–265
  definition, 250, 261
  and scalability, 263–265
envelopes, 45–46
  communicators, 45, 47
  tags or message types,
    46–47
environmental management
  commands, 391–393
error handling, 210–212,
  391–392
errors. *See also* debugging;
  testing programs
  checking with stderr,
    152–153
  constants, 394
  error handling, 210–212,
    391–392
errors in this book
  downloading errata, 401
  reporting, xix
exclusive or, **288–290**
executing programs, 42–43
execution profiles, 269–270
  MPI interface, 271–272, 393
  using Upshot, 272–275
execution times. *See also* performance
  blocking vs. nonblocking
    allgather, 299, 300–301
  and communication,
    251–252
  and communication copro-
    cessors, 268
  factors affecting, 246
  and I/O, 248–249
  for persistent requests, 304
  problems evaluating,
    269–270
  for serial trapezoidal rule,
    248, 249
  taking timings, 254–256,
    392
extent, of derived datatypes,
  164–166

FAQ, MPI, 400
Feasible, 330, 331
fflush for debugging,
    182–184, 199–200
file I/O, **156–158**
Find_alltoall_send_
    params, **236–239**
Find_recv_
    displacements, 239
Flynn's taxonomy, 12
Fortran
    calling C programs from,
        341
    calling subprograms from
        C, 340–342
    and code examples, xviii–
        xix
    data-parallel programs, 6
    wrappers, 341, **348–350**
Fox's algorithm, **115**
    implementation, **125–128**
    intra-communicators,
        116–121
    overview, 113–115
    topologies, 121–125
ftp sites, MPI implementa-
    tions, 399–400
functions. *See also* command
    summary
    capitalization, 44
    user-defined, 141–142,
        396–397
future of MPI, 362

Gantt charts, 272
gather, 78–83
    all-to-all scatter/gather,
        232–233
    command summary,
        376–378
    matrix-vector product ex-
        ample, **79–80**, **83**
    MPI_Allgather, 82–83
    MPI_Gather, 80–81
    overview, 79–80
gdb, 184
general MPI datatypes. *See*
    derived datatypes

generating keys, **231–232**
Get_corresp_rank, 146
Get_Data function
    simple I/O, **61–62**
    tree-structured distribution,
        66–67, **67–69**
    using broadcast, **70–71**
    using derived datatype,
        91–95
    using pack and unpack,
        100–103
Get_io_rank, **148–149**
Get_list_size, **228**, **229**,
    230, **231**, 239–240
Get_local_keys, **229**, 230,
    232
global variables, 60
GNU debugger, 184
graph topology management,
    389–390
grids
    creating subgrids, 124–125
    finding coordinates from
        rank, 122–123
    finding rank from coordi-
        nates, 122–123
grouping data for communi-
    cation
    choosing a method,
        103–104
    using count, **89–90**, 103
    using derived datatypes,
        90–100, 103
    using pack and unpack,
        100–103, **104–105**
groups
    associating with contexts,
        119–120
    command summary,
        381–383
    constants, 395, 396
    creating communicators,
        117–120
    definition, 116

Handles
    constants, 396
    null, 396

for opaque objects, 119
hardware, 11–25
    Flynn's taxonomy, 12
    MIMD systems, 15–24
    pipeline and vector archi-
        tectures, 13–14
    and program performance,
        246
    routing issues, 24–25
    SIMD systems, 14–15
    von Neumann machines, 12
hardwired input, **226**,
    230–231
header files
    mpi.h, 44, 393, 396
    for sorting program, **229**
"hello, world" program,
    41–43
hypercube allgather, 284–293
    addressing scheme,
        284–286
    bitwise exclusive or,
        288–290
    coding, **292–293**
    derived datatypes, 290
    with nonblocking commu-
        nication, **299–301**
    offsets in sends and re-
        ceives, **291–292**
    rank of processes, 286–287
    send-receive issues,
        293–295
hypercube networks, 22–23
hypercubes
    addressing scheme,
        284–286
    defining inductively, 284
    rank of processes, 286–287

Identifiers, 44
idle time
    as overhead, 262–263,
        266–267
    predictable or regular,
        266–267
    unpredictable or irregular,
        267
    and work, 261

inactive requests, 303
#include "mpi.h" statement, 44
inherently serial code, 260
Initialize, 353, **356–357**
input. *See* I/O on parallel systems
inputs, and program performance, 246
Insert_key, **232**, 236
inter-communicators, 116, 385–386
Internet resources, 399–401
intra-communicators
creating, **117–120**
creating multiples, 120–121
overview, 116–117
I/O on parallel systems, **61–62**, 137–176. *See also* array I/O; rank of processes
access to command line arguments, **154–156**
adding debugging output, 199–200, 208–210
array I/O, 158–171
attribute caching, 139–142, **144–148**
attribute retrieval, **148–149**
broadcasts, 69–70, **70–71**, 376
coding tips, 226
file I/O, **156–158**
hardwired, **226**, **230–231**
inputs and performance, 246
overview, 60–61
and performance analysis, 248–249
printf, 60–62, 137, 138–139
stderr, 138, **152–153**
stdin, 138, **149–150**, **154–156**
stdout, 138, **150–152**
tree-structured distribution, 65–67, **67–69**
irregular idle time, 267

Jacobi's method, 218–225
overview, 218–219
parallel program, **223–225**
parallel pseudocode, 220–223
serial program, **219–220**

Keys
bitonic sequences, 316–317
constants, 395
creating for attributes, **140–142**
datatype definition for, 227
generating, **231–232**
redistributing, **233–236**
Krylov subspace methods, 351–352

LAM implementation, 399
LAPACK (Linear Algebra Package), 342–343
latency, 251
libraries, 339–359
advantages of, 339–340
BLACS, 343–345
BLAS, 342–343
documentation needed, 340
LAPACK, 342–343
PBLAS, 343, 345
PETSc, 350–357
ScaLAPACK, 340–350
Linear Algebra Package (LAPACK), 342–343
linear array networks, 21, 22
linear speedup, 250, 261
linking to Fortran libraries, 341
load balancing, 35
dynamic, 328
and performance, 266–267
local send mode, 307
Local_sort, **229**, 236
local variables, 60
log files, mon.out, 269

Mapping. *See* data mapping

massive parallelism, 259–260
MatAssemblyBegin, 351, **355**
MatAssemblyEnd, 351, **355**
matrix multiplication
checkerboard distribution, 113
Fox's algorithm, 113–115, **125–128**
and nondeterminism, 188–191
simple algorithm, **111–113**
using intra-communicators, 116–120
matrix-vector product
parallel example, **83**
serial example, **78**
using allgather, **82–83**
using gather and scatter, **79–82**
Merge_split, **322–323**
mesh networks, 23–24
message passing. *See also* collective communication; sending messages
buffering, 30–31
bugs typical in, 200–202
communication modes, 304–309, 364–365
communicators, 45, 47
C vs. Fortran, 341
envelopes, 45–47
nonblocking communication, 32, 296–301
as overhead, 262, 263
overlapping computation, 267–268
overview, 6–7, 29–32, 45–47
and performance, 250–252, 267–268
persistent communication requests, **301–304**, 369–371
send-receive, 293–295, 371–372
tags or message types, 46–47

Message-Passing Interface
(MPI)
  development of, 6
  free implementations,
    399–400
  future of, 362
  overview, xvii, 6–7, 29–30
  profiling interface, 271–272
  references and resources,
    361–362, 399–401
message types, 46–47
MIMD machines. *See*
  multiple-instruction
  multiple-data (MIMD)
  machines
MISD machines. *See* multiple-
  instruction single-data
  (MISD) machines
monitors, 29
monotonic sequences, 316
mon.out, 269
MPI. *See* Message-Passing Interface (MPI)
MPI_, 44
MPI-2, 362, 401
MPI_Abort, 393
MPI_Address, 372
MPI_Allgather. *See also*
  Allgather_cube; All-
  gather_ring
  with block mapping, 223,
    224, **225**
  example, **83**
  syntax, 82–83, 376–377
MPI_Allgatherv, 377
MPI_Allreduce, 77–78, **225**,
    379
MPI_Alltoall, 232–233,
    234, 377
MPI_Alltoallv
  displacements, 236
  syntax, 233, 377–378
  using, 232–233, **234–235**
MPI_Attr_delete, 386
MPI_Attr_get
  examples, **140–141**, **148**
  syntax, 140, 386
MPI_Attr_put, **140**, 386

MPI_Barrier, 254, 256, 268,
    376
MPI_Bcast
  and buffering, 71–72
  Get_Data using, **70–71**
  grouping data with count,
    89–90, 103
  and synchronization, 72–73
  syntax, 70, 376
  and tags, 71
MPI_Bsend, 307, **308–309**,
    364
MPI_Bsend_init, 308,
    369–370
MPI_Buffer_attach, 308,
    309, 365
MPI_Buffer_detach, 308,
    309, 365
MPI_Cancel, 369
MPI_Cart_coords, 122, 123,
    387
MPI_Cart_create, 122, 123,
    387–388
MPI_Cartdim_get, 388
MPI_Cart_get, 388
MPI_Cart_map, 388
MPI_Cart_rank, 122, 123,
    388
MPI_Cart_shift, 389
MPI_Cart_sub, 124–125,
    389
mpich, 272, 399
MPI_Comm_compare,
    145–146, 383–384
MPI_Comm_create, 119–120,
    384
MPI_Comm_dup, 140,
    141–142, 384
MPI_Comm_free, 384
MPI_Comm_group, 119, 381
MPI_Comm_rank, 44–45, 384
MPI_Comm_remote_group,
    385
MPI_Comm_remote_size,
    385
MPI_Comm_size, 384
MPI_Comm_split, 120–121,
    385
MPI_Comm_test_inter, 385

MPI_COMM_WORLD, 45, 49
MPI constants, 44, 393–396
MPI_Copy_function,
    141–142, 396–397
MPI_Datatype
  MPI_Type_struct exam-
    ple, **92–95**
  overview, 91
  using other constructors,
    96–98
  using relative addresses,
    91–92
MPI datatypes. *See* datatypes
MPI_Delete_function,
    142, 397
MPI_Dims_create, 389
MPI_Dims_get, 389–390
MPI_Errhandler_create,
    391
MPI_Errhandler_free, 391
MPI_Errhandler_get, 391
MPI_Errhandler_set,
    211–212, 392
MPI_Error_class, 392
MPI_ERRORS_ARE_FATAL,
    211
MPI_ERRORS_RETURN,
    211–212
MPI_Error_string, 392
MPI_Finalize, 44, 393
MPI functions. *See also* com-
    mand summary
  capitalization, 44
  user-defined, 141–142,
    396–397
MPI_Gather
  example, **79–80**
  syntax, 80–81, 378
MPI_Gatherv, 378
MPI_Get_count, 363
MPI_Get_elements, 372
MPI_Get_processor_name,
    391
MPI_Graph_create, 389
MPI_Graph_get, 390
MPI_Graph_map, 390
MPI_Graph_neighbors, 390
MPI_Graph_neighbors_
    count, 390

MPI_Group_compare, 381
MPI_Group_difference, 381
MPI_Group_excl, 381
MPI_Group_free, 382
MPI_Group_incl, 119, 382
MPI_Group_intersection, 382
MPI_Group_range_excl, 382
MPI_Group_range_incl, 382
MPI_Group_rank, 383
MPI_Group_size, 383
MPI_Group_translate_ranks, 146, 383
MPI_Group_union, 383
MPI_Handler_function, 397
mpi.h file, 44, 393, 396
MPI_Ibsend, 307–308, 365–366
MPI identifiers, 44
MPI_Init, 44, 393
MPI_Initialized, 393
MPI_Intercomm_create, 385
MPI_Intercomm_merge, 386
MPI_IO attribute, 143–144
MPI-IO home page, 401
MPI_Iprobe, 331, 369
MPI_Irecv
  in Allgather_cube, **300**
  in Allgather_ring, **299**
  completing operations, 297–298
  syntax, 297, 366
MPI_Irsend, 306, 366
MPI_Isend
  in Allgather_cube, **300**
  in Allgather_ring, **299**
  completing operations, 297–298
  syntax, 297, 366
MPI_Issend, 305, 366–367
MPI_Keyval_create
  example, **139–140**, 141
  syntax, 141–142, 386–387
MPI_Keyval_free, 387

MPI_Op_create, 379
MPI_Op_free, 380
MPI_Pack
  examples, **100–101**, **104–105**, **302**
  syntax, 101–102, 375
  when to use, 103–104
MPI_Pack_size, 375
MPI_Pcontrol, 271–272, 393
MPI_Probe, 369
MPI_PROC_NULL, 295–296
MPI_Recv
  in Allgather_cube, **291–294**
  in Allgather_ring, **283–284**, 293–294
  and broadcasts, 70, 72
  grouping data with count, **89–90**, 103
  I/O example, **61–62**
  overview, 45
  and program bugs, 200–202
  return values, 50
  syntax, 48–40, 364
MPI_Recv_init, 302–303, 370
MPI_Reduce
  aliasing arguments, 75
  example, **75–76**
  grouping data with count, **89–90**, 103
  and performance, 253, 254, 263
  predefined operators, 74
  syntax, 73–74, 380
MPI_Reduce_scatter, 380
MPI_Request_free, 303, 367
MPI_Rsend, 306, 364–365
MPI_Rsend_init, 306, 370
MPI_Scan, 380
MPI_Scatter
  and array I/O, 162–166
  examples, **81**, **164–166**
  extent of derived datatypes, **164–166**
  syntax, 81–82, 164, 378–379
MPI_Scatterv, 379

MPI_Send
  in Allgather_cube, **291–294**
  in Allgather_ring, **283–284**, 293–294
  example, **61–62**
  grouping data with count, **89–90**, 103
  overview, 45
  and program bugs, 200–202
  return values, 50
  syntax, 47–50, 364
MPI_Send_init, 302–303, 370
MPI_Sendrecv, 294–295, 371
MPI_Sendrecv_replace, **127–128**, 295, 372
MPI_Ssend, **305–306**, 365
MPI_Ssend_init, 305, 371
MPI_Start, **302**, **303**, 371
MPI_Startall, 371
MPI_Test, 367
MPI_Testall, 367
MPI_Testany, 367
MPI_Test_cancelled, 369
MPI_Testsome, 368
MPI_Topo_test, 387
MPI_Type_commit, 95, 372
MPI_Type_contiguous, 97–98, 373
MPI_Type_extent, 373
MPI_Type_free, 373
MPI_Type_hindexed, 373
MPI_Type_hvector, 373
MPI_Type_indexed, 97, **98**, 374
MPI_Type_lb, 374
MPI_Type_size, 374
MPI_Type_struct
  changing extent of types, **165–166**
  examples, **93–95**, **165–166**
  syntax, 95, 374
MPI_Type_ub, 374
MPI_Type_vector
  and array I/O, 162–163
  examples, **97**, **290**
  syntax, 96–97, 290, 375

MPI_Unpack
  examples, **100–101**, **104–105**, **302**
  syntax, 102–103, 375–376
  when to use, 103–104
MPI_User_function, 397
MPI_Wait
  in Allgather_cube, **300**
  in Allgather_ring, **299**
  completing nonblocking operations, 297–298
  with persistent requests, 303
  syntax, 298, 368
MPI_Waitall, 368
MPI_Waitany, 368
MPI_Waitsome, 368–369
MPI_Wtick, 392
MPI_Wtime, 254–256, 392
multicomputers. *See* distributed-memory MIMD
multiple-instruction multiple-data (MIMD) machines, 15–24
  definition, 12
  distributed-memory systems, 19–24
  general systems, 15–16
  routing issues, 24–25
  shared-memory systems, 16–18
multiple-instruction single-data (MISD) machines, 14
multiprocessors. *See* shared-memory MIMD
multistage networks, 20–21
mutual exclusion, 27–28

Networks of workstations, 265–266
New_request, 333–334
newsgroup, Usenet, 400
nonblocking communication, 32
  command summary, 365–369

completing operations, 297–298
hypercube allgather with, **299–301**
overview, 296–298
with PETSc, 350–351
ring allgather with, **298–299**
nondeterminism
  as a bug, 188–191
  as a feature, 191
nonlocal send modes, 307
non-uniform memory access (NUMA) systems, 18
null handles, 396
null processes, 295–296
NUMA systems. *See* non-uniform memory access (NUMA) systems

Omega networks, 20–21
online support materials, xx
opaque objects, 119
opaque types, 396
operators, reduction, 74
Out_of_work, 333
output. *See* I/O on parallel systems
overhead
  communication, 262, 267–268
  definition, 261
  extra computation, 262, 263
  idle time, 262–263, 266–267
  per-process, 262

P, prefix to MPI functions, 271–272
packing data. *See* MPI_Pack
panel distribution. *See* block-row distribution
parallel algorithms. *See* algorithms
parallel bitonic sort, **320–324**
Parallel BLAS (PBLAS), 343, 345

parallel computers, 5
parallel computing, 11–39
  Amdahl's law, 259–260
  design challenges, 5–6
  hardware, 11–25
  need for, 1–5
  references and resources, 361–362, 399–401
  software issues, 25–36
parallel debuggers, 196–199
parallel libraries. *See* libraries
Parallel Programming with MPI
  about this book, xviii–xix, 7–9
  classroom use, xix–xx
  downloading programs and errata, 401
  support materials, xx
  typographic conventions, 9
  Web page, 401
parallel tree search, 328–335
  based on depth-first search, **328–330**
  distributed termination detection, 334–335
  Par_dfs, **330–332**
  Service_requests, **332**
  Work_remains, **332–334**
Par_bitonic_sort_decr, **323**
Par_bitonic_sort_incr, **323–324**
Par_dfs, **330–332**
partitioning of data. *See* data mapping
Par_tree_search, **328–329**
PBLAS (Parallel BLAS), 343, 345
performance, 245–278. *See also* execution times
  Amdahl's law, 259–260
  asymptotic analysis, 245, 246
  blocking vs. nonblocking allgather, 299, 300–301
  and collective communication, 269

performance (*continued*)
  and communication,
    250–252, 262, 267–268
  efficiency, 250, 261,
    263–265
  execution profiles, 269–275
  factors affecting runtime,
    246
  and I/O, 248–249
  and load imbalance,
    266–267
  and networks of worksta-
    tions, 265–266
  overhead, 261, 262–263
  parallel program analysis,
    249–254
  predicted vs. actual,
    253–254, 255
  problems estimating,
    265–269
  and resource contention,
    265–266
  scalability, 263–265
  serial programs, 245–249
  slowdown, 250
  speedup, 249–250,
    253–254, 261
  taking timings, 254–256,
    392
  tools for evaluating,
    269–275
  of trapezoidal rule program,
    247–248, 252–254
  work, 261, 262
per-process overhead, 262
persistent communication
  requests, **301–304**,
  369–371
PETSc, 350–357
  command line arguments,
    351–352, 357
  example program, **352–357**
  Krylov subspace methods,
    351–352
  nonblocking operations,
    350–351
  overview, 350–352
pipelining, 13
`PMPI_`, 271–272

point-to-point communica-
  tion, 279–314. *See also*
  specific commands
  `Allgather_cube` exam-
    ple, 284–293, **299–301**
  `Allgather_ring` exam-
    ple, 280–284, **298–299**
  blocking sends and re-
    ceives, 363–364
  cancel commands, 369
  command summary,
    363–372
  communication modes,
    304–309, 364–365
  nonblocking communica-
    tion, **296–301**, 365–369
  null processes, 295–296
  persistent communica-
    tion requests, **301–304**,
    369–371
  probe commands, 369
  send-receive, 293–295,
    371–372
portability of programs, 205
Portable Extensible Toolkit for
  Scientific Computation.
  See PETSc
posting, 296–297
preconditioner, 352
predictable idle time, 266–267
preprocessor directive, 44
`printf`
  `Cprintf`, **150–152**,
    199–200, 208–210, 236
  for debugging, 182–184,
    199–200, 208–210
  on parallel systems, 60–62,
    137, 138–139
  and performance analysis,
    248–249
`Print_list`, **229**, 236
probe commands, 369
processes. *See also* rank of
  processes; topologies
  barriers, 28–29, 376
  command line argument
    access, 154–155
  communicators, 45
  definition, 25–26

  dynamic creation of, 26–29
  global and local variables,
    59–60
  mutual exclusion, 27–28
  null processes, 295–296
  synchronizing, 254, 256
`prof`, 269–270
profiling interface, 271–272,
  393
prompt, shell, 9
`psgemv` wrapper, **348–349**

Q–R

quicksort algorithm, 316
`Rand`, **231–232**
rank of processes, 44–45
  caching, **139–140**,
    141–142, **144–148**
  finding from grid coordi-
    nates, 122–123
  finding grid coordinates
    from, 122–123
  and hypercubes, 286–287
  identifying, **142–144**
  organizing output by,
    138–139
  retrieving, **140–141**,
    148–149
ready send mode, **306–307**,
  364–365
`Redistribute_keys`, **229**,
  230, **233–236**
reduction, 73–78
  aliasing arguments, 75
  all reduce, 76–78
  command summary,
    379–380
  constants, 395–396
  dot product example, **75–76**
  predefined operators, 74
references for study, 361–362,
  399–401
registers, 12
regular idle time, 266–267
relative addresses, 91–92
releasing buffers, 308, **309**
Remote Procedure Call (RPC),
  34

request parameter, 32

resource contention, 265–266

resources for study, 361–362, 399–401

retrieving I/O process rank, **140–141**, **148–149**

ring networks, 21, 22

ring pass allgather, 280–284
  coding, **282–284**
  four-processor ring pass, 280, 281
  four-process pairwise exchange, 280, 282
  function parameters, 280
  with nonblocking communication, **298–299**
  persistent communication requests, **301–302**
  runtimes, 299, 304
  send-receive issues, 293–295
  with synchronous sends, **305–306**

root of broadcast, 69

routing in MIMD systems, 24–25

RPC. *See* Remote Procedure Call (RPC)

runtimes. *See* execution times; performance

Scalability, 263–265

ScaLAPACK, 340–350
  descriptors, 344
  example program, **345–350**
  Fortran issues, 340–342
  overview, 342–344
  wrappers, 341, **348–350**

scanf
  and Cscanf, **149–150**
  and performance analysis, 248–249

scatter, **81–82**
  all-to-all scatter/gather, 232–233

command summary, 377–379

searching trees. *See* tree search algorithms

self-initialization, **155–156**

Send_all_rejects, 333

sending messages. *See also* message passing
  bugs typical in, 200–202
  communication modes, 304–309, 364–365˙
  overview, 47–50
  packing and unpacking, 100–103, **104–105**
  send-receive, 293–295, 371–372
  using count parameter, **89–90**, 103
  using derived datatypes, 90–100, 103

Send_request, 334

serial debugging, 179–188
  adding debugging output, 182–184
  examining source code, 180–182
  in parallel programs, 203–205
  symbolic debuggers, 184–187

serial programs
  bitonic sort, **316–320**
  dbx with, 185–187
  definite integrals, **55–56**
  inherently serial code, 260
  Jacobi's method, **219–220**
  matrix-vector product, **78**
  performance, 245–249
  trapezoidal rule, **55–56**
  tree search, **325–328**

Service_requests, 332

shared-memory MIMD, 16–18
  bus-based, 16, 18
  cache coherence in, 18
  routing issues, 24–25
  switch-based, 16–18

shared-memory programming, 26–29

single-instruction multiple-data (SIMD) machines, 14–15

single-instruction single-data (SISD) machines, 12

single-program multiple-data (SPMD) programs, 30, 43

SLESCreate, 353, **355**

SLESSetFromOptions, 353, **355**

SLESSetOperators, 353, **355**

SLESSolve, 353, **355**

slowdown, 250. *See also* execution times; performance

snoopy protocol, 18

software issues, 25–36
  data mapping, 34–36
  data-parallelism, 32–33
  lack of software, 339
  message passing, 29–32
  RPC and active messages, 34
  shared-memory programming, 26–29

Solve wrapper, **349–350**

sort.h, **229**

sorting algorithms, 316–324
  parallel bitonic sort, 320–324
  quicksort, 316
  serial bitonic sort, 316–320
  simple parallel algorithm, 227, 316

sorting program, 226–240
  all-to-all scatter/gather, 232–233
  Find_alltoall_send_params, **236–239**
  finishing up, **239–240**
  input functions, **230–232**
  main program, **227–230**
  overview, 226–227
  redistributing keys, **233–236**

speedup. *See also* execution
     times; performance
     definition, 249–250
     linear speedup, 250, 261
     predicted vs. actual,
          253–254, 255
splitting communicators,
     120–121
SPMD programs. *See* single-
     program multiple-data
     (SPMD) programs
srand, **231–232**
standard communication, 304
startup commands, 392–393
start-up phase, performance
     costs, 251
static process creation, 26
status.MPI_Source, 296
status.MPI_Tag, 296
stderr
     error checking, **152–153**
     MPI support for, 138
     writing to, **152–153**
stdin
     limited access to, **154–156**
     MPI support for, 138
     reading from, **149–150**
stdout
     MPI support for, 138
     writing to, **150–152**
store-and-forward routing, 25
subgrids, creating, 124–125
subprograms, testing, 226
switch-based shared-memory
     MIMD, 16–18
symbolic debuggers
     parallel, 196–199
     serial, 184–187
synchronization, and broad-
     casts, 72–73
synchronous send mode, 72,
     305–306, 365

Tags, 46–47
     and broadcasts, 71
termination detection, dis-
     tributed, 334–335
testing programs. *See also*
     debugging
     drivers for, 226
     final testing, 210
     initial tests, 196
     multiple processes,
          206–207
     subprograms during cod-
          ing, 226
timing functions, 392
timing program execution,
     254–256, 392
topologies
     caching, 121–123
     Cartesian, 387–389
     command summary,
          387–390
     constants, 396
     definition, 111, 121
     and Fox's algorithm, 126
     graph, 389–390
     virtual, 121
torus networks, 23–24
total exchange, 232–233
tours, 324
trapezoidal rule, 53–55
     I/O example, **60–62**
     parallel program, **56–60**
     parallel program per-
          formance, 252–254,
          272–275
     serial program, **55–56**
     serial program perfor-
          mance, 247–248
     Upshot example, 272–275
travelling salesman problem.
     See tree search algo-
     rithms
tree search algorithms,
     324–335
     and combinatorial opti-
          mization, 324–325

     parallel, **328–335**
     serial (depth-first),
          325–328
tree-structured distribution,
     66–67, **67–69**
troubleshooting. *See* debug-
     ging; errors; testing pro-
     grams
types. *See* datatypes; derived
     datatypes
type signature, 99

Unpacking data. *See* MPI_
     Unpack
unpredictable idle time, 267
Upshot, 272–275, 399
Usenet newsgroup, 400
user-defined functions,
     141–142, 396–397

Variables, global vs. local,
     60
vector architecture, 13–14,
     344
virtual topologies. *See* topolo-
     gies
von Neumann machines, 12

W–Z
W32MPI, 400
weather prediction, 2–3
Web resources, 400, 401
wildcards, with MPI_Recv,
     49
Windows implementations,
     400
WinMPI, 400
work, 261, 262
Work_remains, **332–334**
Work_requests_pending,
     332
wrappers, 341, **348–350**

Related Titles from Morgan Kaufmann

Computer Architecture: A Quantitative Approach, Second Edition
John L. Hennessy and David A. Patterson
This landmark revision focuses on the new generation of architectures and design techniques with a view toward the future. It includes increased coverage of pipelining and storage, a comprehensive presentation of caches, and new chapters on shared-memory multiprocessing and networking technology. Anyone involved in building computers will profit from the unmatched experience and quantitative approach that Hennessy and Patterson apply to their presentation.
ISBN 1-55860-329-8; cloth; 760 pages; 1995

Scalable Shared-Memory Multiprocessing
Daniel E. Lenoski and Wolf-Dietrich Weber
This book explores a new class of machines supporting both cache-coherent shared memory and scalability to a large number of processors. It examines general concepts involved in building scalable multiprocessors, especially scalable shared-memory machines. The authors address the challenges in designing scalable architectures and then discuss the trade-offs between shared memory and message passing, as well as the challenges of scalable cache coherency. Of value to both designers and programmers of scalable machines who wish to understand the performance of various architectures as well as the variety of design alternatives.
ISBN 1-55860-315-8; cloth; 341 pages; 1995

Parallel Computing Works!
Geoffrey C. Fox, Roy D. Williams, and Paul C. Messina
A clear illustration of how parallel computers can be successfully applied to large-scale scientific computations. This book demonstrates how a variety of applications in physics, biology, mathematics, and other sciences were implemented on real parallel computers to produce new scientific results, and it investigates issues of fine-grained parallelism relevant for future supercomputers with particular emphasis on hypercube architecture.
ISBN 1-55860-253-4; cloth; 977 pages; 1994

Introduction to Parallel Algorithms & Architectures: Arrays, Trees & Hypercubes
F. Thomson Leighton
A unique combination of networks and parallel algorithms that offers a fundamental understanding of parallel computing technology and programming techniques to a general advanced audience. Featuring communication networks that form the architectural basis of almost all parallel computing, the author describes their capabilities, limitations, and use in solving specific algorithmic problems with a simple, intuitive style. Throughout, discussions consider practical restrictions on hardware, with examples drawn from real implementations on commercially available machines. Intended for designers, programmers, and engineers who need to understand these issues at a fundamental level in order to utilize the full power afforded by parallel computation.
ISBN 1-55860-117-1; cloth; 831 pages; 1992